AN *Outline History* OF *Spanish American Literature*

An *Outline History* of *Spanish American* Literature

FOURTH EDITION

John E. Englekirk
UNIVERSITY OF CALIFORNIA, LOS ANGELES
CHAIRMAN AND EDITOR

Irving A. Leonard
UNIVERSITY OF MICHIGAN

John T. Reid

John A. Crow
UNIVERSITY OF CALIFORNIA, LOS ANGELES

**IRVINGTON PUBLISHERS, INC.,
551 Fifth Ave., New York, N.Y. 10176**

Copyright © 1980 by Irvington Publishers, Inc.
1965 by Meredith Publishing Co.

All rights reserved. No part of this book may be reproduced in any manner whatever, including information storage or retrieval, in whole or in part (except for brief quotations in critical articles or reviews), without written permission from the publisher. For information, write to Irvington Publishers, Inc., 551 Fifth Avenue, New York, New York, 10176.

Library of Congress Cataloging in Publication Data
Instituto Internacional de Literatura Iberoamericana.
  An outline history of Spanish American literature.

  Bibliography: p.
  Includes index.
  1. Spanish American literature—Outlines, syllabi, etc. I. Englekirk, John Eugene, 1905– II. Title.
PQ7081.I5   1979   860'.9   79-19074
ISBN 0-89197-874-7
ISBN 0-89197-326-5 pbk.

Printed in the United States of America

TO
THE MEMORY OF

E. Herman Hespelt
(1886–1961)

discriminating pioneer and friend

and

John T. Reid
(1908–1978)

resourceful and loyal colleague

Preface to the Fourth Edition

The dozen-odd years since the appearance of the third edition (1965) of this *Outline History* have been witness to a spectacular upsurge in the enrichment and appreciation of contemporary Spanish American literature. This amazing development was soon explosively baptized "the boom." However, a noticeable slackening in the fevered pitch of the initial outburst as quickly invited a more sobering assessment of the phenomenon. This fourth edition is an attempt to record the nature and the significance of the principal activities and achievements that have undeniably served to propel Spanish American letters ever further into the mainstream of the international cultural scene.

The editors have opted to retain the objectives, format and contents of the third edition. The only changes in the basic text lie in the correction of typographical errors, the mending of unhappy phraseology, and the addition of new information, almost exclusively chronological in character, that serves to update the record. All other purely bibliographical data reflect the gains of recent scholarship bearing on author entries of past editions. This information has been added to the author entries under two new headings: Works (texts, editions, translations) and Studies (bibliographic and critical). There is also an "Addenda to the Bibliography," which includes new tools (historical and critical studies, manuals, bibliographies, reference works, anthologies in
English) that have appeared since 1965. The few exceptions embrace a number of earlier studies that were overlooked in the past and of several works previously listed that have appeared in revised and enlarged editions.

The amount of new writing, both creative and critical, published since the early 1960s has been overwhelming, especially when compared with the scanty and uneven body of materials that served as the source of bibliographical items included in the early editions. The temptation to bring most of this new material together for the first time in the *Outline History* was difficult to hold in check. Fortunately, the decision to maintain high standards of selectivity and availability prevailed. The editors elected to uphold the original concept of the *Outline History* as a guide and resource manual for students and instructors of the typical upper-division introductory survey course in Spanish American literature.

As important and, certainly, even more demanding has been the selection of those writers whose work and stature over the years under review would seem to justify their inclusion in the roster of new authors that follows the introductory statement, "Into the Mainstream," of new Section IV of the Third Period. It is in this new Section IV that the editors proffer their views and analyses of the best and most representative writers and writings of the exhilarating years from the mid-60s to the present. Some names will be challenged, many more will be found wanting. Time alone will provide the necessary perspectives with which to designate those writers of today who hold out the greater promise of surviving the acid test of changing tastes and values. And yet, in spite of the rigorous screening that has always guided the steps of this committee, the addition of sixteen new names, names that have towered above dozens of other literary figures of the same period, would seem to attest amply to the rich harvest that contemporary Spanish American letters have contributed to the cultural heritage of the Western World.

The committee wishes to express its gratitude to all those colleagues who in the past, and now once again, have generously shared views and opinions that have weighed significantly in resolving problems and decisions encountered in the preparation of this fourth edition. Our thanks go out to all of them, but limited space allows us to only name a few: René Acuña, Enrique Anderson Imbert, Andrew P. Debicki, Donald F. Fogelquist, Gerardo Luzuriaga, Robert G. Mead, Richard M. Reeve, Alfredo A. Roggiano, Anibal Sánchez Reulet.

Finally, the committee wishes to extend a very hearty word of appreciation to their former colleague, Claude L. Hulet, who in the face of disheartening odds brought his special assignment through to an examplary conclusion with the publication of his three-volume *Brazilian Literature* (Georgetown Univ. Press, 1975).

J.E.E.
J.A.C.
I.A.L.
J.T.R.

Preface

The *Outline History* is completely revised and restructured in this third edition. Its original five sections are reduced to three, which correspond more directly to the three major economic, social and political periods in the history of Latin America: "1st period: From Discovery to Independence"; "2nd period: From Independence to the Mexican Revolution"; "3rd period: From the Mexican Revolution to the Present." Within this broad historical framework, further sectioning, made along strictly literary-cultural lines, establishes subdivisions for the three principal genres of poetry, prose, and drama. The introductory summaries to the periods are now extended in order to include most of the significant data, together with the references, previously condensed in schematic form immediately following the summaries. The student should acquire by means of this essay form a more comprehensive picture of the setting in which Spanish American literature developed. Also, introductory remarks to a given genre, heretofore introduced occasionally, are now incorporated systematically as parts of the total pattern. The student should thus grasp more readily the salient characteristics and the distinctive contributions of each form in the period or movement under study.

Author entries, rewritten throughout, remain essentially bibliographical. As in earlier editions, extended critical evaluation is reserved for the introductions to selections in the companion *Anthology*. In the case of authors cited in the *Outline History* but not represented in the *Anthology*, somewhat more space is now given to the appreciation of their work. All bibliographical references have been rechecked. Preference is given to the titles listed in the "Bibliography" and, in general, to those items that reflect historical and critical findings of recent years. References to material appearing in journals are limited, in the main, to publications readily available in the average college or university library. Because each of the carefully selected references contributes something different to the student's understanding of the subject, the large dot (●), heretofore used to mark critical works that were especially recommended, was discarded. The double (**) and single (*) asterisks, however, continue to call attention to those authors whom the editors consider indispensable to the student's knowledge.

More than two decades have passed since the printing of the second edition. Time, and the exacting hand of more recent literary criticism and scholarship, have taken their toll of a number of authors previously included in the *Outline History*. But others—a few of the past, a larger number of the present—have been added to fill the ranks. The final roster of those included was anything but a foregone conclusion. Colleagues everywhere spoke up warmly for their favorites. To have allowed space to even a niggardly share of the names proposed would have turned this "outline" into a small-scale catalog of authors and titles. The committee had no choice but to adhere closely to the general conclusions, drawn from the original study of 1940 and from the more recent questionnaire of 1957, that were formed to guide it in determining the scope and character of this manual. The committee believes that both the *Outline History* and the *Anthology* (which will soon be revised to mirror this third edition of the *Outline History*) should continue to serve the needs of students and instructors for whom the typical course in Spanish American literature meets three times a week for two semesters (or their equivalent) and is elected by upperclassmen after a minimum of two years of college Spanish. Even though the committee has refrained from loading the outline with authors and titles that find easy access to most manuals and anthologies, it has included much more material than the "average" student of the "typical" class can assimilate. The editors, while they have not lost sight of the original purpose of this outline, have tried to give the instructor ample help in choosing among authors, readings, and critical items best suited to his course and students.

The "Bibliography" has undergone a thorough pruning. Many entries of dated vintage were discarded, along with others that are now generally unavailable or are of dubious value in the face of

PREFACE

the growing body of sound historical and critical studies of recent years. The one general exception to this practice is the case of anthologies of Spanish American literature edited in the United States. Because they are highly useful to the student with minimum language background and because they are readily available, most of them were retained. At the same time an unusually large number of new items were added. For the reader not yet prepared to enjoy Spanish American literature in the original, entries formerly grouped together under "Anthologies" have now been listed separately under either "Anthologies in Spanish" or "Anthologies in English Translation." Although few average libraries can be expected to house the greatly extended, albeit selected, list provided herein, even the modest college library should offer many titles within the wide range of these listings.

Two features of the earlier editions were omitted. Responses to the 1957 questionnaire suggested that Appendix B ("Chronological Outline") was of little practical value. Since an essential feature of the manual itself is the orderly presentation, both chronologically and esthetically, of significant facts and trends in the development of Spanish American literature, the committee concluded that rearrangement of periods and movements and consequent relocation of authors within this revised framework would greatly enhance the utility of the *Outline History* and that suppression of the chronological tables would remove an unwanted redundancy.

On the other hand, response to the query concerning the validity and value of Appendix A ("A Bibliographical Introduction to Brazilian Literature for Those Reading Only English and Spanish") was a clear mandate to provide a more effective instrument for our approach to the literature of Brazil. The committee was urged almost universally to prepare a full outline history of Brazilian literature, and a corresponding anthology, similar to the anthology of Spanish American literature. A sharp difference of opinion soon developed, however, over how best to achieve this broader objective. Should there be a single, integrated outline for *Latin* American literature, one accompanied by a multivolume anthology that would reflect the concurrent development of Spanish American and Brazilian literatures? Or should there be separate but companion outlines, one for the Spanish American and one for the Brazilian area, supported by separate but companion anthologies? The issue was resolved in part by a prudent look at the present and probable future profile of courses in *Latin* American literature in colleges and universities throughout the United States.

Professor Marion Zeitlin of the University of California, Los Angeles, author of Appendix A of the earlier editions, was initially responsible, in large measure, for achieving an instrument that would serve as a guide line in the approach to both literatures. When Professor Zeitlin found it impossible to devote further time to the project, the committee invited Professor Claude L. Hulet, also of the University of California, Los Angeles, to continue the task of editing the Brazilian volumes under a special project of the United States Office of Education directed by the chairman of this committee. The *Outline History* and accompanying *Anthology* of Brazilian literature are scheduled for publication by the University of California Press.

The committee wishes to thank all those many colleagues who, either through informal exchange of views or through their response to the 1957 questionnaire, contributed toward the reshaping of the *Outline History* and made helpful suggestions for preparing a revised edition of the *Anthology*. A very special note of appreciation is due the following for their thoughtful replies and for their notes on errors and other failings uncovered in both volumes: José A. Balseiro, Arnold Chapman, Frank Dauster, George De Mello, José Ferrer Canales, Max Henríquez Ureña, Claude L. Hulet, Thomas B. Irving, Willis Knapp Jones, Luis Leal, Kurt L. Levy, Francisco Monterde, Luis Monguió, Gerald M. Moser, Ruth Richardson, George O. Schanzer, and John Van Horne.

The members of the committee would also like to take this opportunity to express their deepest sorrow at the death of Professor E. Herman Hespelt, who served as editor of the original *Outline History* and *Anthology*. Herman Hespelt was profoundly admired and widely respected; he was one of the outstanding teachers and scholars in the Latin American field and was, in addition, a loyal friend and leader. It is impossible to replace him. We dedicate this book to his memory.

J.E.E.
I.A.L.
J.T.R.
J.A.C.

Contents

Preface to the Fourth Edition   vii

Preface   xi

1st period:
    From Discovery to Independence   1

    Introductory Summary   3

I. Literature of Discovery, Conquest, Exploration, and Evangelization (1492-1600)   10
    A. Prose   10
        a. Letters and Reports   12
        b. Chronicles and Histories   15
    B. Poetry   18
    C. Drama   21

II. Flowering and Decline of Colonial Letters (1600-1750)   24
    A. Poetry   24
        a. Epic and Descriptive   25
        b. Lyric and Satiric   27
    B. Prose   29
    C. Drama   33

III. Period of Enlightenment and Revolt (1750-1832)   37
    A. Poetry   37
        a. Heroic and Popular   38
        b. Lyric   40
    B. Prose   44
    C. Drama   49

2nd period:
   From Independence to the Mexican Revolution — 51

   Introductory Summary — 53

   I. Romanticism (1832-1888) — 62
      A. Poetry — 62
         a. Lyric — 64
         b. Gaucho — 74
      B. Prose — 78
         a. Fiction — 79
         b. Essay and *Tradición* — 83
      C. Drama — 88

   II. Realism and Naturalism (1854-1918) — 90
      A. Prose — 90
      B. Poetry — 101
      C. Drama — 101

   III. Modernism (1882-1910) — 104

3rd period:
   From the Mexican Revolution to the Present — 133

   Introductory Summary — 135

   I. Poetry — 141
      A. Postmodernism — 143
      B. Vanguard Poetry — 155

   II. Prose — 168
      A. Essay — 175
      B. Fiction — 186
         a. Social Protest — 186
         b. Psychological and Philosophical — 197
         c. Historical, Regional, Autobiographical — 208

   III. Drama — 222
   IV. Into the Mainstream — 231

Bibliography — 263
Addenda to Bibliography — 279
Works and Studies — 295
Index of Authors — 322

An *Outline History* of *Spanish American Literature*

1st period

From Discovery to Independence

Introductory Summary

The vast process of westernizing the terrestrial globe, which characterizes the modern period of history, was initiated by the peoples of the Spanish Peninsula in the late fifteenth century. With astonishing rapidity the Conquistadors swept over the Caribbean islands, the mainland of Middle America (which included southern regions of the United States), and much of South America, setting up European institutions wherever they went and founding a colonial society soon composed of a complexity of human elements. These included Spaniards and Creoles, the latter being colonials born in America of European parentage, sedentary and nomadic Indians, Negro slaves, and a confusing array of castes resulting from the intermarriage of diverse races. For three long centuries these overseas realms were Spain in America.

There is a certain aptness in considering the colonial period, taken as a whole, as the Middle Ages of Spanish America, and its literature as essentially medieval. Feudal institutions in Spain were beginning to disintegrate at the time of the conquest, but this process had not advanced sufficiently to prevent the transfer to the newly acquired provinces of a fundamentally medieval civilization with the predominance of the Church in temporal affairs and of theology in intellectual life. The existence of a large, subjugated population of sedentary Indians in the richest areas of the New World was bound to perpetuate a social and economic order that was breaking up in Europe; the innumerable serfs at the disposal of the Spanish overlords rendered such a society practically inevitable. With necessary local modifications, then, the mode of life and thought of the Middle Ages in Europe was reestablished in the new communities organized by the Spaniards, and it survived far beyond the chronological period of the Middle Ages elsewhere. In such a conservative order, rigidly controlled by a medieval Church and by representatives of a distant Crown, literature was cultivated mainly as an aristocratic privilege or, more often, as a means of promoting the work of that Church and of glorifying it as an institution. Under these circumstances colonial letters could only develop as a somewhat stunted branch of Spanish literature. Hence much of the literary production of the colonies consists of sermons, religious guides, missionary chronicles, theological tracts and, later, an almost uninterrupted flood of gongoristic verse, reflecting current bad taste. Some exceptional figures and works, however, mark the progress of three centuries of colonial cultural life.

Sixteenth century colonial literature was the product of much the same influences as those at work in the mother country, and it was conditioned directly by them. In Spain, the bare, medieval chronicle was giving way to the more luxuriant form of the Renaissance, and the prodigious exploits of the conquerors and the vast new world whose exotic wonders they revealed served as a powerful stimulant to the newer style of detailed, descriptive histories. Reports and chronicles such as those of Hernán Cortés (1485-1547), Bernal Díaz del Castillo (1495?-1584), Bartolomé de las Casas (1484-1565), Toribio de Benavente (?-1569), and Pedro Cieza de León (1520?-1554) are frequently literary monuments of permanent value and do not lack novelistic elements to interest the general reader.

Spanish letters also cultivated narrative verse which keenly felt Italian influences in this period of high adventure, and the stirring models of Ariosto (1477-1533) and Tasso (1544-1595) helped to create a school of poets, men of action in the New World. The metrical compositions of this group reflected the zestful spirit of their time, and they record, often in memorable verse, the incredible feats of valor of the Conquistador and the legends of his Indian opponents. The work of Alonso de Ercilla (1534-1594), poet of action as well as of words, best epitomizes this heroic genre, for the realism and descriptive vigor of his *La araucana* are never quite equalled in the diminuendo of similar but less inspired poems during the century following. Nevertheless, these later, rhymed narratives also reveal the enthusiasm and love of action witnessed by the first exuberant decades of Spain in America, and they have left a

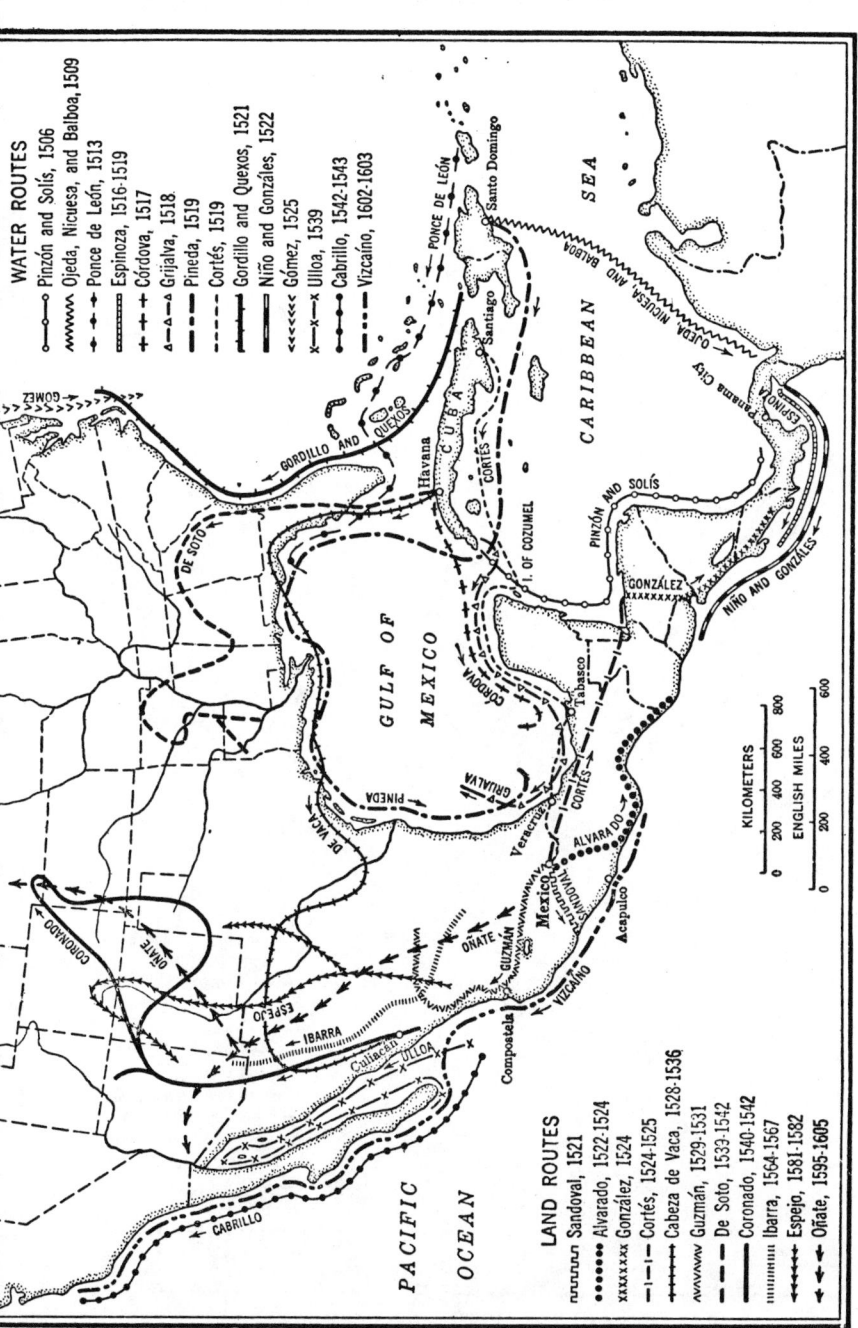

EXPLORATIONS IN NORTHERN SPANISH AMERICA

Based on the maps on pp. 114 and 118 of *The Development of Hispanic America* by A. Curtis Wilgus (Farrar, Straus & Co., Inc., 1941). By permission of the author.

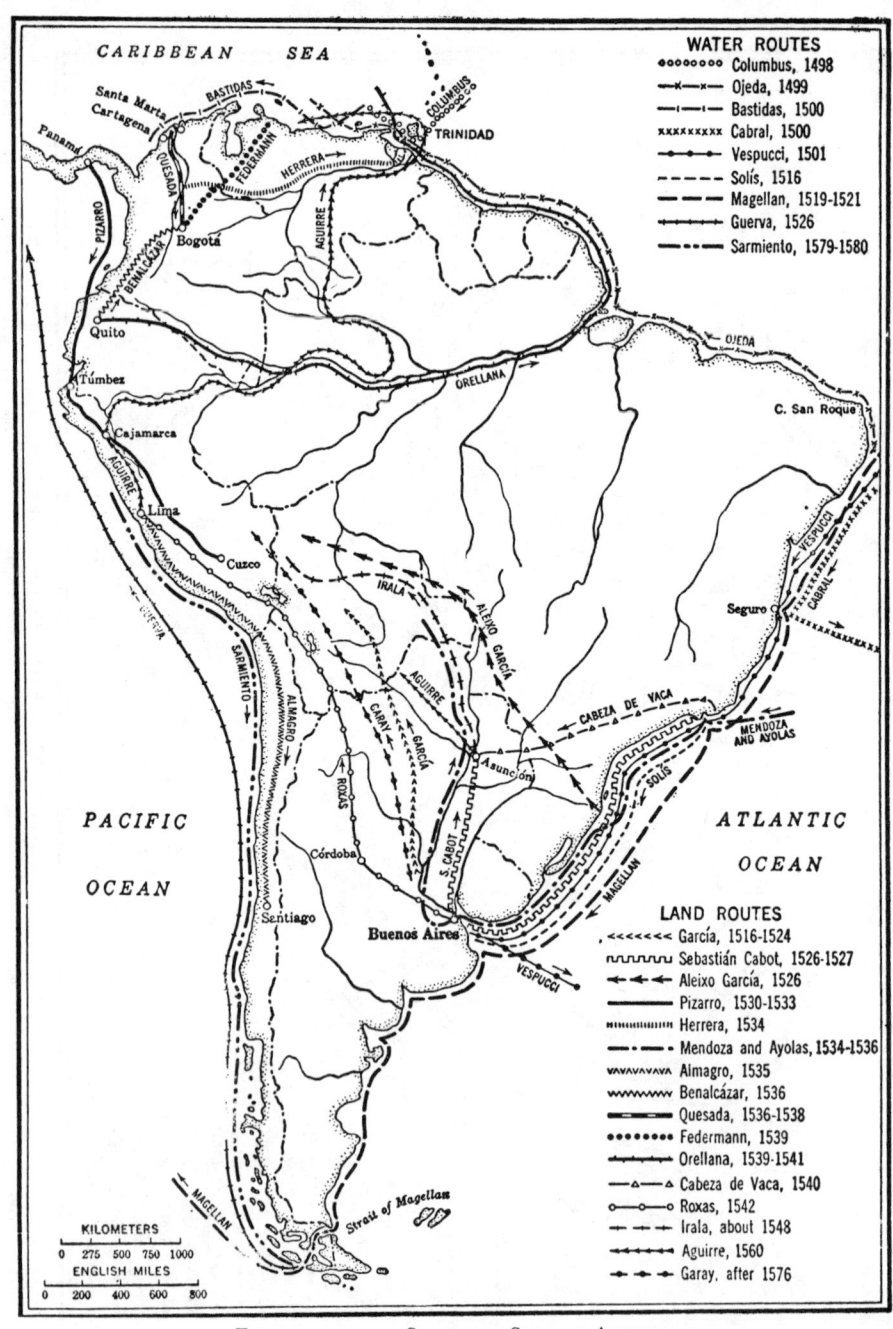

EXPLORATIONS IN SOUTHERN SPANISH AMERICA
Based on the maps on pp. 131 and 133 of *The Development of Hispanic America* by A. Curtis Wilgus (Farrar, Straus & Co., Inc., 1941). By permission of the author.

literary legacy that can still be enjoyed. Indeed, their success, and later that of versified plays, was so great that both tended to discourage the use of prose as a medium of creative expression during the whole colonial period.

By the beginning of the seventeenth century the era of tremendous expansion was at an end. The weakened motherland was obliged to content itself with consolidating gains already made and with thrusting here and there a defensive frontier against foes, foreign and domestic. With the passing of the Conquistador a settled state of society gradually emerged, accompanied by an increasing cultivation of the arts and of social refinements. Universities were soon established almost simultaneously in Mexico City and Lima, and these, with other educational institutions founded later, began to flourish in the seventeenth century. About them as a nucleus grew a small but increasing leisure class with varying degrees of concern for intellectual pursuits. Their eyes, however, turned to the motherland for inspiration, and it was its models that they sought to imitate, neglecting the materials so richly at hand in their own environment. Moreover, the determination of the Spanish Peninsula to adhere to the restrictions of the Counter-Reformation on thought and expression tended to limit the creation of a more vital literature in the colonies.

The last two centuries of Spanish rule saw no dearth of important works of erudition and imagination from colonial presses, but such writings are far outnumbered by the continuous deluge of verse accompanying them. Some poetry possessed merit, but too often it degenerated into mere verbal gymnastics. Seemingly, no occasion was too insignificant to commemorate by such effusions. Births, marriages, deaths in the royal and viceregal families, and particularly the arrival of a new viceroy to take office, as well as the more frequent religious and secular festivals, were all signals for an outburst in print of more or less poetic rhapsody. The custom of *certámenes,* or poetical contests, and later the various literary academies, were productive of much bad verse, too much of which has been preserved to posterity.

All this activity might have resulted in more worthy verse if the colonies had not imitated so sedulously the literary vices and decadence of the mother country. Unfortunately, all these defects were faithfully reproduced and exaggerated in the intellectual centers of Spain's overseas possessions. The innovations of Luis de Góngora y Argote (1561-1627), the Cordovan bard, inspired an army of untalented imitators, and the curse of Gongorism, with its ridiculous conceits, distorted syntax, affected style heavily freighted with classical and mythological allusions, numbing Latinisms, and other marks of pedantry, descended upon colonial letters, prose as well as verse, with blighting effect. The contagion of such excessively bad taste spread even to that inspired genius, Sor Juana Inés de la Cruz (1648-1695). Nearly every writer succumbed to this devastating plague, including sober-minded intellectuals, many of whose works otherwise command respect, such as Carlos de Sigüenza y Góngora (1645-1700) of the University of Mexico, and especially Pedro de Peralta Barnuevo (1663-1743) of the University of San Marcos at Lima, author of the ponderous epic *Lima fundada* (1732). It was indeed the triumph of form over idea, and little of the literature of the time conveys any message for today.

The literary habits of the seventeenth were carried over well into the following century, but the influence of French letters and ideas was early felt, much earlier than usually acknowledged. The accession of the Bourbons to the Spanish throne in 1700 was instrumental in opening colonial ports to French ships which brought French styles, customs, and literature into the overseas realms, particularly the viceroyalty of Peru, almost as soon as into Spain itself. One of the earliest adaptations of Corneille's tragedies in the Spanish language was made by Peralta Barnuevo and performed in Lima about 1720, and the accompanying dramatic skits clearly betray the influences of Molière (1622-1673), Boursault (1638-1701), and Scarron (1610-1660). As the eighteenth century advanced, more and more French works were introduced and read, at first freely and openly, later more surreptitiously as the revolutionary rationalism of Voltaire (1694-1778), Diderot (1713-1784), and Rousseau (1712-1778) and other philosophers alarmed the reactionary Spanish authorities and moved them to exclude such literature from the colonies.

But the neo-medieval culture implanted nearly three centuries before was visibly crumbling. By the beginning of the nineteenth century, the economic restrictions of Spanish colonial policy, the growth of an American spirit among the Creole elements heartened by the successful revolt of the English colonies in North

America, and the spread of the ideas of the French Revolution needed little more than the confusions arising from the Napoleonic invasion of Spain in 1807-1808 and the removal of the Bourbons from the Spanish throne to sever the frail strands of empire. The revolts of Hidalgo, Morelos and Iturbide in Mexico, and the military campaigns of Bolívar and San Martín in the northern and southern regions of South America respectively completed the separation of the former colonies from the mother country.

Before these events, however, two important social phenomena abetted the spread of revolutionary thought during the late eighteenth century: the founding of periodicals and the establishment of literary and scientific societies. Both appeared in Buenos Aires, Lima, Bogotá, and Mexico City which, immediately before and during the wars of separation, provided pulpits for many revolutionists.*

Mariano Moreno (1778-1811) and Bernardo de Monteagudo (1787-1825) in the *Gaceta de Buenos Aires,* Antonio Nariño (1765-1823) in *La bagatela* of Bogotá, and José Joaquín Fernández de Lizardi (1776-1827) in *El pensador mexicano* made important contributions to the earnest and often passionate prose of the struggle for independence. Printing presses multiplied, even in the smaller cities and sometimes surreptitiously, and sent forth pamphlets to inflame the colonists.

In the closing decades of the eighteenth century literary and scientific societies, founded ostensibly to promote general culture and serious studies, soon became centers of political discussion and disseminators of revolutionary propaganda. During the wars for independence fiery patriotic poems were first read in the intimacy of these clubs, of which perhaps the most notable was the *Sociedad Patriótica y Literaria* of Buenos Aires.

From France by way of the mother country came a new and encyclopedic interest in scientific investigation. The expeditions of La Condamine (1735) and Baron von Humboldt (1799) to the colonies and their observations of their flora and fauna opened the

---

* Dates of the more notable periodicals: *Gaceta de literatura de México,* 1788-1794; *Gaceta de Guatemala,* 1794-1816; *Papel periódico* (Bogotá), 1791-1797; *Diario de Lima,* 1790-1793; *Mercurio peruano,* 1791-1795; *Gaceta de Buenos Aires,* 1810; *Aurora de Chile,* 1812; *Semanario del Nuevo Reino de Granada,* 1808-1811.

eyes of the Spanish Americans to a new world of critical thought. The work of such scientists not only influenced indirectly the urge for freedom but also turned the attention of writers in the new-born nations to the natural wonders of their homelands and away from the intricacies of gongoristic expression. Despite this intellectual awakening little literature of lasting value emerged before the wars for independence. The picaresque *Lazarillo de ciegos caminantes* is the only work of the period which merits more than passing mention.

By contrast the first decades of the nineteenth century were active and fertile years for literature. During the revolutionary wars (1808-1824) numerous patriotic odes and journalistic essays testify to a new spirit, but little of this expression is likely to endure. It was an improvised production with occasional sparks of impassioned inspiration, but generally it lacked originality and the finish of works composed in more tranquil times. Since the writers were, for the most part, Creole aristocrats trained in the colonial universities and under French influence, their form and style reflect the neo-classicism of the late eighteenth century. The poetry of Andrés Bello (1781-1865), José Joaquín Olmedo (1780-1847), and José María Heredia (1803-1839), however new its subject matter, is studded with classical allusions and it betrays a classical complexity of syntax. Even their patriotic fervor was, to some extent, an echo of neo-classical patriotic poets of Spain such as Juan Nicasio Gallego (1777-1853) and Manuel José Quintana (1772-1857).

While most of the literature of the revolutionary period was composed by members of the educated, aristocratic classes, it is probable that the mestizos and Indians, who formed the bulk of those in revolt, had their martial expression in the form of ballads and in quatrains. This was true in Argentina where samples of such verse are preserved. Lacking the refinement of more academic poetry they made use, as a refreshing contrast, of colloquial language and of a vigorous folkloric spirit.

Certain poets of this epoch (especially Heredia) sound the new notes of romanticism. This European movement seemed to fit Hispanic American temperaments and conditions for it stressed freedom, individualism, and emotional intensity. It exalted virgin nature and glorified national peculiarities. Most of the early Spanish American romantics were liberals in politics, often suffering exile in opposition to the dictatorships which afflicted the new republics and sometimes sacrificing their lives. Like their European models, they also sought freedom in literary form, breaking away from neoclassical stereotypes. Particularly important for a distinctively New World literature was the romantic preference for American themes which produced narrative poems called *leyendas* based on Indian traditions and on heroic events in the history of their countries. Shorter lyrics dealt with nature, patriotism and, of course, love. This literary movement entered the various Hispanic American countries by different routes and at different times. It reached Mexico first in the early 1820's and by mid-century it had spread all over the southern continent, and this influence was powerful until the closing decades of the century.

In the expression of the revolutionary era and afterward, the Indian motif was prominent. In their hatred of the Conquistador and in their efforts to improvise a native American ideal, they glorified the down-trodden Indian as Chateaubriand (1768-1848) did before them. However, it is important to note that men like Olmedo, who called upon the Inca, Huayna Cápac, to witness the victories of the liberating armies of Bolívar, actually knew little of the Indian masses who lived in the nascent republics, and perhaps cared less. They were part of a romanticized legend which did duty in creating a synthesized nationalism. However false and stylized this interest in the Indian might be, its later and more realistic influence in interpreting the Indian's place in American life is indubitable.

GENERAL REFERENCES

Crow, *Epic,* Chaps. XXI-XXV; XXX-XXXVIII. Henríquez Ureña, *Lit. Curr.,* Chap. IV. Herring, Part II, Chaps. 5-11; Part III, Chaps. 13-17. Leonard, *Books of the Brave, passim.* Moses, *Intel. Back., passim.* Picón-Salas, *Cult. Hist., passim.* Spell, *Rousseau, passim.* Torres-Ríoseco, *Epic,* 44-57. Arthur P. Whitaker (ed.), *Latin America and the Enlightenment,* 2nd ed., Ithaca, N.Y., Great Seal Books, 1961, *passim.* Worcester and Schaeffer, Part II, Chaps. VIII-XII; Part III, Chaps. XIV-XVIII; Part IV, Chaps. XX-XXIII.

I.
Literature of Discovery, Conquest, Exploration, and Evangelization (1492-1600)

A. PROSE

The sixteenth century was preeminently an age of narrative literature in which substance prevailed over form. The discovery, conquest, settlement, and evangelization of the New World provided material for the ready quills of writers eager to recount the exciting events of this extraordinary enterprise for the benefit of readers in Spain and Europe. In many instances the chief actors in this great drama, the explorers, discoverers, and missionaries, were themselves the writers of the letters, reports, and lengthy chronicles that created so rich a literature concerning this saga of European expansion. Strongly conditioned by the ethical and collective tradition of the Middle Ages, they were men of action who incarnated the new Renaissance spirit of individualism. They lived on the borderland, it may be said, between the medieval and the modern eras, they struggled and proselyted in the hidden depths of unknown continents, and they fought and preached on the front lines of clashing cultures and faiths. These contacts with the elementals of historical experience moved them to write in a deeply personal and subjective fashion that often borrowed stylistic techniques from the contemporary romances of chivalry with which so many were familiar. These literary peculiarities included the use of invented harangues with identical phrases and metaphors, dialogues, anecdotes, long descriptions of battles and individual combats, declarations of lofty sentiments of honor, and references to fanciful scenes and creatures.

Such elements were not lacking even in the letters and reports of Cristóbal Colón (1451-1506) and Hernán Cortés (1485-1547), and they are conspicuous in the voluminous accounts of Bernal Díaz del Castillo (1495?-1584), Gonzalo Fernández de Oviedo (1478-1557), Pedro Cieza de León (1520?-1554), Francisco López de Jerez (1504-1539), and other eyewitnesses of much that they related. These chroniclers, however, did not fail to give realistic descriptions of the topography, flora, and fauna of regions visited, nor did they omit authentic observations on the customs and ways of Indian civilizations conquered. Perhaps the most personal of these narratives, yet replete with details concerning the existence of nomadic Indians and notable for its stark realism, is the *Naufragios* of Álvar Núñez Cabeza de Vaca (1490?-1559?).

Later, cultivated observers such as the Jesuit José de Acosta (1539-1616) in his *Historia natural y moral de las Indias* were to study more scientifically the problems presented by the New World and to speculate on the origins of these phenomena. Meanwhile, ecclesiastical writers such as the polemical **Bartolomé de las Casas (1484–1565) and the life-long students of Indian lore**, Bernardino de Sahagún (1500-1590) and Toribio de Benavente, known as Motolinía (died 1569), wrote on the indigenous civilizations with deep insight and understanding. But the highest esthetic achievement of all this historiographical literature was that of a native chronicler, the Peruvian half-caste Inca, Garcilaso de la Vega (1539-1616), whose novelesque *La Florida del Inca* (1605) and nostalgic *Comentarios reales de los Incas* (1609) defined him as the first true American writer of artistic merit.

REFERENCES

Anderson Imbert, I, 19-63. Henríquez Ureña, *Lit. Curr.*, 3-21. Ramón Iglesias, *Cronistas e historiadores de la conquista de México: Ciclo de Hernán Cortés*, México, El Colegio de México, 1942, *passim*. Moses, *Span. Col. Lit.*, Chaps. II, III, IV. Reyes, Chap. II. Torres-Ríoseco, *Epic*, 6-14.

a. LETTERS AND REPORTS

1. (Caribbean) Cristóbal Colón (Christopher Columbus) (1451-1506). The great discoverer is the first reporter of events and scenes glimpsed in the New World which he relates and describes in his diaries and letters. Born probably in Genoa, a seaport of Italy, to the family of a humble weaver, he worked as a woolcarder until he was twenty-two. Sea life beckoned and, after serving as a sailor in the Mediterranean, his adventurous career took him to Portugal. After making voyages north to Ireland and Iceland, he married and settled down in Lisbon about 1485, and there he acquired a command of Castilian as well as of the science of navigation. He had dreamed of pursuing the setting sun to the shores of Asia, and when he had failed to interest John II of Portugal in this plan he turned to Isabella, Queen of Castile, and won her support. The reports and letters about his discoveries frequently refer to the appearance and customs of the natives encountered in the West Indies, and he presents impressions and ideas mainly projected from a mind conditioned by medieval myths and legends.

SUGGESTED READING

Diario del primer viaje.

TEXTS

Anderson Imbert and Florit, 12-13.

EDITIONS

El primer viaje de Cristóbal Colón, Madrid, Instituto Histórico de Marina, 1943. *Los cuatro viajes del Almirante y su testamento* (1946), 3rd ed., Buenos Aires, Espasa-Calpe, 1958 (Col. austral, 633).

TRANSLATIONS

Journal of the First Voyage to America by Christopher Columbus, New York, Boni, 1924; introduction by Van Wyck Brooks. Cecil Jane (trans.), *Journal,* London, Hakluyt Society, 1960; revised and annotated by L. A. Vigneras, with appendix by R. A. Skelton. *Four Voyages to the New World: Letters and Selected Documents,* bilingual edition, New York, Corinth Cook, 1961; edited by R. H. Major, with introduction by John E. Fagg. Samuel Eliot Morison (trans.), *Journals and Other Documents on the Life and Voyages of Christopher Columbus,* New York, The Heritage Press, 1964.

FROM DISCOVERY TO INDEPENDENCE 13

CRITICAL REFERENCES

Anderson Imbert, II, 20-22. Antonio Ballesteros y Beretta, *Cristóbal Colón y el descubrimiento de América*, 2 vols., Barcelona, Salvat, 1945. *Vida del Almirante Don Cristóbal Colón*, México, Fondo de Cultura Económica, 1947; edited by Ramón Iglesias. Benjamin Keen (trans.), *The Life of the Admiral Christopher Columbus by his Son Ferdinand*, New Brunswick, N.J., Rutgers Univ. Press, 1959. Samuel Eliot Morison, *Admiral of the Ocean Sea*, 2 vols., Boston, Little, Brown, 1942.

**2. (Mexico) Hernán Cortés (1485-1547). The conqueror of Mexico was born in Medellín, Extremadura, in Spain, and spent two years as an indifferent student at the University of Salamanca. Eager for adventure, he sailed to Santo Domingo in 1504, later joining Diego Velásquez in the conquest of Cuba, where Cortés became a planter. He took advantage of the expedition authorized by Governor Velásquez to the mainland to undertake the conquest of Mexico. During the years 1519-1526 Cortés sent five famous dispatches called *cartas de relación* to Charles V of Spain. These terse, soberly written yet vivid reports possess literary merits comparable to the *Commentaries* of Julius Caesar and to the *Anabasis* of Xenophon. Cortés died a broken and disappointed man near Seville at the age of 62.

SUGGESTED READING

Segunda y tercera carta de relación (selections).

TEXTS

Anthology, 3-14. Anderson Imbert and Florit, 20-24. Arjona and Arjona, 3-11. *Despatches from Mexico to Charles V* (ed. Day), New York, American Book, 1933. Jiménez Rueda, *Antología*, 31-42.

EDITIONS

Cartas de relación de la Conquista de Méjico, Buenos Aires, Espasa-Calpe, 1945 (Col. austral, 547). *Historiadores primitivos de Indias*, Madrid, 1946 (Biblioteca de autores españoles, 22). *Cartas y relaciones con otros documentos relativos a la vida y a las empresas del conquistador*, Buenos Aires, Emecé, 1946; edited by Nicolás Coronado.

TRANSLATIONS

Francis A. MacNutt (ed. and trans.), *Letter of Cortés*, 2 vols., New York, Putnam, 1908. J. Bayard Morris (ed. and trans.), *Five Letters*, New York, Robert M. McBride, 1929.

OUTLINE HISTORY OF SPANISH AMERICAN LITERATURE

CRITICAL REFERENCES

See texts and editions above. Fernando Benítez, *In the Footsteps of Cortés,* New York, Pantheon, 1952. Salvador de Madariaga, *Hernán Cortés,* 2nd ed., Buenos Aires, Sudamericana, 1943; also his *Hernán Cortés, Conqueror of Mexico,* 2nd ed., Chicago, Regnery, 1956 (1st ed., New York, Macmillan, 1941). Carlos Pereyra, *Hernán Cortés,* 5th ed., Buenos Aires, Espasa-Calpe, 1953 (Col. austral, 236). Henry P. Wagner, *The Rise of Fernando Cortés,* Los Angeles, Cortés Society, 1944.

°3. (Mexico and Paraguay) **Álvar Núñez Cabeza de Vaca (1490?-1559?).** Few biographical facts are known concerning the author of the curious memoirs of an extraordinary and terrible odyssey through the south and southwest of the United States and north of Mexico entitled *Naufragios.* He appears to have been a native of Seville, Spain, and a grandson of the conqueror of the Canary Islands. Coming to the New World, he joined the ill-fated expedition of Pánfilo de Narváez to Florida and survived to tell the tale of his hardships and wanderings. Recounted in the first person with great narrative skill in clear, rapid prose he provides a descriptive chronicle of adventures with genuine literary power. Years later he was appointed *adelantado* and governor of La Plata at Asunción, Paraguay, but was soon deposed. These explorations and later adventures were recorded by Pero Hernández in a book called *Comentarios.*

SUGGESTED READING

Naufragios (selections).

TEXTS

Anderson Imbert and Florit, 35-38. Arjona and Arjona, 51-62. *Los naufragios y relación* (ed. Espinosa and Mercado), Boston, Heath, [1941].

EDITIONS

Historiadores primitivos de Indias, Madrid, 1946 (Biblioteca de autores españoles, 22). *Naufragios y comentarios, con dos cartas,* Madrid, Espasa-Calpe, 1936; *ibid.,* 1st ed., 1942 (Col. austral, 304).

TRANSLATIONS

Fanny Bandelier (trans.), *The Journey of Álvar Núñez Cabeza de Vaca and His Companions from Florida to the Pacific, 1528-1536,* New York, Allerton Book, 1922. Cyclone Covey (trans.), *Adventures in the Unknown Interior of America,* New York, Collier, 1962 (paperback). Frederick W. Hodge, *Spanish Explorers in Southern United States, 1528-1543: the Narrative of Álvar Núñez Cabeza de Vaca*, New York, Barnes and Noble, 1953.

CRITICAL REFERENCES

See texts and editions above. Morris Bishop, *The Odyssey of Cabeza de Vaca*, New York, Century, 1933. Cleve Hallenback, *Álvar Núñez Cabeza de Vaca: Journey and Route*, Glendale, Calif., Arthur H. Clark, 1940. Haniel Long, *The Power within us; Cabeza de Vaca's Relation*, New York, Duell, Sloan, and Pearce, 1944.

b. CHRONICLES AND HISTORIES

°°1. (Mexico) **Bernal Díaz del Castillo** (1495?-1584). The soldier-chronicler was born in Medina del Campo, Spain, and came to the New World in 1514 with Pedro Árias Dávila, Governor of Darien. Shortly thereafter Bernal Díaz went to Cuba and was a member of the Grijalva expedition along the Yucatan coast in 1518. Casting his lot with Cortés, he took part in 119 battles and skirmishes during the conquest of Mexico and was rewarded with an *encomienda*, or allotment of Indians, in Guatemala, where he remained much of his long life. Disagreeing with the account of López de Gómara in the latter's *Crónica de la conquista de la Nueva España* (1552), the doughty soldier of Cortés wrote his *Historia verdadera de la conquista de la Nueva España* in a vigorous, unpolished style. This narrative, distinguished for its natural, colloquial language and remarkable detail, was not published until 1632, almost a half century after the death of its author.

SUGGESTED READING

"Recibimiento que les hizo Moctezuma a los conquistadores," "Doña Marina," and other selections included in the texts below.

TEXTS

Anthology, 17-22. Anderson Imbert and Florit, 25-33. Arjona and Arjona, 31-50. Jiménez Rueda, *Antología*, 43-52.

EDITIONS

Historia verdadera de la conquista de la Nueva España, 2 vols., México, Porrúa, 1955; edited by Joaquín Ramírez Cabañas. *Historia verdadera de la conquista de la Nueva España*, México, Fernández, 1961.

TRANSLATIONS

Albert Idell (ed. and trans.), *The Bernal Díaz Chronicles*, Garden City, N. Y., Doubleday, 1957 (paperback). Alfred P. Maudslay (ed. and trans.), *The True History of the Conquest of New Spain*, 5 vols., London, Hakluyt Society, 1908-1916. *The Discovery and Conquest of Mexico, 1517-1521*, New York, Farrar, Straus, and Cudahy, 1956; introduction by Irving A. Leonard (abridgement of Maudslay edition); *ibid.* (paperback), Evergreen E-86 (1958).

CRITICAL REFERENCES

See texts and editions above. Alberto M. Carreño, *Bernal Díaz del Castillo, descubridor, conquistador, y cronista de Nueva España*, México, Eds. Xochitl, 1946.

2. (Caribbean) Bartolomé de las Casas (1484-1565). The "Apostle of the Indians," as the great Dominican friar was called, was born in Seville, Spain, and went to Santo Domingo as a layman and later to Cuba. Profoundly distressed by the cruelties suffered by the Indians at the hands of his countrymen, Las Casas joined the religious order and dedicated the remainder of his long life to the protection of the new wards of the Crown from exploitation by the Spaniards. His excessive zeal moved him at times to exaggerate conditions, notably in his celebrated *Brevísima relación de la destruición de las Indias* (1552) which exercised a profound effect on opinion abroad and upon posterity. Scarcely less influential was his ponderous *Historia de Indias* whose many digressions and heavy-footed prose are occasionally relieved by anecdotes and lighter passages. Las Casas became Bishop of Chiapas and made numerous voyages across the Atlantic in his struggles in behalf of the Indians. Death at 81 found him still gallantly fighting for his cause.

SUGGESTED READING

"La rebelión de Enriquillo."

TEXTS

Anderson Imbert and Florit, 14-19.

EDITIONS

Historia de las Indias, 3 vols., México, Fondo de Cultura Económica, 1951; edited by Agustín Millares Carlo, with introduction by Lewis Hanke. *Doctrina*, 2nd ed., México, 1951 (Biblioteca del estudiante universitario, 22); edited by Agustín Yáñez.

TRANSLATIONS

John Phillips (trans.), *The Tears of the Indian (Brevísima relación de la destruición de las Indiàs)*, Stanford, Calif., Academic Reprints, n.d. (1953?).

CRITICAL REFERENCES

See texts and editions above. Marcel Brion, *Bartolomé de las Casas, "Father of the Indians,"* New York, Dutton, 1929; introduction by Ernesto Montenegro. Lewis Hanke, *Bartolomé de las Casas, an Interpretation of his Life and Writings*, The Hague, M. Nijhoff, 1951; also his *Bartolomé de las Casas, Historian: an Essay in Spanish Historiography*, Gainesville, Univ. of Florida Press, 1952. Manuel María Martínez, *Fray Bartolomé de las Casas, Padre de América*, Madrid, Imp. La Rafa, 1958.

°°3. (Peru) **Inca Garcilaso de la Vega** (1539-1616) was born in Cuzco, Peru, of a Spanish father, cousin of the gifted Castilian poet of the same name (1501?-1536), and of a princess of Incan royalty. The half-caste youth attended school and acquired the different languages and cultures of his mixed parentage. At the age of twenty-one he went to Spain in a vain effort to obtain an inheritance to which he thought himself entitled through his father. He enlisted in the Spanish army and rose to the rank of captain. Much of the rest of his life was passed in the vicinity of Córdoba, where his remains are entombed. He devoted the long years of retirement to collecting information about his Incan forebears and in writing. Besides an excellent translation of León Hebreo's *Diálogos de amor* from Italian, he wrote a novel-like account of Hernando de Soto's wanderings entitled *La Florida del Inca* (1605), that suggests the influence of the romances of chivalry, and his highly esteemed *Comentarios reales que tratan del origen de los Incas* (1609). The second part of this work called *Historia general del Perú* (1617) appeared after his death.

SUGGESTED READING

Comentarios reales (selections) and *La Florida del Inca* (selections).

TEXTS

Anthology, 23-29. Anderson Imbert and Florit, 61-77. Arjona and Arjona, 13-18; 63-88. *Páginas escogidas*, in García Calderón, *Biblioteca*, 3; study by José de la Riva Agüero. *Páginas de los Comentarios reales* (ed. Julio Noé), 6th ed., Buenos Aires, Estrada, 1952

(Col. Estrada, 10). *Comentarios reales: selección,* Lima, Ministerio de Educación Pública, 1958 (Biblioteca del estudiante peruano, 3).

EDITIONS

Los Comentarios reales de los Incas, 2nd ed., 3 vols., Lima, Imp. Gil, 1941-1943; edited by Horacio H. Urteaga. *Comentarios reales de los Incas,* 2nd ed., 2 vols., Buenos Aires, Emecé, 1944; edited by Ángel Rosenblat. *Comentarios reales,* 3rd ed., Buenos Aires, Espasa-Calpe, 1950 (Col. austral, 324); edited by Augusto Cortina. *Comentarios reales de los Incas,* 3 vols., Lima, Univ. Mayor de San Marcos, 1959; edited by José Durand. *Comentarios reales de los Incas,* Lima, Librero Internacional del Perú, 1959; prologue by Aurelio Miró Quesada Sosa. *La Florida del Inca. Historia del Adelantado Hernando de Soto,* México, Fondo de Cultura Económica, 1956; edited by Emma S. Speratti Piñero, prologue by Aurelio Miró Quesada Sosa, bibliography by José Durand. *Obras completas,* 3 vols., Madrid, 1960 (Biblioteca de autores españoles, 132); edited by Carmelo Sáenz de Santa María, S.J. *Diálogos de amor de León Hebreo,* 1st ed., Buenos Aires, Espasa-Calpe, 1947 (Col. austral, 704).

TRANSLATIONS

Clements R. Markham (ed. and trans.), *First Part of the Royal Commentaries of the Yncas,* 2 vols., London, Hakluyt Society, 1869-1871. H. de Onís, 42-52. John G. and Jeannette J. Varner (ed. and trans.), *The Florida of the Inca,* Austin, Univ. of Texas Press, 1951.

CRITICAL REFERENCES

See texts and editions above. Luis A. Arocena, *El Inca Garcilaso y el humanismo renacentista,* Buenos Aires, Centro de Profesores Diplomados de Enseñanza Secundaria, 1949. Julia Fitzmaurice-Kelly, *El Inca Garcilaso de la Vega,* London, Oxford Univ. Press, 1921. Aurelio Miró Quesada Sosa, *El Inca Garcilaso,* 2nd ed., Madrid, Cultura Hispánica, 1948. Raúl Porras Barrenechea, *El Inca Garcilaso en Montilla (1561-1614),* Lima, Ed. San Marcos, 1955. Rojas, III, 206-218.

B. POETRY

The more highly esteemed medium of verse appeared with the Conquistadors in the rustic *romances,* or ballads of eight-syllable lines, which they transmitted orally from Spain or crudely improvised from their New World experience. A little later more cultivated Spaniards came upon the scene, among whom were Gutierre de Cetina (1520-1557?), a gifted poet, Juan de la Cueva (1550?-1610), who became a dramatist, and Pedro de Trejo (late sixteenth century), a prolific versifier, and these visitors introduced Italian meters and forms that strongly influenced the artistic expression of American-born lyrists such as Francisco de Terrazas (1525?-1600?) who composed sonnets, a love poem in tercets, and began an epic.

It was epic poetry, however, that most clearly satisfied the Renaissance preference for narrative literature and achieved the highest literary distinction in that age. Here the Latin and Italian masters, Vergil (70 B.C.-19 A.D.), Torcuato Tasso (1544-1595), and particularly Ludovico Ariosto (1474-1533), provided the models. The latter's *Orlando furioso* (1516) offered a synthesis of Renaissance refinements which included a mingling of the mythological and the contemporary, the martial and the idyllic, the psychological and the merely narrative, that Alonso de Ercilla emulated so effectively in his famous historical poem, the three-part *La araucana* dealing with the conflict between Spaniards and the Araucanian Indians of southern Chile. Its popularity brought a succession of continuations, imitations, and feeble emulations, among which were: *Purén indómito* (end of sixteenth century) of Hernando Álvarez de Toledo (last half 16th century); *La argentina* (1602) of Martín del Barco Centenera (1544?-1605?); *Cortés valeroso* (1588) of Gabriel Lobo Lasso de la Vega (1558-1615); the enormous rhymed chronicle of Juan de Castellanos (1522-1607) entitled *Elegías de varones ilustres de Indias* (1589), and many more. Generally rated the best sequel of *La araucana* is *Arauco domado* (1596) by the Chilean Creole, Pedro de Oña (1570-1643?), which is far more lyric than epic in treating mostly the same themes and episodes. The wealth of bold metaphors, the ornate diction, and the varying rhyme schemes of the traditional octaves set the *Arauco domado* well apart from the realism and the narrative power of *La araucana* and suggest the advent of a more artificial poetic fashion.

REFERENCES

Alegría, *Poesía chilena,* 1-106. Anderson Imbert, I, 64-71. Moses, *Span. Col. Lit.,* Chaps. V, VI, VII, VIII. Solar Correa, *Semblanzas,* 11-106. Torres-Ríoseco, *Epic,* 14-22.

**1. (Chile) Alonso de Ercilla (1533-1594) was born in Madrid. As a page in the royal household of Philip II, he accompanied this monarch, in 1554, to England where Ercilla met the newly appointed *adelantado* of Chile, Gerónimo de Alderete, and became interested in the New World. With royal permission Ercilla reached Lima, Peru, in 1556, and then proceeded to Chile where he fought some two years in the army of the youthful García Hurtado de Mendoza against hardy, warlike Araucanian Indians. In the midst of campaigning he wrote parts of *La araucana,* later completed upon his return to Spain. The three successive parts appeared in 1569, 1578, and 1589 respectively. After further travels in Europe, Ercilla married and settled in Madrid, where he spent the remainder of his life. His epic was an expression of the ethics and esthetics of the Spanish Renaissance and the first in which the poet was an actor; it is the first work of genuine artistic merit in the literature of America.

SUGGESTED READING

La araucana (selections).

TEXTS

Anthology, 41-61. Anderson Imbert and Florit, 78-87. Menéndez y Pelayo, IV, 5-29. Oyuela, I, 4-34. Pierce, 1-64. Weisinger, 28-42.

EDITIONS

La araucana, New York, Hispanic Society, 1902 (facsimile of first and second parts); edited by Archer M. Huntington. *La araucana,* Madrid, Aguilar, 1946; prologue by Concha de Salamanca. *La araucana,* Buenos Aires, Espasa-Calpe, 1947 (Col. austral, 722); prologue by Antonio de Undarraga.

TRANSLATIONS

Charles Maxwell Lancaster and Paul Thomas Manchester (trans.), *The Araucaniad,* Nashville, Vanderbilt Univ. Press, 1945. Walter Owen (trans.), *La araucana,* Buenos Aires, W. Owen, 1945. Walsh, *Hisp. Anth.,* 221-225.

CRITICAL REFERENCES

See texts and editions above. Alegría, *Poesía chilena,* 1-55. José Toribio Medina, *Vida de Ercilla,* México, Fondo de Cultura Económica, 1948; prologue by Ricardo Donoso. Moses, *Span. Col. Lit.,* Chap. V. Solar Correa, *Semblanzas,* 11-48.

2. (Chile) **Pedro de Oña** (1570-1643?). Born in Angol, the son of a Spanish captain fighting Indians in southern Chile, Oña is the first

native Chilean to achieve distinction in literature and is generally considered the foremost poet of that country in the colonial period. He attended (1590-1596) the University of San Marcos in Lima and then took part in an expedition sent to put down an insurrection in Quito, Ecuador. The first part of his *Arauco domado,* inspired by Ercilla's epic, appeared in 1596. More lyric, rhetorical, and rich in metaphors than its model, it has less realism and narrative power; its striving for literary effects weakens its impact and its ornate diction dilutes the intensity of action. Oña's skill as a versifier, however, is great and his inventiveness charms. Other poems are: *Ignacio de Cantabria* (1639), a pious work celebrating Loyola, founder of the Jesuit order; *Temblor de Lima en 1609; Río Lima al río Tibre;* and *El vasauro,* an epic poem of eleven cantos which appeared first in its entirety in 1941.

SUGGESTED READING

Arauco domado, Cantos I and V.

TEXTS

Anderson Imbert and Florit, 106-109. Caillet-Bois, 76-81.

EDITIONS

Arauco domado, Santiago, Academia Chilena, 1917; edited by José Toribio Medina. *Arauco domado,* Madrid, Cultura Hispánica, 1944 (facsimile edition).

TRANSLATIONS

Charles Maxwell Lancaster and Paul Thomas Manchester (trans.), *Arauco Tamed,* Albuquerque, Univ. of New Mexico Press, 1948.

CRITICAL REFERENCES

See texts and editions above. Alegría, *Poesía,* 56-102. Anderson Imbert, I, 106-109. Salvador Dinamarca, *Estudio del Arauco domado de Pedro de Oña,* New York, Hispanic Institute, 1952. Gutiérrez, 351-380. Moses, *Span. Col. Lit.,* 189-197. Solar Correa, *Semblanzas,* 51-98.

c. DRAMA

Before the clash of arms in the Conquest had subsided, missionaries were transplanting the theatrical traditions of Medieval Spain in the New World to spread the Catholic faith among the vanquished natives. The dramatic art of the conqueror and the conquered fused in the *autos sacramentales,* or sacred plays, on themes taken from the Bible and from the lives of saints. These performances took place in the open air and in Indian languages, with singing and dancing in which the humble spectators often participated. Presently, religious occasions such as the Corpus Christi were celebrated with allegorical plays in Latin or in Spanish, frequently with secular episodes interspersed. Schools and *colegios* gave similar performances by students as part of the instructional program.

As the sixteenth century advanced, ecclesiastical influences yielded to those of worldly or secular character. Interludes, called *entremeses,* provided realistic scenes with local types and customs for comic relief. Such contrasting elements increasingly featured the conventional allegorical plays, notably in the *Coloquios* by Fernán González de Eslava (1534?-1601?), many of which were composed to celebrate secular events. The short pieces often reflected life in the New World and so have a certain documentary interest. Quite evidently they hastened the secularizing of drama, and, before the century ended, playhouses for the performance of popular comedies for the general public were established in the vice-regal cities of the Spanish Indies.

REFERENCES
Anderson Imbert, I, 46-47; 72-75. Arrom, *Teatro,* Chaps. I-II. Lohmann Villena, Part I, Chaps. I-III. Reyes, Chaps. III-IV. Rojas Garcidueñas, *Autos y coloquios, passim;* also his *Teatro de Nueva España, passim.* Trenti Rocamora, *passim.* Vargas Ugarte, *passim.*

1. (Mexico) **Fernán González de Eslava** (1534?-1601?) was born in Spain, probably in the vicinity of Seville, and came to Mexico about 1559, but, despite considerable renown in his own time, little more is known about his life. He was author of sixteen *coloquios,* eight *loas,* four *entremeses,* and scattered verse. The *coloquios* were in the nature of allegorical plays usually commissioned by ecclesiastical authorities to celebrate secular as well as religious events. Frequently realistic sketches were interspersed and these are often remarkable for their natural dialogue, simple plot, and comic touches. Characters that are not allegorical are usually well drawn and natural and their language is racy and colloquial. It is regrettable that more of his *entremeses* were not preserved along with the sixteen *coloquios* which were published in 1610 after his death.

SUGGESTED READING

"Entremés, del ahorcado" and selections from the *Coloquios*.

TEXTS

Anthology, 90-93. Rojas Garcidueñas, *Autos y coloquios* ("Coloquio de los cuatro doctores de la Iglesia" and "Coloquio del conde de la Coruña"); also his *Teatro de Nueva España* ("Coloquio de los siete fuertes," "Coloquio de la pestilencia," and an *entremés*). A. Méndez Plancarte, I, 39-51.

EDITIONS

Coloquios espirituales y sacramentales y poesías sagradas, 2nd ed., México, Imp. F. Díaz de León, 1877; edited by Joaquín García Icazbalceta. *Coloquios espirituales y sacramentales*, 2 vols., México, Porrúa, 1958; edited by José Rojas Garcidueñas.

CRITICAL REFERENCES

See texts and editions above. Amado Alonso, "Biografía de Fernán González de Eslava," *Revista de filología hispánica*, II (1940), 213-321. Anderson Imbert, I, 73-75. Arrom, *Teatro*, 64-70. Rojas Garcidueñas, *Teatro de Nueva España*, Chap. VI. Frida Weber de Kurlat, *Lo cómico en el teatro de Fernán González de Eslava*, Buenos Aires, Instituto de Literatura Española, 1963.

II.
Flowering and Decline
of Colonial Letters (1600-1750)

A. POETRY

Even before 1600 the fashion of poetry was perceptibly changing. Poetic narration was already tending to fall into long descriptive passages with a heaping up of colorful adjectives, complex metaphors, and verbal catalogues. As the seventeenth century began, ornate intricacy, lush detail, and rich imagery were complicated by ingenious wordplay, strained conceits, pedantry, and extreme artificiality. Substance surrendered abjectly to form, and impression to expression. The zestful, relatively optimistic quality of Renaissance literature gave way to a spirit of pessimism and disillusionment, and the comparative clarity of the earlier verse yielded to obscurity and affectation in the metrical compositions of the new era which came to be called the Baroque period. *Certámenes poéticos*, or poetic contests, so popular among the literate public of the colonies, provided ample opportunity for exhibitions of metrical manipulation and verbal gymnastics, and they thus contributed to a nearly universal artistic *mal gusto*.

But the transition from the Renaissance to Baroque poetry was marked by at least two epic poets of extraordinary merit, Bernardo de Balbuena (1562?-1627) and Diego de Hojeda (1571-1615). The first is associated with Mexico and the Caribbean and is famed for the color, music, and profusion of ornamental detail in his verse. The second lived most of his life in Peru and achieved fame as the author of the best religious epic in Castilian.

PRINCIPAL SETTLEMENTS IN COLONIAL SOUTH AMERICA

As the seventeenth century progressed, literary abuses grew more excessive, but representative of the better aspects of the Baroque style were the Ecuadorian, Jacinto de Evia (1620-?), and the Colombian, Hernando Domínguez Camargo (?-1657). Towering above all others was the Mexican Creole nun, Sor Juana Inés de la Cruz (1648-1695), one of the finest lyric poets in the language of Spain, whose personality as well as her poetry mark her as the greatest figure in colonial letters. Not so gifted in versifying but more skilful in prose-writing was another nun, the mystical Sor Francisca Josefa del Castillo y Guevara (1671-1742), called Madre Castillo, who lived in New Granada (Colombia).

The extreme artificiality of so much of the writings of the time and the profound frustrations of the Baroque age in Spanish America did not fail to stimulate the Spanish genius for satire in colonial writers of whom the most important was Juan del Valle y Caviedes (1652?-1697?), whose mordant wit assailed the sham and hypocrisy of contemporary society. Another poet of Peru of the same tenor, famed for his gift of improvisation, was the "Blind Mercedarian," Friar Francisco del Castillo Andraca y Tamayo (1716-1770) who, in his varied verse and short dramatic pieces, portrayed contemporary manners with less of the bitterness and indignation of Caviedes.

REFERENCES

Anderson Imbert, I, 76-152. Carilla, *Gongorismo, passim.* Henríquez Ureña, *Lit. Curr.*, Chap. III. Leonard, *Baroque Times, passim.* Picón-Salas, *Cult. Hist.*, Chaps. V-VII. Reyes, Chap. VI. Torres-Ríoseco, *Epic*, 22-43.

a. Epic and Descriptive

°1. (Mexico) **Bernardo de Balbuena** (1562-1627), one of the best descriptive poets of the whole colonial period, is identified with Mexico, though born in Valdepeñas, Spain. Arriving in Mexico as a child, he early displayed precocious literary talent. Trained for the Church, he began about 1592 serving as a priest in various parishes and later became an abbot in Jamaica. During a sojourn in Spain he received a doctorate of theology from the University of Sigüenza, and in 1620 he was appointed Bishop of Puerto Rico, during which episcopate his palace was sacked by the Dutch. Two years later he died in San

Juan. His verse possesses the wealth of descriptive detail and inventiveness of a luxurious tapestry and offers a pictorial, imaginative, and idealized conception of reality. Three important works are associated with his name: *La grandeza mexicana* (1604), a lyrical description in tercets of Mexico City; *El siglo de oro en las selvas de Erífile* (1608), a collection of eclogues in altisonant prose and verse; and *Bernardo, o victoria de Roncesvalles* (1624), a vast epic in five thousand octaves on the legend of Bernardo del Carpio. Italianate influences predominate in these exquisitely wrought works.

SUGGESTED READING

La grandeza mexicana (selections).

TEXTS

Anderson Imbert and Florit, 99-102. Caillet-Bois, 71-76. A. Méndez Plancarte, I, 97-115. Merino, 79-110. Pierce, 167-231.

EDITIONS

Grandeza mexicana y fragmentos del Siglo de Oro y El Bernardo, México, Imp. Universitaria, 1963; edited by Francisco Monterde. *La grandeza mexicana de Bernardo de Balbuena,* Urbana, Univ. of Illinois Press, 1930; edited by John Van Horne.

CRITICAL REFERENCES

See texts and editions above. José Rojas Garcidueñas, *Bernardo de Balbuena: la vida y la obra,* México, Instituto de Investigaciones Estéticas, 1958. John Van Horne, *El Bernardo of Bernardo de Balbuena; A Study of the Poem with Particular Attention to its Relations to the Epics of Boiardo and Ariosto and to its Significance in the Spanish Renaissance,* Urbana, Univ. of Illinois Press, 1927; also his *Bernardo de Balbuena: biografía y crítica,* Guadalajara, México, Imp. Font, 1940.

2. (Peru) **Diego de Hojeda** (1571?-1615). Few facts are known concerning the life of this poet, who was born in Seville, Spain, and who came to Peru as a youth and joined the Dominican order in 1591. He served as prior in a convent in Cuzco and later in Huánuco de los Caballeros, where he died. A gifted poet, to him is assigned the distinction of writing the best sacred epic in the Spanish language. His *La cristiada* (1611), composed in a convent of Lima and divided into twelve books, deals with the life and Passion of the Savior, and may conceivably be likened to Milton's *Paradise Lost* (1667). Despite diffuseness and an abundance of theological disquisi-

tions, it offers passages of great beauty in the ornate, colorful and metaphorical language of the period.

SUGGESTED READING

La cristiada (selections).

TEXTS

Anderson Imbert and Florit, 103-104. García Calderón, *Biblioteca*, VII, 21-45. Merino, 111-146. Pierce, 91-166.

EDITIONS

La cristiada, 2 vols., Lima, Ed., P.T.C.M., 1947; edited by Rafael Aguayo Spencer. *La Christiada, de Fray Diego de Hojeda*, Washington, Catholic Univ., 1935; edited by Sister Mary Helen Patricia Corcoran.

CRITICAL REFERENCES

See texts and editions above. Sister Mary Edgar Meyer, *The Sources of Hojeda's La cristiada*, Ann Arbor, Univ. of Michigan Press, 1953.

b. LYRIC AND SATIRIC

1. (Mexico) Sor Juana Inés de la Cruz (1648-1695). The greatest lyric poet and feminist of the colonial period was Juana Inés de Asbaje y Ramírez de Santillana, the name by which she was known before taking the veil as a nun. Born in San Miguel de Nepantla, Mexico, of Spanish and Creole parentage, she was a precocious child who learned to read when three years old. Studying everything within her reach, she astonished learned professors of the University of Mexico by her knowledge. After living in the court as a favorite maid-in-waiting of the viceroy's wife and famed for her beauty and poetic talent, she chose to take religious vows and in a life of reclusion devote herself to her books. During the years in the convent, she wrote poetry in varied meters on varied themes, including love lyrics that occasionally bordered on the erotic, tender Christmas carols, morality plays, allegorical pieces, and even secular three-act comedies. Much of this metrical expression abounded in literary conceits and suffered from the prevailing florid and ornate fashions, but many sonnets and lyric poems have an almost limpid clarity and an exquisite beauty. A spiritual crisis near the end of her life hastened her death which occurred during an epidemic in the Mexican capital.

SUGGESTED READING

Poetry: "Redondillas contra las injusticias de los hombres al hablar de las mujeres," "Redondillas en que describe racionalmente los efectos irracionales del amor," "Romance en que expresa los efectos del amor divino," "Retrato," "Detente sombra de mi bien esquivo," "Esta tarde, mi bien, cuando te hablaba." Prose: *Respuesta a Sor Filotea de la Cruz*. Drama: *Los empeños de una casa*.

TEXTS

Anthology, 62-72. Anderson Imbert and Florit, 125-147. Caillet-Bois, 91-97. Jiménez Rueda, *Antología*, 103-110; also his edition of *Los empeños de una casa*, 2nd ed., México, 1952 (Biblioteca del estudiante universitario, 14). A. Méndez Plancarte, II, 33-70; 106-120.

EDITIONS

Poesías completas, 2nd ed., México, Botas, 1948; edited by Ermilo Abreu Gómez. *Obras escogidas*, 8th ed., Buenos Aires, Espasa-Calpe, 1951 (Col. austral, 12); edited by Pedro Henríquez Ureña. *Obras completas*, 4 vols., México, Fondo de Cultura Económica, 1951-1957; edited by Alfonso Méndez Plancarte. *El primer sueño*, México, Imp. Universitaria, 1951; edited by Alfonso Méndez Plancarte. *Poesías líricas*, 2nd ed., México, Porrúa, 1950; edited by Joaquín Ramírez Cabañas.

TRANSLATIONS

Pauline Cook (trans.), *The Pathless Grove. A Collection of 17th Century Mexican Sonnets*, Prairie City, Ill., Decher Press, 1950. Underwood, 219-223. Walsh, *Cath. Anth.*, 214-216; also his *Hisp. Anth.*, 357-362.

CRITICAL REFERENCES

See texts and editions above. Ermilo Abreu Gómez, *Sor Juana Inés de la Cruz: bibliografía y biblioteca*, México, 1934 (Monografías bibliográficas mexicanas, 29). Anderson Imbert, I, 118-127. Anita Arroyo, *Razón y pasión de Sor Juana Inés*, México, Porrúa, 1952. Clara Campoamor, *Sor Juana Inés de la Cruz*, Buenos Aires, Emecé, 1944. Carilla, *Gongorismo*, 48-59. Ezequiel A. Chávez, *Ensayo de psicología de Sor Juana Inés de la Cruz*, Barcelona, Araluce, 1931. Gutiérrez, 295-343. Julio Jiménez Rueda, *Sor Juana Inés de la Cruz en su época*, México, Porrúa, 1951. Leonard, *Baroque Times*, Chap. XII. Ludwig Pfandl, *Sor Juana Inés de la Cruz. La Décima Musa de México*, México, Instituto de Investigaciones Estéticas, 1963.

°2. (Peru) **Juan del Valle y Caviedes** (1652?-1697?) was a satiric poet born in Andalusia, Spain, who came, in his childhood, to the mining camps of Peru and later settled in Lima. Few other facts are known with certainty and his writings, which circulated in manuscript in his own time and were not published until the nineteenth century, rarely supply direct information concerning his life. A victim of physical ills and the ministrations of contemporary medicine, many of his verses express his contempt for charlatanism, whether practiced by medical quacks, *beatas,* or the stuffed shirts of official and social circles. His appeal lies in his lusty wit but behind his sardonic humor was a sensitive spirit reacting indignantly to the abuses and injustices of society around him. He wrote short dramatic pieces and also numerous religious poems revealing a depth and intensity of feeling. His pointed satire, earthy wit, and penetrating observations mark him as a forerunner of the *costumbristas* and a versatile poet.

SUGGESTED READING

Diente del parnaso (selections).

TEXTS

Anthology, 73-79. Anderson Imbert and Florit, 111-113. Caillet-Bois, 98-99. García Calderón, *Biblioteca,* V, 203-271.

EDITIONS

Obras de don Juan del Valle y Caviedes, Lima, Ed. Studium, 1947 (Clásicos peruanos, 1); edited by Rubén Vargas Ugarte.

CRITICAL REFERENCES

See texts and edition above. Gutiérrez, 259-289. Glenn L. Kolb, *Juan del Valle y Caviedes. A Study of the Life, Times, and Poetry of a Spanish Colonial Satirist,* New London, Connecticut College, 1959. Daniel R. Reedy, *The Poetic Art of Juan del Valle y Caviedes,* Chapel Hill, Univ. of North Carolina Press, 1964.

3. (Peru) **Francisco del Castillo Andraca y Tamayo** (1716-1770). See II, C, 3, below.

B. PROSE

Prose works of the long middle period of the colonial centuries were mainly chronicles, histories, memorials, religious treatises, and didactic writings usually suffering from the artistic vices of their time and generally of little interest to those seeking diversion in reading. Occasionally more lively in parts were such works as the *Unión de dos cuchillos, pontificio y regio* (1656-1657) of the Ecuadorian Gaspar de Villarroel (1587?-1665) and the *Histórica relación de Chile* (1646?) of the Chilean Alonso de Ovalle (1601-1651). Highly respected is the critical acumen of the Peruvian mestizo, Juan de Espinosa Medrano (1632-1688), in his *Apologético en favor de don Luis de Góngora* (1662).

No authentic novel appeared during the entire colonial period, a curious fact since large importations of this kind of literature from Spain circulated widely in its overseas realms in America. Explanations of the failure to cultivate the novel in colonial literature include the psychological and economic difficulties of the Creole writers, the necessity of obtaining publication licenses from authorities in Spain, the monopoly of printers and booksellers in the Spanish Peninsula, and the popularity of printed versions of plays that poured continuously into the colonies after 1605.

If the true novel is absent in colonial letters of Spanish America, numerous examples exist of what is conveniently termed "prose with novelistic elements." These narratives frequently make use of devices characteristic of fiction such as anecdotes, intercalated incidents, dialogues, rhetorical declamations, and other techniques of contemporary imaginative literature. The pastoral novels of the mother country exerted considerable influence as in Bernardo de Balbuena's *Siglo de oro en las selvas de Erífile* (1608), Francisco Bramón's (?-1655?) *Los sirgueros de la Virgen* (1621), and Juan de Palafox y Mendoza's (1600-1659) *El pastor de Nochebuena* (1644), but later the inspiration of Spain's great picaresque tradition is noticeable in works closely approximating novels such as Juan Rodríguez Freile's (1566-1640?) gossipy chronicle of seventeenth-century Bogotá, *El carnero* (1636-1638), Francisco Núñez de Pineda y Bascuñán's (1607-1682) *El cautiverio feliz* (around 1650), an account of Indian captivity, and particularly Carlos de Sigüenza y Góngora's (1645-1700) *Infortunios de Alonso Ramírez* (1692), which resembles a travel adventure tale.

REFERENCES

Anderson Imbert, I, 80-94. Moses, *Span. Col. Lit.*, Chaps. IX-XII. Picón-Salas, *Cult. Hist.*, Chap. VII. Sánchez, *Novela*, Chaps. III-IV.

Solar Correa, *Semblanzas,* 101-208 (Alonso de Ovalle, Diego de Rosales).

°1. (Mexico) **Carlos de Sigüenza y Góngora** (1645-1700). Born in Mexico City of Spanish and Creole parentage, he was the foremost intellectual figure and humanist of colonial Mexico, having distinguished himself as a mathematician, astronomer, historian, antiquarian, philosopher, and a poet. Educated as a Jesuit, he early left the Order, subsequently becoming a professor of mathematics in the University of Mexico and chaplain of the Hospital del Amor de Dios, where he lived much of his adult life. An intimate friend of Sor Juana Inés de la Cruz, he also wrote poetry but fell far short of her genius, succumbing completely to the affected style which stemmed from the inspiration of his illustrious relative, the Spanish bard, Luis de Góngora (1561-1627). Though his best contributions were in applied science and history, his most readable writings today are those in which, as a court chronicler of the viceroy, the Count of Galve, he recorded contemporary events. His *Infortunios de Alonso Ramírez,* a narrative written in the first person of the misadventures of a Puerto Rican in a journey around the world, is in the picaresque tradition and is sometimes considered a forerunner of the Mexican novel. Sigüenza's scientific work took him in 1693 to Pensacola, Florida, which he surveyed and mapped. A painful illness ended his life at the age of 55.

SUGGESTED READING

Infortunios de Alonso Ramírez (selections) and *Alboroto y motín de México.*

TEXTS

Anthology, 80-85. Anderson Imbert and Florit, 114-124. Jiménez Rueda, *Antología,* 89-102. A. Méndez Plancarte, II, 3-24.

EDITIONS

Poemas, Madrid, G. Sáez, 1931; edited by Irving A. Leonard and Ermilo Abreu Gómez. *Alboroto y motín de México del 8 de junio de 1692,* México, Museo Nacional de Arqueología, 1932; edited by Irving A. Leonard. *Obras con una biografía,* México, Sociedad de Bibliófilos Mexicanos, 1928; edited by Francisco Pérez Salazar. *Triunfo parténico,* México, Eds. Xochitl, 1945; edited by José Rojas Garcidueñas. *Relaciones históricas,* 2nd ed., México, Imp. Universitaria, 1954; edited by M. Romero de Terreros. *Obras históricas,* 2nd ed., México, Porrúa, 1960.

TRANSLATIONS

Irving A. Leonard (ed. and trans.), *The Mercurio volante,* Los Angeles, The Quivira Society, 1932. Edwin H. Pleasants (trans.), *The Misfortunes of Alonso Ramírez,* México, Imp. Mexicana, 1962.

CRITICAL REFERENCES

See texts and editions above. Irving A. Leonard, *Don Carlos de Sigüenza y Góngora, a Mexican Savant of the Seventeenth Century,* Berkeley, Univ. of California Press, 1929: also his *Baroque Times,* Chap. XIII. José Rojas Garcidueñas, *Don Carlos de Sigüenza y Góngora, erudito barroco,* México, Eds. Xochitl, 1945.

2. (Chile) **Francisco Núñez de Pineda y Bascuñán** (1607-1682). The author of a curious tale of Indian captivity entitled *Cautiverio feliz y razón de las guerras dilatadas de Chile* was born in Chillán, the son of a Spanish general with a reputation for fairness among the Araucanian Indians whom he fought, and a Chilean mother, descendant of an early conqueror. Núñez de Pineda was educated by Jesuits who acquainted him with classic Greek and Latin writers as well as sacred literature. Following his father's military profession, he rose from the rank of a private to that of a captain in the campaigns against the Indians of southern Chile. Taken prisoner May 15, 1629, he remained a captive among the Araucanians some seven months, during which he shared their mode of life and had many adventures, although he was well treated. After being exchanged, he resumed his military service, rising to be *maestro de campo* and, shortly before his death, governor of Valdivia. Possibly around 1650 he wrote a detailed and novelesque account of his experiences in captivity, frequently interrupting his narrative by disquisitions of a pious, moral, and political nature and by stanzas of original verse usually amplifying familiar lines from Latin classics. In general he depicts the Araucanian Indians sympathetically and occasionally reveals the resentment of a Creole against privileged Spanish officeholders in the colonies.

SUGGESTED READING

Cautiverio feliz (selections).

TEXTS

Anderson Imbert and Florit, 95-97.

EDITIONS

Cautiverio feliz y razón de las guerras dilatadas de Chile, Santiago, Imp. de El Ferrocarril, 1863 (Colección de historiadores de Chile y documentos relativos a la historia nacional, 3); prologue by Diego Barros Arana. *El Cautiverio feliz de Francisco Núñez de Pineda y Bascuñán,* Santiago, Zig-Zag, 1948; edited by Ángel C. González.

CRITICAL REFERENCES

See texts and editions above. Anderson Imbert, I, 91-94. Alejandro Vicuña, *Bascuñán, el cautivo,* Santiago, Nascimento, 1948. José Toribio Medina, *Historia de la literatura colonial de Chile,* Santiago, Imp. de la Librería del Mercurio, 1878, I, 309-322.

c. DRAMA

With almost no time lag the popularity of the secular drama created by the prolific genius of Spanish playwrights spread to the New World realms. There, printed versions of versified plays were avidly read, while the local *corrales de comedias* drew enthusiastic throngs from all social classes to lively performances by traveling stock companies. In the palaces of the viceroys, private dramatic presentations with rich costumes and elaborate stage effects were common features of aristocratic life. While Creole writers occasionally composed standard three-act plays for the popular theater, more often they supplied short pieces variously termed *loas, entremeses, bailes, sainetes, fines de fiesta,* and the like. These skits served to amuse audiences between the acts or were preludes or afterpieces of the longer plays. Little of this literature was preserved, but enough survives to indicate that these short works brought an indigenous flavor to the colonial theater by their realistic and satirical portrayal of local types, customs, and situations.

Interesting examples both of the longer and shorter plays are those of the Mexican nun, Sor Juana Inés de la Cruz. During the early decades of eighteenth-century Mexico the Spanish-born, Eusebio Vela (1688-1737), directed and staged as elaborate spectacles, the plays that he had written, some fourteen in number. In this same period the Peruvian *sabio,* Pedro de Peralta Barnuevo (1664-1743), prepared for the private theater of the viceroy, three long plays with accompanying shorter pieces. The themes and manner of these dramatic works clearly reveal early French influence while their performance with music especially composed suggests Italian operetta. Before the middle of the same century, Friar Francisco del Castillo (1716-1770), the "Blind Mercedarian," had improvised numerous lively skits, realistic in nature and speech, on life in Lima as well as more formal plays.

REFERENCES

Anderson Imbert, I, 143-146. Arrom, *Teatro época col.*, Chaps. III-IV. Lohmann Villena, Parts II and III and appendix. Hildburg Schilling, *Teatro profano en la Nueva España: fines del siglo XVI a mediados del XVIII*, México, Imp. Universitaria, 1958, *passim*. Trenti Rocamora, *passim*.

1. (Mexico) **Sor Juana Inés de la Cruz** (1648-1695). See II, A, b, 1, above.

2. (Peru) **Pedro de Peralta Barnuevo** (1664-1743), the remarkably versatile Creole of colonial Peru, was renowned as a mathematician, astronomer, engineer, jurist, theologian, historian, poet, and dramatist, and he was familiar with eight languages, in several of which he composed poems. He was born of Spanish and Creole parentage in Lima, where his whole life was spent. His writings as a whole glaringly reveal the inflated style of his time, mingling its baroque and neo-classic fashions. He wrote a belated epic, *Lima fundada* (1732), and later a mystical *Pasión y triunfo de Cristo* (1738) indicating disillusionment with the beginnings of science to which he had given much attention. His three long plays, *Triunfos de amor y poder*, with mythological characters, *Afectos vencen finezas*, a Calderonian *comedia*, and *Rodoguna*, a recasting of Corneille's *Rodogune*, are interesting for their variety of meters. The last-mentioned long play and some of the more engaging short pieces represent the earliest French influences in Spanish American literature. His *entremeses* and *bailes* are comic and *costumbrista* in character, preserving contemporary popular speech and customs.

SUGGESTED READING

"Fin de fiesta" of *Afectos vencen finezas* and "Entremés" of *Rodoguna*.

TEXTS

García Calderón, *Biblioteca,* VII, 184-194 (includes excerpts from *Pasión y triunfo de Cristo*).

EDITIONS

Obras dramáticas de Pedro Peralta Barnuevo, Santiago, Imp. Universitaria, 1937; edited by Irving A. Leonard, with appendix of unpublished poems.

CRITICAL REFERENCES

See texts and editions above. Anderson Imbert, I, 141-143. Arrom, *Teatro época col.,* 142-151. Gutiérrez, 7-212. Lohmann Villena, Part III, Chap. III.

3. **(Peru) Francisco del Castillo Andraca y Tamayo (1716-1770).** Regarded as a prodigy by his contemporaries in Lima because of his gift of rapid improvisation of verses and clever wit, this Mercedarian friar was blind from infancy. His extraordinary facility in versifying placed him in demand at funerals, weddings, banquets, and gatherings of every kind at which, in effortless fashion, he struck off suitable sentiments in varied meters. He was, however, more than a facile improviser of random verses. In his lengthy *romances,* or ballads, he depicted contemporary types and customs, satirizing them after the manner of Valle y Caviedes, though with less indignation. Del Castillo faithfully reproduces the speech and attitudes of the motley throngs on the streets and squares of Lima, and he thus clearly anticipates later *costumbrismo.* More boldly than Caviedes, he essayed the dramatic art in three-act plays after the manner of French neo-classicism as in *Mitridates* and, like Peralta Barnuevo, he also introduced musical effects suggestive of Italian operetta. More successful and more to modern tastes are his *sainetes,* of which *El entremés del Justicia y litigantes* is representative.

SUGGESTED READING

El entremés del Justicia y litigantes, Entremés del viejo niño, and *Romances.*

TEXTS

Vargas Ugarte, 262-275 (*El entremés del Justicia y litigantes*).

EDITIONS

Obras de Fray Francisco del Castillo Andraca y Tamayo, Lima, Ed. Studium, 1948 (Clásicos peruanos, 2); edited by Rubén Vargas Ugarte.

CRITICAL REFERENCES

See texts and editions above. Arrom, *Teatro época col.,* 167-173. Lohmann Villena, Part III, Chap. VI. Ricardo Palma, *Apéndice a mis últimas tradiciones peruanas,* Barcelona, Maucci, 1910, 269-280; also his *Tradiciones peruanas completas,* Madrid, Aguilar, 1957, 603-608.

III.
Period of Enlightenment and Revolt (1750-1832)

A. POETRY

The wars for independence represented a revolution in the writing of poetry as well as in political relations. The colonial spell and tradition were broken with an eruption of verse with new themes and a contagious enthusiasm. In the later colonial decades, the muse had been lethargic, showing some signs of vitality only in a few poets, such as Fray Manuel de Navarrete (Mexico, 1768-1809), whose poems were musical and pleasing, classical and imitative in form; Esteban de Terralla y Landa (Peru, last half of the eighteenth century), a somewhat rowdy but skillful satirical poet who lampooned colonial society (*Lima por dentro y fuera*); and Manuel José de Lavardén (Argentina, 1754-1809), whose ode, "Al Paraná" (1801), was a precursor of later national descriptive poetry.

During the revolutionary period, scores of poets and bards echoed the notes of the bugle call, pronouncing anathemas against the Spaniards, eulogizing the leaders of the revolution, and painting a golden picture of the new nations' future. Strongly influenced by neo-classicism, derived in part from the Spanish liberal poets of the Napoleonic Wars, such as Gallego and Quintana, this poetry is characterized by grandiloquence, classical references and syntax and, in the worst of it, a tendency toward bombast. Among the many poets who wrote in this style, only Olmedo is truly outstanding.

Several other heroic poets should be mentioned because

of their representative qualities: Vicente López y Planes (1784-1856) is known for his ballad, "Triunfo argentino," and especially for his composition of the text of the Argentine national anthem; Esteban de Luca (1786-1824), a more prolific Argentine patriotic poet, was highly praised in his day, and his "Al pueblo de Buenos Aires" can be read today with some profit; far to the north, the Mexican poet, Andrés Quintana Roo (1787-1851) is a minor national hero, especially remembered for his ode, "Al 16 de septiembre de 1821."

Love songs in simple meters, a heritage of Spanish traditional folklore, were current among the common people during the colonial period. When the support of the masses, especially the gauchos in the La Plata region, was enlisted in the wars for independence, these forms were used to express in colloquial, sometimes crude language, the hatred for the Spaniard and the glories of the revolution. The commonest verse form was the *cielito*.

Poetry of a nonpatriotic theme, such as was sung sometimes by Cruz Varela and Heredia, was a subordinate motif, overwhelmed for the most part by the more strident tones of a liberated America. Andrés Bello, in his integrated, humanistic way, managed to combine a sincerely patriotic aspiration with a quiet lyricism, which presaged the best of later romantic poetry.

Considered all together, the poetry of the period, which was mostly patriotic and only in small part personal and lyric, was amazing in quantity, but less astounding in lasting quality. There are a few still-ringing notes, as in Olmedo, Bello, and Heredia, but the rest, by and large, is interesting only from a historical and sociological point of view.

REFERENCES

Anderson Imbert, I, *passim*. Arrieta, I, 225-422. Coester, *Lit. Hist.*, Chaps. II-III. Cometta Manzoni, 136-147. Henríquez Ureña, *Lit. Curr.*, 94-111. Leguizamón, I, 319-434. Rojas, IV, 409-491, 526-658. Sánchez, *Nueva hist.*, 115-171.

a. Heroic and Popular

°1. (Ecuador) **José Joaquín Olmedo** (1780-1847) was born in Guayaquil and received the usual colonial classical education in the University of San Marcos in Lima. This classical background is obvious in his poetry. Shortly after the beginning of the independence movement (1811), he went to Spain to represent his natal city in the Cortes of Cádiz. In 1814 he returned to Guayaquil to take an important part in the revolutionary activities of Ecuador and Peru, and it was he who in 1823 brought the Peruvian plea to Bolívar for aid against the Spaniards.

As a result, Bolívar and his men achieved crucial victories in the battles of Junín (August 6, 1824) and Ayacucho (December 9, 1824), both fought in the central valleys of Peru—victories which decided the final outcome of the wars for independence in South America. These martial events, as well as Bolívar's own suggestions, moved Olmedo to compose in 1825 his best-known poem, "La victoria de Junín: Canto a Bolívar," which in reality encompassed both battles. In spite of the quibbles of some critics, including Bolívar himself, the poem is generally considered the finest example of heroic poetry in the classical style written in America. Olmedo's knowledge and love of the Roman poets, especially Horace and Vergil, are evident throughout the composition.

Olmedo's later life was one of service to his country. After undertaking a special mission to Europe for Bolívar, he participated in Ecuadorian politics and ran for President in 1845. Held in high esteem by his countrymen, he died two years later.

Aside from his "Canto a Bolívar," Olmedo wrote relatively little, his "Al General Flores" (1835) and his translations (1823) of parts of Pope's *Essay on Man* being the most notable.

SUGGESTED READING

"La victoria de Junín: canto a Bolívar."

TEXTS

Anthology, 97-112. Anderson Imbert and Florit, 198-204. Beltrán, I, 44-51. Caillet-Bois, 145-153. Hills, *Odes,* 45-82. Menéndez y Pelayo, III, 272-297. Monterde, 202-226. Oyuela, I, 205-236.

EDITIONS

Poesías, Paris, Garnier, 1896; edited by Clemente Ballén. *Obras completas: poesías,* Quito, Casa de la Cultura Ecuatoriana, 1945; edited by Aurelio Espinosa Polit; same text entitled *Poesías completas,* México, Fondo de Cultura Económica, 1947.

CRITICAL REFERENCES

See texts and editions above. Barrera, *Hist. lit. ecuat.,* III, 33-73; also his *Lit. hisp.,* 210-237. *Diccionario . . . Ecuador,* 51-55. Darío Guevara, *Olmedo,* Quito, Casa de la Cultura Ecuatoriana, 1958.

Leguizamón, I, 409-414. Menéndez y Pelayo, II, cix-cxli. Moses, *Intel. Back.,* Chap. XI. Oyuela, I, 489-492.

2. (Uruguay) **Bartolomé Hidalgo** (1788-1822) was the most notable poet known by name to use the popular gaucho verse forms and language for patriotic purposes during the wars for independence. Born of humble parents in Montevideo, he was a bartender in his youth. Later he participated in the military operations of the independence movement. Aside from his *Diálogos* (1822), which are his best-known compositions, he wrote various *cielitos heroicos,* or folklore ballads with patriotic themes. In addition to his reputation as a folk bard of the revolution, he is considered to be the first of the many gaucho poets of the early nineteenth century— one who helped to form a literary pattern in which folk material could naturally fit (see Second Period, I, A, b).

SUGGESTED READING
"Diálogos patrióticos."

TEXTS
Beltrán, *Antología,* II, 28-34. Caillet-Bois, 167-178. Henríquez Ureña and Borges, 45-56. Oyuela, I, 412-422.

EDITIONS
Cielitos y diálogos patrióticos, Buenos Aires, Ciordia y Rodríguez, 1950; with study on origins of gaucho poetry.

CRITICAL REFERENCES
See texts and editions above. Domingo A. Caillava, *Historia de la literatura gauchesca en el Uruguay,* Montevideo, C. García, 1945, 29-38. Mario Falcão Espalter, *El poeta uruguayo Bartolomé Hidalgo, su vida y sus obras,* 2nd ed., Madrid, Gráficas Reunidas, 1929. Oyuela, I, 515-531. Rojas, II, 335-348.

b. LYRIC

1. (Argentina) **Juan Cruz Varela** (1794-1839). Although his deeply patriotic sentiments ally him closely with such poets of the revolution as Olmedo, he was a classical lyric poet whose inspiration ranged in a wide field. A native of Buenos Aires, he received a thorough classical education in Córdoba. His works fall into five periods: (1) those of his apprenticeship—translations from Vergil and Horace

and early love poems; (2) two dignified tragedies in the classical tradition, *Dido* (1823) and *Argia* (1824); (3) patriotic odes inspired by contemporary events; (4) poems on civic themes written in support of social reforms; and (5) his last and greatest poem, a song of exile written a few months before his death and after he had been banished to Montevideo. A man of great culture, he was an intellectual, rather than an inspired poet. To modern ears, his poetry sounds excessively declamatory and rhetorical.

SUGGESTED READING

"Campaña del ejército republicano al Brasil y triunfo de Ituzaingó: canto lírico," "El 25 de mayo de 1838, en Buenos Aires."

TEXTS

Beltrán, *Antología,* I, 58-60. Caillet-Bois, 201-209. Menéndez y Pelayo, IV, 91-95. Oyuela, I, 428-441.

EDITIONS

Poesías, Buenos Aires, 1943 (Biblioteca de clásicos argentinos, 9); prologue by Manuel Mujica Láinez. *Tragedias,* Buenos Aires, 1915 (Biblioteca argentina, 6); prologue by Ricardo Rojas.

TRANSLATIONS

Green and Lowenfels, 294-303. Poor, 28-30.

CRITICAL REFERENCES

See texts and editions above. Arrieta, I, 368-398, 416-422. *Diccionario . . . Argentina,* I, 187-189. Menéndez y Pelayo, IV, cxxviii-cxliv. Oyuela, I, 534-545. Rojas, IV, 632-658.

2. (Venezuela) **Andrés Bello (1781-1865). Although he was a Venezuelan by birth, he may be considered a citizen of all South America because of his broad, human outlook and his solid accomplishments for several of the new republics. His early training in Latin and the Spanish classics, plus his sound acquaintance with the rationalistic trends of eighteenth-century European thought, gave him encyclopedic knowledge as well as idealistic vision. In 1810 he was sent to London as an agent of the revolting colonies and there he remained for nearly twenty years. These years he spent in intelligent support of the independence cause, as well as in study and literary investigation. In 1826 he founded a journal, *El repertorio americano* (1826-1828), through which he hoped to defend the idea of freedom for the Spanish New World. In it he published for the first time his well-known "Silva a la agricultura de la zona tórrida" (1826). Three years later, at the invitation of the republican government, he went to Chile to be the Minister of Foreign Affairs. He spent the remainder of his very active life in Chile, being editor of *El araucano* (1830-1853), first president of the University of Chile (1843-1865), and a leader of the nation's intellectual life for many years. His amazingly varied accomplishments included penetrating studies in law and philosophy, continued creative work in poetry, and the compilation of the *Gramática de la lengua castellana* (1847), which, with the notes of Rufino José Cuervo (Colombia, 1844-1911), is still considered one of the most complete and logical treatises on the language.

During his entire life he was a defender of classicism and humanism, of the principle of traditional authority in literature. Consequently he came into frequent conflict with Argentine exiles in Chile —among them the famous Sarmiento—who were fired with zeal for the new and antitraditional theories of romanticism. This polemic, violent and acrimonious at times, was one of the outstanding battles in Latin American literary history. In his later years Bello composed, in imitation of Victor Hugo, a tender, lyrical poem, "La oración por todos" (1843), in which the classicist, ironically enough, yields to certain romantic tendencies in tone and form. His earlier "Silva," while lacking the martial fervor of Olmedo's poem, reveals a deeply patriotic concern for the future of the newborn republics, illustrates the idealistic and optimistic dreams which accompanied the independence movement, and in style shows a graceful lyricism.

SUGGESTED READING

"Silva a la agricultura de la zona tórrida" and "La oración por todos."

TEXTS

Anthology, 113-130. Anderson Imbert and Florit, 204-215. Beltrán, *Antología,* I, 37-43. Caillet-Bois, 153-161. Hills, *Odes,* 27-41. Menéndez y Pelayo, II, 301-312. Oyuela, I, 252-256.

EDITIONS

Antología poética, Buenos Aires, Estrada, 1945; edited by Eugenio Orrego Vicuña. *Poesías,* Caracas, Ministerio de Educación, 1952 *(Obras completas,* I); prologue by Fernando Paz Castillo.

TRANSLATIONS

Walsh, *Hisp. Anth.,* 389-394. John Cook Wylie (trans.), *A Georgic of the Tropics,* Charlottesville, Va., Lindsay Printing Corp., 1954.

CRITICAL REFERENCES
Miguel Luis Amunátegui, *Vida de Don Andrés Bello,* Santiago, Imp. P. G. Ramírez, 1882. Anderson Imbert, I, 193-198. Barrera, *Lit. hisp.,* 264-276. Blanco-Fombona, *Grandes escritores,* 11-28. Davis, *Latin American Leaders,* 119-127. Pedro Grases, *Doce estudios sobre Andrés Bello,* Buenos Aires, Nova, 1950. Menéndez y Pelayo, II, cxvii-clviii. Pedro Lira Urquieta, *Andrés Bello,* México, Fondo de Cultura Económica, 1948. Oyuela, I, 492-502.

°°3. (Cuba) **José María Heredia** (1803-1839). In the early nineteenth century neo-classicism coexisted with romanticism; the latter was clearly heard as an increasingly typical note and was directly associated with the liberal, revolutionary spirit of the times. Although his homeland was not to break bonds with Spain until 1898, Heredia was an exemplary romantic revolutionary: he hated political oppression, was an exile, and wrote poetry in which his emotions were fused with nature. His ideal of political freedom was inherited from his father, a political liberal, and was nurtured during his youth by residence in Venezuela (1812-1817) and Mexico (1818-1821). He returned to Cuba to finish his law course, but, as a member of a revolutionary society, he became involved in the first and abortive movement to free Cuba from Spain. As a result, he was sentenced to perpetual exile and fled to the United States. There he spent two scant unhappy years earning his living as a teacher of Spanish at a New York private academy. After publishing a volume of poems in 1825, he again went to Mexico where he was appointed to several political offices. Some ten years later, he was allowed to return to Cuba, but the professional exile was unsatisfied with his homeland and died in Mexico as a young man.

Although neo-classical in his form and in some of his phraseology, Heredia was one of the first truly romantic poets of the Spanish language. His lines are the outpouring of a young man's intense emotion, often melancholy and introspective, and are usually inspired by the grander forces of nature—the sea, the hurricane, the waterfall—or by his sense of time's pitiless antipathy to the works of man. His best poems show a strong, sensitive awareness of the American landscape.

SUGGESTED READING

"En el teocalli de Cholula," "A Flérida," "En una tempestad," "Niágara," "A Emilia," "Al sol."

TEXTS

Anthology, 131-145. Anderson Imbert and Florit, 218-225. Beltrán, *Antología*, I, 52-57. Caillet-Bois, 224-235. Hills, *Odes*, 85-116. Menéndez y Pelayo, II, 15-46. Oyuela, I, 357-374. Torres-Ríoseco, *Ant. lit. hisp.*, 148-152.

EDITIONS

Obras poéticas, 2 vols., New York, N. Ponce de León, 1875. *Poesías líricas*, Paris, Garnier, 1893; prologue by E. Zerolo. *Poesías, discursos y cartas*, 2 vols., Habana, Cultural, 1939. *Poesías completas*, 2 vols., Habana, Municipio de La Habana, 1940-1941.

TRANSLATIONS

Blackwell, 486-489. Green and Lowenfels, 368-373. Hills, *Odes*, 130-136. Walsh, *Hisp. Anth.*, 405-414. For other translations see Francisco González del Valle, *Poesías de Heredia traducidas a otros idiomas* (Habana, 1940).

CRITICAL REFERENCES

See texts and editions above. Anderson Imbert, I, 207-211. Barrera, *Lit. hisp.*, 249-263. José María Chacón y Calvo, *Estudios heredianos*, Habana, Ed. Trópico, 1939. Manuel Pedro González, *José María Heredia, primogénito del romanticismo hispano*, México, El Colegio de México, 1955. Menéndez y Pelayo, II, xiv-xxvii. Oyuela, I, 502-507. Remos, I, Chap. XII.

B. PROSE

In the last half of the eighteenth century, prose writing was considerably more lively and original—at least in the work of certain authors—than the production in poetry. During the independence period, it was quite as important as the heroic poetry and generally less exaggerated and more thoughtful. Both "Concolorcorvo" and Fernández de Lizardi represent a refreshing, ironic, popular type of writing which was far removed from the earlier and more tedious literature of colonial times, and which presaged the *costumbrista* prose of the nineteenth century.

During and immediately after the wars for independence,

journalistic essays flowed from the pens of the patriots like spring freshets. The works of Bernardo de Monteagudo (Argentina, 1785-1825), particularly noted below, are good examples of the writings of a host of others who reasoned and argued about the problems confronting the nations being born, often with real eloquence. Some of them were hardly more than propagandistic tracts of more interest to the historian than to the student of literature. In the works of other men, such as those of Bolívar, we find serious hard thinking expressed with care and a classical elegance.

It is perhaps odd, but nevertheless understandable that, with the exception of Fernández de Lizardi, the independence period produced no fiction writer of any note. It appears that educated men were far too preoccupied with the "war effort" to dabble in what they doubtless considered an idle pastime.

REFERENCES
Anderson Imbert, I, *passim*. Arrieta, I, 225-422. Coester, *Lit. Hist.*, Chaps. II-III. Henríquez Ureña, *Lit. Curr.*, 94-111. Leguizamón, I, 319-434. Rojas, IV, *passim*. Sánchez, *Nueva hist.*, 115-171.

°1. (Peru) "Concolorcorvo" (Alonso Carrió de la Vandera) (1715-after 1778). His *Lazarillo de ciegos caminantes* is a lively account of an arduous journey in viceregal days from Montevideo across the plains and mountains to Lima. It is in effect a kind of witty guidebook which describes in vivid, realistic, often ironic language, the towns, the economic resources of the country, the customs and manners, as well as the privations and dangers of the journey. There are notes on the popular traditions of the Argentine pampas and the Andean highlands, anecdotes, humorous dialogues, and snatches of early gaucho verse. The clarity of its descriptions, the many light touches, the satire, and the picaresque humor set this work in startling contrast to the prevailing literary fashions of the day. Some of its pages are the most diverting in colonial literature. The author was long thought to be a mestizo, Calixto Bustamante Carlos Inga, and the book was allegedly published in Gijón in 1773. Actually its date and place of publication are uncertain and the true author was a Spaniard sent to reorganize the postal service between Buenos Aires and the Peruvian capital. The mestizo was his traveling companion.

SUGGESTED READING

El lazarillo de ciegos caminantes, Chaps. I, II, or VIII.

TEXTS

Anthology, 86-90. Anderson Imbert and Florit, 159-177. García Calderón, *Biblioteca,* 6.

EDITIONS

El lazarillo de ciegos caminantes desde Buenos Aires hasta Lima, Buenos Aires, 1908 (Biblioteca de la Junta de Historia y Numismática Americana, 4); edited by Martiniano Leguizamón. *El lazarillo de ciegos caminantes,* Buenos Aires, Eds. Argentinas Solar, 1942; edited by José Luis Busaniche. *El lazarillo de ciegos caminantes,* Buenos Aires, Espasa-Calpe, 1946 (Col. austral, 609).

TRANSLATIONS

Walter C. Kline (trans.), *El Lazarillo: A Guide for Inexperienced Travelers Between Buenos Aires and Lima,* Bloomington, Indiana Univ. Press, 1965; introduction by Richard A. Mazzara, foreword by Irving A. Leonard.

CRITICAL REFERENCES

See texts and editions above. Moses, *Span. Col. Lit.,* 525-530. José J. Real Díaz, "Don Alonso Carrió de la Vandera, autor del *Lazarillo de ciegos caminantes,*" *Biblioteca de autores españoles,* vol. 122, 245-277.

2. (Argentina) **Bernardo de Monteagudo** (1785-1825) was born in Tucumán and educated in the colonial schools of Argentina. He was among the first conspirators for independence in La Paz, where he was condemned to die as a traitor. Escaping, he joined the revolutionary army and went to Buenos Aires. There, and later in Chile and Peru, he was a fiery journalist who keenly analyzed in his articles the problems of freedom, and was for a time San Martín's secretary. He was one of the founders of the *Sociedad Patriótica Literaria* (1812) and of a similar organization in Lima. While in Lima, he worked with Bolívar toward the formation of an American federation of states. Still at the height of a remarkable career, he died at the hand of an assassin in Lima.

SUGGESTED READING

"Ensayo sobre la necesidad de una federación general entre los estados hispanoamericanos y plan de su organización" (1824).

TEXTS and EDITIONS

Escritos políticos, Buenos Aires, "La Cultura Argentina," 1916;

edited by Mario A. Pelliza, with introduction by Álvaro Melián Lafinur. *Obras políticas,* Buenos Aires, Roldán, 1916 (Biblioteca argentina, 7), 75-88; edited by Ricardo Rojas. *El pensamiento de Bernardo Monteagudo,* Buenos Aires, 1944 (Biblioteca del pensamiento argentino, 6); edited by Gregorio Weinberg.

CRITICAL REFERENCES

See texts and editions above. *Diccionario . . . Argentina,* I, 144-146. Moses, *Intel. Back.,* Chaps. V, VII, IX. Rojas, V, 39-58. Mariano de Vedia y Mitre, *La vida de Monteagudo,* 3 vols., Buenos Aires, Kraft, 1950.

3. (Mexico) **José Joaquín Fernández de Lizardi (1776-1827) is often known by his pseudonym, "El Pensador Mexicano." He was born of a middle-class family in Mexico City. Although his formal education was incomplete, he managed to become well acquainted with the books of the French *philosophes* of the eighteenth century. When Padre Hidalgo initiated the revolutionary movement in 1810, Lizardi was among his eager supporters. He founded the revolutionary journal *El pensador mexicano* in 1812 and became famous as an ardent propagandist and pamphleteer. His criticism of the authorities brought him to prison on several occasions. Although he was a prolific journalist to the end of his life, his lasting reputation rests largely on his picaresque novel, *El Periquillo Sarniento* (1816), frequently called the first American novel.

El Periquillo Sarniento is a satire of Mexican middle-class life at the end of the colonial period. In many respects an autobiographical novel, its sincerity, frank social criticism, abundant humor, and graphic pictures of social life make it one of the most readable books of the time. It has the virtues and defects of the picaresque genre. In the main the characters are conventionalized types intended to be representative of a group; as such they lack psychological subtlety. Following the Spanish picaresque tradition of *Lazarillo de Tormes* (1554) and countless others, the novel has no formal plot and is a series of loosely related episodes unified only by the principal character. The story is interrupted by long moralizing passages expounding Lizardi's ideas on pedagogy and social justice. Many such ideas he derived from his reading of eighteenth-century French authors and from the Spanish thinker, Padre Benito Feijóo (1675-1764). Since some parts of the novel are more or less faithful reproductions of popular speech, the modern reader is occasionally harassed by bits of difficult jargon and many *mexicanismos*. It is still one of Mexico's most popular literary works.

Two other novels of Lizardi, *La Quijotita y su prima* (1819), and *Don Catrín de la Fachenda* (1825), show the same didactic criticism of morals as the *Periquillo*.

SUGGESTED READING
El Periquillo Sarniento (selections).

TEXTS
Anthology, 146-160. Anderson Imbert and Florit, 194-198. Flores, 11-34. *El Periquillo Sarniento* (ed. Mapes and López-Morillas), New York, Appleton-Century-Crofts, 1952. *El pensador mexicano* (ed. Yáñez), 3rd ed., México, Univ. Nacional, 1962 (Biblioteca del estudiante universitario, 15).

EDITIONS
El Periquillo Sarniento, 2 vols., México, Porrúa, 1942; edited by Octavio N. Bustamante. *El Periquillo Sarniento,* 2nd ed., México, Porrúa, 1959; edited by Jefferson R. Spell. *Obras. I. Poesías y fábulas,* México, Univ. Nacional, 1963; edited by Jacobo Chencinsky and Luis Mario Schneider.

TRANSLATIONS
Katherine Anne Porter (trans.), *The Itching Parrot,* Garden City, N.Y., Doubleday, Doran, 1942.

CRITICAL REFERENCES
See texts and editions above. Azuela, 35-72. Davis, *Latin American Leaders,* 111-118. González, *Trayectoria,* 25-35. Luis González Obregón, *Don José Joaquín Fernández de Lizardi,* México, Botas, 1938. J. R. Spell, *The Life and Works of José Fernández de Lizardi,* Philadelphia, Univ. of Pennsylvania Press, 1931.

°4. (Venezuela) **Simón Bolívar** (1783-1830). Great as were his military exploits, the Liberator is almost equally noted for his well-written analyses of social and political conditions in the new republics. García Calderón says, "He was the thinker of the Revolution . . . the first sociologist of these romantic democracies." His clear and energetic style is exemplified in his many letters and speeches, the best known of which are the letter from Jamaica (a prophecy of future political conditions in Spanish America, 1815), and his draft of a model constitution presented to the Congress of Angostura (1819).

SUGGESTED READING

"Carta a un caballero que tomaba gran interés en la causa republicana en la América del Sur" and "Discurso en el Congreso de Angostura."

TEXTS

Anthology, 161-166. *Address to the Venezuelan Congress at Angostura*, Cambridge, England, Cambridge Univ. Press, 1933 (Cambridge Plain Texts).

EDITIONS

Discursos y proclamas, Paris, Garnier, 1933; edited by Rufino Blanco-Fombona. *Bolívar*, México, Secretaría de Educación Pública, 1943 (El pensamiento de América, 5); edited by Francisco Monterde. *Cartas del Libertador corregidas conforme a los originales,* New York, Colonial Press, 1948; edited by Vicente Lecuna.

TRANSLATIONS

Lewis Bertrand (trans.), *Selected Writings*, 2nd ed., 2 vols., New York, Colonial Press, 1951; edited by Harold A. Bierck.

CRITICAL REFERENCES

See texts and editions above. Víctor Andrés Belaúnde, *Bolívar and the Political Thought of the South American Revolution*, Baltimore, The Johns Hopkins Univ. Press, 1938. Gerhard Masur, *Simón Bolívar*, Albuquerque, Univ. of New Mexico Press, 1948.

c. DRAMA

Although the theater was popular in Mexico City and Lima during this period, drama was not one of the dominant forms of original literary production. In the late colonial years, translations and adaptations of French classical drama had some popularity, a tradition which was carried on by the Argentine, Juan Cruz Varela, in his tragedies, *Dido* (1823) and *Argia* (1824), which had indirect relevance for the struggle for independence.

In the early nineteenth century, romantic and nationalistic themes began to enter the meager dramatic literature. José María Heredia in his Mexican days tried out some theatrical essays on subjects of Mexican history, as well as a few adaptations of French plays, while the Colombian poet, José Fernández Madrid (1789-1830), produced two dramas under romantic influence: *Atalá* (1820), based on Chateaubriand, and *Guatimoc* (1827), recollecting

Aztec tales of the Conquest. In Lima, where the vice-regal tradition of a lively theater persisted, Felipe Pardo (1806-1868) presented, among other dramatic works, a comedy of manners with *costumbrista* characteristics, *Frutos de la educación* (1829).

On the borderline of colonial times and independence, the Argentine poet, Manuel José de Lavardén (1754-1809), wrote a rather remarkable drama, *Siripo,* produced in 1789. Dealing with relations between the Spanish settlers of the River Plate and the indigenous population, it foreshadowed a later and more vivid portrayal of the theme in the romantic and gaucho writers.

It is significant that Lavardén was a friend and pupil of a parish priest in Chuquisaca, Bolivia, Antonio Valdés (died 1816), who either discovered or possibly composed the controversial drama, *Ollantay.* The play came to light between 1770 and 1780 when Valdés had it performed before an Incan chieftain, José Gabriel Condorcanqui (1744-1781). Originally written in Quechua verse, its action is in Cuzco, the Incan capital, and deals with the love of Ollantay, a chieftain of lowly birth, and the princess Cusi-Coyllu, daughter of the Inca, Pachacutic. The spirit of the play and its technical characteristics indicate that it was composed in the eighteenth century on the model of the Spanish *comedia.* In all likelihood, however, the theme itself was based on an ancient Incan legend, and there has been much speculation about the possibility that the play represents a later modernization of a genuinely pre-Conquest drama. In this light, it has acquired a peculiarly important status in retrospective efforts to find indigenous roots for Spanish American nationality. *Ollantay* can be read in Jorge Basadre's *Literatura inca,* Paris, 1938 (Biblioteca de cultura peruana, 1). The nationalistic significance of the drama is apparent in Ricardo Rojas' study, *Un titán de los Andes,* Buenos Aires, Losada, 1939. Rojas, incidentally, made his own dramatization of the theme. One of the best studies on the origin of the play is that by E. C. Hills, "The Quechua Drama *Ollanta*," *Romanic Review,* II (1911), 127-176.

REFERENCES

Arrom, *Teatro época col.,* Chap. V. Jones, *Breve hist.,* Chaps. II-III. Lohmann Villena, Part III, Chaps. VI-VIII. Morales, 21-127. Olavarría y Ferrari, Part I, Chaps. IV-XVII; Part II, Chaps. I-VIII.

2nd period

From Independence to the Mexican Revolution

Introductory Summary

It is impossible to consider the literature of this period, so crucial in molding the cultural personality of Spanish America, without constant reference to literary and political pressures from abroad, as well as to the intimate relationship of internal political and social conditions to literature in the growing independent republics. Consequently, on the one hand one can see obvious reflections in America of the dominant European literary modes—romanticism, realism, naturalism, modernism—but, on the other hand, it is abundantly evident that, within the framework of these modes, there developed—often in a slow and groping fashion—a distinctively New World manner and viewpoint, apparent in subject matter, style, and even in new forms. A clear case in point is the gaucho literature of the River Plate.

A fairly valid generalization holds that most of this period was, for most of the new republics, one of political turmoil and instability. The principal political problem was the creation of responsible national governments which could at the same time be responsive to the needs of heterogeneous populations, ensure domestic peace, and command respect abroad. Great difficulties hampered and delayed the solution of this problem, difficulties which were entirely comparable to those which have beset the more recently established independent states of Africa and Asia. Most of the new nations passed through longer or shorter periods of wars against their neighbor states and bloody civil disturbances among factions within the states, frequently followed by spells of military dictatorship. The economic, social and industrial development, upon which the stability of a republican form of government traditionally has rested, was retarded by a complex of factors, among which may be especially noted the racial heterogeneity of the population; the absence of a significant middle class of tradesmen and artisans; the low level of literacy and education among the bulk of the people; the lack of experience in self-government; the persistence of the aristocratic tradition that manual labor is degrading and that the natural resources of the land are rightfully the property of the rich and powerful; and—particularly in the latter part of the century—the imperialistic overtones of foreign economic and political penetration.

External wars, big and little, were frequent throughout the period: Brazil-Argentina, 1827; Mexico-United States, 1846-1848; Brazil-Paraguay, 1865-1870; French invasion of Mexico, 1862; Maximilian as Emperor of Mexico, 1864-1867; Chile-Peru, 1879-1883—to mention only a few. To catalogue all the multitude of revolutions, civil wars, and dictatorships of the time would not serve a useful purpose here. Among the more notable of these episodes were: Juan Manuel Rosas (1793-1877), Argentine dictator, and intermittent civil war, 1829-1852; revolt and reforms of the Zapotec Indian, Benito Juárez (1806-1872) in Mexico, 1855-1860; civil war and dictatorship of Ramón Castilla (1797-1867) in Peru, 1854-1861; dictatorship of Gabriel García Moreno (1821-1875) in Ecuador, 1861-1875; Porfirio Díaz (1830-1915), Mexican dictator, 1876-1911; dictatorships of Antonio Guzmán Blanco (1829-1899) and Cipriano Castro (1858-1924) in Venezuela, 1870-1909. In some of the republics, during the latter decades of the nineteenth century, relative peace and at least outward stability was achieved, either by the often harsh imposition of dictatorial, *caudillo* rule, or—in a few cases—by the development of a pattern of constitutional, representative government. Some economic progress accompanied these periods of political tranquility.

Many of the literary men of the period were more or less actively and personally engaged in the political unrest outlined above. Among the writers of Spanish American romanticism, most felt themselves to be the custodians and defenders of liberty, called to work toward the creation of a new order. Not a few of them suffered persecution or exile for their political beliefs. The most illustrious group, the Argentine proscripts—Esteban Echeverría (1805-1851), José Mármol (1817-1871), Hilario Ascasubi (1807-1875) —continued to wage from their exile an unremitting and finally successful war against the dictator Rosas. "Plácido" (Gabriel de la Concepción Valdés, 1809-1844) in Cuba was a poet-martyr to the liberal cause. Among the *costumbrista* and realist novelists, Ignacio M. Altamirano (1834-1893) of Mexico and Eduardo Acevedo Díaz (1851-1921) of Uruguay, as well as a score of lesser names, were deeply involved in the political vicissitudes of their countries. The best-known essayists of the period, Domingo Faustino Sarmiento (1811-1888) and Juan María Gutiérrez (1809-1878) of Argentina, Juan Montalvo (1832-1889) of Ecuador, and Eugenio María Hostos (1839-1903) of Puerto Rico, were all profoundly concerned with political matters. While the *modernista* poets for the most part remained aloof from the hurly-burly of political struggle, there were men like Guillermo Valencia (1873-1943) of Colombia who actively engaged in national politics, and others like Rubén Darío (1867-1916) of Nicaragua and José Santos Chocano (1875-1934) of Peru who concerned themselves on occasion with the reaction against "Yankee imperialism." And finally it should be recalled that many of the *modernistas* were in effect subsidized by the dictators, often occupying long-term diplomatic positions.

Underlying the political turmoil, but not often a real issue in it, was widespread social inequality and economic imbalance and poverty in the majority of the Spanish American republics. The often highly educated, relatively sophisticated, Europeanized upper crust of the capital cities was economically and socially worlds apart from the numerically dominant agricultural population. Economic feudalism was the prevailing system in most countries; the working farmer or plantation hand, and later the small class of industrial workers, lived at an unbelievably depressed level. Living conditions were primitive, public education practically nonexistent, and the percentage of illiteracy was very great. The Indian elements in Mexico, Central America, and the Andean countries were usually in the worst situation of all: economically not much more than slaves, they represented a great unassimilated mass which only by courtesy could be considered citizens of democratic republics. Occasionally, as in the case of Benito Juárez, leaders of political revolts were concerned with reforming these conditions, but far more often the so-called "revolutions" were merely struggles for power within the ruling classes.

These social factors had their effect in several different

ways on the literature of the period. In the first place, the reading public was small and was made up almost exclusively of the wealthy landholding families, government officials and employees, army officers, priests, and an occasional merchant. These were the people for whom books were written; they were also—with a few notable exceptions like "Plácido" and Altamirano—the people by whom books were written. Many of them were educated in Europe and felt themselves more closely related in taste and breeding to the cultured classes of France and Spain than to the Indians and mestizos who worked on their estates or in their mines. They were accustomed to import books and magazines along with the other comforts and even luxuries which gave novelty and interest to their lives. It was natural, therefore, that they should accept European styles in thought as well as in dress, and natural too that each prevailing European literary mode in its turn should stimulate them to follow the general fashion. While they frequently modified those styles by their choice of subjects and managed to give an American accent to many of their writings, they remained emotionally and intellectually unable to penetrate very deeply into the inchoate and inarticulate spirit of their own countries considered as total populations.

Having emphasized the general European orientation of literary men in the nineteenth century, one must in all honesty remark on the conscientious and equally general efforts made to evolve a literary *americanismo* by choosing themes and to some extent language which would reflect the social conditions and even problems of the Spanish New World. Many critics are given to believe that such efforts were abortive and befogged by somebody else's literary theories, or inhibited by the social separateness of the author from the broad national and social environment. It must be granted, however, that some of them laid the bases for later and more direct literary interpretations of the Latin American social scene.

As theoreticians of literary nationalism, the romantic writers—especially in the River Plate region—were vehement. Echeverría, for example, advocated the creation of a literature which would be "the highest expression of our characteristic ideas, of the feelings and passions which are born in our social struggle." But, as a practitioner of his theories, he, in "La cautiva" (1837), and others such as Jorge Isaacs (1837-1895), in *María* (1867), were inclined to blur their vision of American social realities by their own emotional states and somewhat dramatic stances.

One of the typical romantic fashions in prose fiction was *costumbrismo,* sketches of manners and customs which portrayed various aspects of contemporary life, amusing or picturesque, usually of provincial regions. From these sketches or *cuadros* developed longer stories and novels reproducing the local color and the particular ways of a limited social group. Although the *costumbristas* were conscious imitators of a European school, their works, because of their choice of subject matter and their detailed description, are authentically American and present a somewhat realistic picture of life in their native countries. But, by reason of their restricted social scope and their emphasis on the picturesque, the *costumbristas* usually avoided the more stark and sordid reality of Spanish American society. Theirs was a kind of poetic realism.

The natural outgrowth of *costumbrismo,* realism, or *criollismo* in Spanish America was also influenced by European models; but it was essentially American, regional, often naturalistic and colloquial in style and content. In a generally more honest way, the realistic writers of the late nineteenth century embodied a much more organic vision of the American world than their predecessors. Novelists such as Carlos María Ocantos (1860-1949) of Argentina, Federico Gamboa (1864-1939) of Mexico, and Baldomero Lillo (1867-1923) of Chile did not hesitate to depict the seamy side of Spanish American society—the tribulations of the common man in Buenos Aires, prostitution in Mexico, the plight of the Chilean miner. It is true that their style and structure were often tiresome and amateurish, but they did at least transcend the narrow, polite interests of the cultured groups. They doubtless paved the way for the more full-bodied naturalistic novel of social protest in the twentieth century.

Another phase of realistic expression was the *literatura indianista,* or literature of indigenous theme, which sprang from the soil and from the growing social consciousness of Peru, Bolivia, and Ecuador toward the end of the nineteenth century. It represented a contrast to the romantic novel and poetry of Indian life like Juan León Mera's (1832-1894) *Cumandá* (1871) and Juan Zorrilla de San Martín's (1855-1931) *Tabaré* (1888) in which the Indian is stylized and made into a sentimental pastiche. At last, writers managed to see beyond their proud city noses into the dog-like lives of the exploited natives. This indigenous element comprised from sixty to eighty percent of the population of the three so-called "Indian countries" of South America and a substantial portion of the inhabitants of Mexico and Central America. Clorinda Matto de Turner (1854-1909) of Peru started the championship of Indian rights with her novel, *Aves sin nido* (1889), which dealt with the exploitation of the Peruvian natives. Manuel González-Prada (1848-1918), usually treated as a Peruvian modernist essayist, carried a similar torch which he hurled into many a neatly piled heap of Latin American prejudices. In Mexico also, a few writers carried Altamirano's romantic treatment of Indian life into more realistic channels. The fuller development of the novel of the Indian was to come in the twentieth century.

Perhaps the most original and continuing link between literature and society during this period was the gaucho theme in the River Plate countries. The nationalistic inspiration of this almost legendary figure was present in the wars for independence, took various forms in the nineteenth-century national literatures, and extends into the present century. Gaucho literature cannot be attached exclusively to one style or fashion of literary theory. It has included romantic writers (in many respects the essential element of gaucho literature is romantic), realists, and naturalists, and even poets and novelists interested in esthetic and psychological nuances. Authors from the lowliest poetaster to the finest writers of those countries have dealt with the theme, as have musicians and painters. Nearly always, a strong element of *costumbrismo,* although not usually in the traditional form, has been an ingredient of the gaucho material.

There is a streak of deception in this literature. Although on the surface it almost invariably seems to be realistic, down-to-earth, and colloquial, portraying common rural life, it is centered, practically in its entirety, around a symbolic character, an idealized figure that probably never existed except in men's minds. It is true that in late colonial days and during the independence period there lived in the River Plate countries a breed of men known as gauchos (or *gauderios*). Contemporary accounts indicate that the gaucho was a colonial bootlegger whose business was contraband trade in cattle hides and who was somewhat of a shady character. Reckless, fond of fighting, and skillful on a horse, this man on the fringe of society was a fierce and indispensable element in San Martín's campaigns. In the ensuing civil strife, the gaucho continued as a barbaric but successful warrior. There began the legend of the brave, doughty patriotic man of the plains, the national ideal.

In the middle years of the nineteenth century, economic changes left hardly any room for the old gaucho. His illegal activities in cattle-trading, his skill with the lasso and the knife, and even his war-like propensities were unneeded in a society where organized cattle-raising with wire fences, the spread of wheat-growing, the gradual settling down of society, and the increase in European immigration made him an anachronism. After the fall of Rosas in 1852 (the dictator had provided some rough military employment for the "old boys"), the gaucho was practically done for as a real being. Some were absorbed into the new cattle culture as cowhands, but that was a different story and life.

These facts of history did not stop the growth of the nationalistic legend. In addition to assuming the role of the reckless patriot on horseback, the gaucho began to symbolize the picturesque and irresistible lover, the plaintive folk singer, and finally the folk hero of all the ill-treated rural people. So he is portrayed, after the real gaucho had in effect disappeared, in *Santos Vega* (1872) and *Martín Fierro* (1872-1879). In the later realistic novels and tales of Martiniano P. Leguizamón (1858-1935) and Roberto J. Payró (1867-1928) of Argentina and in the plays of Florencio Sánchez (1875-1910) of Uruguay, the legendary character persists with slightly different literary trappings.

In spite of, or perhaps because of his legendary nature, the gaucho without any doubt was responsible for weaving, in Argentina and Uruguay at an early date, a truly national literature that was characterized by closer ties with the life and problems of the people than in most of the other Spanish American nations.

By and large, international affairs were seldom mirrored in the literature of the last century. Writers were preoccupied with matters of formal style and with local and national subject matter. The principal exception to this generalization was the increasing importance of the United States in Latin American affairs. In the latter years of the century, an emotional image of the United States grew as an imperialistic, predatory, materialistic "Colossus of the North." The Mexican War, the aftermath of the Spanish American War, the fairly frequent North American intervention in the management of the Caribbean republics, the heavy investment of North American capital in certain republics with its alleged attempts to control the destinies of those countries, a series of Pan American Conferences which were interpreted as moves to gain hegemony over the whole hemisphere, and the obviously burgeoning wealth and power of the United States were all factors which inflamed Latin American opinion, including the literary sector, to regard their northern neighbor as a dangerous threat to their independence and way of life. This attitude was vigorously reflected in the works of many of the *modernista* writers: Rubén Darío (1867-1916), José Enrique Rodó (1872-1917), José Santos Chocano (1875-1934), Manuel Ugarte (1878-1951), and others whose writing otherwise moved mainly in more ethereal realms. It is important to note this phenomenon as an explanatory background factor in contemporary anti-United States attitudes among so many contemporary literary men of Latin America.

However much the literature of this period may be related to the political and social life of the several countries, it would be inaccurate to leave without emphasis the purely belletristic aspect of this literature. The romantic poets and novelists, aside from their social interests, followed their European counterparts in revelling in beautiful, even though somewhat exaggerated, imagery, and some of them, such as Gertrudis Gómez de Avellaneda (1814-1873) of Cuba and Manuel Acuña (1849-1873) of Mexico, were preoccupied with personal introspection and emotions to the practical exclusion of other matters.

The modernist poets and novelists were in general the very epitome of abstraction from the work-a-day world and its problems. Along with similar movements in Europe, they represented a violent reaction against the drabness of the realistic preoccupation with social questions and what they considered the sweet commonplaces of romantic writing. They echoed a distaste common to groups in the whole Western World for what appeared to be the colorless, bourgeois uniformity of modern civilization and they fled, not to the personal, nature-inspired ecstasies of the romantics, but to a formal, refined, music-filled world of fancy. In a purely artistic sense their innovations meant a conscious disciplining of style and techniques, an exercise long overdue in the literature of Spanish America. This discipline is evident in their descendants who, in the twentieth century, have produced so much truly distinguished poetry. Through *modernismo,* Spanish American literature entered fully into the mainstreams of universal literature with an excellence that any nation could be proud of.

GENERAL REFERENCES

Anderson Imbert, I, 206-281. Barrera, *Lit. hisp.,* 293-441. Carilla, *Romanticismo, passim.* Castro, Chap. VII. Chapman, *Rep. Hisp. Am.,* Chaps. I, VII-X. Coester, *Lit. Hist.,* Chaps. IV-XIV. Crawford, *passim.* Crow, *Epic,* Chaps. XLII-LI. Fagg, Chaps. XXII-XXIV. García Calderón, *Del romanticismo, passim.* Manuel Pedro González, *Trayectoria del gaucho y su cultura,* Habana, Úcar, García, 1934. Henríquez Ureña, *Lit. Curr.,* 112-184. Herring, *passim.* Madaline W. Nichols, *The Gaucho,* Durham, Duke Univ. Press, 1942. José de Onís, *The United States as Seen by Spanish American Writers, 1776-1890,* New York, Hispanic Institute, 1952. Sánchez, *Nueva hist.,* Chaps. IX-XIII. Torres-Ríoseco, *Epic,* Chap. II; also his *New World,* Chaps. IV-V. Worcester and Schaeffer, Chaps. XXV-XXXIII.

I.
Romanticism (1832-1888)

A. POETRY

In some of the poets who wrote during the struggle for independence (especially Heredia), the new notes of romanticism were audible. As the century waxed and began to wane, poetry written in the romantic mode swelled in volume in almost every one of the new nations. This European literary fashion seemed exceptionally congenial to Hispanic American temperaments and conditions. It stood for freedom, individualism, and emotional intensity. It exalted virgin nature with almost religious fervor and sought out the picturesque oddities of local or primitive life. As has already been noted, many of the romantic poets were passionate liberals in politics. They also, like their European models, sought freedom in literary form, breaking away from neoclassical stereotypes in subject and metrical pattern—even though they quickly formed their own stereotypes. Restraint in the expression of their emotions in lyric form was considered old-fashioned: tears flowed, imprecations were hurled, exclamatory utterances studded their lines.

Of particular importance for the development of a distinctively American literature, the romantic poets preferred to write about themes of their native lands. Some of them composed narrative poems, called *leyendas,* based on Indian traditions or on heroic events in their national history. Their shorter lyrics dealt with nature—the Andes, the pampas, the tropical forests, patriotism, and of course love, especially love in its sad and unrequited moments.

The original *poesía gauchesca* was composed by the

payador or gaucho minstrel and sung to the accompaniment of his own guitar as he wandered from place to place like the troubadours of the Middle Ages, but his songs were improvised, never recorded, and have been lost. The term *poesía gauchesca* is now given to poems written in imitation of his, by educated men-of-letters who have succeeded in recapturing something of the spirit of his genuine *payadas*. They celebrate the gaucho as lover, as poet, as outlaw. They are written in his own language. Their settings are the plains, the campfire, and the tavern. They owe their existence in part to the romanticists' interest in primitive nature and primitive man, but they, are a very special outgrowth of the romantic spirit.

Romanticism entered the various Hispanic American countries by different routes and at different times. It reached Mexico first in the early 1820's and by mid-century had spread all over the southern continent. Spanish and French romanticists, especially Espronceda (1810-1842) and Chateaubriand (1768-1848), were the favorite models in Spanish America, although Byron (1788-1824) was also much admired.

Literary historians are wont to speak of "first" and "second" generation romanticists. The second generation is also often referred to as postromantic. The postromanticists began to appear on the literary scene shortly after mid-century. They were less passionately involved in theory and polemics, more sincere and subdued in their emotional responses, more studied in their description of nature and in their depiction of the local setting and the national past. In poetry, and especially in lyric expression, many served to bridge the gap between the earlier romantics and the initiators of modernism in the eighties. Bécquer (1836-1870) and Heine (1797-1856) exerted a significant influence on the second generation romanticists from 1870 on. Echeverría, "Plácido," La Avellaneda, Caro, and Mármol were all quite obviously of the early romantic period. The others may more properly be classified as postromanticists.

Aside from the poets indicated for special attention below, a few others who are typical should be mentioned. As a poet of American nature, the Colombian, Gregorio Gutiérrez González (1826-1872) is notable. Along with Manuel Acuña, another Mexican, Manuel Flores (1840-1885), is almost the epitome of romantic erotic poetry and is still widely read by love-sick young people. Still another prominent Mexican romantic poet was Juan de Dios

Peza (1852-1910), who was prolific, popular, and delicate in his expression of family affection.

REFERENCES

Anderson Imbert, I, *passim*. Arrieta, III, 51-356. Carilla, *Romanticismo, passim*. Cometta Manzoni, *passim*. García Calderón, *Del romanticismo, passim*. Rojas, I-II, *passim*. Sánchez, *Nueva hist.*, 251-276

a. LYRIC

°°1. (Argentina) **Esteban Echeverría** (1805-1851). Although his first twenty years were spent in Buenos Aires, he was born to literature in France where he lived for four magic years (1826-1830). Romanticism in Paris had stormed the citadel of neoclassical literature and triumphed; Víctor Hugo (1802-1885) was the literary lion and Alfred de Musset (1810-1857) had published his first verses. There, Echeverría read Schiller (1759-1805), Byron (1788-1824), and Walter Scott (1771-1832) and, with a natural flair for the romantic vision and style, began to write his first poetry. He returned to Argentina in 1830, brought with him a clearly formed romantic philosophy of life and literature, and set about publishing his poetry. In 1832, *Elvira o la novia del Plata* appeared, a sentimental tale with a national background, to be followed in 1834 by *Los consuelos*, a collection of Byronic lyrics. Three years later he published *Rimas*, a volume which, in addition to a number of lyric poems, contains his best-known piece, "La cautiva," a story in verse dealing with Argentine themes and scenes.

In 1837, he also founded a political club of young Argentine romantics, the *Asociación de Mayo,* which opposed the dictatorship of the tyrant, Rosas; Echeverría's written program of their political principles, his *Dogma socialista* (1837-1846), is a statement of impassioned idealism. In 1840, because of the dictator, he fled to Uruguay; an ill and homesick exile, he died there eleven years later. Apart from "El matadero," a posthumous story of remarkable realism, the work of his last years was of little merit.

Echeverría is of signal importance in Spanish American literature because he formulated a program and stimulated a school of native Argentine literature. Believing that America should break away from its literary dependence on Spain, he preached, in a romantic vein, the literary possibilities of a New World. While his work reveals an allegiance to French models, his influence and his writings mark an initial milestone in the creation of an original literary *americanismo*.

SUGGESTED READING

"La cautiva" and "El matadero."

TEXTS

Anthology, 169-181. Anderson Imbert and Florit, 225-242. Beltrán, *Antología*, I, 68-94. Caillet-Bois, 255-265. Flores, 35-50. Menéndez y Pelayo, IV, 175-238. Oyuelà, II, vol. 1, 20-43, Weisinger, 56-73.

EDITIONS

La cautiva, seguido de El matadero, La guitarra, Elvira, Rimas, Buenos Aires, Sopena, 1939. *Obras completas*, 5 vols. (1870-1874), Buenos Aires, Antonio Zamora, 1951 (Col. argentoria, 1); edited by Juan María Gutiérrez. *La cautiva, El matadero*, Buenos Aires, Ed. Huemul, [1961]; edited by Juan Carlos Pellegrini.

TRANSLATIONS

Angel Flores (ed. and trans.), *El matadero (The Slaughter House)*, New York, Las Américas, 1959. Green and Lowenfels, 378-381.

CRITICAL REFERENCES

See texts and editions above. Anderson Imbert, I, 221-224. Coester, *Lit. Hist.*, 107-113. *Diccionario . . . Argentina*, I, 39-44. Menéndez y Pelayo, IV, clxi-clxxx. Ernesto Morales, *Esteban Echeverría*, Buenos Aires, Claridad, 1950. Rojas, II, 463-479; V, 155-237. Pablo Rojas Paz, *Echeverría, el pastor de soledades*, Buenos Aires, Losada, 1951.

2. (Cuba) "Plácido" (Gabriel de la Concepción Valdés) (1809-1844), was not a great romantic poet but because of his odd and touching life, as well as some poems of genuine feeling, he is worthy of note. He was the illegitimate son of a mulatto barber and a Spanish dancer, and was brought up in a foundling home without formal education. He earned his living by odd jobs and became a skillful carver of tortoise-shell combs. Learning to read, he sought out especially books of poetry. The verse of the Spanish poet, Francisco Martínez de la Rosa (1789-1862), awakened his own poetic ambitions, and he chose as his pseudonym, "Plácido," the name of an apothecary who had befriended him. Sometimes his poems attracted widespread attention and admiration, but when inspiration failed him, he wandered from town to town, poor and neglected. In 1844 he was accused of

complicity in a plot to bring about Negro domination in Cuba. He and ten companions were convicted and sentenced to death. On the way to his execution, it was reported that he recited some moving lines which he had composed during his imprisonment, insisting on his innocence and submitting himself to the will of God. Although he does not deal specifically with the problems of his race, some of his poems are eloquent protests against injustice and oppression. As such they are in the central current of American romantic literature.

SUGGESTED READING

"Muerte de Gesler," "La fatalidad," "Jicoténcal," "La flor de la caña," "Plegaria a Dios."

TEXTS

Caillet-Bois, 287-290. Hills, *Bardos*, 34-43. Menéndez y Pelayo, II, 69-84. Oyuela, II, vol. 2, 490-498.

EDITIONS

Poesías completas con doscientas diez composiciones inéditas, Habana, Cultural, [1930]. *Poesías selectas de Plácido,* Habana, Cultural, 1930; edited by A. M. Eligio de la Puente.

TRANSLATIONS

Walsh, *Cath. Anth.,* 256-257; also his *Hisp. Anth.,* 431-433.

CRITICAL REFERENCES

See texts and editions above. Jorge Casals, *Plácido como poeta cubano,* Habana, Ministerio de Educación, 1944. Coester, *Lit. Hist.,* 385-391. Manuel García Garófalo y Mesa, *Plácido, poeta y mártir,* México, Botas, 1938. Menéndez y Pelayo, II, xxxiii-xxxviii. Oyuela, II, vol. 2, 952-954. Remos, II, 5-21. Santos González, 253-294. Frederick S. Stimson, *Cuba's Romantic Poet, the Story of Plácido,* Chapel Hill, Univ. of North Carolina Press, 1964.

°3. (Cuba.) **Gertrudis Gómez de Avellaneda** (1814-1873) lived in Cuba only until she was twenty-two years old. The rest of her life was spent in Spain—in Andalusia and Madrid—except for a return period of residence from 1859 to 1863, at which time she was proclaimed Cuba's national poet. Most of her works were written and all were published in Spain, so they belong more properly to Spanish rather than to Spanish American literature except insofar as they are inspired or colored by the environment and experiences of her youth. She was not only a poet, but a dramatist and novelist as well. Her work in all three fields was very highly esteemed by her contemporaries, but it is chiefly for her poems that she is remembered today. Her best-known novels are *Sab* (1841), *Espatolino* (1844), and *Guatimozín* (1846); her greatest dramas, *Munio Alfonso* (1844), *Saúl* (1849), and *Baltasar* (1848). It has been said that the sources of her poetic inspiration were three: human love, divine love, and the love of her art. Her poems show real psychological insight and unusual skill in fitting form to mood.

SUGGESTED READING

"Al partir," "A la poesía," "A Él" (1840), "A la muerte del célebre poeta cubano don José María de Heredia," "A Wáshington," "La pesca en el mar," "A Él" (1845), "A Dios" (1846), "A Dios," "La cruz."

TEXTS

Anthology, 182-193. Anderson Imbert and Florit, 259-267. *Baltasar* (ed. Bransby), New York, American Book, [1908]. Caillet-Bois, 308-321. Menéndez y Pelayo, II, 87-121. Oyuela, II, vol. 2, 499-531. Weisinger, 114-128.

EDITIONS

Obras de la Avellaneda, 6 vols., Habana, Aurelio Miranda, 1914 (Edición nacional del centenario). *Sus mejores poesías*, Barcelona, Ed. Bruguera, 1953 (Col. laurel).

TRANSLATIONS

Blackwell, 490-491. Mrs. Wilson W. Blake (trans.), *Cuauhtemoc, The Last Aztec Emperor*, México, Hoeck, 1898. William Freeman Burbank (trans.), *Belshazzar*, San Francisco, A. M. Robertson, 1914. Green and Lowenfels, 280-281 and *passim* (6). Poor, 50. *Trans. from Hisp. Poets*, 215-217. Walsh, *Hisp. Anth.*, 434-436.

CRITICAL REFERENCES

See texts and editions above. Emilio Cotarelo y Mori, *La Avellaneda y sus obras*, Madrid, Tip. de Archivos, 1930. Rafael Marquina, *Gertrudis Gómez de Avellaneda, la peregrina*, Habana, Ed. Trópico, 1939. Menéndez y Pelayo, II, xl-xlvi. Edwin B. Williams, *The Life and Dramatic Works of Gertrudis Gómez de Avellaneda*, Philadelphia, Univ. of Pennsylvania Press, 1924.

4. (Colombia) José Eusebio Caro (1817-1853) was born in Ocaña. Orphaned early, he had to earn his own living. He started to study law in Bogotá, but gave up his course to become a journalist instead. In 1836 he and his friend, José Joaquín Ortiz (1814-1892), founded a literary periodical, *La estrella nacional*. In 1837 he became sole editor of *El granadino,* a journal of political reform. He was elected deputy to the congress in 1841 and from then until 1849 held various posts of trust in public office. When a change took place in the government on the election of José Hilario López in 1849, he went as an exile to the United States for three years. As he was returning home in 1853, he contracted yellow fever, and died just as the ship reached the port of Santa Marta. He was a man of uncompromising moral integrity, a "puritan" who repeatedly sacrificed personal advantage for principle, an ardent believer in political freedom and liberty of conscience. His greatest poems, some of which were written in exile, are all songs of freedom and the fearless man.

SUGGESTED READING

"En boca del último Inca," "La libertad y el socialismo," "Despedida de la patria," "El hacha del proscrito," "En alta mar," "El ciprés."

TEXTS

Anderson Imbert and Florit, 269-271. Caillet-Bois, 339-349. García-Prada, *Antología,* I, 105-126. Menéndez y Pelayo, III, 25-54. Oyuela, II, vol. 1, 235-256.

EDITIONS

Poesías, Madrid, M. Tello, 1885 (Col. de escritores castellanos, 25). *Antología; verso y prosa,* Bogotá, Ministerio de Educación Nacional, 1951 (Biblioteca popular de cultura colombiana, 148).

TRANSLATIONS

Blackwell, 414-417. Walsh, *Hisp. Anth.,* 452-453.

CRITICAL REFERENCES

See texts and editions above. Coester, *Lit. Hist.,* 275-278. *Diccionario . . . Colombia,* 17-19. Gómez Restrepo, IV, 53-73. Menéndez y Pelayo, III, xli-lii. Oyuela, II, vol. 2, 926-930. Jaime Ospina Ortiz, *José Eusebio Caro, guión de una estirpe,* Bogotá, Editores Publicaciones Técnicas, [1958].

5. (Argentina) **José Mármol** (1817-1871). See B, a, 1, below.

°6. (Colombia) **Rafael Pombo** (1833-1912) was born of a prominent family in Bogotá. An exceptionally versatile, talented man of many interests and moods, he began writing as a boy of ten; his last verses were composed when he was seventy-nine. As a young man of twenty-one he was sent to be secretary of the Colombian Legation in the United States. There he remained until 1859, even after his diplomatic post fell away as a result of a change of government. He occupied himself in learning English and in writing lively romantic verse and literary criticism. It was there too that he wrote his wellloved fables and rhymes for children. Returning to Bogotá he spent the remainder of his life as editor of magazines, stimulator of the arts, educator, and—above all—as one of the grand figures of Colombian poetry. Pombo's total vision was broad and original. His verse ran the whole gamut of romantic themes—love, adoration of nature, political rebellion. And he translated widely and faithfully from classical and modern literatures—Homer, Horace, Vergil, Bryant, Byron, Longfellow, Tennyson, Lamartine, Heredia, Hugo, Goethe. In 1905 his country honored him as its first poet laureate.

SUGGESTED READING

"El bambuco," "Edda," "Las norteamericanas en Broadway," "Elvira Tracy," "En el Niágara," "Preludio de primavera," "Noche de diciembre."

TEXTS

Caillet-Bois, 503-514. García-Prada, *Antología,* I, 191-236. Oyuela, III, vol. 1, 363-484.

EDITIONS

Poesías de Rafael Pombo, 2 vols., Bogotá, Imp. Nacional, 1916-1917; edited by Antonio Gómez Restrepo. *Traducciones poéticas,* Bogotá, Imp. Nacional, 1917; edited by Antonio Gómez Restrepo. *Poesías completas,* Madrid, Aguilar, 1957; edited by Eduardo Carranza, with introductory study by Antonio Gómez Restrepo.

TRANSLATIONS

Blackwell, 394-401. Walsh, *Hisp. Anth.,* 471-483.

CRITICAL REFERENCES

See texts and editions above. Nicolás Bayona, "Rafael Pombo," *Revista iberoamericana,* 18 (1945), 217-241. Coester, *Lit. Hist.,* 296-298. *Diccionario . . . Colombia,* 81-84. John E. Englekirk, *El epistolario Pombo-Longfellow,* Bogotá, Instituto Caro y Cuervo, 1954. Gómez Restrepo, IV, 117-176. Sanín Cano, 101-105.

°7. (Argentina) **Olegario Víctor Andrade** (1839-1882) was born in exile in the Brazilian frontier city of Alegrete. Since his family was out of political favor, his formative years were spent, not in Buenos Aires, but in a kind of hand-to-mouth existence in the provinces. At seventeen he left school without finishing his course, and earned a meager living as a minor government employee and as a provincial journalist. Simply keeping body and soul together consumed most of his energies, and it was not until he was thirty-six that his considerable poetic talent was revealed in the publication of "El nido de cóndores" (1877), a powerful poem which was to win him great acclaim. This was followed during the next five years by four other significant works: "Prometeo" (1877), "San Martín" (1878), "Víctor Hugo" (1881), and "Atlántida" (1881). In 1880, the by-then established poet of Argentine nationalism was called to become editor-in-chief of *La tribuna nacional,* the government newspaper. He died two years later at the height of his fame and creative activity.

In some respects, Andrade resembles Walt Whitman (1819-1892): he had a great vision of his country's destiny; he seemed anointed to be the prophetic bard of his fatherland; and, in technique, he was wont to use a heavy brush on a wide canvas. Also like Whitman, he often lapsed into awkward and unpolished expression, and his learning was sometimes inadequate for his lofty themes. But as a popular patriotic poet, there is no question about the effectiveness of his noble inspiration among his countrymen.

SUGGESTED READING
"El nido de cóndores" and "Atlántida, canto al porvenir de la raza latina en América."

TEXTS
Anthology, 205-211. Caillet-Bois, 568-586. Menéndez y Pelayo, IV, 305-353. Oyuela, III, vol. 2, 772-785, 1141-1159.

EDITIONS
Obras poéticas, Buenos Aires, La Cultura Argentina, 1923; edited by Evar Méndez. *Obras poéticas,* Buenos Aires, Academia Argentina de Letras, 1943; edited by Eleuterio F. Tiscornia.

TRANSLATIONS
Blackwell, 314-327. Walsh, *Hisp. Anth.,* 506-512.

CRITICAL REFERENCES
See texts and editions above. *Diccionario . . . Argentina,* I, 14-16. Menéndez y Pelayo, IV, clxxvii-cxci. Oyuela, III, vol. 2, 1132-1140. Rojas, VII, 276-288. Valera, I, 97-152.

°8. (Venezuela) **Juan Antonio Pérez Bonalde** (1846-1892) was born in Caracas but, for political reasons, spent a good part of his life abroad. As a young boy, he was taken with his family to Puerto Rico and was educated there. He returned to Venezuela briefly in 1870, where he devoted himself to political journalism. But the dictatorship of Guzmán Blanco made him an exile again, this time in New York "on the banks of the cold Hudson." There he worked in the advertising business and as a salesman for a drug firm. In 1877, during a short visit to his native land, he wrote his "Vuelta a la patria," a song of nostalgia for all exiles. Back in the United States, he married an American in 1879; the marriage was not a happy one and, as a climax to the lonely exile's sorrows, his only daughter, Flor, died in 1883. For her he wrote a beautiful and tender elegy, one of his finest poems. Some inner spring was broken and, although he continued his literary work, he became addicted to alcohol. He returned to Venezuela for the last time in 1890, and died two years later at the age of forty-six. During his nomad life, he had traveled widely and became a good linguist. As a translator of Heine and Poe he was highly praised. Most of his original poetry appeared in two volumes: *Estrofas* (1877) and *Ritmos* (1880).

SUGGESTED READING

"El poema del Niágara," "Flor," "Vuelta a la patria," "Primavera," "El cuervo" (Poe).

TEXTS

Caillet-Bois, 586-599. D'Sola, I, 3-31. Oyuela, III, vol. 1, 332-355.

EDITIONS

Poesías y traducciones, Caracas, Ministerio de Educación Nacional, 1947.

CRITICAL REFERENCES

See texts and editions above. Pedro César Dominici, "Juan Antonio Pérez Bonalde," *Cultura venezolana,* VIII (1925), 129-141. Uslar Pietri, *Letras y hombres,* 113-121.

°9. (Mexico) **Manuel Acuña** (1849-1873) was born in Saltillo. He was almost the perfect stereotype of the romantic poet. As a youth he was sickly and melancholy, and fell under the spell of Victor Hugo. In 1865 he went to Mexico City; three years later he entered the school of medicine. There, his desperate attitude toward life was reenforced by scientific teachings which denied the immortality of the spirit; his pessimism was translated into his well-known poem, "Ante un cadáver" (1872). In the course of an unhappy love affair, he wrote verses—"Nocturno a Rosario" (1873)—in the album of his beloved. These were to become the cherished heritage of generations of Spanish American sweethearts. Acuña's poems constitute but a single volume, and he was the author of one drama, *El pasado* (1872), a tragedy of love. Acuña himself died for love, committing suicide at the age of twenty-four.

SUGGESTED READING

"Ante un cadáver" and "Nocturno a Rosario."

TEXTS

Anthology, 199-204. Anderson Imbert and Florit, 325-326. Caillet-Bois, 639-642. Menéndez y Pelayo, I, 263-270. Oyuela, III, vol. 1, 40-47. Weisinger, 158-167.

EDITIONS

Poesías, Buenos Aires, Sopena, 1941. *Obras,* México, Porrúa, 1949; edited by José Luis Martínez.

TRANSLATIONS

Blackwell, 154-156. Green and Lowenfels, 66-175. Underwood, 291-298.

CRITICAL REFERENCES

See texts and editions above. Francisco Castillo Nájera, *Manuel Acuña,* México, Imp. Universitaria, 1950. Benjamín Jarnés, *Manuel Acuña, poeta de su siglo,* México, Eds. Xochitl, 1942. Menéndez y Pelayo, I, cxlviii-cliii.

°10. (Argentina) **Rafael Obligado** (1851-1920). In contrast to Andrade, Obligado was born to a family of comfortable means and was able to devote his entire time to literature. Born and educated in Buenos Aires, he advanced the cause of humanistic studies at the national university there by assisting in the establishment of the Faculty of Philosophy and Letters and in it the first chair in Argentine literature. In a poetic contest with one of his literary colleagues, Calixto Oyuela (1857-1935), Obligado defended the theories of romanticism against the attacks of the adherents of classicism. His own clearly romantic affiliations were evident in his choice of poetic models: Echeverría, "Plácido," and José Hernández. His collected verse— first published in 1885, with additional poems in later editions— may be divided into three groups: (1) poems in praise of the heroes of the wars for independence; (2) poems presenting intimate pictures of nature and human affection; and (3) the *Leyendas argentinas,* romantic versions of national folk themes, including four poems about the legendary Santos Vega (1887).

SUGGESTED READING

"Santos Vega."

TEXTS

Anthology, 370-377. Beltrán, *Antología,* II, 260-272. Caillet-Bois, 656-663. Oyuela, III, vol. 2, 824-836.

EDITIONS

Poesías, Buenos Aires, Espasa-Calpe, [1941] (Col. austral, 142). *Poesías,* Buenos Aires, Juan Roldán, 1944 (Grandes escritores argentinos); edited by Carlos Obligado. *Poesías escogidas,* Buenos Aires, 1954 (Bibl. de grandes obras de la literatura universal); edited by Fermín Estrella Gutiérrez.

TRANSLATION

Blackwell, 348-377.

CRITICAL REFERENCES

See texts and editions above. *Diccionario* . . . *Argentina,* I, 149-152. Oyuela, III, vol. 2, 1164-1199. María Antonia Oyuela, *El Santos Vega de Obligado,* Buenos Aires, Imp. Mercatoli, 1937. Rojas, VII, 299-312. Valera, I, 77-88.

°°11. (Uruguay) **Juan Zorrilla de San Martín** (1855-1931) was, in addition to being one of the most interesting and original poets of the century, a prime example of the persistent vitality of the romantic tradition in Spanish American letters. His first book of verse, *Notas de un himno,* published in 1877, almost a half century after Echeverría's *Elvira,* was strictly within the lyric pattern of the Spanish romantic poets, with sad love and patriotism as the dominant themes. Born in Montevideo, he was educated in Jesuit schools in Argentina, Uruguay and Chile and also studied at the universities in Montevideo and Santiago de Chile. A profoundly Catholic and religious tone characterized his first poetic efforts and indeed his whole work. Establishing himself in Montevideo in 1878, he founded a Catholic daily paper, *El bien público.* The following year, at the unveiling of a monument to Uruguay on independence day, he read in public his stirring patriotic ode, "La leyenda patria" (1879). These lengthy, eloquent verses earned for him widespread public fame. But the romantic in Zorrilla wanted to compose a more original piece and the result was, seven years later, the publication of his masterpiece, the epic poem, *Tabaré* (1886); it embodied an indigenous theme which excited nationalistic aspirations. From this time on he was showered with such honors as a small but proud republic could give. He became a member of Congress and Minister to Spain, Portugal, France, and the Vatican, and achieved fame as a patriotic orator. His later publications include *Resonancias del camino* (1896), a book of impressionistic notes on his European travels; *La epopeya de Artigas* (1900), a reverent study of the Uruguayan patriot; *Conferencias y discursos* (1900), a collection of essays and addresses; and *Las Américas* (1945), writings concerning the first World War. His later books in particular reveal a marked conservative, Catholic attitude.

SUGGESTED READING

Tabaré.

TEXTS

Anthology, 212-238. Anderson Imbert and Florit, 394-398. Beltrán, *Antología,* I, 145-278. Caillet-Bois, 674-684. Oyuela, III, vol. 2, 603-636.

EDITIONS

Tabaré: Novela en verso, La leyenda patria, 4th ed., Barcelona, Cervantes, 1929. *Obras completas,* 16 vols., Montevideo, Banco de la República, 1930. *Tabaré,* Buenos Aires, Estrada, [1944]; prologue by Alberto Zum Felde. *Tabaré,* 2nd ed., Montevideo, Mosca, 1962.

TRANSLATIONS

Blackwell, 444-446. Walter Owen (trans.), *Tabaré,* Washington, Pan American Union, 1956; with original text and notes.

CRITICAL REFERENCES

See texts and editions above. Enrique Anderson Imbert, "La originalidad del *Tabaré,*" *Memoria del séptimo congreso,* 33-55. "Lauxar," *Motivos de crítica,* Montevideo, Palacio del Libro, 1929, 5-127. Valera, II, 263-290.

b. Gaucho

1. (Argentina) **Hilario Ascasubi** (1807-1875), born in Fraile Muerto (later Belle-Ville) in the province of Córdoba, led an exciting and adventurous life. When he was twelve years old, he ran away from school and joined the navy. His boat was captured and taken to

Portugal, where he escaped, and, after traveling through France and England, he made his way home again. He took part in the war against Brazil and was present at the battle of Ituzaingó (1827). He was in prison for two years under Rosas, then escaped to Montevideo. Here he started a very successful bakery, using his profits to fit out a ship against the tyrant. During the siege of Montevideo he wrote and published, in pamphlet form, a series of "barrackroom ballads" purporting to be written by a gaucho in the army, dealing with life in the camp and on the battlefield, and fulminating against the dictator. These were collected under the title *Paulino Lucero, o los gauchos del Río de la Plata cantando y combatiendo contra los tiranos de las Repúblicas Argentina y Oriental del Uruguay* (1839-1851). After the defeat of Rosas (1852), he returned to Buenos Aires and started a periodical called *Aniceto el gallo* (1853-1859), which contained comments in prose and poetry on current political events and defended the political creed of the Unitarians. He also invested his fortune in the construction of the old Teatro Colón, completed in 1857, which later burned down and ruined him financially. In 1860 he was sent by the government on a commission to Paris, and he remained there for many years finishing and publishing there his most important work, the gaucho epic, *Santos Vega o Los Mellizos de la Flor* (1872), some fragments of which had appeared as early as 1851. The poem is now commonly known as *Santos Vega, el payador*.

SUGGESTED READING
Santos Vega, el payador, Cantos IX and X.
TEXTS
Beltrán, *Antología,* II, 45-258. Caillet-Bois, 278-284. Oyuela, III, vol. 2, 666-670.
EDITIONS
Santos Vega o Los Mellizos de la Flor, 2 vols., Buenos Aires, Sopena, 1939.
CRITICAL REFERENCES
See texts and editions above. *Diccionario . . . Argentina,* I, 17-19. Manuel Mujica Láinez, *Vida de Aniceto el Gallo (Hilario Ascasubi),* 2nd ed., Buenos Aires, Emecé, 1955. Oyuela, III, vol. 2, 1076-1082. Rojas, II, Chaps. XVII-XVIII, XXI.

°°2. (Argentina) **Estanislao del Campo** (1834-1880) was born in Buenos Aires, the son of an army officer. He himself fought as captain on the side of the Unitarians in the civil wars against the confederation which followed the regime of Rosas. He later held various political positions, but his chief interest was literature. He was a disciple and follower of Ascasubi, choosing as his pseudonym "Anastasio el Pollo," reminiscent of "Aniceto el Gallo," but he surpassed Ascasubi in the sensitivity of his interpretation of the soul of the gaucho and in his innate good taste. He wrote many poems which do not belong to the "poesía gauchesca," but his masterpiece is *Fausto* (1866), a dialogue in which a gaucho describes his visit to a performance of Gounod's opera.

SUGGESTED READING

Fausto.

TEXTS

Anthology, 305-328. Anderson Imbert and Florit, 277-294. Beltrán, *Antología,* II, 539-555.

EDITIONS

Fausto, seguido de poesías completas, Buenos Aires, Sopena, 1939. *Fausto,* Buenos Aires, Kraft, 1942. *Fausto,* Buenos Aires, Peuser, 1951.

TRANSLATIONS

Walter Owen (trans.), *Faust,* Buenos Aires, Imp. Lamb, 1943.

CRITICAL REFERENCES

See texts and editions above. *Diccionario . . . Argentina,* I, 27-28. Manuel Mujica Láinez, *Vida de Anastasio el Pollo (Estanislao del Campo),* Buenos Aires, Emecé, 1948. Oyuela, III, vol. 2, 1083-1102. F. M. Page, *"Fausto,* a Gaucho Poem," *PMLA,* XI (1896), 1-62. Rojas, II, Chap. XXII.

°°3. (Argentina) **José Hernández** (1834-1886) was born on an estate in the province of Buenos Aires and grew up in the country among gauchos and Indians. He never attended school beyond the primary grades, but read voraciously and had a prodigious memory. During the civil wars, he fought on the side of the Federals for the provinces. After their defeat, he emigrated to Brazil for a time. Later, he returned to Entre Ríos, Rosario, Montevideo, and finally Buenos Aires, where he founded the newspaper *Río de la Plata* (1869). He subsequently held various positions in the government. In writing *Martín*

Fierro (1872) and its sequel, *La vuelta de Martín Fierro* (1879), Hernández claims that it was his purpose to teach his unlettered countrymen to read by so imitating their manner of expression and their way of thought that reading would seem a natural continuation of their lives. He succeeded so well that the poems were to be found on sale in the humblest grocery stores in remote sections of the country. At the same time he accomplished with *Martín Fierro* the goal which Echeverría had set for himself in writing "La cautiva" —the creation of a thoroughly American epic independent of European norms and influences.

Hernández also wrote two books in prose: one, *Vida del Chacho* (1863), a biography of the *caudillo,* Angel Vicente Peñaloza (died 1863), the other, *Instrucción del estanciero* (1881), which offered practical advice on problems of agriculture and animal husbandry.

SUGGESTED READING
Martín Fierro.
TEXTS
Anthology, 329-369. Anderson Imbert and Florit, 294-324. Beltrán, *Antología,* II, 295-535. Oyuela, III, vol. 2, 713-771.
EDITIONS
Martín Fierro, Buenos Aires, Espasa-Calpe, 1938 (Col. austral, 8). *Martín Fierro,* Buenos Aires, Estrada, 1945 (Eds. argentinas de cultura); edited by Carlos Alberto Leumann. *Martín Fierro,* 8th ed., Losada, Buenos Aires, 1953 (Col. de textos literarios); edited by Eleuterio F. Tiscornia.
TRANSLATIONS
Joseph Auslander (trans.), *A Fragment from Martín Fierro (El gaucho),* New York, Hispanic Society, 1932. Walter Owen (trans.), *The Gaucho, Martín Fierro,* New York, Farrar and Rinehart, 1936. Henry Alfred Holmes (trans.), *Martín Fierro, the Argentine Gaucho Epic,* New York, Hispanic Institute, 1948.
CRITICAL REFERENCES
See texts and editions above. *Diccionario . . . Argentina,* I, 85-94. Henry Alfred Holmes, *Martín Fierro, an Epic of the Argentine,* New York, Hispanic Institute, 1923. Ezequiel Martínez Estrada, *Muerte y transfiguración de Martín Fierro* (1948), 2nd ed., 2 vols., México, Fondo de Cultura Económica, 1958. Rojas, II, Chaps. XXIII-XXV.

B. PROSE

In prose, as in poetry, this was a particularly fecund period. While there were lingering reminiscences of colonial times and a continuing search for patriotic identity issuing from the wars for independence, all kinds of new trends generated from romantic enthusiasms were evident in the novel and essay. The theme of the gaucho and the Indian found their way into fiction and essay, although the approach was colored by individualistic romantic theory and models. Popular customs became a fetish for novelists and essayists. The potentialities of the new nationalities for the future, fascinated men like Juan María Gutiérrez (1809-1878), Sarmiento, Mármol, Hostos, and Montalvo. Most of the writers in prose showed a high seriousness and eagerness which were stimulating in their implications for the future. The leisurely and sardonic tones of Ricardo Palma were the exception rather than the rule.

The shortcomings of a good deal of the prose of the romantic decades of the century are painfully apparent to the modern reader. The novelists were usually and obviously under the spell of European models, and sometimes, even in the case of such exceptional men as Isaacs and Mera, wandered into a conventionalized sentimentality. The essays and miscellaneous prose, with the signal exceptions of some pages of Sarmiento and Palma, tended to be sententious and repetitious.

Nevertheless, it was an exciting time of experimentation. Serious writers and practical politicians, like Bartolomé Mitre (1821-1906) and Sarmiento (both Presidents of Argentina), and Juan Bautista Alberdi (1810-1884), author of the famous *Bases* (1852), rubbed shoulders with literary dreamers like Mármol. Novelists who were fairly close to the soil, like Altamirano, coexisted with relatively sophisticated writers like Palma. Most of them were searching in the tangled contemporary scene, or in a legendary and idealized past, for national roots. The prose of this period has interest both for the literary scholar and the student of cultural history.

REFERENCES

Alegría, *Breve hist.*, 27-87. Anderson Imbert, I, 281-300. Brushwood, *passim*. Frank M. Duffey, *The Early Cuadros de Costumbres in*

Colombia, Chapel Hill, Univ. of North Carolina Press, 1956. Meléndez, passim. Read, passim. Sánchez, Proceso y contenido, Chap. VI. Jefferson R. Spell, "The Costumbrista Movement in Mexico," PMLA, L (1935), 290-315. Torres-Ríoseco, Novela, 199-224. Warner, passim.

a. FICTION

*1. (Argentina) **José Mármol** (1817-1871) was perhaps of all the literary opponents of the dictator Rosas, the most typical and consistently vociferous. He was born and educated in Buenos Aires. In 1839, while still a university student, he was imprisoned by Rosas and was said to have scratched on his cell wall violent verses against the tyrant. Upon his release, he fled to Montevideo, the traditional refuge of Rosas' political opponents, and carried on from there his battle in verse against the dictator. In 1843, when Rosas' forces marched into Montevideo, the poet escaped to Rio de Janeiro. After a thwarted attempt to reach Santiago de Chile, he remained an exile in Rio and later again in Montevideo. When the dictator fell in 1852, he returned to Buenos Aires, was appointed to several public offices, and in 1858, became director of the National Library, a post which he held until his death. Although Mármol wrote a considerable body of poetry, both political and lyrical, and two weak romantic plays (*El poeta* and *El cruzado*—both performed in Montevideo in 1842), his position today in Spanish American letters rests almost entirely on *Amalia* (Part I, 1851; complete, 1855), a novel of life in Buenos Aires under the Rosas reign of terror, and on *Cantos del peregrino* (1846-1857), an incomplete long poem in the Byronic style. The lyric beauty of some of its parts and the passages descriptive of the wonders of nature in America mark it as of more than passing value.

SUGGESTED READING

Prose: *Amalia*. Poetry: *Cantos del peregrino* (selections).

TEXTS

Prose: *Amalia* (ed. Leavitt), Boston, Heath, 1926. *Amalia*, (ed. Babcock and Rodríguez), Boston, Houghton Mifflin, 1949. Poetry: *Anthology*, 194-198. Anderson Imbert and Florit, 256-259. Caillet-Bois, 350-361. Menéndez y Pelayo, IV, 265-304. Oyuela II, vol. 1, 59-84.

EDITIONS

Amalia, 2 vols., Buenos Aires, Estrada, 1944 (Biblioteca de clásicos argentinos, 14-15); prologue and notes by Adolfo Mitre. *Poesías completas*, 2 vols., Buenos Aires, Academia Argentina de Letras, 1946-1947; edited by Rafael Alberto Arrieta.

TRANSLATIONS

Green and Lowenfels, 304-313. Poor, 19-23. Mary J. Serrano (trans.), *Amalia: A Romance of the Argentine*, New York, Dutton, 1919.

CRITICAL REFERENCES

See texts and editions above. Alegría, *Breve hist.*, 38-42. Arrieta, II, 215-268. Stuart Cuthbertson, *The Poetry of José Mármol*, Boulder, University of Colorado, 1935. *Diccionario . . . Argentina*, I, 130-135. Oyuela, II, vol. 2, 868-908. Rojas, VI, Chap. XV.

2. (Ecuador) Juan León Mera (1832-1894) was a native of Ambato. A self-taught man, he achieved eminence in many activities—poetry, fiction, scholarship, and politics. He is particularly remembered today for his long narrative poem, *La virgen del sol* (1861), which tells a dramatic Indian love story of the time of the Spanish conquest of Ecuador, and for his *indianista* novel, *Cumandá* (1871). This is a somewhat melodramatic tale in the Chateaubriand tradition of the ill-fated love of a Spanish lad and a girl presumed to be Indian. It is notable for its descriptions of Indian life and of the grandeur of the primeval forest. Scholars still find Mera's *Ojeada histórico-crítica sobre la poesía ecuatoriana* (1868) valuable as an exposition of *americanista* literary doctrine.

SUGGESTED READING

Cumandá o un drama entre salvajes.

TEXTS

Cumandá (ed. Flores), Boston, Heath, 1932. Flores, 134-142.

EDITIONS

Cumandá, Quito, Casa de la Cultura Ecuatoriana, 1948 (Clásicos ecuatorianos, 14); prologue by Augusto Arias; *ibid.*, Buenos Aires, Espasa-Calpe, 1951 (Col. austral, 1035).

CRITICAL REFERENCES

See texts and editions above. Barrera, *Hist.*, III, 257-288. *Diccionario . . . Ecuador*, 40-43. Meléndez, 151-164. Rojas, *Novela ecuatoriana*, 49-57. Valera, II, 211-221.

°°3. (Colombia) **Jorge Isaacs** (1837-1895) was the son of a prosperous planter, an English Jew, who had come to Colombia from Jamaica and married the daughter of a Spanish naval officer. He was born in the Cauca and there he spent his childhood on his father's estate, "El Paraíso," near Cali, on the slope of the Cordillera Central. In 1848 he was sent to boarding school in Bogotá. He remained there for six years. During this time his father's business ventures turned unsuccessful, and the boy came home to find the family in straitened circumstances. Soon afterwards both his parents died. The civil war of El Cauca completed his financial ruin, and in 1864 he and his brothers and sisters were obliged to give up their home and move to Bogotá. In this city he gained the approval of the critics and the public by a volume of *Poesías* (1864). Three years later (1867), he published his masterpiece, *María*. He entered politics and was appointed to several government posts, including that of consul to Chile (1871-1873). He tried to win back his fortune by an ambitious business undertaking, but without success. His dreams of owning again the home of his childhood never came true. He died in poverty.

An idyllic romance with many autobiographical features, *María* owes its unique charm to a mingling of realistic detail and delicate, romantic melancholy. The sentimental story won immediate and continuing success and has been more widely read than any other Spanish American novel of its time.

María.
SUGGESTED READING

TEXTS

Prose: *María* (ed. Keniston), Boston, Ginn, [1918]. *María* (ed. Pitcher), New York, Macmillan, 1922. *María* (ed. Warshaw), Boston, Heath, 1926. *María* (ed. Olmsted), New York, Oxford Univ. Press, 1944. Flores, 81-94. Poetry: Caillet-Bois, 556-558. García-Prada, *Antología*, I, 265-280.

EDITIONS

Prose: *María*, Madrid, Aguilar, 1945 (Col. crisol, 90). *María*, México, Fondo de Cultura Económica, 1951; introductory study by Enrique Anderson Imbert. Poetry: *Poesías completas*, Barcelona, Maucci, [1920]; introductory study by Baldomero Sanín Cano.

TRANSLATIONS

Rollo Ogden (trans.), *María* (1890), 3rd ed., New York, Harper, 1918; prologue by Thomas A. Janvier.

CRITICAL REFERENCES

See texts and editions above. Mario Carvajal, *Vida y pasión de Jorge Isaacs*, Santiago, Ercilla, 1937. *Diccionario . . . Colombia*, 55-58. Gómez Restrepo, IV, 177-200. Sanín Cano, 107-112.

*4. (Mexico) **Ignacio Manuel Altamirano** (1834-1893) was a pureblooded Aztec who lived, until he was fourteen, in the small Indian pueblo of Tixtla in the State of Guerrero. Since he showed great precocity at the village school, he was sent to Toluca and finally to Mexico City to finish his education. Here his course of study was interrupted by the revolution of 1854, the "War of Reform" (1857), and the war against Maximilian. Altamirano fought with the liberals under Juárez. After the expulsion of the French and the reestablishment of the republic he turned his interests to literature and education, edited the periodicals *El correo de México* (1867) and *El renacimiento* (1869), founded literary societies, taught history and law, and by precept and example showed the younger generation of Mexican writers the value of the local customs, village types, and the stirring events of their own times as literary material. He was appointed consul-general in 1889 to Spain and later to France. He died in San Remo. His works include a volume of *Rimas* written before 1867, but published later (1871), the novel *Clemencia* (1869), the novelette *La navidad en las montañas* (1871), several short stories and *artículos de costumbres,* and a posthumous novel, *El Zarco*.

SUGGESTED READING

La navidad en las montañas or *El Zarco,* and "El día de muertos."

TEXTS

Anthology, 378-382. Caillet-Bois, 515-520. *La navidad en las montañas* (ed. Hill and Lombard) Boston, Heath, 1917. *El Zarco: Episodios de la vida mexicana en 1861-1863* (ed. Grismer and Ruelas), New York, Norton, 1933. *Aires de México* (ed. Antonio Acevedo Escobedo), México, Univ. Nacional, 1940 (Biblioteca del estudiante universitario, 18). *Clemencia* (ed. Scherr and Walker), Boston, Heath, 1948.

EDITIONS

El Zarco, 4th ed., Buenos Aires, Espasa-Calpe, [1950] (Col. austral, 108); prologue by Francisco Sosa. *Obras literarias completas*, México, Eds. Oasis, 1959; prologue by Salvador Reyes Nevares.

TRANSLATIONS

Harvey L. Johnson (trans.), *Christmas in the Mountains*, Gainesville, Univ. of Florida Press, 1961. Underwood, 253-259.

CRITICAL REFERENCES

See texts and editions above. Azuela, 113-123. Read, 159-177. Warner, 47-55.

b. Essay and "Tradición"

1. (Argentina) **Domingo Faustino Sarmiento (1811-1888) was a prolific author—his collected works fill fifty-two volumes—but his writings are mostly about political and educational matters and few are of any but historical interest today. Among those few, however, stands *Facundo o civilización y barbarie* (1845), a classic for the student of Spanish American culture. Sarmiento's life is itself a classic version of the "poor boy who makes good." Born in provincial poverty in San Juan near the Andes, he became by his own industry, genius, and perseverance, President of the Argentine Republic (1868-1874). Having almost no formal schooling, he read widely and educated himself. He began to teach in a country school at the age of fifteen; shortly thereafter, he joined in a revolt against Rosas and his caudillos and went into exile in Chile. There he worked as a rural schoolmaster, clerk, and miner. His subsequent career, until the fall of Rosas in 1852, was varied. He was a busy journalist, a director of the Normal School in Santiago, an opponent of Andrés Bello in the famous classicism-romanticism polemic, and a participant in many a political debate. From 1845 to 1848, he traveled as a collector of educational ideas in Europe and the United States; of the latter country—he was Argentina's ambassador for three years, 1865-1868—he became a great admirer. His travel book, *Viajes por Europa, África y América* (1849-1851) offers interesting and acute observations resulting from his travels. Returning to Argentina, he entered fully into the new political life and was eventually elected President in 1868. At the conclusion of his term (1874), he devoted his talents to the organization and improvement of the schools of his country.

Written in haste and in anger, and published in installments in *El progreso* of Santiago during early 1845, *Facundo* is the story of the career of one of Rosas' caudillos, a rough, unprincipled barbarian. In addition, this very readable book includes excellent descriptive chapters and a reasoned exposition of the author's political and socio-economic principles. *Recuerdos de provincia* (1850) is a rambling, interesting series of reminiscences of his boyhood.

SUGGESTED READING

Facundo.

TEXTS

Antología, 239-291. Anderson Imbert and Florit, 242-256. *Facundo* (ed. Fernández and Brown), Boston, Ginn, 1960. *Sarmiento* (ed. Iduarte and Shearer), New York, Dryden, 1949.

EDITIONS

Obras, 53 vols., Santiago, Imp. Gutenberg, 1885-1914. *Facundo,* Buenos Aires, Estrada, 1940 (Clásicos argentinos, 2); edited by Delia S. Etcheverry. *Facundo,* Buenos Aires, Peuser, 1955; edited by Raúl Moglia. *Facundo o civilización y barbarie,* New York, Doubleday, 1961 (Col. hispánica). *Recuerdos de provincia,* Buenos Aires, El Navío, 1944; edited by Jorge Luis Borges. *Recuerdos de provincia,* 6th ed., Buenos Aires, Sopena, 1953. *Obras selectas,* 3 vols., Buenos Aires, 1944 (Biblioteca histórica del pensamiento americano, 1-3); edited by Enrique de Gandía.

TRANSLATIONS

Stuart Edgar Grummon (trans.), *A Sarmiento Anthology,* Princeton, Princeton Univ. Press, 1948; edited by Allison Williams Bunkley. Frank, 127-151. Mrs. Horace Mann (trans.), *Life in the Argentine Republic in the Days of the Tyrants, or Civilization and Barbarism* (1868), New York, Hafner, 1960 (Hafner Library of Classics, 21). H. de Onís, 123-128.

CRITICAL REFERENCES

See texts and editions above. Anderson Imbert, I, 228-232. Allison Williams Bunkley, *The Life of Sarmiento,* Princeton, Princeton Univ. Press, 1952. Crow, *Epic,* Chap. XLIV. *Diccionario . . . Argentina,* I, 173-179. C. Galván Moreno, *Radiografía de Sarmiento,* 2nd ed., Buenos Aires, Claridad, 1961. Henríquez Ureña, *Lit. Curr.,* 131-136. Alberto Palcos, *Sarmiento,* 4th ed., Buenos Aires, Emecé, 1962. Ricardo Rojas, *El profeta de la pampa; vida de Sarmiento,* 5th ed., Buenos Aires, Losada, 1951.

°2. (Ecuador) **Juan Montalvo** (1832-1889), born in the same year and in the same town as Juan León Mera, was an implacable enemy of tyrants and especially of his country's dictator, García Moreno. Possessing an extremely clear and flexible prose style, he used this gift to excoriate the ruler in the pages of his journal, *El cosmopolita* (1866-1869). Consequently he was forced to leave the country. When in exile in 1875, he heard that García Moreno had been assassinated. He is said to have exclaimed with satisfaction, "¡Mi pluma le ha matado!" After the tyrant's death he again found himself at odds with the authorities and was condemned to perpetual banishment. In 1889 his polemical essays were published in Panama under the title *Catilinarias*. From Panama he went to France, where he spent the rest of his life. Here he founded a paper called *El espectador* (1886-1888), and here his famous *Siete tratados*, written about 1873, were finally published in 1882. His remarkably successful imitation of *Don Quixote*, the *Capítulos que se le olvidaron a Cervantes*, appeared posthumously. Montalvo's style has classic purity, balance, and perfection of form, but his spirit has no classical serenity; it is uncompromising and rebellious.

SUGGESTED READING

"Washington y Bolívar," "Elogio de la pobreza," "Las facultades extraordinarias," "El interviéwer."

TEXTS

Anthology, 383-396. Anderson Imbert and Florit, 326-332. Monterde, 227-235.

EDITIONS

Siete tratados, 2 vols., Paris, Garnier, 1930; introduction by R. Blanco-Fombona; *ibid.*, México, Secretaría de Educación Pública, 1947; prologue by Antonio Acevedo Escobedo. *Páginas escogidas,* Buenos Aires, Estrada, 1941 (Col. Estrada, 16); edited by Arturo Giménez Pastor. *Obras escogidas,* Quito, Casa de la Cultura Ecuatoriana, 1948 (Clásicos ecuatorianos, 13); edited by Julio E. Moreno.

CRITICAL REFERENCES

See texts and editions above. Enrique Anderson Imbert, *El arte de la prosa en Juan Montalvo,* México, El Colegio de México, 1948. Barrera, *Hist.*, III, 165-230. *Diccionario . . . Ecuador,* 43-47. José Enrique Rodó, *Cinco ensayos,* Madrid, Ed. América, n.d. (Biblioteca Andrés Bello), 21-109. M. Vitier, 75-94.

3. (Puerto Rico) **Eugenio María Hostos** (1839-1903) was the champion of union and independence for the Caribbean islands. He was born in Puerto Rico but educated in Spain where he lived from 1851 to 1869 and where he fought for the republic of 1868. He hoped that republican Spain would give the Antilles the status of a free dominion within a vast federation of Spanish-speaking countries. Pérez Galdós mentions him in one of his *Episodios nacionales (Prim)* as a "young man of very radical ideas, talented and noisy." Banished from Spain, he came back to America, living first in the United States and then in many countries of Spanish America. In Santo Domingo he worked for the reform of the school system; in Chile he taught international law. Wherever he went he was a force for enlightenment and progress. His writings are concerned with problems of great social import; his style is that of an inspired teacher. *Moral social* (1888) is generally conceded to be his most important work.

SUGGESTED READING

Moral social.

TEXTS

Anderson Imbert and Florit, 342-348. Beltrán, *Antología*, I, 124-130.

EDITIONS

Moral social, 2nd. ed., Buenos Aires, Jackson, 1946 (Grandes escritores de América, 2). *Obras completas,* 20 vols., Habana, Cultural, [1939]. *Eugenio María de Hostos, a Promoter of Pan Americanism; a Collection of Writings and a Bibliography,* Madrid, J. Bravo, [1954].

CRITICAL REFERENCES

See texts and editions above. Blanco-Fombona, *Grandes escritores*, 173-221. Juan Bosch, *Hostos, el sembrador,* Habana, Ed. Trópico, 1939. *Eugenio María de Hostos,* New York, Hispanic Institute, 1940. M. Vitier, 95-116.

°°4. (Peru) **Ricardo Palma** (1833-1919), Peru's greatest literary personality, was born in Lima and spent most of his long life in that city, absenting himself from it only for a short period of political exile in his youth and for brief interludes of travel in his riper years. He left university before his graduation in order to give his attention to literature, journalism, and politics. He published his first book of verses, *Poesías,* in 1855. His delightful *La bohemia de mi tiempo* (1887) recalls the romantic vagaries of those early years. In 1863 his important historical study, *Anales de la Inquisición en Lima*, appeared; in 1865, another book of poems, *Armonías, libros de un desterrado;* and, in 1870, a third called *Pasionarias*. Two years later he found the medium which was to give him a unique place in Spanish American literature as the creator of the *tradición*, or historical anecdote. In a series of ten volumes published intermittently from 1872 to 1910, Palma recreated with wit and imagination his country's past. During the wars with Chile (1879-1883), Palma's own house and manuscripts were destroyed and the books and documents of the Biblioteca Nacional plundered and scattered. On the conclusion of peace Palma was put in charge of the work of restoring the national library. He succeeded in recovering many of its treasures and in reviving and increasing its prestige. Thus, in a double sense, he may be said to have preserved the past for his fatherland. Palma started his literary career as a romanticist, but his temperament was not romantic, and his early poems are of little value. He himself criticized them mercilessly. His muse was not lyrical, but ironic; not sentimental, but critical.

SUGGESTED READING

"Las orejas del alcalde," "Un virrey hereje y un campanero bellaco," "Amor de madre," "La camisa de Margarita," "La pantorrilla del comandante," "La viudita," "El alacrán de fray Gómez," "Dónde y cómo el diablo perdió el poncho."

TEXTS

Anthology, 397-423. Anderson Imbert and Florit, 334-341. Caillet-Bois, 494-499. Flores, 94-106. *Tradiciones escogidas*, in García Calderón, *Biblioteca*, 11. *Tradiciones peruanas* (ed. Umphrey), Chicago, Sanborn, 1936. Weisinger, 129-154.

EDITIONS

Tradiciones peruanas, 6 vols., Madrid, Calpe, 1924. *Tradiciones peruanas*, Buenos Aires, Espasa-Calpe, 1939 (Col. austral, 132). *Flor de tradiciones*, México, Cultura, 1943 (Clásicos de América, ediciones del Instituto Internacional de Literatura Iberoamericana, 4); edited by George W. Umphrey and Carlos García-Prada. *Tradiciones peruanas completas*, 3rd ed., Madrid, Aguilar, 1957; edited by Edith Palma.

TRANSLATIONS

Colford, 52-66. Harriet de Onís (trans.), *The Knights of the Cape,* New York, Knopf, 1945.

CRITICAL REFERENCES

See texts and editions above. Guillermo Feliú Cruz, *En torno de Ricardo Palma*, 2 vols., Santiago, Univ. de Chile, 1933. García Calderón, *Semblanzas*, 93-106. César Miró, *Don Ricardo Palma; el patriarca de las Tradiciones*, Buenos Aires, Losada, 1953. Angélica Palma, *Ricardo Palma*, Buenos Aires, Tor, 1933. Valera, II, 291-300.

c. DRAMA

While in France and Spain the romantic drama was a dominant and flourishing genre, in Spanish America in general, it found barren soil, and such plays as were produced were considerably less original and interesting than the poetry and prose of the time. Almost all fall into two broad categories: historical plays and comedies of manners. In the latter field, for which Bretón de los Herreros (1796-1873) in Spain and Scribe (1791-1861) in France provided models, the Peruvian, Manuel Ascencio Segura (1805-1871) wrote some twelve comedies which were gaily satirical of manners and customs in Lima. *El Sargento Canuto* (1839) and *Ña Catita* (1856) are minor classics of their type and time. In Mexico, Fernando Calderón (1809-1845) pleased his public with his only comedy, *A ninguna de las tres* (1839), which is still amusing for its native types and its anti-romantic raillery.

Calderón also gained a place in Mexican literature with his historical dramas, *El torneo* (1839), *Ana Bolena* (ca. 1840), and *Hermán o La vuelta del cruzado* (1842). And Calderón's contemporary, Ignacio Rodríguez Galván (1816-1842), followed in the same vein with his romantic plays on colonial times, *Muñoz, visitador de México* (1838) and *El privado del virrey* (1842). In Cuba, José Jacinto Milanés (1814-1863) joined their company with *El Conde Alarcos* (1838), a verse drama clearly in the style of Spain's Antonio García Gutiérrez (1813-1884). It will be recalled that La Avellaneda and Mármol were also writing historical plays on these and similar themes during those very years.

Biblical days, medieval history and legend, and colonial times furnished a major share of the themes for the romantic theater in America. But perhaps the most interesting of the historical plays were those concerning the tragic fate of the Indian. The struggle between conqueror and conquered inspired the writing of romantic dramas in almost every corner of the New World. Caupolicán, Atahualpa, Tecum-Umán, Cuauhtémoc, Xicoténcatl, Malinche, Cortés, Alvarado, Pizarro and their counterparts elsewhere peopled many a play composed by regional dramatists long since forgotten. Heredia was the only leading writer of the period to explore the theme in his youthful attempts at dramatizing the tragic lot of Mexico's martyrs—*Moctezuma* (1819) and *Xicoténcatl* (1823). But even so, the Indian, and in the long view other romantic material as well, fared far better in poetry and in the novel.

REFERENCES

Alpern and Martel, 242-347 (*Ña Catita*). Arrom, *Lit. dram. cubana*, Chaps. III-V. Jones, *Antología*, 13-46 (*El Sargento Canuto*). Olavarría y Ferrari, I, Parts II-IV.

II.
Realism and Naturalism
(1854-1918)

A. PROSE

Although for the sake of convenience one can roughly label nineteenth-century novelists as romanticists, realists, or naturalists, and with equal imprecision assign classifications to chronological segments of the century, such practices must be recognized as oversimplifications. For example, as early as 1840, the arch-romanticist, Esteban Echeverría, published a long story, "El matadero," which in its attention to repugnant detail is every bit as "naturalistic" as the ugly situations described in the novels of his compatriot Eugenio Cambaceres (1843-1888)—possibly the earliest and most faithful follower of Zola (1840-1902) in America—and the Mexican Federico Gamboa (1864-1939), who also wrote under the influence of French naturalism. On the other hand, some of the episodes of *Santa* (1903) by Gamboa would rival any of the romantic school in their sentimental melodramatic traits. To further illustrate the complexity of the matter, Luis Alberto Sánchez in his painstaking survey of the Spanish American novel (*Proceso y contenido de la novela hispanoamericana*) found it necessary to invent at least thirteen classifications; even they seem inadequate.

With these warnings in mind one can say, nevertheless, that in general, Spanish American novelistic production from 1854 to 1918 was characterized by attempts to write more or less objectively about external reality, and was in contrast to the rhapsodic idealism and emphasis on emotion of the earlier years. Various adjectives are applied to stress different aspects of these attempts: "naturalistic" usually refers to the emphasis on sordid reality, often the result of imitating Zola or the Goncourts (Edmond, 1822-1896;

Jules, 1830-1870) in France; "realistic," a more general term, frequently denotes an influence of the Spanish novelists, Pereda (1834-1906), Pérez Galdós (1843-1920), and Valera (1827-1905), with their occasionally tiresome prolixity in detailed description; *"costumbrista,"* a tendency prominent in the sketches of the romantic authors and a constant in the literature of the whole century, refers to an intent fascination with picturesque local manners, types, and habits of speech. "Regionalism" (sometimes called *criollismo*) is similar to *costumbrismo*, perhaps with more emphasis on the description of the rural landscape. It is frequently possible to apply all or several of these epithets to the same novelist. And the "regional—*costumbrista*" work of many a realist was often marked by strong romantic overtones as in the "sentimental" novels, *La Calandria* (1891) and *Angelina* (1893), of the Mexican, Rafael Delgado (1853-1914).

Although the formal structure of the novel generally is imitative of overseas models, the subject matter was as varied and American as the New World itself.

REFERENCES

Alegría, *Breve hist.*, 88-107. Navarro, *passim*. Sánchez, *Proceso y contenido*, Chaps. X-XII. Torres-Ríoseco, *Novela*, 199-213. Warner, 103-110. Zum Felde, *Índice crítico*, II, Chaps. III-IV, *passim*.

°1. (Chile) **Alberto Blest Gana** (1830-1920) was born in Santiago, the son of an Irish professor of medicine. From 1847 to 1851, he pursued advanced military studies in France. It was there, under the spell of Balzac (1799-1850), that he was first strongly attracted to letters. Except for a short period as a teacher of mathematics in the military academy, he soon abandoned his career to turn full time to writing. His first story was published in 1853. He was ambitious to record for posterity in imaginative prose the history of his country and the daily life of all classes of its people. In 1860 his *La aritmética en el amor* won the first prize ever offered in Chile for a work of prose fiction. It was followed by a series of other novels, the most important of which were *Martín Rivas* (1862) and *El ideal de un calavera* (1863). Thereafter, Blest Gana entered the diplomatic service, serving many years as Chilean Ambassador to France and to England. A second period of literary production began for him in 1897 with the historical novel, *Durante la reconquista*. After his retirement from public life he lived in Paris and continued to write until an advanced age. His novels are social documents of the greatest interest and importance, but he lacked creative imagination. His influence upon his contemporaries was profound. He taught many of them to prefer prose to poetry.

SUGGESTED READING
Martín Rivas.
TEXTS
Flores, 61-81. *Martín Rivas* (ed. Umphrey), Boston, Heath, 1926.
EDITIONS
Martín Rivas, 2 vols., Paris-México, Bouret, 1924. *Martín Rivas,* 8th ed., Santiago, Zig-Zag, 1961. *El ideal de un calavera,* 3rd ed., Paris-México, Bouret, 1918. *El jefe de la familia y otras páginas,* Santiago, Zig-Zag, [1956]; edited by Raúl Silva Castro. *Blest Gana, sus mejores páginas,* Santiago, Ercilla, 1961; edited by Manuel Rojas.
TRANSLATIONS
Jones, 250-253. Mrs. Charles Whitman (trans.), *Martín Rivas* (1916), New York, Knopf, 1918.
CRITICAL REFERENCES
See texts and editions above. Alegría, *Breve hist.,* 54-58. "Alone," *Don Alberto Blest Gana,* Santiago, Nascimento, 1940. Raúl Silva Castro, *Alberto Blest Gana,* 2nd ed., Santiago, Zig-Zag, 1955.

°2. (Chile) **Baldomero Lillo** (1867-1923) was the first Chilean short-story writer to accentuate the social problems of his country's national life. He was born of a middle-class family, and as a child heard his father relate mining experiences which he had gone through in several parts of Chile and in the state of California, U.S.A. The son, Baldomero, was employed by a Chilean mining company, and finally became manager of the company store. He read voluminously (French and Russian naturalism, especially), and Zola's *Germinal* (1885) left a deep imprint on his work. In 1898 he went to Santiago, where he immediately identified himself with the problems of the city workers and often attended *tertulias* frequented by a group of his brother's friends known as the *generación de novecientos.* He secured a position in the section of publications of the University of Chile. In 1917 he had to give up this university work because of ill health, and from that time until his death he received a pension from the national government. He left only two first-rate works, *Sub terra* (1904) and *Sub sole* (1907).

SUGGESTED READING
"El chiflón del diablo," "El pozo," "La compuerta número 12."
TEXTS
Anthology, 606-613. Anderson Imbert and Florit, 376-383. Arratia and Hamilton, 37-45. Flores, 227-243. Jones and Hansen, 173-186. Torres-Ríoseco and Kress, 95-106.
EDITIONS
Sub terra, 5th ed., Santiago, Nascimento, 1956. *Sub sole*, 3rd ed., Santiago, Nascimento, 1943; "Baldomero Lillo," together with bibliography, by J. S. González Vera, 195-264. *Antología de Baldomero Lillo*, Santiago, Zig-Zag, 1955; edited by Nicomedes Guzmán.
TRANSLATIONS
Colford, 36-42. Esther S. Dillon and Angel Flores (trans.), *The Devil's Pit and Other Stories*, Washington, Pan American Union, 1959.
CRITICAL REFERENCES
See texts and editions above. *Diccionario* . : . *Chile*, 109-111. Ruth Sedgwick, "El mensaje social de Baldomero Lillo," *Memoria del segundo congreso*, 35-44; also her "Baldomero Lillo y Emile Zola," *Revista iberoamericana*, 14 (1944), 321-328.

3. (Uruguay) **Eduardo Acevedo Díaz** (1851-1921) was one of the first good novelists of the so-called *mester de gauchería*. His work inaugurated and closed the epoch of the historical novel in Uruguay and stimulated gaucho prose in the entire River Plate region. Acevedo Díaz studied law, fought in the revolutionary army, engaged in politics and journalism, held several diplomatic posts, was twice exiled, and, in 1903, fled from Uruguay never to return. His entire work was written in exile. His style was naturalistic on the whole, but there were passages of romance and characters symbolic of his country's principal types. His three early novels—*Ismael* (1888), *Nativa* (1890), *El grito de gloria* (1893)—were a nationalistic trilogy called a "hymn to blood;" his best written novel, *Soledad* (1894), became a model for later gauchesque prose.
SUGGESTED READING
Soledad.
TEXTS
Flores, 161-172.
EDITIONS
Soledad, Montevideo, Ministerio de Instrucción Pública, 1954 (Col.

de clásicos uruguayos, 15); prologue by Francisco Espínola. *Ismael,* Montevideo, Ministerio de Instrucción Pública, 1953 (Col. de clásicos uruguayos, 4); prologue by Robert Ibáñez. *Nativa,* 2 vols. Montevideo, C. García, 1931. *El grito de gloria,* Buenos Aires, Sociedad Editora Latinoamericana, 1954 (Obras completas, 1).

TRANSLATIONS

Jones, 233-235.

CRITICAL REFERENCES

See editions above. Alberto Lasplaces, *Eduardo Acevedo Díaz,* Montevideo, C. García, 1931. Zum Felde, *Proceso,* I, 275-307.

°4. (Uruguay) **Javier de Viana** (1868-1926) was reared on a ranch among gauchos. At the age of eleven he went to Montevideo, where he studied languages and medicine and served a short term in the parliament. In 1904 he became a voluntary exile to Buenos Aires, where he took up journalism, writing articles on the theater. An ardent admirer of nature and a keen observer of men, he became one of the most vigorous regionalists America has produced. His work is extremely somber in tone and is often freighted with local terms and descriptive detail. He stands, however, as the precursor of the best of the contemporary *criollo* school. His first short pieces, or "Escenas de la vida de campaña," appeared under the title of *Campo* in 1896. *Leña seca* (1911) and *Yuyos* (1912) are among his best collections of short stories. In addition to many other volumes of tales, sketches and chronicles, he left one novel, *Gaucha* (1899), an abnormally brutal story of rural life written according to the Zola formula.

SUGGESTED READING

"La tísica," "El domador," "Lo mesmo da."

TEXTS

Anthology, 672-679. Anderson Imbert and Florit, 373-375. Coester, *Cuentos,* 25-31, 59-64. Crow, *Cuentos,* 171-180. Flores, 275-279. García Calderón, *Cuentos,* 7-26, 92-96, 199-203. Manzor, 353-359. Wilkins, 112-117.

EDITIONS

Campo, Montevideo, C. García, 1945 (Biblioteca Rodó, 136-137). *Gaucha,* Montevideo, Ministerio de Educación Pública, 1956 (Col. de clásicos uruguayos, 19); prologue by Arturo S. Visca. *Leña seca,*

6th ed., Montevideo, C. García, [192?]. *Yuyos,* Montevideo, C. García, 1926.

TRANSLATIONS

Colford, 97-105. H. de Onís, 163-178.

CRITICAL REFERENCES

See texts and editions above. Zum Felde, *Proceso,* II, 193-217.

5. (Argentina) **Martiniano. P. Leguizamón** (1858-1935), born in the province of Entre Ríos, became a professor of literature and history in Buenos Aires. His many fine naturalistic, regional, gauchesque short stories and sketches and his drama *Calandria* (1896) had a revitalizing effect on Argentine prose and served to perpetuate all that was national in the gaucho literature which had gone before. His novel *Montaraz* (1900) is a dramatic account of the heroic defense of the *montoneras* against Artigas. Leguizamón was also an excellent critic and historian of the gaucho epoch.

SUGGESTED READING

Prose: "El forastero" and "El tiro de gracia." Drama: *Calandria.*

TEXTS

García Calderón, *Cuentos,* 85-92, 179-186.

EDITIONS

Prose: *Recuerdos de la tierra,* Buenos Aires, F. Lajouane, 1896; introduction by Joaquín V. González. *Alma nativa* (1906), 2nd ed., Buenos Aires, J. Roldán, 1912. *De cepa criolla,* Buenos Aires, Solar-Hachette, 1961; prologue by Guillermo Ara. *Montaraz, Costumbres argentinas,* 4th ed., Buenos Aires, J. Roldán, 1962. Drama: *Calandria,* Buenos Aires, Hachette, 1961.

TRANSLATIONS

Calandria, A Drama of Gaucho Life, New York, Hispanic Society, 1932. *Trans. from Hisp. Poets,* 185-186.

CRITICAL REFERENCES

See texts and editions above. *Diccionario . . . Argentina,* I, 104-106. Julia Grifone, *Martiniano Leguizamón y su égloga Calandria,* Buenos Aires, Imp. de la Universidad, 1940. José Torre Revello, *Martiniano Leguizamón, el hombre y su obra,* Paraná, Museo de Entre Ríos, 1939.

6. (Argentina) **Carlos María Ocantos** (1860-1949), novelist and diplomat—he entered the foreign service in 1884—claimed to have initiated

the *novela galdosiana* in his country; and was called the "Balzac of Argentina." Both claims are only superficially true. Ocantos is often prolix, and oftentimes his characters are weakly delineated, his plots almost ridiculous; his passages on customs and daily life are generally good. The author lived most of his life in Spain, separated from the main currents of Argentine literature; in 1897 he was elected a member of the Spanish Royal Academy. He died in Madrid. *León Zaldívar* (1888) was the first in a series of twenty *novelas argentinas* in which Ocantos undertook to depict, and to censure, the social scene of Buenos Aires of his day.

SUGGESTED READING

León Zaldívar.

TEXTS

León Zaldívar (ed. Rice), New York, Appleton-Century-Crofts, 1937.

EDITIONS

León Zaldívar, Barcelona, Sopena, [1916]. *Don Perfecto,* Barcelona, Montanero y Simón, 1902.

CRITICAL· REFERENCES

See texts and editions above. Theodore Andersson, *Carlos María Ocantos, Argentine Novelist,* New Haven, Yale Univ. Press, 1934. Arrieta, III, 400-405. *Diccionario . . . Argentina,* I, 152-154. Lichtblau, 185-194.

°7. (Argentina) **Roberto J. Payró** (1867-1928) was a journalist, traveler, translator of Zola, writer of *costumbrista* sketches, and dramatist of the contemporary scene. In 1896 he became secretary of the first Center of Socialist Studies in Argentina, of which Leopoldo Lugones (1874-1938) and José Ingenieros (1877-1925) were also members. He was caught in Belgium during the first World War, where he was imprisoned as an enemy spy after he had expressed bitter hatred of German militarism. His later writings were permeated with these war experiences. His earlier sketches of the Argentine scene are his best: the sobering *Divertidas aventuras del nieto de Juan Moreira* (1910), the humorous tales of *Pago Chico* (1908), and the picaresque novelette, *El casamiento de Laucha* (1906), generally conceded to be his masterpiece. Journalistic style weakens many of his literary efforts.

Payró also won early recognition as a dramatist. Of his several plays based on social-moral conflicts in Argentine life, *Sobre las ruinas* (1904) and *Vivir quiero conmigo* (1923) are excellent.

SUGGESTED READING

Prose: *El casamiento de Laucha.* Drama: *Sobre las ruinas.*

TEXTS

Anderson Imbert and Florit, 371-373. Flores, 257-268.

EDITIONS

Prose: *El casamiento de Laucha. Chamijo. El falso Inca,* Buenos Aires, Losada, [1940]. *Pago Chico y los nuevos eventos de Pago Chico,* Buenos Aires, Losada, 1961 (Bibl. contemporánea, 36). *Divertidas aventuras del nieto de Juan Moreira,* Buenos Aires, Losada, 1957 (Bibl. contemporánea, 60). *Veinte cuentos,* Buenos Aires, Poseidón, 1943. Drama: *Teatro completo,* Buenos Aires, Hachette, 1956; prologue by Roberto F. Giusti.

TRANSLATIONS

Frank, 1-77, 155-178. H. de Onís, 192-202.

CRITICAL REFERENCES

See texts and editions above. *Diccionario . . . Argentina,* I, 156-160. Germán García, *Roberto J. Payró; testimonio de una vida y realidad de una literatura,* Buenos Aires, Nova, 1961. Raúl Larra, *Payró, el novelista de la democracia,* 3rd ed., Buenos Aires, La Mandrágora, 1960 (Clásicos argentinos del siglo XX).

8. (Peru) **Clorinda Matto de Turner** (1852-1909), wife of an English doctor, wrote one of the first *indianista* novels depicting the lives of the exploited natives of Peru. *Aves sin nido* (1889) was greeted with many shudders of protest on the part of the clergy and the large landowners. Her later novels, *Índole* (1891) and *Herencia* (1895), and her *Tradiciones y leyendas cuzqueñas* (1884-1886)—in the tradition of Palma, her "maestro"—helped further to establish her as one of the early and most dedicated prose writers of her sex and time. Her admiration for native customs and traditions was intelligent and sincere; her indignation over the abject condition of the native cleared the way for later protest literature in behalf of America's Indian masses.

SUGGESTED READING

Aves sin nido.

EDITIONS
Aves sin nido, Cuzco, Univ. Nacional del Cuzco, 1948.
TRANSLATIONS
J. G. Hudson, *Birds Without Nests,* London, Thynne, 1904.
CRITICAL REFERENCES
See editions above. Manuel E. Cuadros Escobedo, *Paisaje i obra, mujer e historia: Clorinda Matto de Turner,* Cuzco, Rozas, 1949. Meléndez, 171-178.

°9. (Colombia) **Tomás Carrasquilla** (1858-1940) was born in Antioquia, a prosperous mountainous region of Colombia lying between the Magdalena and Cauca rivers. Its inhabitants are a traditionally independent people; among them, Carrasquilla spent most of his long life and devoted most of his energy to writing narratives which portray in great and sometimes annoying detail, the landscape, characters, local speech, and manner of living of the region. He is sometimes compared with the Spanish realists, Pereda and Pérez Galdós, and in fact his works have the same leisurely tempo, loving reproduction of provincial talk, and purity of style and tone which characterized the Spanish authors. In contrast to many of his Spanish American confreres influenced by French naturalism, Carrasquilla rarely became involved in the exposition of social problems or the description of life's seamier side. Also in contrast to some of his contemporaries, he was truly a professional craftsman, not a part-time amateur and reformer. In spite of this fact, he has been criticized as weak in his plot structure; this is doubtless due to his *costumbrista* technique in which sketches are loosely connected together to form a novel. *Frutos de mi tierra* (1896), his first work, is generally considered to be his masterpiece, but *La marquesa de Yolombó* (1928), a historical novel of colonial times, is also highly regarded. During a period of blindness he dictated his last and best sustained work, the three-volume novel *Hace tiempos* (1935-1936), for which he was awarded the Premio Nacional de Literatura in 1935.

SUGGESTED READING
"Simón el mago," "En la diestra de Dios Padre," "Dimitas Arias," "El ánima sola," "¡A la plata!," "El rifle."

TEXTS
Anderson Imbert and Florit, 384-388. Flores, 200-218. *Seis cuentos* (ed. García-Prada), México, Studium, 1959.
EDITIONS
Obras completas, Madrid, E.P.E.S.A., 1952; prologue by Federico de Onís. *Cuentos de Tomás Carrasquilla,* Medellín, Bedout, 1956; edited by Benigno A. Gutiérrez. *Obras completas,* 2 vols., Bogotá, Empresa Nacional de Publicaciones, 1956; edited by José Eusebio Ricaurte. *Obras completas,* 2 vols., Medellín, Bedout, 1958; prologues by Roberto Jaramillo and Federico de Onís.
TRANSLATIONS
H. de Onís, 146-163.
CRITICAL REFERENCES
See texts and editions above. *Diccionario . . . Colombia,* 21-24. García-Prada, *Estudios,* 255-259. Kurt L. Levy, *Vida y obras de Tomás Carrasquilla,* Medellín, Bedout, 1958. Sanín Cano, 199-202.

10. (Mexico) **José López-Portillo y Rojas** (1850-1923) was born in Guadalajara of a prominent family; he studied law in Mexico City and later became a distinguished professor of that subject. During his life he traveled widely in England, France, Italy and the Orient, and acquired an extensive culture, which included a profound knowledge of French, English, and Spanish literatures. He held the governorship of Jalisco and other important political posts. Besides novels and some excellent short stories, López-Portillo y Rojas wrote poetry, drama, travel sketches, criticism, and history. *La parcela* (1898), his first full-length novel, was hailed as the first important work of fiction on rural Mexico; it has far outshadowed in popularity his later novels, *Los precursores* (1909) and *Fuertes y débiles* (1919).
SUGGESTED READING
La parcela.
TEXTS
Algunos cuentos (ed. Emmanuel Carballo), México, Univ. Nacional, 1956 (Biblioteca del estudiante universitario, 77). Starr, *Modern Mexican Authors,* 313-333. Torres-Ríoseco and Sims, 51-65.
EDITIONS
La parcela, México, Porrúa, 1945; prologue by Antonio Castro Leal. *Cuentos completos,* 2 vols., Guadalajara, Eds. I.T.G., 1952 (Biblioteca jalisciense, 7-8); prologue by Emmanuel Carballo.

TRANSLATIONS

Starr, *Modern Mexican Authors,* 313-333.

CRITICAL REFERENCES

See texts and editions above. Azuela, 147-163. Navarro, 183-237. Warner, 115-119; also his "Aportaciones a la bibliografía de don José López-Portillo y Rojas," *Revista iberoamericana,* 25 (1947), 165-198.

11. (Mexico) **Federico Gamboa** (1864-1939) stands apart from the aforementioned Mexican realists in his tendency to naturalism and his obsession with the emotional (pathological) conflicts of city life. He felt a strong admiration for the French, Zola and the Goncourts, but his feeling was punctuated with a frequent religious sentiment. Gamboa was born in Mexico City, where his family early suffered adverse fortune. Hardship sharpened the author's sensibilities and helped him to become a self-made man. He followed a very successful diplomatic and literary career. In later life he taught Mexican literature in the National University, and was President of the Mexican Academy of Letters. Gamboa left four Zolaesque, sermon-filled novels of social reform, one on religious salvation, several dramas, and detailed bio-bibliographical accounts of his life and writings. *Santa* (1903) is one of the best-known and most popular Spanish American novels in the naturalist manner.

SUGGESTED READING

Santa.

TEXTS

Starr, *Modern Mexican Authors,* 405-420.

EDITIONS

Suprema ley (1896), México, E. Gómez de la Puente, 1920. *Santa,* 11th ed., México, Botas, 1938. *Reconquista* (1908), 2nd ed., México, Botas, 1937.

TRANSLATIONS

Starr, *Modern Mexican Authors,* 405-420.

CRITICAL REFERENCES

See texts and editions above. Azuela, 189-206. González, *Trayectoria,* 72-76. Ernest Moore, "Bibliografía de obras y crítica de Federico Gamboa," *Revista iberoamericana,* 3 (1940), 271-279. Navarro, 246-312.

b. POETRY

Unfortunately for literary historians, creative literature does not always fit neatly into chronological and pigeon-holed movements. As an example, during the years of the later nineteenth century when the novel in Spanish America was making a fairly definite break with the idealistic fancies of the romanticists, poetry continued to evolve almost imperceptibly away from the earlier ecstasies and clichés of romanticism through a more refined and sophisticated expression of the tendency, until it burst forth into the modernist movement. Realism and naturalism, perhaps in the very nature of their inspiration, hardly touched the poetic muse in Spanish America. In chronological reality, while Blest Gana in Chile was writing his social document, *Martín Rivas;* Clorinda Matto de Turner, her exposé of Indian conditions in Peru; and Eugenio Cambaceres, his frank account of the more sordid aspects of life in Buenos Aires, some of the later romantic poets, the so-called postromanticists, were pursuing delicate and exquisite paths of personal experience far removed from naturalistic reality. The poetry of Manuel González-Prada (1848-1918) (see III below) was possibly the most interesting bridge between the romantic strain and the complicated tone of later poetry. There are few important or obvious poetic counterparts, then, to the strong thrust of naturalism in prose. Only in the virile gaucho tradition of the River Plate are the forms of romantic poetry during this period intertwined with the stuff of realism.

REFERENCES

Sánchez, *Nueva hist.,* 354-371. Torres-Ríoseco, *Epic,* 78-81.

c. DRAMA

While there were scattered examples elsewhere of theatrical works produced during these decades, the only realistic drama of originality and merit developed in the River Plate region. Beginning in the early 1880's, with rustic gaucho themes as its mainstay, it grew from pantomimes and crude melodramas featured in the circus rings of Argentina and Uruguay. Legendary gaucho heroes, such as Juan Moreira and Santos Vega and Juan Cuello were generally the protagonists. Originating as improvised, rudimentary dramatic representations, without established scripts, they gradually entered the realm of artistic, written drama of a refreshingly original type. A landmark of this theater of known authorship was *Jesús Nazareno,* by Enrique García Velloso (1881-1938), produced in 1902. Thereafter, writers of all kinds tried their hand at the theater. Some continued in the stylized gaucho tradition; others used the format for treating rural or even urban social problems. One of the earliest and best of these playwrights was the Uruguayan, Florencio Sánchez (1875-1910). Roberto J. Payró and Martiniano Leguizamón, both better known as novelists (see under II, A, above), and Martín Coronado (1850-1919) were also skillful practitioners of the genre. In Mexico, as elsewhere in the Americas, romantic verse drama and *costumbrista* comedy continued to dominate the stage until the decade of the Revolution and World War I.

REFERENCES

Anderson Imbert, I, 429-435. Jacob S. Fassett (trans.), *Three Plays of the Argentine,* New York, Duffield, 1920 (*Juan Moreira, Santos Vega, La montaña de brujas*); edited by Edward Hale Bierstadt. Magaña Esquivel and Lamb, 99-106. Morales, 173-247. Olavarría y Ferrari, II-V, *passim.* Ordaz, Chaps. II, IV, VII.

°°1. (Uruguay) **Florencio Sánchez** (1875-1910) was born in Montevideo but was really the dramatist of the whole River Plate region. His short life was harried by poverty, excessive drinking, and attempts to be a political radical. He wrote his plays hurriedly (often on the backs of stolen telegraph pads), and was an amazingly prolific dramatist, writing twenty dramas between 1903 (when his first very successful play, *M'hijo el dotor,* was produced) and 1909. His brief prosperity was followed by a trip to Europe, made possible by a slim and tardy subsidy from the Uruguayan government. He died in Italy shortly after his arrival. In his technique the influence of Ibsen and other Europeans is apparent, but his considerable stature in Spanish American literature is due to his serious and effective attempts to deal with the human conflicts of his region—the struggle between city and countryside, between the individual and conventional institutions, between the new order of the immigrant and the old times. There is a strong moralistic and reformer's zeal in most of his work. His best-known plays are *M'hijo el dotor* (1903), *La gringa* (1904), *Barranca abajo* (1905), all on rural themes; and *En familia* (1905), *Los muertos* (1905) and *Nuestros hijos* (1907), which deal with urban subjects.

SUGGESTED READING

La gringa or *Barranca abajo*.

TEXTS

Alpern and Martel, 34-73 (*Los derechos de la salud*). Jones, *Antología*, 145-189 (*Barranca abajo*). *La gringa* (ed. Richardson and Lister), New York, Appleton-Century-Crofts, 1927.

EDITIONS

Teatro completo, Buenos Aires, El Ateneo, 1951; prologue by Vicente Martínez Cuitiño. *Teatro completo*, 2nd ed., Buenos Aires, Claridad, 1952; edited by Dardo Cúneo.

TRANSLATIONS

Alfred Coester (trans.), *Plays of the Southern Americas*, Stanford, Calif., Stanford Univ., 1942 (*La gringa*). Jones, 380-392; also his *Representative Plays of Florencio Sánchez*, Washington, Pan American Union, 1961.

CRITICAL REFERENCES

See texts and editions above. Díez-Canedo, 311-322. Fernando García Esteban, *Vida de Florencio Sánchez, con cartas inéditas del insigne dramaturgo*, Santiago, Ercilla, 1939. Julio Imbert, *Florencio Sánchez, vida y creación*, Buenos Aires, Schapire, 1954. Ruth Richardson, *Florencio Sánchez and the Argentine Theater*, New York, Hispanic Institute, 1933.

III.
Modernism (1882-1910)

Modernism began in the late 1870's with José Martí (1853-1895) of Cuba and Manuel Gutiérrez Nájera (1859-1895) of Mexico. The fresh, vital, flexible style of these two writers, filled with vivid imagery and color symbolism, indicated a clear break with the stodgy, pedestrian writing of the previous generation. Martí's *Ismaelillo* and *Versos libres,* both of which appeared in 1882, and Gutiérrez Nájera's *Cuentos frágiles* (1883), characterize these early steps of the new movement. Salvador Díaz Mirón (1853-1928) of Mexico, Julián del Casal (1863-1893) of Cuba, and José Asunción Silva (1865-1896) of Colombia are three other early modernists. Rubén Darío's (1867-1916) *Azul,* which appeared in Valparaíso in 1888, canalized this first stage of modernism, and attracted European attention (Juan Valera). Darío's later works (he lived longer than the other modernists) carried the movement to its zenith, and then to its conclusion. Because of his relatively long life and tremendous literary genius Darío became also the focus and leader of the movement.

Modernism began as a literature of escape, symbolized by the ivory tower. It concluded by bringing Spanish America's men of letters down from the clouds, and helped to give them a more intense awareness of their own authenticity and their own environment. It effected a complete renovation in both poetic and prose styles. Like a crucible it served to blend many diverse European and native currents into a new esthetic whole; this is the most striking *American* quality. Modernism asserted the maturity of Spanish American literature, and brought the writers of all regions into its cosmopolitan brotherhood. With modernism Spanish American literature entered the mainstream of Western letters, and carried its influence back to Europe. The Generation of 1898 represents modernism in Spain.

REFERENCES

Alegría, *Breve hist.*, 118-142. Argüello, *passim*. Blanco-Fombona, *El modernismo*, *passim*. Coester, *Lit. Hist.*, Chap. XIV; also his *Anthology*, *passim*. Craig, *passim*. Guillermo Díaz Plaja, *Modernismo frente a noventa y ocho*, Madrid, Espasa-Calpe, 1951. García-Prada, *Poetas modernistas*, *passim*. Goldberg, *passim*. González, *Notas al modernismo*, *passim*. M. Henríquez Ureña, *Breve hist.*, *passim*. Johnson, *passim*. Loprete, *passim*. Matlowsky, *Bibl. modernismo*. Maya, *passim*. Meza Fuentes, *passim*. Onís, XIV-XIX. Ivan A. Schulman, "Génesis del azul modernista," *Revista iberoamericana*, 50 (1960), 251-271. Silva Castro, *Ant. crít.*, *passim*. Torres-Ríoseco, *Precursores*, *passim*.

°1. (Peru) **Manuel González-Prada** (1848-1918), inheritor of the mantle of the Ecuadorean, Juan Montalvo, and wielder of choice invective, was born an aristocrat but became Peru's most dynamic, combative champion of the underdog, and the principal pioneer for its social reform movement, *aprismo*. As a child, González-Prada ran away from the seminary where he had been sent to study, and in early maturity (but only after the death of his religious mother) he began to hurl attacks at the Church. For several years he held a position as head of the national library, and was active in politics throughout his life. During the occupation of Lima by the forces of Chile in the War of the Pacific (1879-1883), he locked himself in his house and refused to appear on the streets. He preached national union, hatred of the Lima bureaucracy, defense of the Indians, and repression of the clerical oligarchy. In order to unleash this ceaseless propaganda of attack, he founded several journals, collaborated on many others, and accepted exile and enmity with apparent relish. He attempted to perform an autopsy on Peru's festering social, economic, and religious system. His viewpoint is summed up in his battle cry: "*¡Los viejos a la tumba, los jóvenes a la obra!*" He modeled the mentality of succeeding socialist-*aprista* generations (José Carlos Mariátegui, Raúl Haya de la Torre, Luis Alberto Sánchez, etc.) His prose style is terse and mordant, somewhat like that of the Spanish, Larra, whom he also resembles in spirit. Many of González-Prada's works lay scattered for years, to be assembled and published posthumously in book form by his son. They prove him to be a fine poet, particularly of ironic verse, as well as Spanish America's most colorful essayist.

SUGGESTED READING

"Triolets," "Rondeles," "El mitayo," "Grafitos," "El Perú," "La serenata de Pierrot," "Discurso en el Politeama," "La muerte y la vida," "Discurso en el entierro de Luis Márquez," "La fuerza," "El individuo," "La salud de las letras," "La educación del indio."

TEXTS

Anthology, 570-590. Anderson Imbert and Florit, 349-354. García-Prada, *Poetas modernistas,* 34-45. Holmes, *Span. Am.,* 432-433. Onís, 4-5. Silva Castro, *Ant. crít.,* 49-53.

EDITIONS

Páginas libres (1894), 2nd ed., Madrid, Sociedad Española de Librería, 1915; prologue by Rufino Blanco-Fombona; *ibid.,* 3rd ed., Lima, Ed. P.T.C.M., 1946; prologue by Luis Alberto Sánchez. *Minúsculas* (1901), 4th ed., Lima, Ed. P.T.C.M., 1947. *Horas de lucha* (1908), 2nd ed., Lima, Tip. "Lux," 1924. *Exóticas (1911). Trozos de vida* (1933), Lima, Ed. P.T.C.M., 1948; prologue by Luis Alberto Sánchez. *Anarquía* (1936), 4th ed., Lima, Ed. P.T.C.M., 1948. *Nuevas páginas libres,* Santiago, Ercilla, 1937. *Antología poética,* México, Cultura, 1940; prologue and notes by Carlos García-Prada. *El tonel de Diógenes,* México, Tezontle, 1945; prologue by Luis Alberto Sánchez, notes by Alfredo González-Prada. *Manuel González-Prada,* México, Imp. Universitaria, 1945; edition and prologue by Luis Alberto Sánchez.

TRANSLATIONS

Flores, *Anth. Span. Poetry,* 195-203. Jones, 107-108. *Trans. from Hisp. Poets,* 251.

CRITICAL REFERENCES

See texts and editions above. Eugenio Chang-Rodríguez, *La literatura política de González-Prada, Mariátegui y Haya de la Torre,* México, Studium, 1957. Crawford, 173-182. Adriana de González-Prada, *Mi Manuel,* Lima, Ed. Cultura Antártica, 1947. Henríquez Ureña, *Breve hist.,* 333-335. Mead, *Ensayo,* 53-55; also his *González Prada: el pensador y el prosista,* New York, Instituto de las Españas, 1955; also his *Temas,* 13-75. Jorge Mañach, Federico de Onís, Arturo Torres-Ríoseco, et al., *Manuel González-Prada. Vida y obra, biblio-*

grafía, antología, New York, Instituto de las Españas, 1938. Luis Alberto Sánchez, *Don Manuel* (1930), 3rd ed., Santiago, Ercilla, 1937.

°°2. (Cuba) **José Martí** (1853-1895) was a patriot, journalist, essayist, critic, poet, symbol of Cuban struggle for independence, exile, revolutionary worker, national martyr, and hero. He resided and wrote successively in Mexico (1874-1877), Guatemala, Spain, New York, Venezuela (1877-1880), and again in New York (1881-1895), where he remained to work for the cause of Cuba until his final departure to take part and die in the last war for his country's freedom. Martí's poetry is of a sincere simplicity unparalleled save in folk ballads; it does not enter at all into the torrent of modernist formalism. His prose style is very forceful and ringing, but sometimes becomes altisonant. He was a stirring orator and marvelous conversationalist. He was an extremely well-read man, and his was the earliest voice in initiating the new trends in style which led to the flowering of the modernist movement. His intense awareness of social problems, and his abiding interest in the freedom of all men, make him the most contemporary in spirit of all modernist writers. His articles (written mainly for *La nación* of Buenos Aires between 1882 and 1891) bear on every conceivable subject and are full of original ideas; his letters form a category unique in the Spanish language. His works, as a whole, mix influences of Spanish classic and popular culture and of England and North America, and show no decided characteristics of any literary movement. His literary work, great as it is, is hardly the equal of his life, which is the shining ideal of all Cubans.

    SUGGESTED READING

"Versos sencillos I, VII, IX, XXIII, XXV, XXXIX," "Nuestra América," "Los pinos nuevos," "Escena neoyorquina," "El terremoto de Charleston," "El poeta Walt Whitman," "La muñeca negra," "Mi raza."

    TEXTS

Anthology, 445-458. Anderson Imbert and Florit, 401-419. García-Prada, *Poetas modernistas,* 46-59. Holmes, *Span. Am.,* 279-283. Onís, 34-49. Silva Castro, *Ant. crit.,* 53-60. Walsh, *Cuentos,* 81-86.

    EDITIONS

Páginas escogidas, Paris, Garnier, 1923; edited by Max Henríquez Ureña. *Obras completas de José Martí,* 2 vols., Paris, Excelsior, 1926; edited by Armando Godoy and Ventura García Calderón. *Obras completas,* 8 vols., Madrid, Atlántida, 1925-1929. *Obras completas,* 74 vols., Habana, Ed. Trópico, 1936-1953. *Páginas selectas* (1939), 6th ed., Buenos Aires, Estrada, 1957; edition and prologue by Raimundo Lida. *Nuestra América,* Buenos Aires, Losada, 1939; edited by Pedro Henríquez Ureña. *Obras completas,* 2 vols., Habana, Lex, 1946; prologue by M. Isidro Méndez. *Poesía,* Buenos Aires, Raigal, 1952; edited by Juan Carlos Ghiano. *Poesías* (1929), 2nd ed., Habana, Cultural, 1953; edited by Juan Marinello. *Poesías completas,* Madrid, Aguilar, 1953; edited by Rafael Estenger. *Jose Martí, esquema ideológico,* México, Cultura, 1961; edited by Manuel Pedro González and Ivan A. Schulman. *La cuestión racial,* Habana, Lex, 1951. *Páginas escogidas,* Buenos Aires, Espasa-Calpe, 1962 (Col. austral, 1163). *Versos,* New York, Las Américas, 1962; edited by Eugenio Florit.

TRANSLATIONS

Cecil Charles (trans.), *Tuya, Other Verses and Translations from José Martí,* New York, Richardson, 1898. Jones, 69-71. Juan de Onís (trans.), *The America of José Martí,* New York, Noonday, 1953; introduction by Federico de Onís.

CRITICAL REFERENCES

See texts and editions above. Enrique Anderson Imbert, "La prosa poética de José Martí," *Memoria del Congreso de Escritores Martianos* (Habana, 1953), 570-616. Julio Caillet-Bois, "Martí y el modernismo literario," *Memoria del Congreso de Escritores Martianos* (Habana, 1953), 474-489. Goldberg, 46-52. González, *Estudios,* 133-150; also his "Iniciación de Rubén Darío en el culto a Martí," *Memoria del Congreso de Escritores Martianos* (Habana, 1953), 503-569; also his *José Martí: Epic Chronicler of the United States in the Eighties,* Chapel Hill, Univ. of North Carolina Press, 1953; also his *Fuentes para el estudio de José Martí,* Habana, Ministerio de Educación, 1950; and his *Antología crítica de José Martí,* México, Cultura, 1960. Max Henríquez Ureña, "Martí, iniciador del modernismo," *Memoria del Congreso de Escritores Martianos* (Habana, 1953), 447-465; also his *Breve hist.,* 50-66. Félix Lizaso, *Martí, místico del deber,* Buenos Aires, Losada, 1940; also his *Proyección humana de Martí,* Buenos Aires, Raigal, 1953. Jorge Mañach, *Martí, el apóstol,* 4th ed., Buenos Aires, Espasa-Calpe, 1952 (translated into English by Coley Taylor, *Martí, Apostle of Freedom,* New York, Devin-Adair, 1950); *ibid.,* rev. ed., New York, Las

Américas, 1963. Juan Marinello, *José Martí, escritor americano: Martí y el modernismo,* México, Grijalbo, 1958. Fermín Peraza Sarausa, *Bibliografía martiniana, 1853-1955,* Habana, Eds. Anuario Bibliográfico Cubano, 1956. José Antonio Portuondo, *José Martí, crítico literario,* Washington, Pan American Union, 1953. Emeterio Santiago Santovenia, *Lincoln en Martí,* Habana, Ed. Trópico, 1948 (translated into English by Donald F. Fogelquist, *Lincoln in Martí,* Chapel Hill, Univ. of North Carolina Press, 1953). Ivan A. Schulman, *Símbolo y color en la obra de José Martí,* Madrid, Gredos, 1960. Torres-Ríoseco, *Precursores,* 77-93.

°3. (Mexico) **Salvador Díaz Mirón** (1853-1928), who was once a member of the Mexican Congress, led a stormy and dramatic life. An impulsive sense of honor caused him to fight duels and suffer imprisonment. He lived in aristocratic seclusion, entirely apart from literary currents of his day—a man of extremely broad and profound culture. Díaz Mirón began his literary life as an admirer of Byron and Victor Hugo, and progressed toward a desire for perfect expression (often enigmatic and abstruse) which at times recalls Góngora. He did not belong clearly to any modernist group. His work exerted a considerable influence on Rubén Darío and José Santos Chocano, particularly the poem "A Gloria," which was known and often quoted by all modernists. The later poems of Díaz Mirón, which were collected in a volume entitled *Lascas* ["Chips from a Stone"] (1901), show perfected form at its zenith.

SUGGESTED READING

"A Gloria," "El fantasma," "Ejemplo," "Idilio," "A ella," "Música fúnebre," "Peregrinos."

TEXTS

Anderson Imbert and Florit, 399-400. Coester, *Anthology,* 3-6. García-Prada, *Poetas modernistas,* 59-68. Holmes, *Span. Am.,* 360-362. Onís, 54-64. Silva Castro, *Ant. crít.,* 60-64.

EDITIONS

Lascas, Xalapa, Tip. del Gobierno del Estado, 1901. *Sus mejores poemas,* Madrid, Ed. América, n.d.; prologue by Rufino Blanco-Fombona. *Poesías completas (1876-1928),* México, Porrúa, 1941; biographical sketch, notes, and bibliography by Antonio Castro Leal. *Antología poética,* México, Univ. Nacional, 1953; prologue and notes by Antonio Castro Leal. *Prosa,* México, Biblioteca de Autores Veracruzanos, 1954; prologue by Leonardo Pasquel.

TRANSLATIONS

Jones, 31-33. *Trans. from Hisp. Poets,* 222. Underwood, 35-38. Walsh, *Hisp. Anth.,* 535-537.

CRITICAL REFERENCES

See texts and editions above. José Almoina, *Díaz Mirón; su poética,* México, Ed. Jus, 1958. Blanco-Fombona, *El modernismo,* 51-69. Pedro Caffarel Peralta, *Díaz Mirón en su obra,* México, Porrúa, 1956. José Carrillo, *Radiografía y disección de Salvador Díaz Mirón,* México, Libros Bayo, 1954. Henríquez Ureña, *Breve hist.,* 80-89. Alfonso Méndez Plancarte, *Díaz Mirón, poeta y artífice,* México, Robredo, 1954. Francisco Monterde, *Díaz Mirón: el hombre, la obra,* México, Studium, 1956.

°4. (Mexico) **Manuel Gutiérrez Nájera** (1859-1895) attended a French school as a child, wrote verses at an early age, and later. became a journalist, editor, poet, and prose modernist. His entire life was "a journalistic grind." His first book of stories, *Cuentos frágiles* (1883), is written in a beautiful and sparkling style. With Carlos Díaz Dufóo, he established Mexico's first *modernista* review, *Revista azul,* (1894-1896,) and continued it until his death. Nájera was unsightly in body, and given to heavy drinking. Many of his finest poems show that he was constantly beset by an unresolved religious conflict. His work is deeply permeated with French influences (Musset, Gautier, Verlaine), but he was thoroughly conversant with Spanish literature, and showed a particular liking for the mystics. He was married to Cecilia Maillefert, whose father was of French ancestry. Nájera's whimsical, highly-colored sketches and stories exerted great influence on modernist prose. He often used the pen name "El Duque Job," which is suggestive of his temperament (the aristocrat—the sufferer). The importance of his work lies in that it best represents the transition between romanticism and modernism. Both his prose and his poetry are restrained, elegiac, spontaneously musical, pervaded with delicate elegance and melancholy. A very considerable part of what he wrote has only recently been collected and published in book form.

SUGGESTED READING

"La duquesa Job," "Para entonces," "De blanco," "Mis enlutadas,"

"Serenata de Schubert," "Pax animae," "Non omnis moriar," "La novela del tranvía," "Rip-Rip," "Historia de un peso falso," "Mañana de San Juan."

TEXTS

Anthology, 427-444. Anderson Imbert and Florit, 418-427. García-Prada, *Poetas modernistas,* 69-88. Onís, 5-21. Oyuela, II, vol. 1, 69-105. Silva Castro, *Ant. crít.,* 65-80.

EDITIONS

Poesías, México, Tip. de la Oficina Imp. del Timbre, 1898; prologue by Justo Sierra. *Prosa, I,* México, Tip. de la Oficina Imp. del Timbre, 1898; prologue by Luis G. Urbina. *Prosa, II,* México, Tip. de la Oficina Imp. del Timbre, 1903; prologue by Amado Nervo. *Hojas sueltas,* México, Imp. de Murguía, 1912; prologue by Carlos Díaz Dufóo. *Cuentos, crónicas y ensayos,* México, Univ. Nacional, 1940; prologue by Alfredo Maillefert. *Cuentos color de humo, Cuentos frágiles* (1942), 2nd ed., México, Stylo, 1948; prologue by Francisco Monterde, *Obras inéditas,* New York, Hispanic Institute, 1943; edited by E. K. Mapes. *Prosa selecta,* México, Jackson, 1948; prologue by Salvador Novo. *Poesías completas,* 2 vols., México, Porrúa, 1953; prologue by Francisco González Guerrero. *Cuentos completos y otras narraciones,* México, Fondo de Cultura Económica, 1958; prologue and notes by E. K. Mapes. *Obras. Crítica literaria, I,* México, Univ. Nacional, 1959; edited by E. K. Mapes, with introduction by Porfirio Martínez Peñaloza. *Cuentos y cuaresmas del Duque Job. Cuentos frágiles. Cuentos color de humo,* México, Porrúa, 1963; prologue by Francisco Monterde.

TRANSLATIONS

Blackwell, 2-33. Jones, 34-39. *Trans. from Hisp. Poets,* 223-227. Underwood, 5-33. Walsh, *Hisp. Anth.,* 551-558; also his *Cath. Anth.,* 326-327.

CRITICAL REFERENCES

See texts and editions above. Blanco-Fombona, *El modernismo,* 69-87. Boyd G. Carter, *Manuel Gutiérrez Nájera, estudio y escritos inéditos,* México, Studium, 1956; also his *En torno a Gutiérrez Nájera y las letras mexicanas del siglo XIX,* México, Botas, 1960; and his "Backflash on the Centennial of Manuel Gutiérrez Nájera," *Hispania,* XLIV (1961), 675-682. Irma Contreras García, *Indagaciones sobre Gutiérrez Nájera,* México, Metáfora, 1957. Goldberg, 16-46. González, *Estudios,* 121-132. Margarita Gutiérrez Nájera,

Reflejo, biografía anecdótica de Manuel Gutiérrez Nájera, México, Bellas Artes, 1960. Henríquez Ureña, *Breve hist.*, 67-79. Julio Jiménez Rueda, "El México de Manuel Gutiérrez Nájera," *Memoria del séptimo congreso*, 81-89. Alexander Kosloff, "Técnica de los cuentos de Manuel Gutiérrez Nájera," *Revista iberoamericana*, 38, 39 (1954, 1955), 333-357, 65-94. E. K. Mapes, "The Pseudonyms of Manuel Gutiérrez Nájera," *PMLA*, LXIV (1949), 648-677. Meza Fuentes, 37-55. Harley D. Oberhelman, "Manuel Gutiérrez Nájera, his *Crónicas* in the *Revista azul*," *Hispania*, XLIII (1960), 49-55. Oyuela, III, 930-947. Torres-Ríoseco, *Precursores*, 49-74. Nell Walker, *The Life and Works of Manuel Gutiérrez Nájera*, Columbia, Univ. of Missouri Press, 1927.

*5. (Cuba) **Julián del Casal** (1863-1893) was born and died in Havana. His mother died when he was five years old from causes which were attributed to his birth, and left the writer with deep feelings of guilt and remorse. His health was undermined by a painful form of tuberculosis which made of him an almost morbid introspectionist. He had a thorough acquaintance with the French Parnassian movement, and poems reflecting this contact appeared in the journal *La Habana elegante* and other periodicals beginning in 1885. *Hojas al viento* (1890) and *Bustos y rimas* (1893) are well-known titles of the first collections of his verse and prose. Casal was a great lover of exoticism and Japanese art, a deep admirer of Baudelaire, an excellent Parnassian sonneteer. The French poet Verlaine praised him for his "solid and fresh poetic talent." He spent several months in Spain during 1888-1889, but never went to Paris for fear the city might not correspond to his idealized dream. His poems are a most intense expression of desolation, irony, emptiness. Both metrically and in feeling these writings are strongly characteristic of the coming *modernista* renovation.

SUGGESTED READING

"Páginas de vida," "Nostalgias," "Recuerdo de la infancia," "Rondeles I, II, III," "Elena," "Crepuscular," "Neurosis," "En el campo."

TEXTS

Anthology, 459-464. Anderson Imbert and Florit, 427-431. Coester, *Anthology*, 27-37. García-Prada, *Poetas modernistas*, 89-101. Holmes, *Span. Am.*, 284-285. Onís, 64-78. Oyuela, III, vol. 1, 267-270. Silva Castro, *Ant. crít.*, 81-89.

EDITIONS

Sus mejores poemas, Madrid, Ed. América, 1916; prologue by Rufino Blanco-Fombona. *Selección de poesías de Julián del Casal,* Habana, Cultural, 1931; introduction by Juan J. Geada y Fernández. *Poesías completas,* Habana, Ministerio de Educación, 1945; prologue, bibliography, and notes by Mario Cabrera Saqui. *Selected Prose of Julián del Casal,* University, Univ. of Alabama Press, 1949; prologue by Marshall Nunn.

TRANSLATIONS

Jones, 72-74. *Trans. from Hisp. Poets,* 219. Walsh, *Cath. Anth.,* 337-338; also his *Hisp. Anth.,* 564-569.

CRITICAL REFERENCES

See texts and editions above. Blanco-Fombona, *El modernismo,* 87-103. Bernardo Gicovate, "Tradición y novedad en un poema de Julián del Casal," *Nueva revista de filología hispánica,* 14 (1960), 119-125. Goldberg, 52-57. Henríquez Ureña, *Breve hist.,* 115-134. Meza Fuentes, 95-111. José María Monner Sans, *Julián del Casal y el modernismo hispanoamericano,* México, El Colegio de México, 1952. Marshall Nunn, "Julián del Casal, First Modernist Poet," *Hispania,* XXIII (1940), 73-80. Torres-Ríoseco, *Precursores,* 35-47.

6. (Colombia) **José Asunción Silva** (1865-1896), born of good family into an environment of culture, was, both as child and as man, deeply fascinated by the fairy tales of the Grimm brothers and of Andersen. He visited France in 1886, and returned to narrow provincial Bogotá as one who was prison bent. During the next ten years he produced many of the finest, most spiritually nostalgic, most pessimistic of modernist poems. His suicide at the age of thirty-two cut short a poetic career of tremendous promise; his talents might easily have made him Spanish America's greatest poet. Silva's father died leaving many business debts which the son assumed and unsuccessfully struggled to pay off; he received a further rebuff from fate when a ship carrying the manuscript of a book of his short stories and several other pieces was lost at sea. After his sister's death, the poet sank into morose melancholy, remembered her in the beautiful, plaintive "Nocturno III," one of the most famous *modernista* poems. Nearly all of his poetry is marked by pessimism, recollections of childhood, an ironic tinge, and the intense lyric expression of a frustrated soul attempting to retain childish illusions in maturity only to see them "fade into the light of common day." Silva committed suicide by firing a bullet into his heart. He was a perfectionist whose world of books could not long endure the battering of a hostile and narrow realism. His fluid use of old and new verse forms did much to liberate Spanish American poetry. Postromantic kinship with Heine, Poe, Baudelaire, Bécquer, and Campoamor make Silva the most typical of the creators of the new modernist lyricism, as he was also the most consummate voice in forming its melancholy language.

SUGGESTED READING

"Crepúsculo," "Los maderos de San Juan," "Vejeces," "Nocturno III," "Día de difuntos," "Psicopatía," "Paisaje tropical," "Egalité."

TEXTS

Anthology, 465-480. Anderson Imbert and Florit, 431-437. Coester, *Anthology*, 38-56. García-Prada, *Poetas modernistas*, 102-130. Onís, 79-94. Oyuela, III, vol. 1, 568-576. Silva Castro, *Ant. crit.*, 90-96.

EDITIONS

Poesías, Barcelona, Imp. P. Ortega, 1908; prologue by Miguel de Unamuno, epilogue by Eduardo Zamacois (reprinted several times by Maucci, Barcelona). *Poesías*, Paris-Buenos Aires, L. Michaud, 1913; prologue by Miguel de Unamuno, notes by Baldomero Sanín Cano. *Poesías*, Santiago, Ed. Condor, 1923; prologue by Baldomero Sanín Cano. *José Asunción Silva: Prosas y versos*, México, Cultura, 1942; introduction and notes by Carlos García-Prada. *Poesías completas y sus mejores páginas en prosa*, Buenos Aires, Elevación, 1944; prologue by Arturo Capdevila. *Poesías*, Buenos Aires, Estrada, 1945; prologue by Francisca Chica Salas. *Poesías completas: seguidas de prosas selectas*, Madrid, Aguilar, 1952; prologue by Miguel de Unamuno, notes by Baldomero Sanín Cano. *Poesías*, Buenos Aires, Espasa-Calpe, 1957 (Col. austral, 827).

TRANSLATIONS

Blackwell, 402-413. Craig, 32-37. Jones, 85-89. *Trans. from Hisp. Poets*, 205-208. Walsh, *Cath. Anth.*, 339-340; also his *Hisp. Anth.*, 581-588.

CRITICAL REFERENCES

See texts and editions above. Blanco-Fombona, *El modernismo*, 103-147. Donald F. Fogelquist, "José Asunción Silva y Heinrich Heine," *Revista hispánica moderna*, XX (1954), 282-295. Bernardo Gicovate, "Estructura y significado en la poesía de José Asunción Silva,"

Revista iberoamericana, 48 (1959), 327-333. Goldberg, 57-64. Henríquez Ureña, *Breve hist.,* 135-157. G. G. King, *A Citizen of the Twilight Zone: José Asunción Silva,* New York, Longmans, Green, 1921; with several translations. Roberto Liévano, *En torno a Silva,* Bogotá, El Gráfico, 1946, Alberto Miramón, *José Asunción Silva,* Bogotá, Imp. Nacional, 1937; prologue by Baldomero Sanín Cano. R. J. Schwartz, "En busca de Silva," *Revista iberoamericana,* 47 (1959), 65-78. Torres-Ríoseco, *Precursores,* 95-124; also his "Las teorías poéticas de Poe y el caso de José Asunción Silva," *Hispanic Review,* XVIII (1950), 319-327.

°°7. (Nicaragua) **Rubén Darío** (1867-1916) was born in the village of Metapa, of Spanish-Indian-Negro extraction. He became Spanish America's most followed, most cosmopolitan poet. The child's parents were separated, and Rubén was reared by an aunt. He wrote verses in early childhood, became known as *el poeta niño,* imitated Bécquer and Campoamor, and acquired a wide Spanish and French culture. His literary talents were soon recognized and to some extent subsidized by influential Central Americans. He traveled over Central America and in 1886 went to Chile, where he worked on *La época* of Santiago, immersed himself in contemporary French literature (Flaubert, Catulle Mendès), and won a poetic contest. In 1888 there appeared in Chile his *Azul,* a famous collection of verse and prose sketches which set the stage for modernism in Spanish America. Juan Valera, writing in Madrid's *El imparcial,* pointed out the young poet's *galicismo mental,* cosmopolitan spirit, Parnassian style. *Azul* was pure "art for art's sake" painted against a background of pagan mythology permeated with a sensuous awareness of color and sound, but often expressed in terms of a French formalism suggesting the gardens of Versailles.

Darío next commenced to write for *La nación* of Buenos Aires, with which great paper he remained connected until his death twenty-six years later. In 1890 he returned to Central America and married, unhappily; in 1892 *La nación* sent him to Spain, where he met many famous Spanish men of letters. He returned to America via Cuba, and in Colombia met Rafael Núñez (poet and former President of that nation), who secured his appointment as Colombian consul in Buenos Aires. Darío then headed for Argentina via New York (where he met Martí) and Paris (where he met intoxicated Verlaine and other French writers). His next famous work, *Prosas profanas* (1896), marks the zenith of the *modernista* movement; the imprisoned princess in the poem, "Sonatina," becomes symbolic of the fettered modernist esthetic creed encaged in cold marble. In 1898 Darío returned to Spain for *La nación* and wrote a series of articles on European subjects. In 1905 appeared his finest work, *Cantos de vida y esperanza,* which retains all the beauty of his former periods plus a great new feeling of freedom, simplicity, strength. The poet then returned to South America (Rio de Janeiro and Buenos Aires), and in 1908 was appointed Nicaraguan Minister to Spain. As a result of heavy drinking, his health began to fail. In 1915 he visited the United States on a lecture tour and failed miserably. Soon afterward he caught pneumonia in New York and rallied only sufficiently to return to Nicaragua, where he died in 1916.

Darío's influence on modernism was tremendous. He was the chief inaugurator, most famous exponent, guiding genius, and messiah of the movement; through him Hispanic poetry was born anew. He was *el poeta de América* because of that supremely American characteristic of fusing all sources, inspirations, feelings, bloods, into one spiritual sensibility which was and is the secret of America's great cosmopolitan crucible. The landscape of the New World and the letter of American content were more fully developed by other poets, particularly Chocano, but Darío gave them life.

SUGGESTED READING

"El rey burgués," "El velo de la reina Mab," "Era un aire suave," "Sonatina," "Yo soy aquel," "Canción de otoño en primavera," "Letanía a nuestro señor don Quijote," "Ay, triste del que un día," "De otoño," "Lo fatal," "Nocturnos I, II, III," "Marcha triunfal," "A Roosevelt," "Salutación al águila," "Sum," "Versos de otoño," "¡Eheu!" "Revelación," "El poema del otoño."

TEXTS

Anthology, 481-512. Anderson Imbert and Florit, 440-463. Coester, *Anthology,* 57-136. Flores, 155-161. García-Prada, *Poetas modernistas,* 131-195. Holmes, *Span. Am.,* 119-128. Onís, 143-197. *Poetic and Prose Selections of Rubén Darío* (ed. Rosenberg and López de Lowther), Boston, Heath, 1931. Silva Castro, *Ant. crit.,* 97-154. *Selections from the Prose and Poetry of Rubén Darío* (ed. Umphrey and García-Prada), New York, Macmillan, 1928.

EDITIONS

Azul (1888), 11th ed., Buenos Aires, Espasa-Calpe, 1952 (Col. austral, 19). *Los raros* (1896), Buenos Aires, Espasa-Calpe, 1952 (Col. austral, 1119). *Prosas profanas* (1896), 4th ed., Buenos Aires, Espasa-Calpe, 1952 (Col. austral, 404). *Cantos de vida y esperanza* (1905), 2nd ed., Buenos Aires, Espasa-Calpe, 1943 (Col. austral, 118), *El canto errante* (1907), 3rd ed., Buenos Aires, Espasa-Calpe, 1950 (Col. austral, 516). *Poema del otoño* (1910), Buenos Aires, Espasa-Calpe, 1945 (Col. austral, 282). *Obras completas,* 22 vols., Madrid, Mundo Latino, 1917-1919; edited by Alberto Ghiraldo. *Obras completas,* 23 vols., Madrid, Fernando Fe, 1923-1934; edited by Alberto Ghiraldo and Andrés González-Blanco. *Obras poéticas completas* (1932), Madrid, Aguilar, 1941; edition and prologue by Alberto Ghiraldo. *Cuentos y poemas en prosa,* Madrid, Aguilar, 1945. *Antología poética,* Berkeley and Los Angeles, Univ. of California Press, 1949; selection and prologue by Arturo Torres-Ríoseco. *Cuentos completos,* México, Fondo de Cultura Económica, 1950; edition by Ernesto Mejía Sánchez, prologue by Raimundo Lida. *Obras completas,* 5 vols., Madrid, Afrodisio Aguado, 1950-1955. *Crítico literario,* Washington, Pan American Union, 1951; prologue by Ermilo Abreu Gómez. *Poesía,* México, Fondo de Cultura Económica, 1952; preliminary study by Enrique Anderson Imbert. *Cuentos,* Buenos Aires, Espasa-Calpe, 1957 (Col. austral, 880). *Antología poética,* Buenos Aires, Kapelusz, 1952; edited by Arturo Marasso. *Poesías completas* (1954), 9th ed., Madrid, Aguilar, 1961; introduction by Alfonso Méndez Plancarte. *Cuentos y poesías de Rubén Darío,* Madrid, Eds. Iberoamericanas, 1961; edited by Carlos García-Prada.

TRANSLATIONS

Blackwell, 182-201. Colford, 127-137. Craig, 38-75. Flores, *Anth. Span. Poetry,* 207-227. Jones, 21-30. *Trans. from Hisp. Poets,* 240-250. Walsh, *Cath. Anth.,* 347-351; also his *Hisp. Anth.,* 595-613. Thomas Walsh and Salomón de la Selva (trans.), *Eleven Poems of Rubén Darío,* New York and London, Putnam, 1916.

CRITICAL REFERENCES

See texts and editions above. Blanco-Fombona, *El modernismo,* 147-191. Arturo Capdevila, *Rubén Darío: "un bardo rei,"* Buenos Aires, Espasa-Calpe, 1946 (Col. austral, 607). Francisco Contreras, *Rubén Darío: su vida y su obra* (1930), 2nd ed., Santiago, Ercilla, 1937. Dolores Ackel Fiore, *Rubén Darío in Search of Inspiration,*

New York, Las Américas, 1963. Donald F. Fogelquist, *The Literary Collaboration and the Personal Correspondence of Rubén Darío and Juan Ramón Jiménez,* Coral Gables, Univ. of Miami Press, 1956. González, *Estudios,* 328-346; also his "Iniciación de Rubén Darío en el culto a Martí," *Memoria del Congreso de Escritores Martianos* (Habana, 1953), 503-569. Goldberg, 101-183. Henríquez Ureña, *Breve hist.,* 90-114; also his *Rubén Darío,* Buenos Aires, Academia Argentina de Letras, 1946. Erika Lorenz, *Rubén Darío: "bajo el divino imperio de la música"* (trans. from the German by Fidel Coloma González), Managua, Eds. Lengua, 1960. E. K. Mapes, *L'Influence française dans l'oeuvre de Rubén Darío,* Paris, Champion, 1925. Arturo Marasso, *Rubén Darío y su creación poética* (1934), 3rd ed., Buenos Aires, Kapelusz, 1954. Ernesto Mejía Sánchez, *Los primeros cuentos de Rubén Darío,* México, Univ. Nacional, 1962. Meza Fuentes, 111-354. Antonio Oliver Belmás, *Este otro Rubén Darío,* Barcelona, Ed. Aedos, 1960; prologue by Francisco Maldonado de Guevara. Allen W. Phillips, "Rubén Darío y sus juicios sobre el modernismo," *Revista iberoamericana,* 47 (1959), 41-64. Pedro Salinas, *La poesía de Rubén Darío,* Buenos Aires, Losada, 1948. Raúl Silva Castro, *Rubén Darío a los veinte años,* Madrid, Gredos, 1956. Arturo Torres-Ríoseco, *Vida y poesía de Rubén Darío,* Buenos Aires, Emecé, 1944. Evelyn E. Uhrhan, "Francisca Sánchez and the 'Seminario-Archivo de Rubén Darío'," *Hispania,* XLI (1958), 35-38. Valera, I, 267-294.

°8. (Venezuela) **Manuel Díaz Rodríguez** (1868-1927), the most famous Venezuelan modernist, was born into a wealthy family and wrote purely as an avocation. He held the degree of doctor in medicine, but did not practice this career. He travelled extensively in Europe and was well acquainted with European literature. His travel sketches are fascinating commentaries on the author's experiences and on regional psychology and customs. His lyrical *Cuentos de color* appeared in *El cojo ilustrado* in and around 1898, and were soon reproduced in French translation in Paris. The style of these and of Díaz Rodríguez's later works suggests a carefully laid mosaic of high polish and many blended colors. The central theme is generally the author's sense of artistic frustration in contact with a world which does not understand.

His masterpiece, *Sangre patricia* (1902), is a brief novel which blends color symbolism, music, mythological witchery, and modernist melancholia in a sonata of flowing and poetic prose. The influence of D'Annunzio is strong, but the author's splendid style is the novel's outstanding quality.

SUGGESTED READING

Sangre patricia.

TEXTS

Anthology, 568-569. Anderson Imbert and Florit, 494-501.

EDITIONS

De mis romerías (1898) y Sensaciones de viaje (1896), Caracas, Eds. Nueva Cádiz, 1951. *Cuentos de color* (1899), Caracas, Eds. Nueva Cádiz, 1952. *Ídolos rotos* (1901), 2nd ed., Madrid, Ed. América, 1919; *ibid.,* 3rd ed., Caracas, Eds. Nueva Cádiz, 1955. *Sangre patricia* (1902), 3rd ed., Caracas, Eds. Nueva Cádiz, 1952. *Camino de perfección (1907) y otros ensayos,* Caracas, Eds. Nueva Cádiz, 1952. *Peregrina, o El pozo encantado, novela de rústicos del valle de Caracas,* Madrid, Ed. América, 1922. *Sermones líricos,* Caracas, Eds. Nueva Cádiz, 1955.

CRITICAL REFERENCES

See texts and editions above. Alegría, *Breve hist.,* 121-124. Lowell Dunham, *Manuel Díaz Rodríguez, vida y obra* (1949), 2nd ed., México, Studium, 1959. Ratcliff, 175-189. Henríquez Ureña, *Breve hist.,* 291-292. Mead, *Ensayo,* 77-78. Torres-Ríoseco, *Grandes novelistas,* II, 61-88. Uslar Pietri, *Letras y hombres,* 139-141.

°°9. (Uruguay) **José Enrique Rodó** (1872-1917) was the best-known modernist after Rubén Darío; his classic prose was the envy of all succeeding Spanish American writers. Rodó was educated in Montevideo, where in 1895 he helped found *La revista nacional de literatura y ciencia sociales,* for which he wrote many essays. He was a professor of literature at the National University (1898), director of the National Library (1900), and a member of the Chamber of Deputies (1902-1905 and 1908-1911). In 1899 his name was widely heralded when he prefaced the second edition of Darío's *Prosas profanas.* Rodó exerted a tremendous influence on other modernist essayists: Manuel Díaz Rodríguez of Venezuela, Manuel González-Prada of Peru, and Carlos Reyles of Uruguay. His first and most famous work, *Ariel* (1900), is still considered by many to be the ethical bible of Latin America; it calls for the preservation of an intellectual aristocracy to withstand the materialistic impact of the United States (Caliban), carefully points out the good and bad elements of our civilization, and urges that the two Americas cooperate and complement each other.

During his lifetime Rodó was considered to be *the* great essayist of the modernist group, but with the passage of time his prolix, philosophical approach has lost much of its appeal, and his lack of a deep social concern has dated his best efforts. During the past few decades José Martí has constantly grown in stature as an essayist, while Rodó has steadily diminished.

Toward the end of his life Rodó traveled in Europe representing the Argentine newspaper *La nación* and the Argentine journal *Caras y caretas,* to both of which he was a frequent contributor. He died unexpectedly at a hotel in Palermo, Sicily.

SUGGESTED READING
Ariel.

TEXTS
Anthology, 591-605. Anderson Imbert and Florit, 526-545. Coester, *Anthology,* 148-159. Holmes, *Span. Am.,* 484-488. *Ariel* (ed. Nin-Frías and Fitzgerald), New York, Sanborn, 1928; *ibid.* (ed. Rice), Chicago, Univ. of Chicago Press, 1929.

EDITIONS
Ariel (1900), Santiago, Ercilla, 1936; *ibid.;* Montevideo, C. García, 1936; prologue by Leopoldo Alas; *ibid.,* 1st ed., Buenos Aires, Espasa-Calpe, 1948 (Col. austral, 866); *Los motivos de Proteo* (1909), 2nd ed., Madrid, Ed. América, n.d.; *ibid.,* 4th ed., Montevideo, Barreiro y Ramos, 1956. *Ariel; Motivos de Proteo,* 3rd ed., Buenos Aires, Jackson, 1957. *El mirado de Próspero* (1914), Montevideo, C. García, 1939; *ibid.,* Montevideo, Barreiro y Ramos, 1958. *Hombres de América* (1920), Montevideo, C. García, 1939. *El pensamiento vivo de Rodó,* Buenos Aires, Losada, 1944; edition by Emilio Oribe. *Obras completas* (1948), 2nd ed., Buenos Aires, Zamora, 1956; prologue by Alberto José Vaccaro. *Obras selectas,* Buenos Aires, El Ateneo, 1956; prologue by Arturo Marasso. *Obras completas,* Madrid, Aguilar, 1957; prologue and notes by Emir Rodríguez Monegal.

TRANSLATIONS
F. J. Stimson (trans.), *Ariel,* Boston, Houghton Mifflin, 1922. Ángel Flores (trans.), *The Motives of Proteus,* New York, Brentano's, 1928; prologue by Havelock Ellis. Jones, 326-330.

CRITICAL REFERENCES

See texts and editions above. Glicerio Albarrán Puente, *El pensamiento de José Enrique Rodó,* Madrid, Cultura Hispánica, 1953. C. C. Bacheller, "An Introduction for Studies on Rodó," *Hispania,* XLVI (1963), 764-769. Hugo D. Barbagelata, *Rodó y sus críticos,* Paris, Agencia General de Librería, 1920. Crawford, 79-90. Federico Ferrándiz Alborz, "José Enrique Rodó y el nuevo estilo americano," *Cuadernos americanos,* LXXX (1955), 206-227. García Calderón, *Semblanzas,* 7-25. García Godoy, 73-152. Goldberg, 184-245. M. Henríquez Ureña, *Breve hist.,* 224-232. Mead, *Ensayo,* 72-77. Víctor Pérez Petit, *Rodó. Su vida. Su obra,* Montevideo, G. García, 1937; contains extensive bibliography. Arturo Scarone, *Bibliografía de Rodó,* 2 vols. Montevideo, Imp. Nacional, 1930. M. Vitier, 117-136. Gonzalo Zaldumbide, *José Enrique Rodó,* Madrid, Ed. América, 1919; also his *Montalvo y Rodó,* New York, Instituto de las Españas, 1938.

°10. (Mexico) **Amado Nervo** (1870-1919) studied for the priesthood but left the seminary to become a journalist in Mazatlán. He visited Paris in 1900, where he met Darío. Nervo wrote for the *Revista azul* (1894-1896) as long as it lasted, and when this journal died, he and Jesús E. Valenzuela established the *Revista moderna* (1898-1911), the second famous modernist periodical of Mexico. Besides poetry Nervo wrote short stories, literary criticism, essays, prose poems in considerable number, a long study on Sor Juana Inés de la Cruz. From 1905 to 1918 the poet was secretary to the Mexican legation in Madrid, where much of his best work was produced; in 1919 he went to Argentina and Uruguay as Mexican Minister and died in Montevideo that same year. His writings are characterized by a growing pantheism, Buddhistic feeling, touches of mystic serenity, a deep religious sentiment despite outward skepticism, and an almost Indian resignation and humility. His poetry shows a slow progression from overadornment and frivolity to simplicity, depth, perfection. The titles of his best works are fully characteristic of their content.

SUGGESTED READING

"A Kempis," "La hermana agua," "Seis meses . . . ," "Expectación," "Si eres bueno," "Inmortalidad," "En paz," "La sed," "Una esperanza."

TEXTS

Anthology, 521-539. Anderson Imbert and Florit, 484-486. Coester, Anthology, 211-230. Crow, Cuentos, 25-33. García-Prada, Poetas modernistas, 196-214. Holmes, Span. Am., 371-375. Onís, 396-416. Silva Castro, Ant. crít., 219-228. Sus mejores cuentos (ed. Leal) (1951), Boston, Houghton Mifflin, 1963 (paperback).

EDITIONS

Perlas negras (1898), Buenos Aires, Espasa-Calpe, 1945 (Col. austral, 458). Poemas (1901), 4th ed., Buenos Aires, Espasa-Calpe, 1956 (Col. austral, 373). Serenidad (1914), 9th ed., Buenos Aires, Espasa-Calpe, 1958 (Col. austral, 211). Elevación (1916), 6th ed., Buenos Aires, Espasa-Calpe, 1956 (Col. austral, 311). Plenitud (1918), 10th ed., México, Espasa-Calpe, 1961 (Col. austral, 175). Los cien mejores poemas de Amado Nervo, México, Cultura, 1919; prologue by Enrique González Martínez. La amada inmóvil (1920), 14th ed., Buenos Aires, Espasa-Calpe, 1957 (Col. austral, 32). Obras completas, 29 vols., Madrid, Biblioteca Nueva, 1920-1928; edited by Alfonso Reyes. Poesías completas, Madrid, Biblioteca Nueva, 1935; prologue by Genaro Estrada. Mañana del poeta, México, Botas, 1938; edited by Alfonso Méndez Plancarte. Un epistolario inédito, México, Imp. Universitaria, 1951; prologue by Ermilo Abreu Gómez. Primavera y flor de su lírica (1952), 2nd. ed., Madrid, Aguilar, 1959; prologue by Alfonso Méndez Plancarte. Semblanzas y crítica literaria, México, Imp. Universitaria, 1952. Obras poéticas completas, Buenos Aires, El Ateneo, 1955; prologue by Arturo Marasso. Obras completas, 2 vols., Madrid, Aguilar, 1951-1956; studies and notes by Francisco González Guerrero and Alfonso Méndez Plancarte.

TRANSLATIONS

Blackwell, 34-67. Colford, 138-146. Craig, 76-87. Flores, Anth. Span. Poetry, 337-342. Johnson, 94-101. Dorothy Kress, Confessions of a Modern Poet, Boston, Bruce Humphries, 1935. Jones, 43-45. William F. Rice (trans.), Plenitude, Los Angeles, J. R. Miller, 1928. Trans. from Hisp. Poets, 230-232. Underwood, 59-65. Walsh, Cath. Anth., 370-371; also his Hisp. Anth. 626-634.

CRITICAL REFERENCES

See texts and editions above. Blanco-Fombona, El modernismo, 253-273. Goldberg, 75-81. Henríquez Ureña, Breve hist., 472-477. Luis Leal, "La poesía de Amado Nervo," Hispania, XLIII (1960), 43-47. Martínez, Lit. mex. siglo XX, I, 147-154. Concha Meléndez, Amado

Nervo, New York, Instituto de las Españas, 1926. *Nosotros* (June 1919), memorial volume (contains 36 articles on the poet). Bernardo Ortiz de Montellano, *Figura, amor y muerte de Amado Nervo,* México, Eds. Xochitl, 1943. Alfonso Reyes, *Tránsito de Amado Nervo,* Santiago, Ercilla, 1937. Esther Turner Wellman, *Amado Nervo, Mexico's Religious Poet,* New York, Instituto de las Españas, 1936.

°11. (Bolivia) **Ricardo Jaimes Freyre** (1868-1933), teacher, diplomat, and one-time Bolivian Minister to the United States, was for several years a professor of history and literature at the University cf Tucumán. He is the author of several fascinating pieces on Argentine history of the colonial epoch (*El Tucumán del siglo XVI,* 1914) and also of a work on versification (*Leyes de la versificación castellana,* 1912). He lived for an extended period in Buenos Aires, where he and Darío founded the ephemeral *Revista de América* in 1894. His first work, *Castalia bárbara* (1899), was his best; it marks a step in the development of modernism, and its aptly chosen title is characteristic of the poet's fusion of *Castalia,* or classic "fountain of the gods," with elements of barbaric splendor. Freyre lived and wrote apart from reality in a fantastic, mythological world which was more Nordic than Hellenic. In his later poems Jaimes Freyre moves into the realm of symbolism and also proves himself a master of this mode.

SUGGESTED READING

"Siempre," "Lo fugaz," "Aeternum Vale," "Hoc Signum," "El canto del mal," "Las voces tristes."

TEXTS

Anthology, 513-515. Anderson Imbert and Florit, 477-480. Coester, *Anthology,* 137-141. V. García Calderón, *Cuentos,* 160-167. García-Prada, *Poetas modernistas,* 215-225. Holmes, *Span. Am.,* 102-103. Onís, 365-369. Silva Castro, *Ant. crít.,* 205-212. Walsh, *Cuentos,* 93-98.

EDITIONS

Castalia bárbara (1899) *y los sueños son vida* (1917), Madrid, Ed. América, 1918. *Castalia bárbara y otros poemas,* México, Murguía, 1920; prologue by Leopoldo Lugones. *Los más bellos poemas,* México, Cultura, 1920; prologue by Leopoldo Lugones. *Poesías completas,* Buenos Aires, Claridad, 1944; introductory study by Eduardo Joubin Colombres. *Poesías completas; Leyes de la versificación castellana*

(1912), La Paz, Ministerio de Educación, 1957; prologue by Fernando Díez de Medina.

TRANSLATIONS

Blackwell, 454-461. Colford, 43-51. Craig, 85-88. Johnson, 90-93. Jones, 115-117.

CRITICAL REFERENCES

See texts and editions above. E. M. Barreda, "Ricardo Jaimes Freyre, un maestro del simbolismo," *Nosotros,* LXXVII (1933), 285-290. Blanco-Fombona, *El modernismo,* 341-345. Emilio Carilla, *Ricardo Jaimes Freyre,* Buenos Aires, Eds. Culturales Argentinas, 1962. *Diccionario . . . Bolivia,* 49-52. Henríquez Ureña, *Breve hist.,* 176-184. Raúl Jaimes Freyre, *Anecdotario de Ricardo Jaimes Freyre,* Potosí, Ed. Potosí, 1953, Juan B. Terán, "Ricardo Jaimes Freyre," *Nosotros,* LXXVII (1933), 280-284. Arturo Torres-Ríoseco, "Ricardo Jaimes Freyre," *Hispania,* XVI (1933), 389-398.

°°12. (Argentina) **Leopoldo Lugones** (1874-1938), most famous Argentine modernist, was a close friend of Darío's. For several years he directed the National Council of Education in Argentina, and was once the representative of his country on the Committee on Intellectual Cooperation of the League of Nations. He made various trips to Europe. At one stage in his life Lugones expressed a dislike for Spain, a fondness for France and the United States, and extolled Pan Americanism. His ideology evolved from socialism to extreme nationalism, and from romanticism to realism. In 1924 in Lima he delivered an unfortunate oration, "La hora de la espada," extolling military rule, and thus lost many of his friends. The many facets of his literary expression presage and give base to the later phases of modernism; he can be simple, complex, romantic, symbolistic, or rigorously real, as the mood strikes him. His works show a marked progression and variation in both style and content. Lugones is also a fine literary critic and short-story writer. His *La guerra gaucha* (1905), a very baroque group of sketches, and *Cuentos fatales* (1924), short stories in a vein of convincing fantasy, are both outstanding prose works. He is perhaps the most varicolored of all modernists except Darío. Some critics place him, along with that famous Nicaraguan, above all the others, and call him the exponent of a new *culteranismo literario.*

SUGGESTED READING

"Delectación morosa," "A los gauchos," "La blanca soledad," "Elegía crepuscular," "El solterón," "Juan Rojas," "Las cigarras," "Viola Acherontia," "Yzur."

TEXTS

Anthology, 515-520. Anderson Imbert and Florit, 464-472. Anderson Imbert and Kiddle, 16-26. Coester, *Anthology*, 142-147. Flores, 249-257. García-Prada, *Poetas modernistas*, 267-288. Onís, 369-396. Silva Castro, *Ant. crit.*, 273-290.

EDITIONS

Las montañas del oro (1897), Buenos Aires, Centurión, 1947. *Los crepúsculos del jardín* (1905), 2nd ed., Buenos Aires, Babel, 1926. *La guerra gaucha* (1905), Buenos Aires, Emecé, 1954. *El libro de los paisajes* (1917), 2nd ed., Buenos Aires, Gleizer, 1926. *Romancero* (1924), México, Espasa-Calpe, 1941 (Col. austral, 232). *Cuentos fatales*, Buenos Aires, Babel, 1924. *Romances del Río Seco* (1928), Buenos Aires, Centurión, 1948. *Antología poética*, Buenos Aires, Espasa-Calpe, 1949 (Col. austral, 200); prologue by Carlos Obligado. *Obras poéticas completas* (1948), 3rd ed., Madrid, Aguilar, 1959; prologue by Pedro Miguel Obligado.

TRANSLATIONS

Blackwell, 326-338. Colford, 77-89. Craig, 96-111. Frank, 81-102. Johnson, 102-107. Jones, 149-154. *Trans. from Hisp. Poets*, 187-189. Walsh, *Hisp. Anth.*, 664-670.

CRITICAL REFERENCES

See texts and editions above. Guillermo Ara, *Leopoldo Lugones*, Buenos Aires, La Mandrágora, 1958. Arrieta, IV, 19-59. Blanco-Fombona, *El modernismo*, 295-341. Jorge Luis Borges, *Leopoldo Lugones*, Buenos Aires, Troquel, 1955. Arturo Cambours Ocampo, *Lugones, el escritor y su lenguaje*, Buenos Aires, Theoría, 1957. *Diccionario . . . Argentina*, I, 117-124. Juan Carlos Ghiano, *Lugones, escritor*, Buenos Aires, Raigal, 1955. Henríquez Ureña, *Breve hist.*, 190-202. "Lauxar," 177-198. Leopoldo Lugones (hijo), *Mi padre, biografía de Leopoldo Lugones*, Buenos Aires, Centurión, 1949. Dorothy McMahon, "Leopoldo Lugones, a Man in Search of Roots," *Modern Philology*, LI (1954), 196-203. M. Olivari, *Leopoldo Lugones*, Buenos Aires, Saeta, 1940. Allen W. Phillips. "Notas sobre una afinidad. Jules Laforgue y el Lugones del *Lunario sentimental*," *Revista iberoamericana*, 45 (1948), 43-65.

°13. (Colombia) **Guillermo Valencia** (1873-1943) was of an aristocratic family, and received a strict classical education. He once ran for the Presidency of his country. He was simple and democratic in temperament and on one occasion remarked that he would rather be a good general or doctor than a writer. Valencia in some ways is the most Parnassian of all writers in Spanish, but his style suggests a mixture of Greek and Latin classicism plus overtones of French Parnassianism. *Ritos* (1898), one of the finest volumes in the Parnassian manner written in America, reveals, as well, the poet's unusual gifts as a translator. Christian history and symbolism also play an important part in his work, which, though limited in amount, is of the purest quality. His ideology is not based on cold objectivity but is rooted in sensitive human values and feelings; he was never a professional writer.

SUGGESTED READING

"Los camellos," "Leyenda a Silva," "Judith y Holofernes," "San Antonio y el centauro,"."Cigüeñas blancas."

TEXTS

Anderson Imbert and Florit, 474-477. Coester, *Anthology*, 167-178. García-Prada, *Poetas modernistas*, 243-266. Holmes, *Span. Am.*, 235-236. Onís, 347-365. Silva Castro, *Ant. crít.*, 261-270.

EDITIONS

Ritos (1898) Londres, Wertheimer, Lea, 1914; introduction by Baldomero Sanín Cano. *Oraciones panegíricas* (1915), Bogotá, Ministerio de Educación, 1952. *Sus mejores poemas* (1919), Madrid, Ed. América, 1926. *Sus mejores versos*, Bogotá, La Gran Colombia, 1944; prologue by Rafael Maya. *Obras poéticas completas* (1948), 3rd ed., Madrid, Aguilar, 1955; prologue by Baldomero Sanín Cano. *Poesías y discursos*, Madrid, Eds. Iberoamericanas, 1959; prologue and notes by Carlos García-Prada.

TRANSLATIONS

Blackwell, 412-415. Craig, 112-125. Jones, 92-95. *Trans. from Hisp. Poets*, 209-211. Walsh, *Cath. Anth.*, 386.

CRITICAL REFERENCES

See texts and editions above. Blanco-Fombona, *El modernismo*, 221-237. Henríquez Ureña, *Breve hist.*, 306-320. Sonja Karsen, *Guillermo Valencia, Colombian Poet,* New York, Hispanic Institute, 1951. Robert Nugent, "Guillermo Valencia and French Poetic Theory," *Hispania,* XLV (1962), 405-409. A. Ortiz Vargas, "Guillermo Valencia,

Colombia's Master Poet," *Poet Lore,* XLI (1930), 413-423. John T. Reid, "Una visita a D. Guillermo Valencia," *Revista iberoamericana,* 3 (1940), 199-201. Antonio Rocha, "Guillermo Valencia y el humanismo colombiano," *Revista de las Indias,* XXI (1944), 147-163.

°14. (Peru) **José Santos Chocano** (1875-1934), first among Peruvian modernists, was at various times in his life a revolutionary, a picaresque criminal who became involved in duels and love intrigues, a hectic nationalist, a political prisoner, and an exile. In his poetry, Chocano was all this plus a defender of the Indian, an exalter of Spain, a seeker of Spanish-Indian amalgamation and unity, and a champion of revolt against North American imperialism. As a painter of tropic loveliness and the lush seductive color and strength of that great zone, he is unexcelled. His *Alma América* (1906) was received with great acclaim in Spain, and the poet was feted and lionized in Madrid. In 1922 his "coronation" was celebrated with much pomp by the government of the Peruvian dictator, Augusto B. Leguía. His verse is at times bombastic, wordy, worthless, and irritating, but at others it is simple, spontaneous, touchingly beautiful. Chocano gave a telluric American feeling to modernism. While riding a streetcar in Chile, he was stabbed to death by a man who had invested and lost a considerable sum in the poet's hare-brained scheme to dig for buried treasures.

SUGGESTED READING

"Blasón," "Troquel," "Avatar," "Los Andes," "La visión del Cóndor," "Caupolicán," "Los volcanes," "La epopeya del Pacífico," "Los caballos de los conquistadores," "La canción del camino," "Tres notas de nuestra alma indígena."

TEXTS

Anthology, 540-556. Anderson Imbert and Florit, 481-482. Coester, *Anthology,* 179-207. García Calderón, *Biblioteca,* XII. García-Prada, *Poetas modernistas,* 303-321. Onís, 427-444. Silva Castro, *Ant. crít.,* 301-314.

EDITIONS

Primicias de 'Oro de Indias,' Santiago, Imp. Siglo XX, 1934. *Poesías completas,* 2 vols., Barcelona, Maucci, 1910; prologue by Manuel González-Prada. *Selección de poesías,* Montevideo, C. García, 1941; prologue by Juan Parra del Riego, and critical articles by Ventura García Calderón, Manuel González-Prada, Isaac Goldberg, *et al.*

Poesías, 2nd ed., Buenos Aires, Jackson, 1946; prologue by Luis Fabio Xammar. *Antología poética,* 2nd ed., Buenos Aires, Espasa-Calpe, 1948 (Col. austral, 751); prologue by Alfonso Escudero. *Obras completas,* Madrid, Aguilar, 1954; prologue by Luis Alberto Sánchez. *Chocano: poesía,* Lima, Univ. Nacional, 1959; prologue by Luis Alberto Sánchez. *Sus mejores poemas,* Lima, Caracas, 1962.

TRANSLATIONS

Blackwell, 206-229. Craig, 130-145. Johnson, 108-111. Jones, 108-112. *Trans. from Hisp. Poets,* 252-255. Edna W. Underwood (trans.) *Spirit of the Andes,* Portland, The Mosher Press, 1935.

CRITICAL REFERENCES

See texts and editions above. Blanco-Fombona, *El modernismo,* 273-295. García Calderón, *Semblanzas,* 104-124. Goldberg, 246-295. Henríquez Ureña, *Breve hist.,* 335-348. Roberto Meza Fuentes, "La poesía de José Santos Chocano," *Nosotros,* LXXVIII (1934), 286-311. Luis Alberto Sánchez, "Chocano, traductor," *Revista iberoamericana,* 45 (1958), 113-120; also his *Aladino, o, vida de José Santos Chocano,* México, Libro-Mex, 1960.

°°15. (Uruguay) **Julio Herrera y Reissig** (1875-1910) was the extremely sensitive son of an illustrious family fallen into disgrace. He suffered from a severe heart ailment which caused his early death. Books and literature were his life, and he never left the country of his birth. He founded the journal *La revista* in 1899, which helped make modernism popular in Uruguay and at about the same time he organized a literary group of Bohemian poets, called the *Torre de los Panoramas,* who met in the attic of his father's house for their *tertulias,* readings, and musical outbursts, with the poet himself often playing the guitar. Herrera y Reissig was fervently admired by this small clique which carried on a kind of literary feud with a rival group headed by Horacio Quiroga. Herrera y Reissig's poetry ranges from simple lyricism to extreme complexity. He is the outstanding symbolist of the *modernista* group, links modernism to ultraism, and is distinctly a poet for the fit though few. His work was produced between 1900 and 1910 and was dispersed in periodicals; it was not collected until after his death.

SUGGESTED READING

"Desolación absurda," "Julio," "El cura," "Despertar," "La iglesia," "Color de sueño," "Almas pálidas," "La gota amarga."

TEXTS
Anthology, 557-559. Anderson Imbert and Florit, 477-480. Coester, *Anthology,* 160-166. García-Prada, *Poetas modernistas,* 288-302. Holmes, *Span. Am.,* 459-461. Onís, 469-488. Silva Castro, *Ant. crít.,* 295-300.

EDITIONS
Obras completas, 5 vols., Montevideo, Bertani, 1913. *Prosas; crítica, cuentos, comentarios,* Montevideo, M. García, 1918; prologue by Vicente A. Salaverri. *Páginas escogidas,* Barcelona, Maucci, 1919; prologue by Juan Mas y Pí. *Antología lírica* (1939), 2nd ed., Santiago, Ercilla, 1942; prologue by Carlos Sabat Ercasty, bibliography by Manuel de Castro. *Poesías completas* (1942), 2nd ed., Buenos Aires, Losada, 1945; prologue by Guillermo de Torre. *Poesías completas, y, Páginas en prosa,* 2nd ed., Madrid, Aguilar, 1961; prologue and notes by Roberto Bula Píriz.

TRANSLATIONS
Blackwell, 444-445. Craig, 126-129. Johnson, 112-113. Jones, 167-170. Walsh, *Cath. Anth.,* 396-397; also his *Hisp. Anth.,* 683-686.

CRITICAL REFERENCES
See texts and editions above. Blanco-Fombona, *El modernismo,* 191-221. Roberto Bula Píriz, *Herrera y Reissig, vida y obra, bibliografía, antología,* New York, Hispanic Institute, 1952. Elizabeth Colquhoun, "Notes on French Influences in the Work of Julio Herrera y Reissig," *Bulletin of Spanish Studies,* XXI (1944), 145-158. Bernard Gicovate, "The Poetry of Julio Herrera y Reissig and French Symbolism," *PMLA,* LXVIII (1953), 935-942. García Calderón, *Semblanzas,* 77-90. "Lauxar," 397-444. Bernard Gicovate, *Julio Herrera y Reissig and the Symbolists,* Berkeley, Univ. of California Press, 1957. Henríquez Ureña, *Breve hist.,* 254-272. Herminia Herrera y Reissig, *Vida íntima de Julio Herrera y Reissig,* Montevideo, Amerindia, 1944. Yolando Pino Saavedra, *La poesía de Julio Herrera y Reissig,* Santiago, Universidad de Chile, 1932. George D. Schade, "Mythology in the Poetry of Julio Herrera y Reissig," *Hispania,* XLII (1959), 46-49. Zum Felde, *Proceso,* II, 115-150.

°16. (Mexico) **Enrique González Martínez** (1871-1952) practiced medicine in the Mexican provinces for seventeen years, went to Mexico City in 1911, where he joined the group of young writers who in 1907 had founded the *Sociedad de Conferencias* which later became the *Ateneo de México.* In Mexico City González Martínez held several professorial and political positions, and later became Mexican Minister to Argentina and Spain. Both his life and works are marked by an innate serenity. His poetry is serious, sensitive, terse, sometimes ironic, always carefully wrought. It expressed the reaction against the *modernista* worship of cold marble and graceful swans, set up the owl instead, and called on poets to wring the neck of the deceptively plumaged swan. González Martínez strove to penetrate the husk of things in order to find within an essence which is the theme of his own deep music. He himself was, according to some critics, "the last modernist."

SUGGESTED READING

"Irás sobre la vida de las cosas," "Como hermana y hermano," "Tuércele el cuello al cisne . . . ," "Mañana los poetas . . . ," "¿Te acuerdas?," "Viento sagrado," "El retorno imposible," "Psalle et sile," "Dolor, si por acaso . . . ," "Balada de la loca fortuna."

TEXTS

Anthology, 560-567. Anderson Imbert and Florit, 487-490. Coester, *Anthology,* 208-210. García-Prada, *Poetas modernistas,* 226-242. Holmes, *Span. Am.,* 375-376. Onís, 488-503. Silva Castro, *Ant. crít.,* 245-258.

La muerte del cisne, México, Porrúa, 1915. *Jardines de Francia*

EDITIONS

(translations), México, Porrúa, 1915; prologue by Pedro Henríquez Ureña. *Poesía,* 3 vols., México, Ed. "Polis," 1939-1940. *Antología poética,* Buenos Aires, Espasa-Calpe, 1943 (Col. austral, 333). *Poesías completas,* México, Libreros y Editores Mexicanos, 1944. *Segundo despertar y otros poemas,* México, Stylo, 1945. *Preludios. Lirismos, Silenter, Los senderos ocultos,* México, Porrúa, 1946; prologue by Antonio Castro Leal. *Vilano al viento,* México, Panamericana, 1949. *El nuevo Narciso y otros poemas,* México, Fondo de Cultura Económica, 1952. *Cuentos y otras páginas,* México, Libro-Mex, 1955; prologue by Ana María Sánchez.

TRANSLATIONS

Blackwell, 100-108. Craig, 146-153. Johnson, 114-125. Jones, 40-43. *Trans. from Hisp. Poets,* 233-234. Underwood, 46-56. Walsh, *Cuentos,* 91-92.

CRITICAL REFERENCES

See texts and editions above. Blanco-Fombona, *El modernismo,* 351-

355. Enrique Díez-Canedo, "Enrique González Martínez en su plenitud," *Revista iberoamericana,* 4 (1940), 383-389. Goldberg, 82-92. Enrique González Martínez, *El hombre del buho,* México, Cultura, 1944; also his *La apacible locura,* México, Cuadernos Americanos, 1951 (the poet's own memoirs). Henríquez Ureña, *Breve hist.,* 492-501. Luisa Luisi, *La poesía de Enrique González Martínez,* Montevideo, M. García, 1923. *La obra de Enrique González Martínez,* México, El Colegio Nacional, 1951; edited by José Luis Martínez, with prologue by Antonio Castro Leal. José Luis Martínez, *Lit. mex. siglo XX,* I, 178-181. Pedro Salinas, "El cisne y el buho, apuntes para la historia de la poesía modernista," *Literatura española siglo XX,* México, Robredo, 1940, 45-65.

3rd period

From the Mexican Revolution to the Present

Introductory Summary

The reaction against modernism had definitely asserted itself by 1911, the year when Enrique González Martínez wrote his famous sonnet entitled "Tuércele el cuello al cisne . . . ," in which he decried the empty ritualism of the *rubendarianos* and at the same time welcomed the sincere, more meaningful poetry of the postmodernist group. The Mexican Revolution (1910-1920) hastened and sharpened the social awareness of nearly all writers. "Art for art's sake" no longer held any appeal for a generation alive to the need for serious thought and purposeful action. Thinking men everywhere in the southern countries sought to define and to interpret the American scene and to ponder the immediate social problems.

The contemporary period in Spanish American literature, therefore, opens with the Mexican Revolution of 1910, which was the most conspicuous movement for social reform in the history of the Hispanic republics. Porfirio Díaz (1830-1915), dictator par excellence, after thirty-five years of rule, was deposed by the Mexican people under the leadership of an idealistic and wealthy landowner named Francisco I. Madero (1873-1913). Madero did not understand the hungers of his time: a hunger for bread, a hunger for land, a hunger for justice, and a hunger for liberty. He temporized and was assassinated. The Revolution now erupted like a volcano. The people of Mexico were greatly aroused and carried the holocaust to all corners of their country. It was a rebellion against all established authority. Mexican society was hacked up at the roots as the nation was torn from her colonial past. This was no political rebellion; for the first time a Latin American revolution had become a social revolution.

The Mexican Revolution gave birth to an entire cycle of literature and art. During the nineteenth century the Indian had entered into literature only as a note of local color; he now became the body and soul of Mexican writing, the mainstay of the present and the hope of the future. The novel of the Revolution became the outstanding novelistic type in Spanish American letters. It was terse, vital, and non-European. The Revolution was also the main source of inspiration for Mexico's great mural painting, her new architecture, and her revitalized music. A similar strong spirit of *americanismo* or feeling for the American earth and for the American masses, *los de abajo* in general, manifested itself in the literature of other regions. The Indian, mestizo peon, Negro, and poor city worker became the grist of a new generation of writers throughout Latin America. Mexican highlands, Andean mountains, Argentine pampas, Venezuelan *llanos,* Amazon jungle, and festering urban centers were a few of the areas presented. In this literature, landscape and social protest often walked hand in hand; everywhere it was man against nature and man against the system.

The First World War, too, exerted a direct influence on the course of Spanish American letters and thought. Rapidly expanding trade and soaring foreign investments—largely from the United States, who poured postwar millions into her sister nations' coffers with no concern over the ability of these nations to repay her —ushered in a period of economic prosperity and political corruption that only drew to a close in 1929 with the worldwide depression. The European conflict also brought Spanish America and North America into closer political relations. At the outset, the insistence of the United States on a unilateral interpretation of hemispheric policy goaded the Spanish American nations to lay aside differences in order to present a more effective front to this Yankee threat. The most determined resistance took form in a strong anti-imperialistic movement known as *aprismo* (from APRA standing for Alianza Popular Revolucionaria Americana) that sprang up in Peru in the twenties. APRA's purpose was to combat not only Yankee but all foreign hegemony and to launch a youth reform crusade under the nativist banners of Indo-America. On the other hand, a surge of sympathy was felt for Spain by her former colonies after the defeat of the mother country in 1898. This rapprochement gained intensity with the founding of the Second Republic in 1931. Pan-Hispanism,

Indo-Americanism, and Pan-Americanism—since the inauguration of the Good Neighbor Policy in 1933, this last movement bids fair for the first time to take on a vital meaning in Spanish America—are among the more important currents of this period, that run counter to the rising wave of ardent nationalism that characterizes much of the literature of recent years. These conflicting ideologies are indicative of an America that is rapidly approaching maturity; they give direction to the course that is being pursued in the solution of the multiple problems—social, political, and economic—confronting twentieth-century Spanish America. These problems and their psychological aftermath constitute the essence of contemporary literature and thought.

It was to be expected, therefore, that prose should have become the more important medium of expression since 1910. The essay reveals the intense intellectual self-scrutiny of present-day America; the short story and the novel are focused sharply on the native scene. Up to 1940 regionalism flowered in many vigorous writers: Benito Lynch (1880-1951) and Ricardo Güiraldes (1886-1927) of Argentina, Rómulo Gallegos (1884-1969) of Venezuela, Ciro Alegría (1909-1967) of Peru, José Rubén Romero (1890-1952) of Mexico, and numerous others. Poetry, on the other hand, being more universal in outlook, probes the tragedy of the individual within a social frame that is still in flux. An outstanding group of feminine poets—Delmira Agustini (1886-1914), Gabriela Mistral (1889-1957), Alfonsina Storni (1892-1938), and Juana de Ibarbourou (1895-   )—and several men, with Pablo Neruda (1904-1973) of Chile at the top, have produced some of the finest poetry ever to come out of Latin America. The theater, groping and sporadic in the past, has suffered heavily since the advent of the motion picture. Yet it is true that experimental groups everywhere have swept away much of the chaff of the traditional nativist theater. And in recent years Samuel Eichelbaum (1894-   ) of Argentina and Rodolfo Usigli (1904-   ) of Mexico have brought to the Spanish American stage a heightened professional awareness and new concepts of dramatic art.

From the Mexican Revolution up to the 1940's foreign literary trends no longer dominated the American scene, nor were France and Spain the sole arbiters of Spanish America's literary destiny. Paris had ceased to be the Mecca of the Spanish American artist, and the Spanish-Indian heritage had regained its rightful place in the cultural life of the southern countries. North American influences were stronger than ever. Traditional themes and popular forms had supplanted the exotic note and experimental metrics of the modernists. Gallicisms had surrendered the field in the face of a veritable barrage of regionalisms. Americans everywhere were bent on creating an original literary art, divorced in language, in theme, and in spirit as completely as possible from the European models they had been accused of imitating in servile fashion ever since political independence was won. It is true, of course, that several of the innumerable postwar isms of Europe found their way to America, brought here by the very men who made them known. Vicente Huidobro (1893-1948) of Chile and Jorge Luis Borges (1899-   ) of Argentina are two examples. *Creacionismo* and *ultraismo* are the names of the ultraradical, ephemeral movements headed by these men in the twenties. But it should be noted that as a consequence of the closer relationship between Spanish America and Spain after 1898, these postwar currents reached America largely through the mother country rather than from France. Renascent Spain, as if grateful to the modernists for having revealed to her a new esthetic world, repaid her debt to America through the inspiration which the Hispanic American postmodernists received from the poetry of Juan Ramón Jiménez (1881-1958) and Federico García Lorca (1899-1936), to cite but two of the most illustrious and most representative poets of the peninsula whose influence on American letters since the First World War has far outshadowed that of Paul Valéry (1871-1945) or Guillaume Apollinaire (1880-1918) of France or that of the revolutionary Whitman (1819-1892).

The Spanish Civil War (1936-1939) also had an immediate and concrete effect on Spanish American letters, first in arousing widespread sympathy for the republicans, and second, through the activities of many well-known Spanish writers and publishers who came to this hemisphere to live after the defeat of the Second Republic. The increment that these outstanding figures brought to the culture of the Hispanic countries is incalculable. Their names are legion, and begin with that of the Nobel Prize winner (1956), Juan Ramón Jiménez.

A marked change in feeling and perspective in Latin American literature was eventually brought about by the worldwide economic depression of the 1930's, the Spanish Civil War, and the holocaust of World War II. The Hispanic republics were catapulted into the international arena. Regionalism began to lose its appeal and was supplanted by a restless spirit of philosophical and psychological enquiry in which the locale is inconsequential or is a mere element of color. The essential theme of this literature is not man against nature, nor indeed man against man, but rather man against civilization or man against himself. The writer attempts to penetrate and interpret the depths of the human mind and psyche. The existential novel and short story come to the fore. This is accompanied by a kind of suprarealism (one critic calls it "magical realism") in which the usual measurements of time and place are obliterated in order to make way for a new reality.

European influences in Latin American prose of the twentieth century up to this time had been James Joyce (1882-1941), Marcel Proust (1871-1922), Jules Romains (1885-1972), the French and Russian naturalists, and the realists of Spain. But with the change in perspective noted above, the literature of the southern countries becomes almost planetary in scope. Each literary circle is a microcosm of everything on the world scene. Almost all of the outstanding European and North American writers have left their imprint on this new literature. The existential novel and short story have replaced the earlier regionalism in the great urban centers, and even in the Indianist regions advanced stylistic techniques have opened up new vistas of literary expression. In a recent short story contest held in 1960 by *Life en español*, 3149 original manuscripts were submitted. Not one of these entrants earned his living by writing. They were journalists, teachers, doctors, lawyers, businessmen, clerks, workers of many kinds. Literature to them was simply an added cultural dimension, yet several of them have approached world stature in artistic achievement.

The essay, similarly, has moved gradually from the area of social history and criticism, often with petulant overtones, to a position of objective analysis and more universal outlook. Literary criticism has risen to a very high level, social history is more solidly presented (Mariano Picón-Salas, 1901-   , of Venezuela), and psychological insight is much more acute (Eduardo Mallea, 1903-   , of Argentina and Leopoldo Zea, 1912-   , of Mexico). Self-criticism, indeed, has become devastating in its attempt to bare the weaknesses which hold back the path of progress and the fulfillment of man in the various regions (Ezequiel Martínez Estrada, 1895-   , of Argentina and Octavio Paz, 1914-   , of Mexico). The philosophical essay has reached a high point of excellence, and cultural topics in general have found many worthy exponents (Alfonso Reyes, 1889-1959, of Mexico and Baldomero Sanín Cano, 1861-1957, of Colombia).

In the Latin American scale of values creativity is more highly regarded than cash. For persons of humble origin it is often the only possible means of crossing the rigid caste barriers. A tremendous proportion of Latin American literature, therefore, is written by amateurs, and not by professionals. This often makes for a lack of polish and reveals an uncertain control of the techniques of the trade. But if the output of these writers is sometimes faltering, it is also frequently very much alive, down-to-earth, with a feeling of sincerity and immediacy which give it a quality of great freshness and charm. The writers of our time place the individual in perpetual tension. In so doing they often present the stories of lives that are grim and bitter, but which withal have a strong sense of vitality and of individual dignity. The best works of this literature have gone deep into the heart of man and illuminate what is paramount and essential in human relationships.

GENERAL REFERENCES

Bailey and Nasatir, Chaps. XXVIII-XLI. Castro, 127-258. Gerald Clark, *The Coming Explosion in Latin America,* New York, McKay, 1963, *passim.* Crow, *Epic,* Chaps. XLVI-LIII. Fagg, *passim.* Hanke, *passim.* Henríquez Ureña, *Lit. Curr.,* Chaps. VII-VIII; also his *Hist. de la cult.,* Chaps. VII-VIII. Herring, *passim.* Rippy, Chaps. XXVI-XXXIV. Schurz, *passim.* J. Silva Herzog, *Breve historia de la Revolución Mexicana,* 2 vols., México, Fondo de Cultura Económica, 1960. Torres-Ríoseco, *Epic,* Chaps. IV-VI. Tannenbaum, *passim.* Worcester and Schaeffer, Chaps. XXX-XL.

I.
Poetry

Surfeited with the experimental and exotic aspects and excesses of their own immediate esthetic past, poets descended from the ivory tower of early modernist years to speak in more direct and more meaningful terms to their fellowmen. They cherished, however, the enduring legacy of enriched language, imagery, metrics, and expanded poetic horizons of their senior fellow-modernists. This, then, was their common heritage. But once they experienced the exhilaration of the first firm steps of budding maturity, each began to develop more and more independently. And so diverse were the paths they followed that it is impossible to attempt any clear-cut definition of their esthetics as a whole. Two trends, however, may be said to characterize their departure from the relative conformity of early modernist days: the one, to return to simplicity and sincerity of expression; the other, to carry out to its ultimate possibilities, that urge of their modernist predecessors that tended to divorce poetry from all that man had associated with it in the past.

The first trend is particularly characteristic of the period 1910-1918, and the poets of that period—and many of the immediately subsequent years—are usually spoken of as postmodernists. These so-called "postmodernists" have never sought to regroup themselves in any formalized movement; on the contrary, they have evinced little or no concern for the esthetic preoccupations and pursuits of those who would seek new poetic alignments. And yet, without any conscious effort as a group, without manifestos or literary journals to proclaim their artistic creed, many have written so much in similar strains that they have become susceptible to certain broad classifications. Among these postmodernists, then, there are those—Rafael Arévalo Martínez (1884-   ) of Guatemala, Baldomero Fernández Moreno (1886–1950), Enrique Banchs (1888–1968), Rafael Alberto Arrieta (1889–1968), and Conrado Nalé Roxlo (1898-   ) of Argentina—whose verse is especially distinguished for its spontaneity and simplicity of expression and form and for its intimate revelation of daily themes and basic human passions. There are others—Delmira Agustini (1886-1914) and Juana de Ibarbourou (1895-   ) of Uruguay, Gabriela Mistral (1889-1957) of Chile, Alfonsina Storni (1892-1938) of Argentina—who constitute the first galaxy of female voices to sing of self and sex without prudery or restraint. Some, like José Eustasio Rivera (1888-1928) of Colombia, capture in classic meters, the dramatic brilliance of tropical America. Others, like Luis Carlos López (1883-1950), also of Colombia, ridicule the chronic romanticism of provincial life. And, finally, there are poets like Ramón López Velarde (1888-1921) of Mexico who, in daring imagery and diction, reveal regional America in novel perspective.

The second trend takes shape during the closing years of World War I. Unlike the postmodernists the poets of this trend were disposed in the beginning to denounce all poetry that was in any way tied to the esthetic past, all poetry that was content to bask in its own reflected image. These "rebels" identified their own nihilistic aims with those of similar trends abroad, and loudly they launched their separate yet similar creeds in a multiplicity of ephemeral literary movements and journals. Dadaism, cubism, surrealism, existentialism, the poetry of Paul Valéry (1871-1945), Rainer Maria Rilke (1875–1926), Thomas Stearns Eliot (1888–1965), Pierre Reverdy (1889-1960), Paul Éluard (1895-1953), André Breton (1896-1966), Tristan Tzara (1896-1963), found their American counterparts, and their admirers and their disciples, under banners variously labeled *ultraísmo, creacionismo, estridentismo, cubismo, postumismo, integralismo, invencionismo, transcendentalismo.* These successive isms and generations are often best reflected in the journals to which they gave birth. *Proa* (1924-1925) and *Martín Fierro* (1924-1927) were among the earliest and best-known literary organs of the post-World War I vanguard movements in the Argentine; *Amauta* (1926-1930) became the mouthpiece of the Peruvian *apristas; Contemporáneos* (1928-1931) spoke for the first distinguished generation of Mexican writers to appear after the Revolution of 1910; and

Revista de avance (1927-1930) and *Orígenes* (1944-1952) of Cuba, *Alfar* (1921-1955) of Uruguay, and *Viernes* (1937-1941) of Venezuela were among other important journals that recorded a similar common striving for a new poetics. Many poets of the earlier vanguard movements—Vicente Huidobro (1893-1948), Ricardo Molinari (1898-   ), Jorge Luis Borges (1899-   ), Pablo Neruda (1904-1973)—are commonly classified as *ultraistas*. But there are others who can only more properly be identified with the more recent wide-spread vanguard writing of our time. Of the latter, there are those who are less radical in their denial: Jorge Carrera Andrade (1903-   ) of Ecuador, Carlos Pellicer (1899-1977), José Gorostiza (1901-1973), Jaime Torres Bodet (1902-1974) and Xavier Villaurrutia (1903-1950) of Mexico, all of the generation of *Contemporáneos;* and there are others who are more insistent in their appeal for deeper human understanding: César Vallejo (1892-1938) of Peru, Nicolás Guillén (1902-   ) of Cuba, Luis Palés Matos (1892-1959) of Puerto Rico, Octavio Paz (1914-   ) of Mexico. Collectively, but in varying measures, these *ultraista* and later vanguard poets have broken free of the fetters of established verse forms and have made the metaphor the symbol and the key of poetic expression. They have sought to surmount the barrier of language in an effort to communicate more effectively with modern man in his brooding loneliness. They have placed their art at the service of the masses and of the left. It is they, in short, who to a large degree have been responsible for the critical tone and the sense of commitment of much Spanish American writing of today that strives to create a medium more responsive to the human and spiritual needs of the changing scene.

REFERENCES

Anderson Imbert, II, 12-79. Anderson Imbert and Florit, 553 *et passim*. Arrieta, IV, 607-665. Dauster, 149-181. Johnson, 25-33, 129-139. Leiva, *passim*. Martínez, "La literatura de vanguardia," in *Lit. mex. siglo XX*. Monguió, *Poesía postmodernista peruana*. Onís, XVIII-XXIV. Torre, *passim*.

A. POSTMODERNISM

°1. (Argentina) **Baldomero Fernández Moreno** (1886-1950) or simply Fernández Moreno, as he preferred to be known, was born of Spanish parents in Buenos Aires. From 1892 to 1899 he lived with his family in Spain. He took up medicine as a career and practiced his profession in the provinces and in Buenos Aires until he located permanently in the capital in 1924. It was then that he abandoned medicine and dedicated the rest of his life to teaching and to writing. His first book, *Las iniciales del misal,* appeared in 1915. Volume followed volume as the poet sang of the things he loved most: countryside and hamlet and city, home and family and friends, everything real and tangible and near. His poetry is spontaneous, unadorned, warm with the gentle irony and humor of one in sympathetic understanding with each intimate moment. His mastery of traditional verse forms and language and his ability to capture the beauty of the humble details of daily living won him wide popularity and many honors. *Aldea española* (1925), *Poesía* (1928), *Décimas* (1928), *Dos poemas* (1935), *Seguidillas* (1936), *Romances* (1936) were all prize-winning collections. In 1934 he was elected to the Academia Argentina de Letras. His country's greatest recognition was bestowed upon him one month before his death when *Viaje del Tucumán* (1949) and *Parva* (1949) received the Gran Premio de Honor of the Sociedad Argentina de Escritores. Fernández Moreno also published several autobiographical pieces, philosophical bits, and sketches and impressions of people and places. Much of his prose, however, still lies scattered in journals and reviews.

SUGGESTED READING
"Inicial de oro," "Genealogía," "Habla la madre castellana," "Invitación al hogar," "Le digo a un sauce," "Propósito," "Setenta balcones y ninguna flor," "Auto," "Crepúsculo argentino," "Algún día serás," "Hoy, por primera vez . . . ," "Árboles de la Avenida," "Tráfago," "Yo," "Romance de palomas," "Seguidillas personales," "Plaza mojada," "Poeta," "Una ventana," "Parque Lezama."

TEXTS
Anderson Imbert and Florit, 584-586. Caillet-Bois, 1053-1058. Onís, 864-875.

EDITIONS
Antología, 1915-1950, 6th ed., Buenos Aires, Espasa-Calpe, 1954 (Col. austral, 204). *Ciudad 1915-1949,* Buenos Aires, Eds. de la Municipalidad, 1949; edited by César Fernández Moreno.

CRITICAL REFERENCES
See texts and editions above. *Diccionario . . . Argentina,* I, 50-53.

César Fernández Moreno, *Introducción a Fernández Moreno,* Buenos Aires, Emecé, 1956.

*2. (Argentina) Enrique Banchs (1888-1968) was born in Buenos Aires. He has led a life of quiet seclusion and silence—*el poeta de los grandes silencios*—that has been broken only by brief editorial assignments and by occasional appointments to national commissions on education, libraries, and cultural affairs. In 1941 he was elected a member of the Academia Argentina de Letras, and in 1954 he was awarded the Gran Premio de Honor by the Sociedad Argentina de Escritores. His first book of verse, *Las barcas,* appeared in 1907. Three more volumes of poems followed in rapid order, *El libro de los elogios* in 1908, *El cascabel del halcón* in 1909, and *La urna* in 1911. Since that time he has contributed a scattering of poems and prose pieces to journals and reviews over the years, but his only other book has been a collection entitled *Lecturas,* published in 1920, and that was largely one of prose and prose poems. As Argentina's first outstanding poet after Lugones, Banchs turned early to the simplicity and sincerity of popular forms and themes in an effort to achieve the classic lyric tone and depth of human emotion that characterize the later finely-wrought sonnets of *La urna.*

SUGGESTED READING

"Elogio de una lluvia," "Romance de la bella," "Romance de cautivo," "Cancioncilla" ("El pino dice agorerías . . ."), "Cancioncilla" ("No quería amarte . . ."), "Balbuceo," "Carretero," "El voto," "La estatua," "Como es de amantes necesaria usanza," "Entra la aurora en el jardín . . . ," "Tornasolando el flanco . . . ," "Sé de una fuente. . . ."

TEXTS

Anthology, 758-767. Caillet-Bois, 1108-1115. Noé, 181-197. Onís, 703-714. Santos González, 355-401.

EDITIONS

Poemas selectos (ed. Francisco Monterde), México, Cultura, 1921.

TRANSLATIONS

Craig, 174-181. Johnson, 162-169. Jones, 155-156. *Trans. from Hisp. Poets,* 190.

CRITICAL REFERENCES

See texts and editions above. *Diccionario . . . Argentina,* II, 234-238.

3. (Argentina) **Rafael Alberto Arrieta** (1889-1968), poet, critic, bibliographer and literary historian, was born in Rauch in the province of Buenos Aires. Educated at the universities of Buenos Aires and La Plata, he later served both institutions in an administrative capacity and as professor of European literature. Over the years he has taken an active interest in literary journalism, in foreign literatures, and in international cultural relations. In 1926, and again in 1943, he won recognition for his work as a poet and as a scholar. And in 1935 he was elected to membership in the Academia Argentina de Letras. His best, sustained, poetic effort is largely limited to the years encompassed by his first book of poems, *Alma y momento,* published in Buenos Aires in 1910, and by its spiritual successor, *Fugacidad,* a volume that completed the poet's essential esthetic cycle in 1921. His later poems are contained in volumes published over a widening span of years, *Estío serrano* appearing in 1926 and *Tiempo cautivo* in 1947. His verse is marked by simplicity and serenity and by a predilection for traditional forms and for themes of the intimate present.

SUGGESTED READING

". . . Iba el peregrino," "En la tarde invernal," "La voz ausente," "Lied," "El sueño," "La medalla," "Álamos de Córdoba," "Canción infantil," "Lluvia," "En un cementerio abandonado," "El río seco," "La visión optimista."

TEXTS

Anthology, 768-772. Caillet-Bois, 1141-1149. Noé, 169-180. Onís, 659-665.

EDITIONS

Sus mejores poemas,. Buenos Aires, Agencia General de Librería y Publicaciones, 1923. *Antología poética,* 3rd ed., Buenos Aires, Espasa-Calpe, 1944 (Col. austral, 291).

TRANSLATIONS

Fitts, 467-477. Johnson, 170-175. *Trans. from Hisp. Poets,* 191.

CRITICAL REFERENCES

See texts above. *Diccionario . . . Argentina,* II, 230-234.

°**4.** (Argentina) **Alfonsina Storni** (1892-1938) was born in Switzerland. Her early years were spent in the provinces of San Juan and Santa Fe. When barely eleven, she was forced to earn her own living, first as a member of a theatrical troupe, then as a rural school teacher in Rosario. In 1913 she went to Buenos Aires where, after several disheartening years in the business world, she finally came to know a more satisfying life in journalism, in the teaching of literature, and in directing and writing for the young people's theater movement. She had long been attracted to poetry and in Buenos Aires she easily won the respect of the literary circles that she frequented more than any other woman of her day. Her first book, *La inquietud del rosal,* appeared in 1916. Five other collections of poems followed within a decade. Of these, *Ocre* (1925) is perhaps the best and most representative of her earlier period. Her poetry progresses from a boldly subjective approach to love, and the role of her sex in a male-dominated world, to the intellectual and often tortured manner of her latter days. Aware of the fact that she was a victim of cancer, she sought her own death in the sea off the shores of Mar del Plata.

SUGGESTED READING

"Cuadrados y ángulos," "Peso ancestral," "Bien pudiera ser . . . ," "Veinte siglos," "Moderna," "Hombre pequeñito . . . ," "La que comprende . . . ," "El ruego," "Soy," "El engaño," "Tú que nunca serás . . . ," "Una voz," "Dolor," "Epitafio para mi tumba," "El ensayo," "El hombre," "Faro en la noche."

TEXTS

Anthology, 740-748. Anderson Imbert and Florit, 586-587. Caillet-Bois, 1186-1195. Onís, 932-941.

EDITIONS

Las mejores poesías, Barcelona, Cervantes, [1923]; prologue by F. Maristany. *Antología poética,* Buenos Aires, Espasa-Calpe, 1938 (Col. austral, 142). *Obra poética,* Buenos Aires, Ramón J. Roggero, 1952.

TRANSLATIONS

Blackwell, 386-391. Craig, 220-225. Fitts, 512-521. Johnson, 150-155. Jones, 157-160. *Trans. from Hisp. Poets,* 192-194.

CRITICAL REFERENCES

See texts and editions above. *Diccionario . . . Argentina,* I, 179-181. Helena Percas, *La poesía femenina argentina (1810-1950),* Madrid, Cultura Hispánica, 1958, 75-237. Rosenbaum, 205-227.

°5. (Uruguay) **Delmira Agustini** (1886-1914) was born into a well-to-do family and received the kind of cultural training befitting a young lady of Montevideo society of her day. From her earliest years she was keenly attracted to the arts, to painting and music and poetry. She began writing poems at the age of ten. Her first volume of verse, *El libro blanco,* appeared in 1907, to be followed in 1910 by *Cantos de la mañana* and in 1913 by *Los cálices vacíos,* her best and most representative work. An unhappy marriage soon ended in a separation apparently never fully realized or desired by either as she met death at the hands of her desperately despondent husband who instantly took his own life as well. Modernist tendencies carry over in most of her work, of which the dominant theme is all-consuming love. No other Hispanic poetess has sung so freely and so dramatically of the erotic experience, an experience more passionately desired perhaps than ever wholesomely enjoyed.

SUGGESTED READING

"Desde lejos," "El intruso," "La barca milagrosa," "Lo inefable," "Las alas," "Tu boca," "Cuentas de mármol," "Cuentas de sombra," "Cuentas de fuego," "Cuentas de luz," "Cuentas falsas," "Mis amores," "Tu amor . . . ," "Tarde pálida," "Nocturno."

TEXTS

Anthology, 723-729. Anderson Imbert and Florit, 577-581. Caillet-Bois, 1059-1065. Onís, 907-920.

EDITIONS

Las mejores poesías, Barcelona, Cervantes, [1923]. *Obras completas,* 2 vols., Montevideo, M. García, 1924. *Poesías completas,* 2nd ed., Buenos Aires, Losada, 1955; edition and prologue by Alberto Zum Felde.

TRANSLATIONS

Johnson, 140-149.

CRITICAL REFERENCES

See texts and editions above. Ofelia Machado B. de Benvenuto, *Delmira Agustini,* Montevideo, Ceibo, 1944. Miranda, 154-194. Rosenbaum, 57-167.

6. (Uruguay) **Juana de Ibarbourou (1895-   ) was born in the provincial city of Melo, where she lived and was known as Juanita Fernández until her early and happy marriage at the age of eighteen, when she moved to Montevideo. Her simple, uneventful life has been that of a contented wife and mother. In 1929, as the most beloved of America's living women poets, she was christened *Juana de América* in a ceremony at which Alfonso Reyes presided in the Palacio Legislativo of Montevideo. In 1947 she was honored by election to membership in the Academia Nacional de Letras. *Las lenguas de diamante,* her first and most representative collection of poems, appeared in 1919. Five additional volumes of verse, books of poetic prose with religious themes, poems and tales for children, textbooks, these have been the fruits of the later intervening years. Her verse is instinctive, sensuous, and intensely subjective; her all-embracing theme is nature. The early pagan songs of love and self yield finally to the somber and more studied manner of the autumnal poems of *Oro y tormenta* (1956).

SUGGESTED READING
"La hora," "El fuerte lazo," "La cita," "La inquietud fugaz," "Vidagarfio," "La espera," "Rebelde," "Estío," "Salvaje," "La pequeña llama," "Cenizas," "Días sin fe," "Atlántico," "Día de felicidad sin causa," "Despecho," "Tiempo."

TEXTS
Anthology, 749-757. Anderson Imbert and Florit, 581-583. Caillet-Bois, 1266-1275. Onís, 941-951.

EDITIONS
Las mejores poesías, Barcelona, Cervantes, 1930. *Sus mejores poemas,* Madrid, Ed. América, 1930; prologue by Rufino Blanco-Fombona. *Sus mejores poemas,* Santiago, Nascimento, 1930; edition and prologue by Humberto Díaz Casanueva. *Poemas,* 9th ed., Buenos Aires, Espasa-Calpe, [1961] (Col. austral, 265). *Obras completas,* Madrid, Aguilar, 1953; edition by Dora Isella Russell, prologue by Ventura García Calderón.

TRANSLATIONS
Blackwell, 448-449. Fitts, 490-493. Johnson, 156-161. Jones, 170-175. *Trans. from Hisp. Poets,* 261-264.

CRITICAL REFERENCES
See texts and editions above. Miranda, 195-246. Rosenbaum, 229-256.

°°7. (Chile) **Gabriela Mistral (Lucila Godoy Alcayaga)** (1889-1957) was born in the Valley of Elqui in the north-central province of Coquimbo. For almost two decades she served as teacher and director of elementary and secondary schools in every corner of her land. In 1914 she won her first laurels for poetry when she was awarded first prize in the Juegos Florales of Santiago for her "Sonetos de la muerte." And she gained international recognition for her years of teaching when, in 1922, she was invited to collaborate in Mexico's edutational reform program. From 1925 until her death in New York she was her country's most authentic voice abroad, now as representative to international gatherings, now as consul and cultural attaché in Europe, in Mexico and Brazil, and in the United States. *Desolación* (1922), *Ternura* (1924), and *Tala* (1938) contain her best poems, and for them she received the Nobel Prize in 1945. Because of an early tragic love affair, she never married. Out of the desolation of that tragedy she wrote her incomparable poems for children, her poems of maternal longing and of love, of loneliness and fear of death, of hopeful communion with nature, man, and God.

SUGGESTED READING

"La maestra rural," "El niño solo," "Meciendo," "Yo no tengo soledad," "Piececitos," "Suavidades," "Ruth," "Los sonetos de la muerte," "El ruego," "Nocturno," "In Memoriam," "Mientras baja la nieve," "Tres árboles," "Historias de loca" (4), "Sol del trópico," "La desvelada."

TEXTS

Anthology, 730-739. Anderson Imbert and Florit, 570-577. Caillet-Bois, 1099-1108. Onís, 920-932. Weisinger, 230-239.

EDITIONS

Desolación (1922), Santiago, Ed. del Pacífico, 1954 (Obras selectas, 2). *Lagar,* Santiago, Ed. del Pacífico, 1954. *Antología,* 4th ed., Santiago, Zig-Zag, 1955; prologue by Ismael Edwards Matte.

TRANSLATIONS

Arciniegas, 76-83. Blackwell, 236-279. Craig, 194-205. Fitts, 38-49. Langston Hughes (trans.), *Selected Poems of Gabriela Mistral,* Bloomington, Indiana Univ. Press, 1957. Jones, 120-123. *Trans. from Hisp. Poets,* 199-200. Walsh, *Hisp. Anth.,* 735-736.

CRITICAL REFERENCES

See texts and editions above. "Alone," *Gabriela Mistral,* Santiago, Nascimento, 1946. Margot Arce de Vázquez, *Gabriela Mistral: persona y poesía,* San Juan, P. R., Eds. Asomante, 1958. *Diccionario . . . Chile,* 133-136. Augusto Iglesias, *Gabriela Mistral y el modernismo en Chile,* Santiago, Ed. Universitaria, 1949. Rosenbaum, 171-203. Arturo Torres-Ríoseco, *Gabriela Mistral,* Valencia, Ed. Castalia, 1962.

°8. (Colombia) **Luis Carlos López** (1883-1950) was born in Cartagena where, as poet, humorist, and liberal bourgeois, he spent the whole of a relatively uneventful life except for occasional minor political posts at home and two consular assignments abroad in Munich and in Baltimore. The ancestral home, the pharmacy, and the casino were the vantage points from which *el tuerto López* mused over the monotonous tranquility and the petty tribulations of the provincial scene. His inimitable poetic sketches first appeared in book form in the volume *De mi villorrio,* published in Madrid in 1908. Mockingly and pitilessly, yet without malice, he caught in caricature the ridiculous posture (*Posturas difíciles,* 1909) of fellow provincials, his "hongos de la riba," vegetating in the local scene. His last and best look, mirrored in *Por el atajo* (1920), won him at long last the recognition he so well deserves.

SUGGESTED READING

"Cromo," "Hongos de la riba," "Medio ambiente," "Muchachas solteronas," "A mi ciudad nativa," "Siesta del trópico," "Versos a la luna," "Versos para ti," "Égloga tropical."

TEXTS

Anthology, 789-796. Caillet-Bois, 1008-1010. García-Prada, *Antología,* II, 181-197. Onís, 851-857.

EDITIONS

42 poemas de Luis Carlos López, México, [*Revista iberoamericana*], 1943; edition and prologue by Carlos García-Prada.

TRANSLATIONS

Hays, 50-63. Jones, 95-98. *Trans. from Hisp. Poets.,* 212. Walsh, *Hisp. Anth.,* 711-714.

CRITICAL REFERENCES

See texts and editions above. *Diccionario . . . Colombia,* 62-64. A. Llorente Arroyo, "Luis Carlos López," *Hispania,* VII (1924), 377-386. George D. Schade, "La sátira y las imágenes en la poesía de Luis Carlos López," *Revista iberoamericana,* 43 (1957), 109-132.

*9. (Colombia) **José Eustasio Rivera** (1888-1928), lawyer, poet, and novelist, was born in the tropical city of Neiva, capital of the Department of Huila, in southern Colombia. In 1906 he left for Bogotá where he studied for three years at the newly established Normal School. After a brief and unhappy period of teaching in Tolima, he turned to the study of law, graduating from the National University in 1917. His life from that point on was spent largely in the service of his country, now on special missions to Peru and Mexico (1921) and Cuba (1928), now in the national Chamber of Deputies (1923-1924), and again on government commissions charged with negotiating the settlement of a boundary dispute with Venezuela (1922) or investigating the alleged misuse of government funds in connection with oil leases (1925). During those years his official and other assignments afforded him the opportunity to know and study at first hand the topography and customs and types of the llanos and the upper reaches of the Amazon he has described with such artistry and feeling in his only volume of poems, *Tierra de promisión* (1921), and in his single prose narrative, *La vorágine* (1924). *Tierra de promisión* is one of the best sonnet sequences on tropical America yet written in the Spanish language.

The rhythms, imagery, and colorful details of his poems are reflected repeatedly in the pages of his novel. Romantic in spirit and sociological in content, *La vorágine* is an impassioned denunciation of the tragedy that befell the Colombian rubber gatherers in the upper Amazon jungle during the early years of the century. The poet died in New York where he had gone to assist in the publication of Spanish and English editions of his novel.

SUGGESTED READING

Poetry: "Prólogo" and sonnets 1 and 4 of Part One; 2, 9 and 10 of Part Two; and 3, 9, 21 and 23 of Part Three. Prose: *La vorágine*.

TEXTS

Anthology, 797-802. Anderson Imbert and Florit, 564-566. Flores, 390-410. García-Prada, *Antología,* II, 289-301. Onís, 837-841.

EDITIONS

Poetry: *Tierra de promisión,* 5th ed., Bogotá, Camacho Roldán, 1933. Prose: *La vorágine,* Buenos Aires, Espasa-Calpe, 1941 (Col. austral, 35). *La vorágine,* Buenos Aires, Losada, 1962 (Bibl. contemporánea, 94).

TRANSLATIONS

Arciniegas, 26-43. E. K. James (trans.), *The Vortex,* New York, Putnam, 1935. Jones, 208-217.

CRITICAL REFERENCES

See texts above. Anderson Imbert, II, 88-92. Ricardo Charria Tobar, *José Eustasio Rivera en la intimidad,* Bogotá, Eds. Tercer Mundo, 1963. *Diccionario . . . Colombia,* 97-100. García-Prada, *Estudios,* 33-48. Eduardo Neale-Silva, *Horizonte humano: Vida de José Eustasio*

Rivera, Madison, Univ. of Wisconsin Press, 1960; also his *Estudios sobre José Eustasio Rivera: I. El arte poético,* New York, Hispanic Institute, 1951; also his "The Factual Bases of *La vorágine,*" *PMLA,* LIV (1939), 316-331. Spell, 179-191. Torres-Ríoseco, *Grandes novelistas,* I, 223-272.

°10. (Guatemala) **Rafael Arévalo Martínez** (1884-), poet and novelist, has led a life of quiet dedication to writing and to contemplation. Except for a brief period of teaching in the early days and a one-year appointment (1946-1947) as his country's ambassador to the Organization of American States in Washington, his outstanding role in public life has been as director of the National Library from 1926 to 1946. He began writing poetry as an ardent admirer and disciple of the later Darío of *Cantos de vida y esperanza. Maya,* his first book of poems, appeared in 1911. Other volumes followed— *Los atormentados* (1914), *Las rosas de Engaddi* (1915), *Llama* (1934), *Por un caminito así* (1947), but in spite of their number the poet's total production has been relatively small. Wholly unaffected by the buffeting winds of shifting poetic tastes, his muse has been constant in theme and spirit over the years. Alternately sentimental and ironic, his poems reflect his deeply religious faith and his self-indulgent contrition over ever having doubted the ultimate destiny of mankind.

This preoccupation over the true state of man (*Concepción del cosmos,* 1954) and over man's failure to govern his own worldly state (*El mundo de los mahurachías,* 1938, and *Viaje a Ipanda,* 1939) has found its best expression in his stories and in his novelettes. The creator of an original and fascinating type of short story known as the psychozoological tale, he has become one of the leading exponents of psychological and imaginative fiction in America. His outstanding piece of prose fiction is the novelette *El hombre que parecía un caballo* (1915). He has also written two plays in verse.

SUGGESTED READING

Poetry: "Oración," "Los atormentados," "Ananké," "El Señor que lo veía . . . ," "Retrato de mujer," "Tu mano," "Como· los cipreses . . . ," "Mi vida es un recuerdo," "Lòs hombres-lobos," "Ropa limpia," "Oración al Señor," "Entrégate por entero . . . ," "Cadenas." Prose: *El hombre que parecía un caballo;* "El Señor Monitot" and "La mentira."

TEXTS

Anthology, 781-788. Anderson Imbert and Florit, 602-605. Caillet-Bois, 1045-1051. Onís, 857-864. Torres-Ríoseco, *Ant. lit. hisp.,* 107-113.

EDITIONS

35 poemas, México, [*Revista iberoamericana*], 1944; prologue by Santiago Argüello. *Obras escogidas: prosa y poesía,* Guatemala, Ed. Universitaria, 1959. *Cuentos y poesías,* Madrid, Eds. Iberoamericanas, 1961.

TRANSLATIONS

Poetry: Blackwell, 474-477. Fitts, 496-497. Johnson, 176-177. Jones, 285. Walsh, *Hisp. Anth.,* 729-734. Prose: Victor S. Clark (trans.), "Our Lady of the Afflicted" ("Nuestra Señora de los locos") and "The Panther Man" ("Las fieras del trópico"), *The Living Age,* 321 (1924), 800-806, 1005-1011, 1046-1052. Jones, 280-284.

CRITICAL REFERENCES

See texts and editions above. Englekirk, 369-385. Federico de Onís, "Resurrección de Arévalo Martínez," *Revista de estudios hispánicos,* I (1928), 290-295. Torres-Ríoseco, *Grandes novelistas,* II, 3-18.

°°11. (Mexico) **Ramón López Velarde** (1888-1921) was born in Ciudad García (formerly Jerez) in the State of Zacatecas. From 1902 to 1907 he studied in Aguascalientes. He then went to San Luis Potosí where, in 1911, he earned his degree in law. In 1912, after an unsuccessful stint as a judge in El Venado, he made his first trip to Mexico where, except for a brief return to San Luis Potosí during 1913-1914, he was to spend the rest of his life. In the capital he held several minor government posts. He also taught literature at the Escuela Nacional Preparatoria and at the Escuela de Altos Estudios. His early death cut short an artistic production of unusual promise. *La sangre devota,* his first book of poems, appeared in 1916. It was followed, in 1919, by *Zozobra,* a volume of mature and disconcerting poetry and his only other work to be published during his lifetime. *El minutero* (1923), a collection of short poetic prose pieces, and *El son del corazón* (1932), a slender volume of verse, have been published posthumously. Ostensibly provincial in theme and spirit, in diction and in imagery López Velarde was the most daring innovator of Mexico's post-modernist generation. Until recently his extensive writings in prose have never received the attention they justly deserve.

SUGGESTED READING

"Cuaresmal," "El retorno maléfico," "Humildemente," "Mi corazón se amerita," "Tierra mojada . . . ," "La suave patria."

TEXTS

Anthology, 773-780. Anderson Imbert and Florit, 554-558. Caillet-Bois, 1115-1123. Castro Leal, 189-205. Cuesta, 94-109. Onís, 967-974.

EDITIONS

Obras completas, México, Nueva España, 1944. *Poesías completas y El minutero,* México, Porrúa, 1957; edition and prologue by Antonio Castro Leal.

TRANSLATIONS

Anth. Mex. Poetry, 172-187. Hays, 24-47. Johnson, 178-181. Jones, 45-48. Underwood, 66-69.

CRITICAL REFERENCES

See texts and editions above. Leiva, 33-47. Allen W. Phillips, "López Velarde y su concepto de poesía en el postmodernismo," *Memoria del octavo congreso,* 205-221; also his *Ramón López Velarde: el poeta y el prosista,* México, Instituto Nacional de Bellas Artes, 1962.

B. VANGUARD POETRY

1. (Chile) **Vicente Huidobro** (1893-1948) was born in Santiago. Except for a brief dramatic incursion into politics in 1925 as a candidate for the presidency, most of his life was dedicated to letters and much of it was spent in Europe, in his early years as a high priest of the new poetry, in his latter days as correspondent and observer of the Spanish Civil War and of World War II. It was in Buenos Aires, in 1916, that Huidobro publicly proclaimed his radical poetic doctrine for the first time; and in 1918 he appeared in Spain as the founder of *creacionismo,* the movement that embodied those concepts. *Ecos del alma,* his first collection of poems in the traditional manner, had been published in Santiago in 1910. Five volumes in a similar vein were to follow in quick order before his revolutionary esthetics would bear fruit in the first book of *creacionista* verse, *El espejo de agua,* that appeared in Buenos Aires in 1916. Title after title—now in Spanish, now in French, and products of presses in Paris and Madrid —were to establish the poet as the militant precursor and most fertile

exponent of one of the many ephemeral vanguard movements of the time that failed to survive for long the mad heyday of their obstreperous triumph. *Manifestes* (Paris, 1925) contains significant statements on the poet's esthetics of the time. In his later years Huidobro also wrote plays, and turned more and more to prose. *El Cid Campeador,* published in Madrid in 1929, is generally recognized as his best prose work.

Huidobro repeatedly defined the poet's mission as that of *"un pequeño Dios"* who was to create a poem *"como la naturaleza hace un árbol":*

> Por qué cantáis la rosa, ¡oh poetas!
> hacedla florecer en el poema. ("Arte poética")

In his unbridled attempts to breathe life into the fantastic creations of his imagination, Huidobro rejected the entire poetic structure of the past. All that remains of his own "inventive" seeking along the multiple bypaths to a new poetic expression for his time are a sprinkling of daring metaphors and the amusing artifacts of what was once a startling but brittle find.

SUGGESTED READING

"Arte poética," "El espejo de agua," "Hijo," "Marino," "Horizonte," "Poema funerario a Guillaume Apollinaire" (from original in French), "Cantos IV, VI VII" of *Altazor,* "Canción del huevo y del infinito," "Infancia de la muerte," "Monumento al mar."

TEXTS

Anderson Imbert and Florit, 595-601. Onís, 1127-1133.

EDITIONS

Antología, Santiago, Zig-Zag, 1945; edition, translation, prologue, and notes by Eduardo Anguita. *Poesía y prosa,* Madrid, Aguilar, 1957; preceded by essay on "Teoría del creacionismo" by Antonio de Undurraga.

TRANSLATIONS

Craig, 236-243. Fitts, 64-73. Hays, 66-91. Jones, 124-126. Warre B. Wells (trans.), *Mirror of a Mage (Cagliostro,* 1926), Boston, Houghton Mifflin, 1931; also his *Portrait of a Paladin (Mío Cid Campeador,* 1929), New York, Horace Liveright, 1932.

CRITICAL REFERENCES

See texts and editions above. Anderson Imbert, II, 61-68. David Bary, "Vicente Huidobro: comienzos de una vocación poética," *Revista iberoamericana,* 45 (1958), 9-42; also his "Perspectiva europea del creacionismo," *Revista iberoamericana,* 51 (1961), 127-136; also his "Vicente Huidobro: el poeta contra su doctrina," *Revista iberoamericana,* 52 (1961), 301-312; also his "Vicente Huidobro: el estilo Nord-Sud," *Revista iberoamericana,* 53 (1962), 87-101. *Diccionario . . . Chile,* 91-94. Henry A. Holmes, *Vicente Huidobro and Creationism,* New York, Institute of French Studies, 1933.

2. (Chile) **Pablo Neruda (Neftalí Ricardo Reyes) (1904–1973) was born in Parral. He was only fourteen years old when he began his writing career as literary editor of the daily, *La mañana,* of Temuco. A year later he won his first recognition as a poet. In 1920 he went to Santiago where he studied some three years at the Instituto Pedagógico and where, in 1921, he published his first book, *La canción de la fiesta.* At the age of nineteen he was acclaimed nationally for *Crepusculario* (1923), his first significant volume of verse. From 1927 until his election to the Senate in 1945, he served his country as consul in the Far East, Buenos Aires, Madrid, and Mexico. *Residencia en la tierra* (1925-1945) and *España en el corazón* (1937)—the latter a reminder of his intense sympathy for Republican Spain and of his great admiration for García Lorca—represent the best of his work as esthetic innovator and social rebel. In 1945, for the extraordinary fire and imagery of those middle years, he was awarded the National Prize for Literature. Since then his pronounced Marxist leanings—because of which he lost his seat in the Senate—compelled him to devote himself wholly to writing and to travel. The *Canto general* (1950) and the *Odas elementales* (1954-1957) embrace the outer reaches of the poet's orbit of recent years as he moves from the militantly political and characteristically abstruse expression of his surrealist period to the lyric and limpid simplicity of the latter-day odes. His poems are known in translation in twenty-four different languages. Nourished by his love for man and the land—"*mis poemas/no han comido poemas*"—his poetry remains a constant source of inspiration for the younger poets of our time.

SUGGESTED READING

"Puentes," "Poema 15," "Poema 20," "Arte poética," "Barcarola," "Oda a Federico García Lorca," "Nuevo canto de amor a Stalingrado," "Alturas de Macchu Picchu" (VI, IX, X, XI, XII), "Se unen la tierra y el hombre," "La casa de las odas," "Oda a la crítica," "Oda al aire," "Oda al libro" (I, II), "Oda al diccionario," "Oda al otoño."

TEXTS

Anthology, 816-822. Anderson Imbert and Florit, 682-688. Caillet-Bois, 1522-1538. Onís, 1154-1159.

EDITIONS

Poesías completas, Buenos Aires, Losada, 1951. *Obras completas,* Buenos Aires, Losada, 1956. *Antología,* 3rd ed., Santiago, Nascimento, 1957. *Odas elementales,* Buenos Aires, Losada, 1958.

TRANSLATIONS

Ben Belitt (trans.), *Selected Poems,* New York, Grove Press, 1963; introduction by Luis Monguió. Craig, 226-235. Fitts, 310-337. Ángel Flores (trans.), *Residence on Earth and Other Poems,* Norfolk, Conn., New Directions, 1946. Hays, 240-265. Johnson, 182-185. Jones, 126-133. Carlos Lozano (trans.), *The Elementary Odes of Pablo Neruda,* New York, Las Américas, 1961; introduction by Fernando Alegría. *Three Spanish American Poets,* 25-48.

CRITICAL REFERENCES

See texts and editions above. Amado Alonso, *Poesía y estilo de Pablo Neruda: interpretación de una poesía hermética,* 2nd ed., Buenos Aires, Sudamericana, 1951. *Diccionario . . . Chile,* 144-146. Mario Jorge de Lellis, *Pablo Neruda,* 2nd ed., Buenos Aires, La Mandrágora, 1959. Torres-Ríoseco, *New World Lit.,* 171-184.

°°3. (Argentina) **Jorge Luis Borges** (1899-   ), poet, essayist, and short-story writer, was born in Buenos Aires and educated in Switzerland. He became identified with the *ultraísta* group in Spain sometime late in 1918. In 1921 he returned to Buenos Aires to initiate the movement there. As spokesman for the new poetry, he was active in founding and supporting such historic literary journals of the day as *Prisma, Proa,* and *Martín Fierro.* Those were also the years of his best poetry in the new manner, of his volumes *Fervor de Buenos Aires* (1923), *Luna de enfrente* (1925), and *Cuaderno de San Martín* (1929). From that time on, however, Borges turned more and more to the essay and the short story, and it is to these forms and to his stimulating collaboration in *Sur* that he has earned an international reputation as a disconcertingly subjective critic (*Otras inquisiciones,* 1960), as a profound and engaging essayist (*Nueva* *refutación del tiempo,* 1947), and as a fiction writer in the best tradition of Poe, Kafka and Chesterton *(El Aleph,* 1952). Recognition came as early as 1928 when he won the City of Buenos Aires' second award for his *El idioma de los argentinos,* but long-delayed honors were heaped upon him only after the fall of the dictatorship in 1955 when he was named director of the National Library and professor of English literature at the University of Buenos Aires. That same year he was elected a member of the Academia Argentina de Letras. And in 1961 he shared, with Samuel Beckett, the International Publishers Formentor Prize for his book *Ficciones.*

SUGGESTED READING

Poetry: "Un patio," "La guitarra," "Calle desconocida," "A la calle Serrano," "Dulcia linquimos arva," "El general Quiroga va en coche al muere," "Amorosa anticipación," "La fundación mitológica de Buenos Aires." Prose: "Los dos reyes y los dos laberintos," "El jardín de senderos que se bifurcan," "Funes el memorioso," "Hombre de la esquina rosada," "Tlön, Uqbar, Orbis Tertius," "Las ruinas circulares," "La casa de Asterión."

TEXTS

Anthology, 803-810. Anderson Imbert and Florit, 691-696. Caillet-Bois, 1406-1409. Flores, 486-502. Onís, 1149-1154.

EDITIONS

Poetry: *Poemas (1923-1958),* Buenos Aires, Emecé, 1958. Essay. *Otras inquisiciones,* Buenos Aires, Emecé, 1960. Fiction: *El Aleph,* 2nd ed., Buenos Aires, Losada, 1952. *Historia universal de la infamia,* Buenos Aires, Emecé, 1954. *Ficciones,* 4th ed., Buenos Aires, Emecé, 1962. *Antología personal,* Buenos Aires, Sur, 1961. *Cuentos de Jorge Luis Borges,* Godfrey, Ill., Monticello College Press, 1958; prologue by John Copeland.

TRANSLATIONS

Mildred Boyer and Harold Morland (trans.), *Dreamtigers (El hacedor,* 1960), Austin, Univ. of Texas Press, 1964; introduction by Miguel Enguídanos. Craig, 244-247. Fitts, 64-73. Hays, 118-137. Johnson, 182-187. Jones, 160-163, 343-354. Anthony Kerrigan (ed. and trans., with others), *Ficciones,* New York, Grove Press, 1962. H. de Onís, 222-223; also her *Spanish Stories,* 17-23. Torres-Ríoseco, *Short Stories,* 181-195. *Labyrinths. Selected Stories and Other Writings,* Norfolk, Conn., New Directions, 1962; edited by Donald A. .Yates and James E. Irby, with preface by André Maurois.

CRITICAL REFERENCES

See texts and editions above. Anderson Imbert, II, 228-233. Ana María Barrenechea, *La expresión de la irrealidad en la obra de Jorge Luis Borges*, México, El Colegio de México, 1957. Manuel Blanco-González, *Jorge Luis Borges, anotaciones sobre el tiempo en su obra*, México, Studium, 1963. *Diccionario . . . Argentina*, II, 253-258. César Fernández Moreno, *Esquema de Borges*, Buenos Aires, Perrot, 1957. L. A. Murillo, "The Labyrinths of Jorge Luis Borges: An Introduction to the Stories of The Aleph," *Modern Language Quarterly*, XX (1959), 259-266. Allen W. Phillips, "Notas sobre Borges y la crítica reciente," *Revista iberoamericana*, 43 (1957), 41-60. Adolfo Prieto, *Borges y la nueva generación*, Buenos Aires, Letras Universitarias, 1954. José Luis Ríos Patrón, *Jorge Luis Borges*, Buenos Aires, La Mandrágora, 1955. Emir Rodríguez Monegal, "Borges: teoría y práctica," *Número*, 27 (1955), 124-157.

*4. (Peru) **César Vallego** (1892-1938), was born in Sanitago de Chuco, high in the northern sierra. In 1915 he graduated in letters from the University of Trujillo, where he also studied law until he left for Lima in 1918. His first collection of poems, *Los heraldos negros*, appeared in Lima that same year. On a visit to his home city in 1920, he was unjustly prosecuted and sentenced to spend three months in jail, an incident that embittered the young poet and that found an echo in *Trilce* (1922), his second book of verse, and in other poetry and prose writings of those years. In 1923 he went to Paris, where he lived out a Bohemian existence in misery and want, relieved only by occasional visits to Spain—and a brief period of residence in Madrid during 1931-1932—and by three trips to Russia between 1928 and 1931. Poetry yielded wholly to prose as the artist, with fervor and with conviction, placed his pen at the service of the working class. His proletarian novel, *Tungsteno*, published in Madrid in 1931, is one of the more artistic products of the growing protest literature of that time. The shock of the Spanish Civil War—*España, aparta de mí este cáliz*—found expression in a final passionate outburst of poems that were published posthumously in 1939 under the simple telling title of *Poemas humanos*. The poet died in poverty in Paris in 1938. Love (both sensual and ideal), a racially congenital fixation on death, and a guilt complex over not sharing fully in the hapless lot of his fellowman are among the constants of his repertoire as his poetry progresses in spirit and in technique from the formative postmodernist manner of *Los heraldos negros* to the vanguard social protest writing of his later years.

SUGGESTED READING

"Idilio muerto," "Los heraldos negros," "Heces," "El pan nuestro," "La cena miserable," "Espergesia," "III," "XVIII," "LXI," "Traspié entre dos estrellas," "Masa," "Piedra negra sobre una piedra blanca."

TEXTS

Anderson Imbert and Florit, 590-594. Caillet-Bois, 1210-1219. Onís, 1134-1137.

EDITIONS

Antología de César Vallejo (ed. Xavier Abril), Buenos Aires, Claridad, 1942. *Poesías completas, 1918-1938,* Buenos Aires, Losada, 1949; prologue by César Miró.

TRANSLATIONS

Fitts, 404-427. Hays, 268-297. Jones, 112-115. John Knoepfle, James Wright, and Robert Bly (eds. and trans.), *Twenty Poems of César Vallejo,* Madison, Minn., Odin House, 1963.

CRITICAL REFERENCES

Xavier Abril, *Vallejo,* Buenos Aires, Eds. Front, 1958. Anderson Imbert, II, 57-59. Concha Meléndez, "Muerte y resurrección de César Vallejo," *Revista iberoamericana,* 12 (1943), 419-453. Luis Monguió, *César Vallejo (1892-1938). Vida y obra. Bibliografía. Antología,* New York, Hispanic Institute, 1952.

°5. (Ecuador) **Jorge Carrera Andrade** (1903-   ), poet and diplomat, was born and educated in Quito. In 1926 he left his homeland for the first time to study and travel in Europe. A brief return was cut short by a consular appointment that started him on his life's journey in his country's foreign service from Paita, Peru, to far-off Yokohama, from England to Chile and Venezuela. His poetic journey began when as a youth he came to identify life with the immediate world of his senses. The *Estanque inefable* (1922) of his first poems was soon to be followed by *Boletines de mar y tierra* (1930), *Registro del mundo* (1940), and other volumes of verse and of prose (*Latitudes,* 1940; *Rostros y climas,* 1948; *Viajes por países y libros,* 1962), that record his intimate and sentimental communion with the people and places and things of his *ciclo infinito.* Brief incursions into journalism and politics and his passing attention to other pursuits, now as essayist or as translator of contemporary French poetry, now as director of *Letras del Ecuador* or of *El correo,* the Spanish edition of UNESCO's journal, have never seriously interfered with his lyric commentary on the fragile, lonely condition of man and on the transitory state of all things as he views them through the eyes of the heart.

SUGGESTED READING

"El objeto y su sombra," "Vida perfecta," "Vida del grillo," "Lo que es el caracol," "Lagartija," "Nuez," "Morada terrestre," "Formas de la delicia pasajera," "Biografía para uso de los pájaros," "Soledad de las ciudades," "Juan sin cielo," "Alabanza del Ecuador."

TEXTS

Anderson Imbert and Florit, 678-680. Caillet-Bois, 1455-1463. Onís, 1159-1166.

EDITIONS

Registro del mundo, antología poética, 1922-1939, México, Séneca, 1945. *Edades poéticas (1922-1956),* Quito, Casa de la Cultura Ecuatoriana, 1958. *Mi vida en poemas,* Caracas, Eds. Casa del Escritor, 1962; with "Ensayo autocrítico."

TRANSLATIONS

G. R. Coulthard and Kathleen Nott (trans.), *Visit of Mist,* London, Williams and Norgate, 1950. Fitts, 2-21. Hays, 140-167. Jones, 104-107. Muna Lee (trans.), *Secret Country,* New York, Macmillan, 1946; introduction by John Peale Bishop. *Three Spanish American Poets,* 49-73.

CRITICAL REFERENCES

See texts and editions above. H. R. Hays, "Jorge Carrera Andrade, Magician of Metaphors," *Books Abroad,* XVII (1943), 101-105. *Diccionario . . . Ecuador,* 94-99. William F. Heald, "*Soledad* in the Poetry of Jorge Carrera Andrade," *PMLA,* LXXVI (1961), 608-612. Julian Palley, "Temática de Jorge Carrera Andrade," *Hispania,* XXXIX (1956), 80-83.

°6. (Cuba) **Nicolás Guillén** (1902-   ) was born in Camagüey, of African and Spanish descent. He began to study law at the University of Havana, but was early attracted to journalism and writing, and to these and to the lecture platform, he has devoted most of his life. He has traveled extensively in Europe, Asia, and America. His interest in African folklore and his concern over the fate of his people have made of his poetry one of the best expressions of the spiritual fusion of white and black in the Spanish tongue. In his first volume, *Motivos de son* (1930), Guillén easily and early established himself as an artistic interpreter of Negro dialect, rhythms, and moods. But his mastery of these basic ingredients of all Afro-American verse has not been confined to popular portrayals of the sensuous abandon of those of his race in their exotic island setting. Beginning with *Sóngoro cosongo* in 1931, the poet's voice continues to rise in vigorous protest against oppression of any hue anywhere in the world. Redolent still with the rich nativist flavor of his early verse, his later volumes—*West Indies Ltd,* 1934; *Cantos para soldados y sones para turistas,* 1937; *España: Poema en cuatro angustias y una esperanza,* 1937; *La paloma de vuelo popular: Elegías,* 1948—sweep the poet along full square within the main currents of the better social protest literature of our time.

SUGGESTED READING

"Mulata," "Sóngoro cosongo," "Tú no sabe inglé," "La canción del bongó," "Canto negro," "Velorio de Papá Montero," "Balada del güije," "Sensemayá," "Sabás," "Dos niños," "José Ramón Cantaliso," "No sé por qué piensas tú . . . ," "Un largo lagarto verde."

TEXTS

Anderson Imbert and Florit, 671-673. Ballagas, *Mapa,* 115-126. Caillet-Bois, 1463-1469. Güirao, 84-104. Vitier, 230-239.

EDITIONS

El son entero, Buenos Aires, Pleamar, 1947 (with selections from all previous titles, including inedited poems, musical scores for six of the poems, and vocabulary). *La paloma de vuelo popular: Elegías,* Buenos Aires, Losada, 1948.

TRANSLATIONS

Fitts, 262-277. Hays, 218-237. Langston Hughes and Ben Frederick Carruthers (trans.) *Cuba libre,* Los Angeles, Anderson and Ritchie, 1948 (selections from *El son entero,* with illustrations). Jones, 74-78.

CRITICAL REFERENCES

See texts and editions above. Marinello, 79-93. Olivera, 137-139.

7. (Mexico) **Carlos Pellicer (1899-1977) was born in Villahermosa, Tabasco. Upon graduation from the Escuela Nacional Preparatoria, he was sent as a university student attaché to Bogotá where he completed his studies and prepared for later diplomatic assignments in

America and Europe. From Brazil, where he had gone with the Vasconcelos mission in 1922, he made the rounds of the other Latin American republics, and from 1926 to 1929 he was on a study tour of the Near East. He has taught literature and history at his alma mater and in the secondary schools, and has occupied a number of administrative posts, including that of director of the Palacio de Bellas Artes. More recently he has been active in archeology and has distinguished himself as a museologist. As a creative artist he has devoted himself wholly and exclusively to poetry. His first published work, *Colores en el mar y otros poemas,* appeared in 1921. In his earlier years he sought a common goal with his friends in the pages of *Ulises* (1927-1928) and *Contemporáneos* (1928-1931). *Hora de junio (1929-1936),* published in 1937, *Recinto* (1941), and the volumes that follow are evidence of his steady growth as a profound and subtle poet, as a consummate master of imagery, rhythm and form. Brilliant, sensuous, plastic, his poetry reflects "the color, the light, the water, and the mountains of America." He is a member of the Academia Mexicana de la Lengua.

SUGGESTED READING

"El puerto de Curazao," "Recuerdo de Iza (Un pueblecito de los Andes)," "Deseos," "Segador," "La aurora," "Estudio" (1927), "Grupos de palomas," "A la poesía" (1929), "Esquemas para una oda tropical," "Horas de junio" (I, II, IV, V), "Tema para un nocturno," "He olvidado mi nombre," "La balada de los tres suspiros," "Memorias de la Casa de Viento."

TEXTS

Anderson Imbert and Florit, 662-663. Caillet-Bois, 1334-1339. Castro Leal, 271-286. Onís, 1137-1145.

EDITIONS

Material poético (1918-1961), México, Univ. Nacional, 1962.

CRITICAL REFERENCES

See texts and editions above. Leiva, 91-108. Martínez, *Lit. mex. siglo XX, passim.*

*8 (Mexico) **Jaime Torres Bodet** (1902–1974) graduated from the University of Mexico, where he taught French literature from 1924 to 1928. He published his first volume of verse, *Fervor,* in 1918, and in 1921 accepted his first public office as secretary of the Escuela Nacional Preparatoria from which he had graduated but three years earlier. From that time on Torres Bodet has pursued both lines of endeavor, writing and public affairs, with marked success. He has rendered distinguished service to his country on diplomatic missions to Spain, Italy, Belgium, Holland, Argentina, and France, and as minister of foreign affairs, minister of education—a post to which he has been recalled but recently (1958)—and director-general of UNESCO (1948-1951). In his autobiography, *Tiempo de arena* (1955), he fills in the details of his early years as writer and as public servant until his recognition as one of the leading spirits of the generation of *Contemporáneos* (1928-1931) and his first foreign service appointment, to Spain, in 1929. Expanding intellectual and cultural interests and successive waves of evolving esthetic experience have never impelled his muse to deviate significantly from the lyric simplicity and the subdued emotional tones of his formative years. He was early attracted to the novel and the short story. It is here that he more readily reveals a fruitful response to the new prose of the great French masters of the day, to Gide and Proust and Giraudoux.

SUGGESTED READING

Poetry: "México canta en la ronda de mis canciones de amor," "Paz," "Mediodía," "Ruptura," "Eco," "Despertar," "Música," "La danza," "Fe," "Cascada," "Flecha," "La noria." Prose: "Nacimiento de Venus," *Proserpina rescatada* and *Tiempo de arena* (selections).

TEXTS

Anthology, 811-815. Anderson Imbert and Florit, 698-703. Caillet-Bois, 1474-1477. Castro Leal, 298-307. Cuesta, 119-129. Onís, 995-1002.

EDITIONS

Poetry: *Poesías,* Madrid, Espasa-Calpe, 1926. *Sonetos,* México, Gráfica Panamericana, 1949. *Sin tregua,* México, Tezontle, 1957. Prose: *Margarita la niebla* (novel), México, Cultura, 1927. *La educación sentimental* (novel), Madrid, Espasa-Calpe, 1929. *Proserpina rescatada* (novel), Madrid, Espasa-Calpe, 1931. *Nacimiento de Venus y otros relatos,* México, Cultura, 1941. *Obras escogidas,* México, Fondo de Cultura Económica, 1961.

TRANSLATIONS

Blackwell, 164-167. Fitts, 108-121. Johnson, 186-189. Jones, 48-50. Sonja P. Karsen (trans.), *Selected Poems of Jaime Torres Bodet,*

Bloomington, Indiana Univ. Press, 1964; a bilingual edition of forty-four poems. *Trans. from Hisp. Poets,* 236-239. Underwood, 172-177.
> CRITICAL REFERENCES

See texts above. Anderson Imbert, II, 160-161. Frank Dauster, "La poesía de Jaime Torres Bodet," *Revista iberoamericana,* 49 (1960), 73-94. Leiva, 123-136. Martínez, *Lit. mex. siglo XX, passim.*

°9. (Mexico) **Xavier Villaurrutia** (1903-1950). See III, 3 below.

°10. (Mexico) **Octavio Paz** (1914-   ) was born and educated in Mexico. Under a Guggenheim fellowship awarded in 1943, he pursued advanced studies in the United States on Spanish American poetry. He was witness to the Spanish Civil War *("decisiva para mi generación"),* an experience that bore fruit in *¡No pasarán!* (1936). He has traveled widely in Europe and the Far East, having served his country in diplomatic posts in France, India, Japan and Switzerland. As one of the founders and leading spirits of *Taller* (1938-1941), he soon became recognized as the most representative poet of his generation. As essayist and critic he has analyzed his country's national character in *El laberinto de la soledad* (1950); and in *El arco y la lira* (1956) and *Las peras del olmo* (1957) he has made significant contributions toward a more fruitful appreciation of contemporary poetry. Paz himself has rejected the early lyric exercises of his first collection, *Luna silvestre,* published in 1933. His essential poetic stature is well mirrored in *A la orilla del mundo* (1942) and *Libertad bajo palabra* (1949). His affinity to the surrealists is clear, but by his own admission his poetic effort more nearly resembles that of certain modern poets of his own tongue, specifically Cernuda, whose art reflects similar surrealist leanings.
> SUGGESTED READING

Poetry: "Arcos," "Medianoche," "Dos cuerpos," "El sediento," "Más allá del amor," "Espejo," "Pregunta," "El muro," "Adiós a la casa," "La calle," "El regreso," "La poesía." Prose: "Máscaras mexicanas" and "La 'inteligencia' mexicana."
> TEXTS

Anderson Imbert and Florit, 666-668. Arellano, 265-272. Caillet-Bois, 1752-1761. Castro Leal, 415-423.

EDITIONS
Poetry: *Libertad bajo palabra (Obra poética, 1935-1958)*, México, Fondo de Cultura Económica, 1960. Prose: *El laberinto de la soledad*, 2nd ed., México, Fondo de Cultura Económica, 1952. *Las peras del olmo*, México, Imp. Universitaria, 1957.

TRANSLATIONS
Jones, 50-53. Lysander Kemp (trans.), *The Labyrinth of Solitude; Life and Thought in Mexico*, New York, Grove Press, 1961 (paperback, 1963). Muriel Rukeyser (trans., with foreword), *Sun Stone*, New York, New Directions, 1963; also her *Selected Poems of Octavio Paz*, Bloomington, Indiana Univ. Press, 1963; a bilingual edition of forty-nine poems.

CRITICAL REFERENCES
See texts and editions above. Dauster, 173-175. John M. Fein, "The Mirror as Image and Theme in the Poetry of Octavio Paz," *Symposium*, X (1956), 251-270. Leiva, 205-226.

II.
Prose

Since the outbreak of the Mexican Revolution in 1910 the principal tendencies in prose fiction have been the following: a continuance of the modernist literature of artistic escape, often in extremely poetic style; a vigorous response to the Mexican Revolution itself; an obsession with nature, or landscape, which occasionally becomes the real protagonist; a violent, grotesque presentation of the tragic sentiment of life; an abiding interest in the illiterate masses, the forgotten men of the past century; an intense awareness of social problems, the writer identifying himself with the outcasts and the oppressed in their struggle to become an integral part of the social organism; and last of all, a fascination with philosophical problems, psychological analysis, and the world of imagination.

In récent years Spanish American writers have shown an increasing interest in universal themes, and have moved more and more away from the consideration of exterior reality to an analysis of inner feelings and thoughts. Regional literature, including gauchesque prose, the Indianist novel, the novel of the Mexican Revolution, and the novel of the land (Gallegos, Rivera, Lynch, etc.); has been yielding ground to psychological analysis and a kind of magical suprarealism in the realm of pure fantasy.

Just after the turn of the century, modernism produced two very good novels in *Sangre patricia* (1902), by the Venezuelan, Manuel Díaz Rodríguez (1868-1927) and *La gloria de don Ramiro* (1908), a story which gives an impressionistic interpretation of life in the Spain of Philip II, by the Argentine, Enrique Larreta (1875-1961). Other novels of artistic escape were *Alsino* (1920) by the Chilean, Pedro Prado (1886-1952), about a boy who learns how to fly on Icarian wings, and *El embrujo de Sevilla* (1922), a glorification of Spanish dancing, bullfighting, and *cante jondo,* by the Uruguayan, Carlos Reyles (1868-1938).

In 1914, with *La maestra normal,* by the Argentine, Manuel Gálvez (1882-1962), Spanish American realism came of age and produced a first-rate work very much in the vein of Flaubert's *Madame Bovary* (1857). Gálvez later became one of the most prolific of all Latin American novelists, but he never surpassed this early masterpiece. In 1915 the Mexican doctor, Mariano Azuela (1873-1952), who had been attached to Villa's forces, published in serial form in a newspaper in El Paso, Texas, his famous *Los de abajo,* which started a whole generation of novelists of the Mexican Revolution on their way.

In *Los de abajo* the Mexican underdogs, uprooted from the past and swept into the revolution against Díaz, blindly strike out against all authority, and revert to basic animal passions as they revel in murder and robbery. Azuela and the novelists of the Revolution break with the past and with European literary traditions. They get their material directly from the battlefields, and describe things they have actually seen. They present crowds and types; the hero as such is nonexistent, and the real protagonist is the masses or the Revolution itself. The Indian, formerly only used as an element of local color, becomes all important in these revolutionary novels. The author is submerged; he is merely a camera's eye taking in the scenes before him. He writes with a single-minded intensity, and everything he describes is clear-cut and direct, with even the landscape related to the action. The revolutionary novel is terse and pithy; it rarely exceeds 250 pages. It seldom contains a love theme, and does not moralize. It presents a regional manifestation of universal violence in the Darwinian struggle for survival, objective, sharply etched, rapid in action. A sense of morbid and grotesque doom pervades its pages, for its characters walk hand in hand with death.

But the Revolution was more than death. It became a symbol. The umbilical cord was cut, separating Mexico from her colonial past, and a new life was cast upon the waters of chaos. The novel of the Revolution which caught all this was something distinctly Mexican and distinctly new in Spanish American letters.

The next group of outstanding novels in Spanish American literature falls into the regionalist category: *El inglés de los güesos* (1924) by Benito Lynch (1880-1951) of Argentina, *La vorágine* (1924) by the Colombian José Eustasio Rivera (1888-1929), *Don Segundo Sombra* (1926) by the Argentine Ricardo Güiraldes (1886-1927), and *Doña Bárbara* (1929) by the Venezuelan Rómulo Gallegos (1884-1969). In this quartet, landscape molds, and frequently overshadows, character. In *La vorágine* it becomes the protagonist. The jungle overpowers man; society does not exist. In *El inglés de los güesos*, *Don Segundo Sombra* and *Doña Bárbara* landscape unity—the unity of the pampas and the unity of the llanos—casts in a single mold the people who live in these geographic regions, and collective regional types emerge, the gaucho and the llanero personalities. A body of folk culture evolves around these two types, in opposition to the civilized and more European cultures of the seaboard cities, and between these two societies a conflict is joined. City and hinterland, civilization and barbarism, Europe and Spanish America: such are the opposing poles of this struggle. *El inglés de los güesos* reduces the contest to one of individual emotions, symbolic of their cultures. Both *Don Segundo Sombra* and *Doña Bárbara* present the final stages of the conflict. In *Don Segundo Sombra* civilization has already won, and the gaucho is merely a vestige of the past, out of place in the new industrial society. Güiraldes calls him back to life as an epic writer might bring back to life the heroes of the past in order to recount their deeds. The novel, therefore, is the evocation of a world that has ended.

Among the four above-mentioned regional novelists, Rómulo Gallegos and Benito Lynch are the only ones who go on to produce a whole body of novels. Güiraldes and Rivera are known mainly for a single prose work. Other well-known regionalists are Gregorio López y Fuentes (1895-1967) and José Rubén Romero (1890-1952) of Mexico, Jorge Icaza (1906-   ) of Ecuador, Alcides Arguedas (1879-1946) of Bolivia, Ciro Alegría (1909-1967) of Peru, with his trilogy of novels about the Indians and mestizos of the Andes, the precious and unique Teresa de la Parra (1895-1936) of Venezuela, also Arturo Uslar Pietri (1905-   ) of Venezuela, and Miguel Angel Asturias (1899-1974) and Mario Monteforte Toledo (1911-   ) of Guatemala. Carlos Reyles of Uruguay also produced many realistic novels in the regionalist tradition. Enrique Amorim (1900-1960) of Uruguay and José María Arguedas (1911-1969) of Peru are noteworthy novelists who have linked regionalism with astute psychological insight. All of these writers show an increasing desire to penetrate and interpret the psychology of the characters presented. The psychological novel eventually emerges from native regionalism with obvious European overtones. Around 1930 this change has already begun to manifest itself and the changes in the novelistic techniques in Europe are clearly reflected in Spanish American writers. One of these, Eduardo Barrios (1884-1963) of Chile, had already produced a psychological masterpiece, *El hermano asno,* as far back as 1922. He went on to write many others, the most famous of which is *Los hombres del hombre* (1950). Among the many Europeans who were popular in Latin America in the 1920's and 1930's were the Russian Dostoievsky (1821-1881); the Frenchmen, Marcel Proust (1871-1922), André Gide (1869-1951), Jules Romains (1885-1972), Jean Cocteau (1891-1963); the Germanic Franz Werfel (1890-1945), Arnold Zweig (1887-1968), Franz Kafka (1883-1924); the Englishmen, D. H. Lawrence (1885-1930), Virginia Woolf (1882-1961), Aldous Huxley (1894-1963); and of course, the famous Irishman, James Joyce (1882-1941). The North Americans, Ernest Hemingway (1898-1961), John Dos Passos (1896-1970), and William Faulkner (1897-1962) asserted their very strong influence.

      Agustín Yáñez (1904-   ) of Mexico is the author of the most famous Spanish American novel of the past twenty years, *Al filo del agua* (1947). It is a powerful poetic evocation of hermetic life in a small Mexican town in Jalisco. Yáñez uses Freudian psychology as a sharp tool to mold his characters. Joyce and Faulkner are his primary masters. Stylistically *Al filo del agua* is the best prose work to come out of Mexico in this century. Luis Spota (1925-   ) of Mexico has several good psychological novels to his credit. Spota's *Más cornadas da el hambre* (1951), about bullfighting in the small towns of Mexico, and *Casi el Paraíso* (1956), about a man who poses as a prince in modern Mexican high society, exemplify this writer's versatility.

      The existential and philosophical novelist par excellence is Eduardo Mallea (1903-   ) of Argentina, whose first noteworthy success was *Fiesta en noviembre* (1938), concerning the vapid life of the young Argentine intellectuals. This work was followed by *La bahía de silencio* (1940) and *Todo verdor perecerá* (1941) which extended the novelist's reputation. *El túnel* (1948), by Ernesto

Sábato (1912-   ) of Argentina, also is another excellent existential novel, with overtones of Sartre and Camus. Juan Carlos Onetti (1909-   ) of Uruguay is another widely read existential novelist of the River Plate area. Manuel Rojas (1896-1973) of Chile, known first as a short-story writer, came out in 1951 with the best existential novel to appear in Chile to date, *Hijo de ladrón,* called *Born Guilty* in its English version. This was followed by a series of other novels in the same vein, none of which has the power of *Hijo de ladrón.*

Novelists who fuse the anguish of existentialism with a Kafkian imagination and a desire to transcend the limits of time, space, and physical reality are Alejo Carpentier (1904-   ), Cuba's best-known novelist of this century; María Luisa Bombal (1910-   ) of Chile; José Revueltas (1914-1976), Juan Rulfo (1918-   ), and Carlos Fuentes (1928-   ) of Mexico, creators of a kind of Mexican suprarealism. Bombal's *La última niebla* (1935) and *La amortajada* (1938) are fascinating creations of a refined feminine soul, while Carpentier's *Los pasos perdidos* (1953) is an artistic and mythological evocation of man's search for happiness. Fuentes' *La región más transparente* (1958) was the first of several well-received novels from the pen of this gifted young man, and *Pedro Páramo* (1955), a series of lives in a timeless, never-never land, is Rulfo's only novel.

As might be expected in the presence of a hard, tragic, and bitter social reality, humor is a rare commodity in the contemporary Spanish American novel, but *El socio* (1929) by Jenaro Prieto (1889-1946) of Chile, and *La luna era mi tierra* (1948) by Enrique Araya (1910-   ), also of Chile, are good examples of what has been achieved in this direction. The tongue-in-cheek irony of both novels is distinctly Chilean.

The short story has followed a course similar to that of the novel. Between 1915 and 1935 the main short-story writers were Horacio Quiroga (1878-1937) of Uruguay, Manuel Rojas of Chile, and Alfonso Hernández-Catá (1885-1940) of Cuba. The first two of these writers blend local color with psychological analysis and a vivid imagination, while Hernández-Catá sticks to a dramatic presentation of the abnormal elements present in every-day life. Rafael Arévalo Martínez (1884-   ) of Guatemala carries the modernist short story to its highest peak. He is also a novelist of utopian ideas.

The most famous short-story writer of the past three decades is Jorge Luis Borges (1899-   ) of Argentina, who has produced a series of fascinating stories which are exercises in intellectual ingenuity. Borges is a writer who has taken the best science fiction as a starting point and has carried it to the level of first-rate intellectual literature. Borges has had many recent imitators, but none has approached the master in overall finish or suspense. In Mexico Juan Rulfo and Juan José Arreola (1918-   ) have followed the latest novelistic trends with their tales of fantasy which take place in a kind of twilight zone, eerie and timeless. Other well-known short-story writers of the fifties and sixties are Marco Denevi (1922-   ) of Argentina, winner of the recent *Life en español* contest for the best Latin American short story; Juan Carlos Onetti (1909-   ) and Mario Benedetti (1920-   ) of Uruguay; Francisco Coloane (1910–   ) and José Donoso (1925–   ) of Chile; Julio Cortazar (1914-   ) of Argentina; Augusto Monterroso (1922-   ) of Guatemala; and Sebastián Salazar Bondy (1924-1965) of Peru. Hector Velarde (1898-   ) of Peru is the outstanding humorist among the contemporary short-story writers.

The contemporary psychological novel and short story represent a retreat from landscape and primitivism, and a defense against these elements, reflecting a conscious effort on the part of the writer of today to find inspiration in civilization as over barbarism, in man as over nature, in the twentieth century and its universal neuroses as over the ubiquitous past which obstructs the establishment of society and the progress of man.

The desire to rediscover America in all its savage and virgin beauty, led to a repudiation of Europe and of European literary tendencies, writes Uslar Pietri, a contemporary Venezuelan novelist and literary critic. In contemporary Spanish American fiction, man is placed in perpetual tension, spiritual and physical, against the background of a society in flux or of unconquered and unassimilated natural forces. There is no stable or known reality. The great ferment of the European author is the rebellion of the individual against tradition. Spanish American writers are struggling to establish a tradition. They may reiterate the myth of human impotence, but they also extol the verity of human longing, and seek to focus that longing on a new reality. This new order is beginning to emerge, but nowhere is its emergence complete.

The Spanish American essay, like the novel and short story, has moved gradually from a position of defense to a position of critical self-scrutiny. Manuel Ugarte's (1878-1951) campaigns against the causes of U. S. imperialism in Latin America, so much in the public eye in the 1920's, no longer hold much interest. The essays of José Vasconcelos (1882-1959), amateurish reflections on the issues of race-mixing, world history, and the roots of Hispanic culture, also now appear somewhat pallid. Alfonso Reyes (1889-1959), former dean of Mexican letters, is a writer whose essays, on almost every possible cultural theme, are more firmly rooted in wide reading and profound factual knowledge. There have been many fine literary critics among the essayists: Arturo Torres-Ríoseco (1897-1971) and Fernando Alegría (1918-   ) of Chile, the latter is a professor at Stanford University; Pedro (1884-1946) and Max Henríquez Ureña (1885-1968) of the Dominican Republic; Alberto Zum Felde (1888-   ) of Uruguay; the Argentines, Victoria Ocampo (1891-   ), Enrique Anderson Imbert (1910-), professor emeritus of Harvard University, and Roberto Giusti (1897-   ), editor of the journal Nosotros. (1907-1943).

Francisco Romero (1891-1962) of Argentina writes more in the philosophical vein. Colombia has produced the very eclectic Germán Arciniegas (1900-   ) and Baldomero Sanín Cano (1861-1957), cosmopolitan essayist with an encyclopedic mind. Mariano Picón-Salas (1901-1965) of Venezuela has linked history to cultural and literary themes. In Mexico Leopoldo Zea (1912-   ) and Antonio Alatorre (1922-   ) are outstanding. There have been innumerable essayists of social protest: José Carlos Mariátegui (1895-1930) and Raúl Haya de la Torre (1895-   ) of Peru; Benjamín Subercaseaux (1902-   ) of Chile; and a host of Mexicans. Eduardo Mallea of Argentina has also written essays probing the dark depths of his country's heart, and the works of Ezequiel Martínez Estrada (1895-1964), *Radiografía de la pampa* (1933), *La cabeza de Goliath* (1940), and *Muerte y transfiguración de Martín Fierro* (1948), are a devastating commentary on Argentina life. Octavio Paz (1914-   ) of Mexico, primarily a poet, has also taken up the pen to scrutinize his nation's soul. The Spanish American essayist is today thoroughly identified with the environment in which he lives.

During the past two or three decades, with the rise of psychological analysis, graphic imagery, and anguished self-scrutiny to a preeminent place in Spanish American literature, today's author of fiction is coming more and more to realize the great truth of literature and of life: it is not the particular emotion or tragedy that is important to man, but rather emotion or tragedy itself, which, cruel and omnipresent, ennobles his life or casts upon it the cold dark shadow, whatever his social state. The attempt to specify this anguish and this longing of Everyman is the heart of all great literature.

REFERENCES

Alegría, *Breve hist.*, 114-276. Anderson Imbert, II, *passim*. Barbagelata, *passim*. Brushwood and Rojas Garciduéñas, *passim*. Castro Leal, *Novela*, *passim*. Crawford, *passim*. Flores, 383-695. González, *Trayectoria*, Chaps. VI-XXI; also his *Estudios*, 183-383. Latcham, *passim*. Martínez, *Lit. mex. siglo XX;* also his *Ensayo*, *passim*. Mead, *Ensayo*, Chaps. VII-VIII. *Memoria del quinto congreso: La novela iberoamericana*, *passim*. Morton, *passim*. Sánchez, *Proceso y contenido*, *passim*. Spell, *passim*. Torres-Ríoseco, *Grandes novelistas*. M. Vitier, *passim*. Zum Felde, *Índice crítico*, I, *El ensayo*, 411-600; II, *La narrativa*, *passim*.

A. ESSAY

°1. (Venezuela) **Rufino Blanco-Fombona** (1874-1944), officeholder, diplomat, and several times a political prisoner during his early years, was forced to seek refuge in Europe, where he spent much of his life. It was not until after the death of Gómez in 1935 that he returned to his native land. As editor and publisher of his world-famous series of American books (Biblioteca "Andrés Bello," "Ayacucho," etc.), he contributed much toward making Spanish American literature more widely known. He was one of the most prolific, if not the most objective, literary critics of his generation. His criticism is highly charged with personal feelings and preferences. His poems and short stories are artistically superior to his novels, most of which, passion, satire, and diatribe tend to reduce to the level of polemical journalism. It is, however, as an essayist and a thinker that he has exerted his greatest influence. Even before the turn of the century he began his fiery anti-Yankee campaign, pleading for union against the northern tyrant. He was also one of the most ardent defenders of Spain's role in America and a strong proponent of dynamic Spanish Americanism.

SUGGESTED READING

"Noticias yanquis," *Camino de imperfección* and *El conquistador español del siglo XVI* (selections).

TEXTS

Anthology, 617-625. Anderson Imbert and Florit, 513-517. Holmes, *Span. Am.*, 529-532. Jones and Hansen, 74-82. Onís, 447-460. *El hombre de oro* (ed. Warren), New York, Oxford Univ. Press, 1948. Weisinger, 215-229.

EDITIONS

Cuentos americanos (1904), París, Garnier, [1913]. *El hombre de hierro* (1907), Madrid, Ed. América, [1916]. *La evolución política y social de Hispanoamérica*, Madrid, B. Rodríguez, 1911. *La lámpara de Aladino*, Madrid, Renacimiento, 1915. *El hombre de oro*, Madrid, Ed. América, [1916]. *El conquistador español del siglo XVI* (1922), Caracas, Edime, 1956; prologue by Joaquín Gabaldón Márquez, bibliographical study by Edgar Gabaldón Márquez. *El modernismo y los modernistas*, Madrid, Mundo Latino, 1929. *Camino de imperfección: diario de mi vida (1906-1913)*, Madrid, Ed. América, [1933]. *El espejo de tres faces*, Santiago, Ercilla, 1937.

TRANSLATIONS

Blackwell, 428-429. Isaac Goldberg (trans.), *The Man of Gold*, New York, Brentano's, 1920. Jones, 276-280. *Trans from Hisp. Poets*, 265.

CRITICAL REFERENCES

See texts and editions above. Francisco Carmona Nenclares, *Vida y literatura de Rufino Blanco-Fombona*, Madrid, Mundo Latino, 1928. García Godoy, *Amer. lit.*, 197-244. Goldberg, 307-359. Gilberto González y Contreras, *Radiografía y disección de Rufino Blanco-Fombona*, Habana, Lex, 1944. M. Henríquez Ureña, *Breve hist.*, 289-296. Mead, *Ensayo*, 80-82. Onís, 444-447. Ratcliff, 145-172.

°2. (Argentina) **Manuel Ugarte** (1878-1951), militant propagandist, campaigned widely throughout Spanish America in the second decade of this century in an effort to arouse concerted opposition to the growing peril of Yankee imperialism of that day. It was he who popularized the phrase *el coloso del norte* that Spanish American anti-imperialists have used ever since when referring to the United States. Ugarte, however, did not hate the United States as many of his critics have claimed. He did fear that a weak Latin America would be overwhelmed by the great nation to its north, and he attached much of the blame for this to the Latins themselves. His best creative work has been in the short story—*Cuentos de la pampa* (1903) and *Cuentos argentinos* (1908)—collections that made him famous in France, where he completed his education and where he spent a good part of his life after 1898. He also wrote verse, several novels, and books of travel impressions and literary criticism (*Escritores iberoamericanos de 1900,* 1943).

SUGGESTED READING

"La nueva Roma," "Ante la victoria anglosajona," "La prueba de la guerra," "El porvenir," and *Las mejores páginas de Manuel Ugarte* (selections).

TEXTS

Anthology, 626-638. García Calderón, *Cuentos,* 241-250. Holmes, *Span. Am.*, 65-66. Leavitt, 3-49.

EDITIONS

El porvenir de la América latina, Valencia, Sempere, 1911. *El destino de un continente,* Madrid, Mundo Latino, 1923. *Las mejores páginas de Manuel Ugarte,* Barcelona, Araluce, 1929. *Cuentos de la pampa,* Santiago, Zig-Zag, 1940. *Escritores iberoamericanos de 1900,* Santiago, Orbe, 1943.

TRANSLATIONS

Catherine A. Phillips (trans.), *The Destiny of a Continent,* New York, Knopf, 1925; edited by J. Fred Rippy.

CRITICAL REFERENCES

See texts above. Carrión, 77-117. Crawford, 148-149. M. Henríquez Ureña, *Breve hist.,* 201-203. Mead, *Ensayo,* 84-86. Zum Felde, *Índice crítico,* I, 313-317.

°3. (Peru) **Francisco García Calderón** (1883-1953), son of a former President of Peru and brother of the distinguished writer and literary critic Ventura García Calderón (1886-1959) lived almost continuously in France, where he represented his country in the diplomatic service for over thirty years. Critic, sociologist, and disciple of Rodó, he was a champion of postmodernist American ideology, interpreting America's problems from the European—specifically Latin—point of view. He was an ardent admirer of France; many of his works are written in the language of that country. One of the earliest and one of the best surveys of Latin American civilization, *Latin America: Its Rise and Progress* (1913), was written by Francisco García Calderón.

SUGGESTED READING

"El Wilsonismo," *La creación de un continente* ("Conclusión"), *Latin America: Its Rise and Progress* (selections).

TEXTS

Anthology, 639-643. Holmes, *Cont. Span. Amers.,* 67-76.

EDITIONS

Les Démocraties latines de l'Amérique, Paris, Flammarion, 1912. *La creación de un continente,* Paris, Ollendorff, [1913]. *En torno al Perú y América,* Lima, Mejía Baca, 1954.

TRANSLATIONS

Bernard Miall (trans.), *Latin America: Its Rise and Progress (Les Démocraties latines de l'Amérique),* New York, Scribner's, 1913.

CRITICAL REFERENCES

See texts above. Carrión, 117-167. García Godoy, *Amer. lit.,* 153-196. M. Vitier, 137-156.

°4. (Mexico) **José Vasconcelos** (1882-1959), born in Oaxaca, was educated in Mexico City where he was one of the members of the celebrated Ateneo de la Juventud, which had such a strong influence in revivifying Mexican intellectual life. Alfonso Reyes and Pedro Henríquez Ureña were two other well-known members of this group. Vasconcelos went on to become a successful lawyer, politician, minister of education, rector of the National University, and finally director of the National Library.

During the early 1920's (with the aid of Gabriela Mistral), when he was Mexican minister of education, Vasconcelos achieved considerable results in establishing the bases of a dynamic rural public school system. He also turned over the walls of many of Mexico's public buildings and schools to the young Mexican artists (particularly Rivera and Orozco) who later became famous throughout the world as muralists. In 1925, when the government took a strong anti-clerical stand, Vasconcelos went into voluntary exile, and did not return to his country for many years. Later, he became a zealous Catholic and turned against his early revolutionary opinions and companions. His best-known books of essays are *La raza cósmica* (1925) and *Indología* (1926), which deal with the essential ethnic and social problems of Hispanic America, and *Ulises Criollo* (1935), which is autobiographical in content. In his final years Vasconcelos became the mouthpiece of Catholic conservatism in Mexico, and took a stand against many of the progressive policies of the national and local governments. His style is facile, interesting, vigorous; his ideas are sometimes stimulating, sometimes contradictory, sometimes nonsensical. He is at all times popular rather than profound.

SUGGESTED READING

La raza cósmica ("Prólogo"), *La historia de México* ("Prólogo"), "El calor," "La cañada de la muerte," "El asunto."

TEXTS

Anthology, 653-665. Anderson Imbert and Florit, 547-551. Castillo, 373-380. Castro Leal, *Novela*, I, 532-805. Manzor, 295-301. Martínez, *Ensayo*, I, 124-146.

EDITIONS

La raza cósmica (1925), México, Espasa-Calpe, 1948 (Col. austral, 802). *Indología* (1927), 2nd ed., Barcelona, Agencia Mundial de Librería, [193?]. *Bolivarismo y monroismo* (1934), 2nd ed., Santiago, Ercilla, 1935. *Ulises Criollo* (1935-1939), 9th ed., México, Botas, 1945. *Breve historia de México* (1938), México, Botas, 1950. *Páginas escogidas*, México, Botas, 1940; edition and prologue by Antonio Castro Leal. *Obras completas*, 4 vols., México, Libreros Mexicanos Unidos, 1957-1961.

TRANSLATIONS

Arciniegas, 140-157. W. Rex Crawford (trans.), *A Mexican Ulysses: The Autobiography of José Vasconcelos*, Bloomington, Indiana Univ. Press, 1963 (paperback).

CRITICAL REFERENCES

See texts and editions above. Carrión, 23-76. Crawford, 260-276. Martínez, *Lit. mex. siglo XX*, I, 265-280. Mead, *Ensayo*, 96-100. Morton, 184-193. Patrick Romanell, *Making of the Mexican Mind*, Lincoln, Univ. of Nebraska Press, 1952, 95-138. M. Vitier, 217-233. Zum Felde, *Índice crítico*, I, 419-429.

°5. (Dominican Republic) **Pedro Henríquez Ureña** (1884-1946) and his distinguished brother Max Henríquez Urena (1885-1968) were born in the Dominican Republic but lived most of their lives in other countries. They belong to the most distinguished family of that country and have carried on the tradition of finest scholarship and human tolerance despite the despotic political regime which for so many years plagued their beautiful island. Pedro went to Cuba in 1905 and there pledged his life to a literary career. In 1906 he moved on to Mexico where he became the leader of a group of young intellectuals which eventually formed the famous Ateneo de la Juventud. Between 1917 and 1920 he and Alfonso Reyes, later dean of Mexican letters, studied in Madrid at the Centro de Estudios Históricos. The humanistic concern of both of these men led them away from the strictly positivistic cant of the *porfirista* epoch.

In 1924 Henríquez Ureña moved to Buenos Aires where he remained until his death. He was for many years the leading figure in that city's famous Instituto de Filología of the University of Buenos Aires, where he helped to train an entire generation of young Argentine intellectuals. Henríquez Ureña's writings have been voluminous and of uniformly superior quality. In the early 1940's he delivered a series of lectures in English at Harvard University which were published in 1945 with the title *Literary Currents in Hispanic America.* In 1947 his well-known *Historia de la cultura en la América hispánica,* a sensitive interpretation of Latin American civilization, appeared posthumously.

SUGGESTED READING

"La América española y su originalidad," *Seis ensayos en busca de nuestra expresión*.and *Historia de la cultura en la América hispánica* (selections).

TEXTS

Anderson Imbert and Florit, 641-644. *Pedro Henríquez Ureña: antología,* Ciudad Trujillo, Libr. Dominicana, 1950; edition and prologue, "Hermano y maestro," by Max Henríquez Ureña. *Obra crítica,* México, Fondo de Cultura Económica, 1960; edition and bibliography by Emma Susana Speratti Piñero, prologue by Jorge Luis Borges.

EDITIONS

Seis ensayos en busca de nuestra expresión (1928), Buenos Aires, Raigal, 1952. *Literary Currents in Hispanic America,* Cambridge, Harvard Univ. Press, 1945. *Las corrientes literarias en la América hispánica,* 2nd ed., México, Fondo de Cultura Económica, 1954. *Historia de la cultura en la América hispánica* (1947), 3rd ed., México, Fondo de Cultura Económica, 1955. *Plenitud de América: ensayos escogidos,* Buenos Aires, Peña, del Giudice, 1952; edited by Javier Fernández.

CRITICAL REFERENCES

See texts and editions above. Emilio Carilla, *Pedro Henríquez Ureña,* Tucumán, Univ. Nacional, s.f. [1956]. Antonio Castro Leal, "Pedro Henríquez Ureña, humanista americano," *Cuadernos americanos,* XXVIII (1946), 268-287. Mead, *Ensayo,* 106-109. *Revista iberoamericana,* 41-42 (1956); memorial volume. Alfredo A. Roggiano, *Pedro Henríquez Ureña en los Estados Unidos;* Mexico, Cultura, 1961.

°°6. (Mexico) **Alfonso Reyes** (1889-1959), poet, literary critic, scholar, humanist and diplomat, was born in Monterrey, and received his degree in law from the University of Mexico. He and Pedro Henríquez Ureña (1884-1946) worked closely together for many years in Mexico City and to them both is due the credit for establishing the famous Ateneo de la Juventud (1910-1940) of young intellectuals in that country. Later he accompanied Henríquez Ureña to Spain, and also occupied diplomatic posts in various foreign capitals. His longest residence, however, was in Spain where he worked with Menéndez Pidal, and became famous as an authority on the Spanish Golden Age. On his return to Mexico he was soon regarded as the dean of Mexican letters, the master of the younger generation, and one of the most encyclopedic essayists of the Hispanic countries. He went out of his way to give encouragement to young scholars of the United States who evinced an interest in Latin American literature, both by writing them personal letters and by offering them a means of publication in Mexico. He is one of Latin America's finest prose stylists and one of her most representative and widely respected men of universal culture. His essays cover almost every subject under the sun from Anáhuac through Goethe to Ultima Thule. They reveal a knowledge that is profound and extensive and a mind that is astute, sensitive, and eager. During the final years of his life Reyes served as director and guiding spirit of the Colegio de México, collaborated on many outstanding journals, and participated actively in a wide range of cultural activities.

SUGGESTED READING

Visión de Anáhuac (selections), "La cena," "Jacob o idea de la poesía," "Psicología dialectal," "Los desaparecidos."

TEXTS

Anthology, 666-669. Anderson Imbert and Florit, 649-657. Castillo,

389-394. Holmes, *Span. Am.,* 396-398; also his *Cont. Span. Amers.,* 109-120. Martínez, *Ensayo,* I, 266-311. Onís, 724-729.

EDITIONS

Visión de Anáhuac (1917), 2nd ed., Madrid, Índice, 1923. *Simpatías y diferencias (1921-1926),* 2nd ed., 2 vols., México, Porrúa, 1945; edition and prologue by Antonio Castro Leal. *Cuatro ingenios,* Buenos Aires, Espasa-Calpe, 1950 (Col. austral, 954). *Ancorajes,* México, Tezontle, 1951. *Obra poética,* México, Fondo de Cultura Económica, 1952. *Quince presencias (1915-1954),* México, Obregón, 1955. *Obras completas,* 19 vols., México, Fondo de Cultura Económica, 1955-1969. *Antología de Alfonso Reyes,* México, Fondo de Cultura Económica, 1963 (Col. popular).

TRANSLATIONS

Arciniegas, 225-232. Jones, 53-61. H. de Onís, 334-337; also (ed. and trans.), *The Position of America, and Other Essays,* New York, Knopf, 1950. Charles Ramsdell (trans.), *Mexico in a Nutshell, and Other Essays,* Berkeley and Los Angeles, Univ. of California Press, 1964; foreword by Arturo Torres-Ríoseco.

CRITICAL REFERENCES

See texts and editions above. *Alfonso Reyes: vida y obra, bibliografía, antología,* New York, Hispanic Institute, 1957. Martínez, *Lit. mex. siglo XX,* I, 280-287. Mead, *Ensayo,* 109-111. Manuel Olguín, *Alfonso Reyes, ensayista,* México, Studium, 1956. James Willis Robb, *Patterns of Image and Structure in the Essays of Alfonso Reyes,* Washington, Catholic Univ. of America Press, 1958. M. Vitier, 269-287.

*7. (Argentina) **Ezequiel Martínez Estrada** (1895-1964) of Argentina began his literary life as a poet and achieved a noteworthy distinction in this genre before he entered the field of the essay. His voluminous writings indicate a profound concern for the problems of Argentina, and are a mordacious dissection of that country's history and psyche. His style is filled with startling metaphors, and his criticism is thus both colorful and ruthless.

In *Radiografía de la pampa* (1933) he gives a pessimistic view of Argentina and its ills; in *La cabeza de Goliath* (1940) he examines with equal ruthlessness the megalomania of the great capital city which sits astride the windpipe of his nation. In *Muerte and transfiguración de Martín Fierro* (1948) he seeks and finds an essential gauchesque bedrock in Argentina life, which is a kind of parallel to the "essential Spain" of Unamuno, and which is a primary concern of another Argentine essayist, Eduardo Mallea. This element of the gauchesque, which is just as present today as it was yesterday, has survived every political, social, economic, cultural, and educative change in the country's life. Ezequiel Martínez Estrada's language and ideas have both exerted a profound influence on the younger generation of writers in that country who share his concern for their country's ills and its final destiny.

SUGGESTED READING

"Aislamiento," "Distancias," "Las fuerzas telúricas," "La lucha," "Los valores," from *Radiografía de la pampa*.

TEXTS

Anderson Imbert and Florit, 647-649. Onís, 885-890.

EDITIONS

Radiografía de la pampa (1933), 2nd ed., Buenos Aires, Losada, 1957. *La cabeza de Goliath* (1940), 2nd ed., Buenos Aires, Emecé, 1947. *Sarmiento*, Buenos Aires, Argos, 1946. *Muerte y transfiguración de Martín Fierro* (1948), 2nd ed., 2 vols., México, Fondo de Cultura Económica, 1958. *El mundo maravilloso de Guillermo Enrique Hudson*, México, Fondo de Cultura Económica, 1951. *Diferencias y semejanzas entre los países de la América latina*, México, Escuela Nacional de Ciencias Políticas y Sociales, 1962.

CRITICAL REFERENCES

See texts above. *Diccionario . . . Argentina*, II, 332-335. Mead, *Ensayo*, 118-120. H. A. Murena, "Martínez Estrada: la lección a los desposeídos," in *Sur*, 204 (1951), 1-18. Zum Felde, *Índice crítico*, I, 472-480.

°8. (Colombia) **Germán Arciniegas** (1900-) was born in Bogotá and was educated at the National University. At the age of twenty-one he became editor of the journal *Voz de la juventud*, and later was director of the publishing house Ediciones Colombia and also a member of the board of editors of the distinguished journal *El tiempo* (1930-1933). He has been a frequent contributor to *La nación* of Buenos Aires, and to other outstanding periodicals in Latin America and in the United States. In addition to his activities as a writer, Arciniegas has also served his country well in several diplomatic posts. He taught Spanish American literature and sociology in the United States for an extended period at Columbia, University of

Chicago, Mills College, and other institutions. He was for a time, Colombian Minister of Education, and served for several years as editor-in-chief of the *Revista de América* (1944-1948) of Bogotá.

Arciniegas is the most distinguished writer of Colombia now that the grand old man of Colombian letters, Baldomero Sanín Cano (1861-1957), is dead. His principal interest has been in the broad sociological and literary history of Latin America and of Colombia. He is a writer of stimulating ideas and wide cultural training and reading. Several of his best books have been translated into English, and the anthology published in English under his editorship, *The Green Continent* (1944), consists of many excellent selections by Latin American authors which give their views of their own regions, culture, and problems.

SUGGESTED READING
"La América del Pacífico," "Los mareantes," "Preludio del siglo XX."

TEXTS
Anderson Imbert and Florit, 739-742.

EDITIONS
El estudiante de la mesa redonda (1932), Santiago, Ercilla, 1936. *América, tierra firme*, Santiago, Ercilla, 1937. *El caballero de El Dorado*, Buenos Aires, Losada, 1942. *Este pueblo de América*, México, Fondo de Cultura Económica; 1945. *América mágica: los hombres y los meses* (1959), Buenos Aires, Sudamericana, 1961.

TRANSLATIONS
Mildred Adams (trans.), *The Knight of El Dorado*, New York, Viking, 1942; also *Caribbean, Sea of the New World*, New York, Knopf, 1946; also *The State of Latin America*, New York, Knopf, 1952; also *Amerigo and the New World*, New York, Knopf, 1955.

CRITICAL REFERENCES
See texts above. Federico Córdova, *Vida y obras de Germán Arciniegas*, Habana, Ministerio de Educación, 1950. *Diccionario . . . Colombia*, 141-142. Mead, *Ensayo*, 124-125. M. Vitier, 251-268.

*9. (Venezuela) **Mariano Picón-Salas** (1901-1965) is Venezuela's best-known essayist of this century. Like his famous compatriot Andrés Bello, he spent much of his life in Chile where he obtained his doctor's degree in philosophy and where his personality as a writer was formed. He also became known in Chile as a teacher of literature and cultural history. After many years of exile he returned to his native country where he occupied a position in the Ministry of Education. After this he joined the Venezuelan diplomatic corps in Prague, and was able to travel widely in France, Italy, Germany, and Austria. On his return to Venezuela, via Buenos Aires and Chile, he became editor of the well-known journal, *Revista nacional de cultura,* published in Caracas. During the early 1950's he visited the United States and was a visiting professor at Columbia, UCLA, and other institutions. When the Pérez Jiménez dictatorship ended in 1958, he again returned to Venezuela and became one of the leaders of that country's intellectual life. He taught in the National University, was dean of its division of humanities, and continued to collaborate on many cultural journals. His essays, written in a pungent style and with a sober and probing perspective, are among the most stimulating interpretations of Hispanic American culture and history. His best-known work is perhaps his *De la conquista a la independencia* (1944), a study of the evolution of Latin American civilization, which has been translated into English by Irving A. Leonard.

SUGGESTED READING

"El sueño de la libertad política," "Arte y libertad creadora," "Los batracios," and *De la conquista a la independencia* (selections).

TEXTS

Anderson Imbert and Florit, 733-736. Latcham, 30-31, 172-182.

EDITIONS

De la conquista a la independencia (1944), 3rd ed., México, Fondo de Cultura Económica, 1958. *Viaje al amanecer* (1943), 2nd ed., Buenos Aires, Losada, 1959 (Bibl. contemporánea, 216). *Crisis, cambio, tradición* (Ensayos sobre la forma de nuestra cultura), Caracas-Madrid, Edime, s.f. [1952?]. *Obras selectas,* Madrid, Edime, 1953. *Comprensión de Venezuela,* Madrid, Aguilar, 1955; prologue by Hernando Téllez. *Ensayos escogidos,* Santiago, Zig-Zag, 1958; edition by Juan Loveluck, prologue by Ricardo A. Latcham.

TRANSLATIONS

Irving A. Leonard (trans.), *A Cultural History of Spanish America: from Conquest to Independence,* Berkeley and Los Angeles, Univ. of California Press, 1963 (paperback).

CRITICAL REFERENCES

See texts above. González, *Estudios,* 305-309. Mead, *Ensayo,* 125-126.

Antonio Sánchez Carillo, "El mensaje de Mariano Picón-Salas," *Cuadernos americanos,* LXXXII (1955), 143-148.

°10. (Mexico) **Octavio Paz** (1914-   ). See I, B, 10, above.

B. FICTION

a. SOCIAL PROTEST

°°1. (Argentina) **Manuel Gálvez** (1882-1962) took his degree in law from the University of Buenos Aires in 1904. He wrote a thesis on the white slave trade, and evinced an early interest in social problems. In 1903 he was co-founder of the literary journal *Ideas*. Later, he was made supervisor of secondary education in Argentina. He traveled in Europe, mainly in Spain, and one of his earliest books, *El solar de la raza* (1911), presents Spain and Spanish character as the bedrock of the race. In 1917 Gálvez established a large publishing house, the Cooperativa Editorial de Buenos Aires. His first popular success in the field of fiction was *La maestra normal* (1914), one of the best realistic novels to come out of Spanish America. Both as a psychological study and as the portraiture of life in a small Argentine town, La Rioja, this work is outstanding. In the many novels that followed, Gálvez attempted to present a complete cross section of Argentine life. The best known of these are *La sombra del convento* (1917) and *Nacha Regules* (1919). He also wrote (1928-1929) a forceful trilogy on the Paraguayan war, and is the author of several books of straight history, including interesting biographies of the Venezuelan revolutionary, Francisco de Miranda (1752-1816), and of the Argentine Presidents, Sarmiento (1811-1888) and Irigoyen (1850-1933). Gálvez writes in a simple, flowing style, without any attempt at literary or regional ostentation, and is one of the easiest of all Hispanic novelists to read. This has undoubtedly made him one of the most popular writers of his region.

Gálvez was proposed for the Nobel Prize by a large group of eminent writers and scholars in the Hispanic field, but did not receive the award. He was, however, the recipient of many national and international prizes. His death in 1962 ended a fruitful epoch in Argentine literature.

SUGGESTED READING

La maestra normal or *La sombra del convento.*

TEXTS

Crow, 17-24. *Las dos vidas del pobre Napoleón* (ed. Lichtblau), New York, Scribner's, 1963.

EDITIONS

La maestra normal (1914), 8th ed., Buenos Aires, Tor, 1950. *El mal metafísico* (1916), Buenos Aires, Espasa-Calpe, 1950 (Col. austral, 433). *La sombra del convento* (1917), Buenos Aires, Agencia General de Librería y Publicaciones, 1922. *Nacha Regules* (1919), Buenos Aires, Losada, 1960 (Bibl. contemporánea, 76). *La tragedia de un hombre fuerte* (1922), Buenos Aires, Tor, 1938. *Escenas de la guerra del Paraguay:* I, *Los caminos de la muerte* (1928), Buenos Aires, Losada, 1957 (Bibl. contemporánea, 159); II, *Humaitá* (1929), Buenos Aires, Losada, 1959 (Bibl. contemporánea, 193); III, *Jornadas de agonía* (1929), Buenos Aires, Losada, 1959 (Bibl. contemporánea, 213). *La argentina en nuestros libros,* Santiago, Ercilla, 1935. *Vida de Hipólito Irigoyen,* Buenos Aires, Kraft, 1939. *Hombres en soledad* (1939), Buenos Aires, Losada, 1957 (Bibl. contemporánea, 88). *Obras escogidas,* Madrid, Aguilar, 1949; prologue by the author. *El novelista y las novelas,* Buenos Aires, Emecé, 1959. *Me mataron entre todos,* Buenos Aires, Emecé, 1962.

TRANSLATIONS

Leo Ongley (trans.), *Nacha Regules,* New York, Dutton, 1922. Warre B. Wells (trans.), *Holy Wednesday,* New York, Appleton-Century, 1934.

CRITICAL REFERENCES

See texts and editions above. Alegría, *Breve hist.,* 107-112. Ignacio B. Anzoátegui, *Manuel Gálvez,* Buenos Aires, Eds. Culturales Argentinas, 1961. Alfred Coester, "Manuel Gálvez, Argentine Novelist," *Hispania,* V (1922), 325-335. Crawford, 149-164. *Diccionario . . . Argentina,* II, 292-298. Otis H. Green, "Manuel Gálvez, 'Gabriel Quiroga,' and *La maestra normal*," *Hispanic Review,* XI (1943), 221-252; also his "Manuel Gálvez, 'Gabriel Quiroga,' and *El mal metafísico*," *Hispanic Review,* XI (1943), 314-327. Henry Alfred Holmes, "Una trilogía de Manuel Gálvez—*Escenas de la guerra del Paraguay*," *Revista hispánica moderna,* III (1937), 201-222. Spell, 15-64. Torres-Ríoseco, *Grandes novelistas,* II, 137-160. Zum Felde, *Índice crítico,* II, 217-225.

°°2. (Chile) **Manuel Rojas** (1896-) was born in Buenos Aires of Chilean parents. His father died before he was five. His mother reared him and the boy studied in Argentine schools until he was fourteen. At sixteen he left home and began to work as a common railway laborer in the Andes mountains which serve as a backdrop for so many of his stories, particularly those of his first collection, *Hombres del sur* (1926). He crossed over into Chile where he worked as a bargeman, laborer, and night watchman. This phase of his life is strongly reflected in his novelette, which is a little gem, *Lanchas en la bahía* (1932). Rojas also worked as a sailor, actor, house painter, typographer and journalist. Later, he was a clerk in the National Library, and eventually became director of the University of Chile Press. In the early 1960's he taught Spanish American literature in several colleges in the United States. Rojas is an enormous man, well over six feet in height, soft spoken, shy, but with a profound sense of dignity and inner vitality.

Among his full-length novels, Rojas' masterpiece is *Hijo de ladrón* (1951), a story written in the existential vein in which the poor son of a thief is presented as the dualistic symbol of (1) the economic wretchedness of his society and (2) the indestructible dignity of the common man, regardless of his economic state. Rojas has also written works of literary and social criticism, among which the best known are *De la poesía a la revolucion* (1938) and *El árbol siempre verde* (1960).

SUGGESTED READING

"El cachorro," "El vaso de leche," "El colocolo," "El bonete maulino," and *Lanchas en la bahía.*

TEXTS

Anthology, 707-715. Anderson Imbert and Florit, 637-641. Crow, 157-170. Manzor, 233-238. Torres-Ríoseco and Kress, 3-12.

EDITIONS

Hombres del sur, Santiago, Nascimento, 1926; prologue by Raúl Silva Castro. *El delincuente* (1929), Santiago, Zig-Zag, 1949. *Lanchas en la bahía,* Santiago, Zig-Zag, 1932; prologue by Alone; *ibid.,* 5th ed., 1963. *De la poesía a la revolución,* Santiago, Ercilla, 1938. *Hijo de ladrón* (1951), Santiago, Zig-Zag, 1961. *Mejor que el vino,* Santiago, Zig-Zag, 1958. *El vaso de leche y sus mejores cuentos,* Santiago, Nascimento, 1959. *El árbol siempre verde (Mi experiencia literaria),* Santiago, Zig-Zag, 1960. *Obras completas,* Santiago, Zig-Zag, 1961;

prologue by González Vera. *Antología autobiográfica,* Santiago, Ercilla, 1962.

TRANSLATIONS

Colford, 1-24. Frank Gaynor (trans.), *Born Guilty (Hijo de ladrón),* New York, Library Publishers, 1955. Torres-Ríoseco, *Short Stories,* 121-130.

CRITICAL REFERENCES

See texts and editions above. Alegría, *Breve hist.,* 214-219; also his "Manuel Rojas: transcendentalismo en la novela chilena," *Cuadernos americanos,* CIII (1959), 244-258. *Diccionario . . . Chile,* 169-170. Silva Castro, *Retratos,* 163-179; also his *Panoram. lit.,* 196-203.

3. (Bolivia) **Alcides Arguedas** (1879-1946) was born and educated in La Paz and pursued special studies in the social sciences in Paris. He represented his country in the diplomatic service in London, Paris, and Colombia. A journalist, sociologist, and historian, he was Bolivia's most prominent writer of his time. In his early novel, *Wata-Wara,* written in 1904 and completely rewritten and published in 1919 under the title *Raza de bronce (Wata-Wara),* he stands out as a precursor of the new *indigenista* literature in which the Indian is presented as a pressing social problem. Of his three novels—the other two are *Pisagua* (1903) and *Vida criolla* (1912)—*Raza de bronce* is the author's favorite. *Pueblo enfermo* (1909) is one of the best literary-sociological studies yet written on the American Indian problem. Arguedas also wrote a history of Bolivia (1920) which presents an inside view of that country's sad story.

SUGGESTED READING

"Venganza aymará" and *Raza de bronce.*

TEXTS

Anderson Imbert and Florit, 521-525. Flores, 367-374. Holmes, *Span. Am.,* 109-112. Torres-Ríoseco, *Ant. lit. hisp.,* 39-42.

EDITIONS

Vida criolla, Paris, Ollendorff, 1912. *Pueblo enfermo* (1909), Santiago, Ercilla, 1937. *Raza de bronce (Wata-Wara)* (1904), 3rd ed., Buenos Aires, Losada, 1957 (Bibl. contemporánea, 156). *Los caudillos bárbaros,* Barcelona, Luis Tasso, 1929. *Obras completas,* 2 vols., México, Aguilar, 1959-1960; prologue and notes by Luis Alberto Sánchez.

TRANSLATIONS

Arciniegas, 205-222. Jones, 189-190. H. de Onís, 230-237.

CRITICAL REFERENCES

See texts and editions above. Alegría, *Breve hist.*, 202-203. Carrión, 167-217. Crawford, 106-108. *Diccionario . . . Bolivia,* 5-8. Hugo Lijerón Alberdi, "*Raza de bronce,*" Hispania, XLVI (1963), 530-533. Mead, *Ensayo,* 88-90. Torres-Ríoseco, *Novela,* 225-226. Zum Felde, *Índice crítico,* I, 347-354.

*4. (Peru) **Enrique López Albújar** (1872-1966) shares with Clorinda Matto de Turner (*Aves sin nido,* 1889) and Abraham Valdelomar (1888-1919), the distinction of having initiated the *indigenista* trend in Peruvian letters which later culminated in the works of Ciro Alegría (1909-1967) and José María Arguedas (1911-1969). López Albújar's paternal grandmother coaxed her husband into buying an old rambling house of fifty rooms which they turned into a hotel. On the ground floor they put a grocery store and a cigar factory, and the money rolled in. They sent their son, the father of our author, to Berlin to be educated. On his return he fell in love with a mulatto girl who became the mother of Enrique López Albújar. This is related by Albújar in his autobiographical *De mi casona* (1924). The boy was sent to Lima to the University, and after graduation he became a professor of history in his hometown, Piura, where he also founded and edited a newspaper, and served as a local judge. Later, he returned to Lima to become editor of *La prensa.* His two volumes of stories, *Cuentos andinos* (1920), and *Nuevos cuentos andinos* (1927), many of them based on episodes with which he came in contact during his service as judge, present the tragedies of native life in pages that are stark and pessimistic. His latest work, *Las caridades de la señora Tordoya,* won the Ricardo Palma Prize in 1950.

SUGGESTED READING

"La coca," "El trompiezo," "Ushanam Jampi," "El brindis de los yayas."

TEXTS

Anthology, 715-723. Anderson Imbert and Florit, 517-521. Flores, 345-356. Manzor, 325-332.

EDITIONS

Cuentos andinos (1920), Lima, Imp. Lux, 1924. *De mi casona,* Lima, Imp. Lux, 1924. *Nuevos cuentos andinos,* Santiago, Ercilla, 1937; *ibid.,* Lima, Populibros, 1936. *El hechizo de Tomaiquichua,* Lima, Ed. Peruanidad, 1943. *Las caridades de la señora de Tordoya* (1950),

Lima, Mejía Baca, 1955. *Matalaché,* Lima, Mejía Baca y Villanueva, 1957. *Los mejores cuentos,* Lima, Patronato del Libro Peruano, 1957; edited by Juan Ríos.
TRANSLATIONS
Haydn and Cournos, 915-922. H. de Onís, 238-247.
CRITICAL REFERENCES
See texts and editions above. Faith F. Frikart, "The Short Stories of Enrique López Albújar and Their Milieu," *Hispania,* XXVII (1944), 482-488. Betty Gómez Lance, "El indio y la naturaleza en los cuentos de López Albújar," *Revista iberoamericana,* 49 (1960), 141-145. Estuardo Núñez, "La prosa literaria del Perú en los últimos veinte años," *Memoria del segundo congreso,* 319-338.

5. (Ecuador) Jorge Icaza (1906-   ) is the principal exponent of the Indianist trend in Ecuadorean letters. He began his studies at the University in the field of medicine, but soon abandoned this in favor of the theater in which medium he was actor, director and writer. His success was not outstanding. In 1933 his first book, a group of short stories, *Barro de la sierra,* appeared. This was followed in 1934 by his most famous novel, *Huasipungo,* a totally black and repugnant picture of native Indian life. One year later he published another novel of the same kind, *En las calles* (1935), which was awarded the national prize in literature. *Cholos* (1938), a third novel, is essentially in the same vein, but its characters are somewhat better drawn. Two additional novels, published in 1942 and 1948, add little to the author's stature, but a collection of short stories, *Seis relatos* (1952) shows that he can handle that difficult genre effectively. Icaza's principal weakness is his dependence on repugnant naturalistic scenes for effect. *Huasipungo* has been translated into several foreign languages, but the author's reputation has not grown with the years. He is a writer in one dimension.
SUGGESTED READING
En las calles.
TEXTS
Flores, 584-586.
EDITIONS
Huasipungo (1934), Buenos Aires, Ed. Sol, 1936; critical epilogue by Enrique S. Portugal; *ibid.,* 9th ed., Buenos Aires, Lautaro, 1948; *ibid.,* 2nd ed., Buenos Aires, Losada, 1960 (Bibl. contemporánea,

221). *En las calles,* Quito, Imp. Nacional, 1935. *Cholos,* Quito, Sindicato de Escritores y Artistas, 1938. *Seis veces la muerte (Seis relatos)* (1952), 2nd ed., Buenos Aires, Alpe, [1954]. *El chulla Romero y Flores,* Quito, Casa de la Cultura Ecuatoriana, 1958. *Viejos cuentos,* Quito, Casa de la Cultura Ecuatoriana, 1960. *Obras escogidas,* México, Fondo de Cultura Económica, 1961; with vocabulary, and with prologue by Francisco Ferrándiz Alborz.

TRANSLATIONS

Bernard M. Dulsey (trans.), *The Villagers (Huasipungo),* Carbondale, Southern Illinois Univ. Press, 1964. Jones, 190-198. Mervyn Savill (trans.), *Huasipungo,* London, Dobson, 1962.

CRITICAL REFERENCES

See texts and editions above. Alegría, *Breve hist.,* 246-249. *Diccionario . . . Ecuador,* 128-132. Bernard Dulsey, "Jorge Icaza and his Ecuador," *Hispania,* XLIV (1961), 99-103. Enrique Ojeda, *Cuatro obras de Jorge Icaza,* Quito, Casa de la Cultura Ecuatoriana, 1961. Spell, 239-253. Torres-Ríoseco, *Novela,* 234-235.

°°6. (Colombia) **José Eustasio Rivera** (1888-1928). See I, A, 9, above.

7. (Venezuela) **Romulo Gallegos (1884–1969) teacher, minister of education, journalist, and once President of Venezuela, is one of the great Spanish American novelists of this country. Gallegos went into voluntary exile during the latter years of the Gómez dictatorship (1931-1935), but after the death of the despot he entered politics and in 1947 was elected President by the immense majority of 72 percent of the popular vote. His party was *Acción Democrática,* which had a platform of rigorous social reforms. However, less than a year after assuming the Presidency, Gallegos was unable to maintain order and was deposed by a military group. He again went into exile and lived in Mexico and the United States until the end of the Pérez Jiménez dictatorship in 1958.

Gallegos is the author of many novels, essays, and short stories, but his principal claim to fame rests on the trilogy: *Doña Bárbara* (1929), *Cantaclaro* (1931), and *Canaima* (1935). *Doña Bárbara,* rewritten three times before publication, is one of the most tightly developed novels in Spanish American literature. It presents the essential struggle between civilization and barbarism on the Venezuelan plains. *Cantaclaro* is the story of a folk-singer of the plains who epitomizes his country's popular love and songs. The Peruvian novelist, Ciro

Alegría, called it the best novel in Spanish American literature. *Canaima* is a story of the jungles, which in character development and novelistic technique is definitely superior to the many other jungle novels of Spanish America.

Gallegos is at all times a careful writer and his prose style is both poetic and powerful. He is particularly adept at plot development, but some of his characters suffer from insufficient delineation and growth. This is especially noticeable in *Cantaclaro,* where one of the most convincing characters in Latin -American literature, Dr. Payara, is dropped completely about halfway through the book.

SUGGESTED READING
Doña Bárbara or *Cantaclaro* or *Canaima.*

TEXTS
Anderson Imbert and Florit, 610-613. Flores, 441-445. *Doña Bárbara* (ed. Dunham), New York, Appleton-Century-Crofts, 1942. Torres-Ríoseco, *Ant. lit. hisp.,* 50-52.

EDITIONS
Doña Bárbara (1929), México, Ed. Orión, 1950; prologue and notes by Mariano Picón-Salas; *ibid.,* 19th ed., Buenos Aires, Espasa-Calpe, 1962 (Col. austral, 168). *Cantaclaro* (1931), 5th ed., Buenos Aires, Espasa-Calpe, 1947 (Col. austral, 192). *Canaima* (1935), 5th ed., Buenos Aires, Espasa-Calpe, 1947 (Col. austral, 213). *Pobre negro* (1937), 5th ed., Buenos Aires, Espasa-Calpe, 1961 (Col. austral, 307). *La rebelión y otros cuentos* (1946), Buenos Aires, Espasa-Calpe, 1950 (Col. austral, 851). *Una posición en la vida,* México, Eds. Humanismo, 1954. *Obras completas,* Habana, Lex, 1949. *Novelas escogidas,* Madrid, Aguilar, 1951; prologue by Federico Sainz de Robles. *Obras selectas,* Madrid, Edime, 1959. *Obras completas,* 2nd ed., 2 vols., Madrid, Aguilar, 1959.

TRANSLATIONS
Arciniegas, 467-480. Jones, 217-227. Robert Malloy (trans.), *Doña Bárbara,* New York, Cape and Smith, 1931; *ibid.,* New York, Peter Smith, 1948. H. de Onís, 280-291; also her *Spanish Stories,* 240-247.

CRITICAL REFERENCES
See texts and editions above. Alegría, *Breve hist.,* 176-181. Orlando Araujo, *Lengua y creación en la obra de Rómulo Gallegos,* Buenos Aires, Ed. Nova, 1955. Angel Damboriena, *Rómulo Gallegos y la problemática venezolana,* Caracas, Univ. Católica Andrés Bello, 1960. Lowell Dunham, *Rómulo Gallegos, vida y obra,* México, Studium, 1957. John E. Englekirk, "Doña Bárbara, Legend of the

Llano," *Hispania*, XXXI (1948), 259-270. González, *Estudios*, 297-305. Andrés Iduarte, *Veinte años con Rómulo Gallegos*, México, Eds. Humanismo, 1954. Ulrich Leo, *Rómulo Gallegos, estudios sobre el arte de novelar*, México, Eds. Humanismo, 1954. Felipe Massiani, *El hombre y la naturaleza venezolana en Rómulo Gallegos*, Caracas, Elite, 1943. Ratcliff, 235-263. Spell, 205-239. Torres-Ríoseco, *Grandes novelistas*, I, 43-76.

°°8. (Mexico) **Mariano Azuela** (1873-1952) was born in Lagos de Moreno, Jalisco. He received most of his education in Guadalajara, where he studied medicine, returning to practice in his native city. He wrote his first pieces when still a medical student, and throughout his life he continued to pursue his double role of doctor and novelist. For several months in 1915 he served as army doctor in one of Villa's bands. He is the only true novelist the Revolution has produced. He has treated and interpreted every phase of the movement from the last days of Díaz to the close of Cárdenas' term as President. *Los de abajo* (1915), a "modern classic," is a series of deeply-etched sketches of the "blood-and-horror" years of the Revolution. It has been translated into almost every major living language.

Some of Azuela's later novels, particularly *La malhora* (1923), reflect a stylistic extremism which makes them very difficult reading. *Las tribulaciones de una familia decente* (1938), perhaps his second best full-length novel, interprets the chaotic social and psychological climate of the post-Revolutionary years. Azuela's novels represent a break with those of the previous generation in their terse style, in their omission of moralizations and elements of the pleasantly picturesque, and in their gripping dramatic quality obtained through the acute observation of reality and an almost camera-like reproduction of its immediate effect on the observer-novelist.

SUGGESTED READING

Los de abajo.

TEXTS

Castro Leal, *Novela*, I, 47-199. Flores, 316-320. *Los de abajo* (ed. Englekirk and Kiddle), New York, Appleton-Century-Crofts, 1939 (paperback). Torres-Ríoseco, *Ant. lit. hisp.*, 31-33.

EDITIONS

Mala yerba (1909), México, Botas, 1937. *Los de abajo* (1915), México, Fondo de Cultura Económica, 1961. *Los caciques* (1917) and *Las moscas* (1918), México, La Razón, 1931. *La malhora* (1923), México, Botas, 1941. *La luciérnaga,* Madrid, Espasa-Calpe, 1932. *Las tribulaciones de una familia decente,* México, Botas, 1938. *La mujer domada,* México, El Colegio Nacional, 1946. *Sendas perdidas,* México, Botas, 1949. *La maldición,* México, Fondo de Cultura Económica, 1955. *Esa sangre,* México, Fondo de Cultura Económica, 1956. *Obras completas,* 3 vols., México, Fondo de Cultura Económica, 1958-1960; prologue by Francisco Monterde.

TRANSLATIONS

Jones, 257-270. Enrique Munguía (trans.), *The Underdogs,* New York, Brentano's, 1929; *ibid.,* New York, Signet Classics, 1963 (paperback; with a foreword by Harriet de Onís. Frances Kellam Hendricks and Beatrice Berler (trans.), *The Trials of a Respectable Family and The Underdogs,* San Antonio, Texas, Principia Press of Trinity Univ., 1963; prologue by Salvador Azuela, biographical sketch by Luis Leal. Anita Brenner (trans.), *Marcela (Mala yerba),* New York, Farrar and Rinehart, 1932. Lesley B. Simpson (trans.), *Two Novels of Mexico, The Flies—The Bosses,* 4th ed., Berkeley and Los Angeles, Univ. of California Press, 1964 (paperback).

CRITICAL REFERENCES

See texts and editions above. Alegría, *Breve hist.,* 146-153. González, *Trayectoria,* 108-200. Dewey Roscoe Jones, *El doctor Mariano Azuela, médico y novelista,* México, Univ. Nacional, 1960. Luis Leal, *Mariano Azuela, vida y obra,* México, Studium, 1961. Morton, 29-70. Spell, 64-101. Torres-Ríoseco, *Grandes novelistas,* I, 3-40.

*9. (Mexico) **Martín Luis Guzmán** (1887-1976) was born in Chihuahua and studied law at the National University. He was a journalist with the forces of the Revolution in the north. From 1914 to 1934 he spent most of his years as an exile in New York and in Madrid. After Azuela, he was the earliest novelist to record his experiences and impressions of the Revolution years (*El águila y la serpiente,* 1928) and of political intrigue and corruption of the twenties (*La sombra del caudillo,* 1929). The first of the above works gives a graphic characterization of Pancho Villa, the brute force of the Mexican Revolution, and of Guzmán's firsthand experiences with him.

SUGGESTED READING

El águila y la serpiente.

TEXTS

Anderson Imbert and Florit, 625-628. Castro Leal, *Novela,* I, 209-533. Holmes, *Cont. Span. Amers.,* 145-158. *El águila y la serpiente* (ed. Moore), New York, Norton, 1943.

EDITIONS

El águila y la serpiente (1928), México, Cía. General de Ediciones, 1962. *La sombra del caudillo* (1929), 3rd ed., México, Botas, 1938. *Memorias de Pancho Villa,* 4 vols., (1938-1940), 6th ed., México, Cía. General de Ediciones, 1963. *Islas Marías,* México, Cía. General de Ediciones, 1959. *Filadelfia, paraíso de conspiradores,* México, Cía. General de Ediciones, 1960.

TRANSLATIONS

Arciniegas, 510-522. Jones, 270-276. Harriet de Onís (trans.), *The Eagle and the Serpent,* New York, Knopf, 1930.

CRITICAL REFERENCES

See texts and editions above. Alegría, *Breve hist.,* 153-157. González, *Trayectoria,* 200-215. Helen P. Houck, "Las obras novelescas de Martín Luis Guzmán," *Revista iberoamericana,* 5, (1941), 139-158. Martínez, *Lit. mex. siglo XX,* I, 193-199. Morton, 115-141.

*10. (Mexico) **Gregorio López y Fuentes** (1897-1967) was born ol an hacienda in the Huasteca region of Mexico in the state of Veracruz. His father ran a small general store frequented by Indians and mule drivers, and also engaged in farming and cattle raising. The son, Gregorio, later went to Mexico City to study to become one of the young group of intellectuals and writers. Like many Spanish American authors, he began his career writing poetry, but his first significant work was the novel *Campamento* (1931), which was his third venture in the novelistic field. *Tierra* (1932) is a poetic evocation of the legendary hero, Emiliano Zapata. From this time on López y Fuentes is one of the mainstays of the Mexican literary scene. He has a strongly personal style, inclines to view things allegorically, and appears to have a good understanding of the native Mexican Indian psychology. His novel, *El indio* (1935), took a national prize, and its English translation by Anita Brenner was popular in the United States. López y Fuentes became managing editor of the Mexico City daily *El gráfico,* which absorbed a great portion of his time. In *Los peregrinos inmóviles* (1944) the novelist gives a symbolic and synthetic interpretation of Mexican history in the story of a single Indian village. As in nearly all of the author's work, proper names are insignificant; the anonymous mass is the real protagonist. In 1948 appeared the novel *Entresuelo,* in which rural themes are abandoned in order to make way for an interpretation of urban problems as people flow in from the countryside in search of a better living. The title and individual characters in this novel are symbolic, but the author does not handle his material as well as he did his crowds of soldiers, Indians, rural masses and types.

SUGGESTED READING

El indio.

TEXTS

Castro Leal, *Novela,* II, 137-327. *El indio* (ed. Hespelt), New York, Norton, 1940. *Tierra* (ed. Holmes and Bará), New York, Holt, 1949. *Cuatro siglos lit. mex.,* 754-757, 1052 (inc. poems). Jones and Hansen, 212-220. Walsh, *Cuentos,* 15-19.

EDITIONS

Tierra, México, Ed. México, 1933. *¡Mi general!,* México, Botas, 1934. *El indio* (1935), México, Botas, 1945; *ibid.,* México, Novaro, 1955. *Arrieros* (1937), México, Botas, 1944. *Cuentos campesinos de México,* México, Botas, 1940. *Los peregrinos inmóviles,* México, Botas, 1944. *Entresuelo,* México, Botas, 1948. *Milpa, potrero y monte,* México, Botas, 1951.

TRANSLATIONS

Anita Brenner (trans.), *El indio,* Indianapolis, Bobbs-Merrill, 1937. Colford, 147-152. Jones, 285-289.

CRITICAL REFERENCES

See texts and editions above. Alegría, *Breve hist.,* 163-170. González, *Trayectoria,* 249-267. Morton, 95-115.

b. PSYCHOLOGICAL AND PHILOSOPHICAL

°°1. (Uruguay) **Horacio Quiroga** (1878-1937) was born in the provincial city of Salto. At the age of nine he moved to Montevideo, where he lived until 1900. Thereafter, save for a short trip to Paris that same year, he spent the rest of his life in Argentina. His French sojourn left no imprint on his work. After several unsuccessful attempts at making a living from the soil, he turned finally—and with success—to his pen. He is possibly the greatest of Spanish American short-story writers; in technique, strength, and variety, an accomplished master. His best stories afford us unforgettable portraits of the jungle province of Misiones, Argentina, where he spent a good part of his life, or present tense and dramatic psychological insights into human character. He is also the author of some excellent animal allegories, a collection of children's stories, and of a few choice humorous tales. Poe, Kipling, Maupassant, and the great Russian realists were his masters. His most famous work is *Cuentos de amor, de locura y de muerte* (1917), the title of which is indicative of its content.

SUGGESTED READING

"El desierto," "Tres cartas y un pie," "La gallina degollada," "Juan Darién," "El hijo," "La muerte de Isolda," "Los mensú."

TEXTS

Anthology, 680-696. Anderson Imbert and Florit, 504-513. Crow, 143-156. Flores, 336-344. Jones and Hansen, 197-211. Torres-Ríoseco, *Ant. lit. hisp.*, 53-57. Walsh, *Cuentos,* 33-39, 107-116. Wilkins, 28-35.

EDITIONS

Los arrecifes de coral (1901), Montevideo, C. García, 1943; prologues by Carlos Herrera Mac-Lean and Antonio M. Grompone. *Cuentos de amor, de locura y de muerte* (1917), Buenos Aires, Losada, 1960. (Bibl. contemporánea, 252). *Cuentos de la selva* (1918), Buenos Aires, Losada, 1960 (Bibl. contemporánea, 255). *El salvaje* (1920), Buenos Aires, Eds. Hemisferio, 1953. *Anaconda* (1921), Buenos Aires, Ed. Anaconda, 1942; preliminary study by Lázaro Liacho. *El desierto* (1924), Buenos Aires, Losada, 1956 (Bibl. contemporánea, 261). *Los desterrados* (1926), Buenos Aires, Losada, 1956 (Bibl. contemporánea, 263). *Más allá* (1934), Buenos Aires, Losada, 1954 (Bibl. contemporánea, 258). *Cuentos,* 13 vols., Montevideo, C. García, 1937 1945. *Sus mejores cuentos,* México, Cultura, 1943; prologue by John A. Crow. *Cuentos escogidos* (1950), 2nd ed., Madrid, Aguilar, 1958; prologue by Guillermo de Torre. *Diario de viaje a París,* Montevideo, Instituto Nacional de Investigaciones y Archivos Literarios, 1950; prologue by Emir Rodríguez Monegal. *Cartas inéditas,* 2 vols., Montevideo, Instituto Nacional de Investigaciones y Archivos Literarios, 1959. *Anaconda. El salvaje. Pasado amor,* Buenos Aires, Sur, 1960. *El regreso de Anaconda y otros cuentos,* Buenos Aires, Ed. Universitaria, 1960.

Colford, 106-117. Flores and Poore, 398-408. Frank, 239-268. Jones,

TRANSLATIONS

302-309. Arthur Livingstone (trans.), *South American Jungle Tales (Cuentos de la selva)* (1922), 3rd ed., New York, Dodd, Mead, 1950. H. de Onís, *Spanish Stories,* 133-141. Torres-Ríoseco, *Short Stories,* 55-64.

CRITICAL REFERENCES

See texts and editions above. José M. Delgado and Alberto J. Brignole, *Vida y obra de Horacio Quiroga,* Montevideo, C. García, 1939. Englekirk, 340-368. José Enrique Etchevery, *Horacio Quiroga y la creación artística,* Montevideo, Univ. de la República, 1957. Noé Jitrik, *Horacio Quiroga; una obra de experiencia y riesgo,* Buenos Aires, Eds. Culturales Argentinas, 1959. Pedro G. Orgambide, *Horacio Quiroga. El hombre y su obra,* Buenos Aires, Stilcograf, 1954. Spell, 153-179.

°°2. (Chile) **Eduardo Barrios** (1884-1963) was born in the port city of Valparaíso. His father was one of the Chilean soldiers who had fought in the victorious struggle against Peru in the War of the Pacific. He died when Eduardo was only five years old, and the boy's mother, who was Peruvian, took him to Lima to be educated. At fifteen he was sent back to Chile where he entered a military school, but not finding the discipline to his liking he soon dropped out, and this caused a break with his family. Barrios then commenced to roam about and was employed in a number of different kinds of jobs: as trader, prospector, rubber worker in Peru, bookkeeper in the nitrate mines of north Chile, salesman of stoves in Buenos Aires, member of a traveling circus troupe in which he was a weight lifter. In his spare time he wrote stories. Eventually he became minister of education in Chile and director of the National Library.

His *El niño que enloqueció de amor* (1915) is an intensely poetic picture of a boy of about ten losing his mind because of love for a much older young lady. *El hermano asno* (1922) is a psychological novel based on life in a Franciscan monastery. Barrios himself lived in a monastery for an extended period as preparation for writing this novel. He extols the simple Franciscan life, but introduces problems of pride, saintliness, mundane love, sexual frustration, and attempted rape in the dramatic development of his plot. *Gran señor y rajadiablos* (1948) is the rip-roaring tale of life on a Chilean *fundo* in the past century. *Los hombres del hombre* (1950) is a psychological study of the multiple and ambivalent aspects of one man's being. In this novel Barrios has each aspect of the character assume a different name as the protagonist contemplates the diversity of his own personality. He manages the plot skillfully, and carries it to a dramatic conclusion. Barrios has also written some excellent short stories and has won considerable fame as a dramatist. He deserves great credit for the present popularity and superior merit of psychological fiction in Chilean literature.

SUGGESTED READING

El hermano asno or *El niño que enloqueció de amor.*

TEXTS

Anderson Imbert and Florit, 618-622. Flores, 320-333. Holmes, *Span. Am.,* 171-173. *Cuatro cuentos* (ed. Resnick), New York, Harper, 1951. Torres-Ríoseco, *Ant. lit. hisp.,* 53-57. Torres-Ríoseco and Kress, 23-30. Walsh, *Cuentos,* 120-126. G. M. Walsh, 131-136.

EDITIONS

El niño que enloqueció de amor (1915), Buenos Aires, Losada, 1954 (Bibl. contemporánea, 207). *Un perdido* (1917), Santiago, Nascimento, 1946. *El hermano asno* (1922), Buenos Aires, Losada, 1961 (Bibl. contemporánea, 187); *ibid.,* Santiago, Zig-Zag, 1961. *Páginas de un pobre diablo,* Santiago, Nascimento, 1923. *Y la vida sigue,* Buenos Aires, Tor, 1925. *Teatro escogido,* Santiago, Zig-Zag, 1947; prologue by Domingo Melfi Demarco. *Gran señor y rajadiablos* (1948), Buenos Aires, Espasa-Calpe, 1952 (Col. austral, 1120). *Los hombres del hombre,* Santiago, Nascimento, 1950; *ibid.,* Buenos Aires, Losada, 1957. *Obras completas,* 2 vols., Santiago, Zig-Zag, 1962.

TRANSLATIONS

Colford, 25-33. Flores and Poore, 488-608. Jones, 330-333.

CRITICAL REFERENCES

See texts and editions above. Alegría, *Breve hist.,* 194-198. Ned Davison, "The Dramatic Works of Eduardo Barrios," *Hispania,* XLV (1958), 60-64. Donald Decker, "Eduardo Barrios Talks about his Novels," *Hispania,* XLV (1962), 254-259. *Diccionario . . . Chile,* 16-18. Donald F. Fogelquist, "Eduardo Barrios en su etapa actual," *Revista iberoamericana,* 35 (1952), 13-26. Silva Castro, *Panorama nov. chil.,* 117-129. Spell, 135-153. Torres-Ríoseco, *Grandes novelistas,* II, 21-58.

3. (Chile) **Pedro Prado** (1886-1952), poet, architect, diplomat, painter,

and writer, was the intellectual and esthetic leader of his generation in Chile. In 1915 he founded the famous artistic and intellectual circle known as *Los Diez,* of which he was the guiding spirit and chronicler. This group of musicians, painters, poets, and novelists, inspired by the philosophical theories of Tolstoi, dreamed of regenerating humanity through beauty and art. Prado and Augusto D'Halmar (1880-1950) were perhaps the two best-known writers of the movement, which eventually led to the development of Chilean postmodernism and a kind of regionalism permeated with lyric tones and colorful symbolism. Prado himself began his writing career as a poet who moved from the rhetorical followers of Darío, but later he became Chile's most highly reputed prose stylist.

Prado's unique novel, *Alsino* (1920), about a young boy who sprouts wings and learns how to fly, is a beautifully written allegory and interpretation of the human spirit, "half-dust, half-deity, alike unfit to sink or soar." In *Alsino* the Icarian legend is reborn in a modern setting. It still stands as one of the most exquisite and effective works of imagination to come out of Spanish American literature. Prado's second best-known novel, *Un juez rural* (1924), represents a diminution of the author's poetic fire, but exemplifies many of the finer aspects of Chilean regionalism.

SUGGESTED READING

Alsino.

TEXTS

Anderson Imbert and Florit, 616-619. Holmes, *Span. Am.,* 155-157. Onís, 649-651. Torres-Ríoseco, *Ant. lit. hisp.,* 67-72.

EDITIONS

Alsino (1920), 6th ed., Santiago, Nascimento, 1956. *Un juez rural,* Santiago, Nascimento, 1924. *Androvar,* Santiago, Nascimento, 1925. *Otoño en las dunas,* Santiago, Nascimento, 1940. *No más que una rosa,* Buenos Aires, Losada, 1946. *Antología; las estancias del amor,* Santiago, Ed. del Pacífico, 1949; prologue by Raúl Silva Castro.

TRANSLATIONS

Blackwell, 278-289. Craig, 154-167. Jones, 333-337.

CRITICAL REFERENCES

See texts and editions above. Alegría, *Breve hist.,* 137-141. *Diccionario . . . Chile,* 160-161. Raúl Silva Castro, *Pedro Prado (1886-1952),* New York, Hispanic Institute, 1959. Torres-Ríoseco, *Grandes novelistas,* II, 163-198.

*4. (Chile) **María Luisa Bombal** (1910-   ) was born in Viña del Mar. She was educated in Chile and in France, and holds a degree from the Sorbonne in Paris. Later, she returned to Chile where she engaged in amateur theatrics. She also lived for many years in Argentina. Her early years were unconventional, Bohemian, and stormy. Her first collection of stories, *La última niebla* (1935), definitely killed criollism in Chile. It was written in a delicately feminine and poetic style which is one of the author's chief claims to distinction. Her second book, a novelette called *La amortajada* (1938), consists of the imagined memories of a woman about to be buried. It is a convincing insight into feminine psychology.

In 1944 María Luisa Bombal married a French broker, Fal de Saint Phalle, and moved to New York City to live. In 1947 she and her husband wrote in English a novel entitled *The House of Mist,* which is an extension of the title story in her first collection mentioned above. It was promptly purchased by one of the motion picture companies in Hollywood.

María Luisa Bombal turned her back on realism and moved into a realm of mist, fantasy and imagination which became her unique literary world. In this twilight zone of emotions and memories, and by means of a strong subjectivism and an impressionistic poetic style, she has created some of the most admirable pieces of brief fiction to come out of Spanish America.

SUGGESTED READING

La amortajada or "El árbol."

TEXTS

Anderson Imbert and Kiddle, 170-181. Latcham, 45-46, 303-311.

EDITIONS

La última niebla (1935), 2nd ed., Santiago, Nascimento, 1941; introduction by Amado Alonso. *La amortajada* (1938), 2nd ed., Santiago, Nascimento, 1941. *The House of Mist,* New York, Farrar and Straus, 1947.

TRANSLATIONS

The Shrouded Woman, New York, Farrar and Straus, 1948. Torres-Ríoseco, *Short Stories,* 83-94.

CRITICAL REFERENCES

See texts and editions above. Alegría, *Breve hist.,* 221-222. Martha E. Allen, "Dos estilos de novela: Marta Brunet y María Luisa Bombal," *Revista iberoamericana,* 35 (1952), 63-91. Margaret V. Campbell, "The Vaporous World of María Luisa Bombal," *Hispania,* XLIV (1961); 415-420.

*5. (Guatemala) **Rafael Arévalo Martínez** (1884-   ). See I, A, 10, above.

*6. (Cuba) **Alfonso Hernández-Catá** (1885-1940) was the son of a Cuban mother and a Spanish father, who was loyal to the Spanish cause in that island's struggle for independence. The child, Alfonso, was born in Spain; at the father's insistence, his mother was transported to the peninsula in her fifth month of pregnancy, and as a result of the rigorous trip she suffered disastrous physical consequences. The child was taken back to Cuba, but in his early teens was sent to a military school in Toledo. The rigid discipline repelled him, and he ran off to Madrid to become a journalist. The Spanish novelist Benito Pérez Galdós (1845-1920) helped him begin his literary career. Eventually he became one of the finest short-story writers in the Spanish language.

Hernández-Catá lived in Spain for many years, but never became a Spanish citizen. During the Machado dictatorship in Cuba he wrote a scathing attack on that regime called *El cementerio en las Antillas,* which made him the idol of all young Cuban intellectuals. Both before and after the dictatorship he served in the island's diplomatic corps. He died in an airplane accident in Rio de Janeiro Bay in 1940.

Hernández-Catá loved Cuba deeply, but most of his stories deal with psychological themes, and might be placed almost anywhere. His first collection, *Cuentos pasionales* (1907), recalls Maupassant; other good collections are *Los siete pecados* (1920) and *Piedras preciosas* (1927). The Chilean novelist and critic, Eduardo Barrios, made an anthology of his best *cuentos* in 1936. Hernández-Catá was interested primarily in abnormal psychology, and in unusual situations which suddenly reveal that abnormality within the masked personality. Some of his tales suggest an almost clinical insight into the human psyche. Among his favorite topics are jealousy, insanity, Don Juanism, adultery, homosexuality, man's inhumanity, violence, narcissism, cruelty. He is a masterful short-story teller and an excellent psychologist; as a novelist his stature is somewhat less convincing.

SUGGESTED READING

"Noventa días," "El maestro," "Naufragio," "La culpable," "El testigo," "Los muertos," "La galleguita."

TEXTS

Anderson Imbert and Florit, 605-611. Crow, 55-60. Holmes, *Cont. Span. Amers.*, 88-98.

EDITIONS

Cuentos pasionales (1907), 3rd ed., Madrid, Ed. América, 1920. *Los frutos ácidos*, Madrid, Renacimiento, 1915. *Los siete pecados* (1919), 5th ed., Madrid, Renacimiento, 1930. *La voluntad de Dios* (1921), 5th ed. Madrid, Renacimiento, 1930. *Una mala mujer*, Madrid, Mundo Latino, 1922. *Piedras preciosas*, Madrid, Mundo Latino, 1927. *Mitología de Martí*, Madrid, Renacimiento, 1929. *Manicomio*, Madrid, Ibero-Americana, 1931. *Un cementerio en las Antillas*, Madrid. G. Sáez, 1933. *Sus mejores cuentos*, Santiago, Nascimento, 1936; preface by Eduardo Barrios. *Los frutos ácidos y otros cuentos*, Madrid, Aguilar, 1953.

CRITICAL REFERENCES

See ·texts and editions above. Ernest R. Aragón, "Hernández-Catá, el hombre," *Memoria de Alfonso Hernández-Catá* (Habana), I (1 March 1954), 123-126. José A. Balseiro, "Revisión de Hernández-Catá," *Memoria del quinto congreso*, 105-123; also his "Notas acerca del arte de Alfonso Hernández-Catá," *Revista bimestre cubana*, XXIII (1928), 386-396; also his "La casa de fieras," *Memoria de Alfonso Hernández-Catá*, I (1 March 1954), 126-130; also "Alfonso Hernández-Catá," *Revista iberoamericana*, 7 (1941), 37-48. Antonio Barreras, "Génesis de los concursos Hernández-Catá," *Memorias de Alfonso Hernández-Catá*, I (1 February 1954), 83-87. Salvador Bueno, "El mensaje de Hernández-Catá," *Memoria de Alfonso Hernández-Catá*, I (1 April 1954), 166-170. Rafael Esténger, "Cubanidad de Alfonso Hernández-Catá," *Memoria de Alfonso Hernández-Catá*, I (1 May 1954), 193-200.

°°7. (Argentina) **Jorge Luis Borges** (1899-   ). See I, B, 3, above.

°8. (Argentina) **Eduardo Mallea** (1903-   ) was born in the city of Bahía Blanca where his father was a leading surgeon. His mother died when Eduardo was a young boy. When he was twelve Mallea began to attend an English school in Buenos Aires, where he learned both the language and literature of the English people. He helped found the *Revista de·América* (1923) and became a collaborating editor of the Argentine literary journal *Sur*. Since 1931 he has been the head of the literary supplement of the famous newspaper *La nación*. In 1934 he lectured in Rome and Milan, and on his return to Argentina he became the undisputed master of the younger generation of Argentine writers. In more recent years he has served as his country's diplomatic representative in several foreign capitals. Mallea's anguished autobiography of his nation, *Historia de una pasión argentina* (1937), is a vital and moving document which gives a fine insight into Argentine thinking. His *Fiesta en noviembre* (1938) novelizes the execution of the Spanish poet García Lorca and the indifference of that epoch's educated class. His long novel *La bahía de silencio* (1940) was translated into English and praised by its reviewers in the United States. It is a picture of man in quest of his authenticity in a world devoid of many of its traditional beliefs. Another novel, *Todo verdor perecerá* (1941), is an even more cogent example of the author's restless philosophical tone and Kierkegaardian anguish. Other good examples of his work are *Las águilas* (1943), *Los enemigos del alma* (1950), and *La torre* (1951). Mallea's primary concern is man's isolation in the modern world, his inability to communicate, and the resultant rootlessness of his tragic·state. The novelist is at his best in creating "emotional˙ climates" and in representing the predicament of modern civilization in terms of individual character.

SUGGESTED READING

Todo verdor perecerá or *Las águilas*.

TEXTS

Anderson Imbert and Florit, 723-726. Flores, 668-684. Manzor, 83-85.

EDITIONS

Cuentos para una inglesa desesperada (1926), Buenos Aires, Espasa-Calpe, 1944 (Col. austral, 202). *Historia de una pasión argentina* (1937), 3rd ed., Buenos Aires, Espasa-Calpe, 1944 (Col. austral, 102); *ibid.*, 8th ed., Buenos Aires, Sudamericana, 1961; prologue by Francisco Romero. *Fiesta en noviembre* (1938), Buenos Aires, Losada, 1956 (Bibl. contemporánea, 89). *La bahía de silencio* (1940), 4th ed., Buenos Aires, Sudamericana, 1960. *Todo verdor perecerá* (1941), 2nd ed., Buenos Aires, Espasa-Calpe, 1951 (Col. austral, 502); *ibid.*, Madrid, Aguilar, 1952; prologue by Guillermo de Torre. *Las águilas,*

Buenos Aires, Sudamericana, 1943. *Los enemigos del alma,* Buenos Aires, Sudamericana, 1950. *La torre,* Buenos Aires, Sudamericana, 1951. *Chaves,* Buenos Aires, Losada, 1953. *Notas de un novelista,* Buenos Aires, Emecé, 1954. *Posesión (3 novelas cortas),* Buenos Aires, Sudamericana, 1958. *La razón humana,* Buenos Aires, Losada, 1959 (Bibl. contemporánea, 291). *Las travesías,* 2 vols., Buenos Aires, Sudamericana, 1961-1962. *Obras completas,* 2 vols., Buenos Aires, Emecé, 1961; prologue by Mariano Picón-Salas.

TRANSLATIONS

Stuart Edgar Grummon (trans.), *The Bay of Silence,* New York, Knopf, 1944. Flores and Poore, 11-119. Jones, 294-302. H. de Onís, *Spanish Stories,* 188-208.

CRITICAL REFERENCES

See texts and editions above. Alegría, *Breve hist.,* 231-236. Arrieta, IV, 274-284. *Diccionario . . . Argentina,* II, 319-323. Arnold Chapman, "Terms of Spiritual Isolation in Eduardo Mallea," *Modern Language Forum,* XXXVI (1951), 21-27. Patrick O. Dudgeon, *Eduardo Mallea, a Personal Study of His Work,* Buenos Aires, Agonía, 1949. Arturo Morsella, *Eduardo Mallea,* Buenos Aires, Mac-Co, 1956. John H. Polt, *The Writings of Eduardo Mallea,* Berkeley and Los Angeles, Univ. of California Press, 1959. José M. Topete, "Eduardo Mallea y el laberinto de la agonía," *Revista iberoamericana,* 39 (1955), 117-151.

*9. (Cuba) **Alejo Carpentier** (1904-   ) was born in Havana, the son of a French architect and a Russian lady professor. He studied in Cuba, and later in Paris. His first specialty was architecture, but later he took advanced work in musical theory, and became a journalist, radio-station director, and musicologist. He has taught both the history of music and general anthropology, and was the author of the first history of Cuban music published in that country. Carpentier is a widely-traveled man, and has visited for extended periods, France, the United States, Venezuela, Mexico, Spain, Belgium, Holland, and the Andean countries. For a considerable period he wrote regularly for *El nacional* of Caracas.

Carpentier's best-known novels are *¡Ecue-Yamba-O!* (1933), an Afro-Cuban story; *El reino de este mundo* (1949), an Antillean surrealistic tale placed in the epoch of the slaves' struggle for independence on the island of Santo Domingo and written with a masterful interweaving of reality and fantasy; and his masterpiece, *Los pasos perdidos* (1953), in which the protagonist, a musician, moves backward in time as he makes a trip from a large U.S. city to a primitive valley in the upper reaches of the Orinoco, where he finds a group of forest people living in the Stone Age. The reason for the trip is to bring back some primitive musical instruments, but at the end of his journey the composer stumbles upon a sylvan and human paradise. He witnesses the birth of music, of dance, and of religion among the Stone-Age inhabitants of this isolated place. While he is there the gift of composition flowers in him, he composes feverishly, and loves without reservation. He leaves the valley briefly in order to carry musical instruments back to the museum and to obtain more paper for his musical compositions, but when he attempts to return the rivers have risen and he cannot again find his lost paradise. It is impossible for him to relive the same miracle, or to recapture the same dream. The whole story is symbolic of civilization's quest for its ancient roots, and for creative man's search for the mythological sources of human culture and art.

SUGGESTED READING

Los pasos perdidos.

EDITIONS

El reino de este mundo (1949), Lima, Organización Continental de los Festivales del Libro, 1958. *Los pasos perdidos* (1953), México, Cía. General de Ediciones, 1959. *El acoso,* Buenos Aires, Losada, 1956. *Guerra del tiempo,* México, EDIAPSA, 1958. *El siglo de las luces,* México, EDIAPSA, 1962.

TRANSLATIONS

Harriet de Onís (trans.), *The Lost Steps,* New York, Knopf, 1956; also *The Kingdom of This World,* New York, Knopf, 1957. John Sturrock (trans.), *Explosion in a Cathedral,* London, Gollancz, 1963. Torres-Ríoseco, *Short Stories,* 95-110.

CRITICAL REFERENCES

See texts and editions above. Alegría, *Breve hist.,* 257-263. Salvador Bueno, "Alejo Carpentier, novelista antillano y universal," *La letra como testigo,* Santa Clara, Cuba, Univ. Central de Las Villas, 1957, 153-179. Julieta Campos, "El realismo subjetivo de Alejo Carpentier," *Universidad de México,* (July, 1959), 17-19. Elena Poniatowska, *Palabras cruzadas,* México, Eds. Era, 1961. Frances Wyers Weber,

"*El acoso:* Alejo Carpentier's War on Time," *PMLA,* LXXVIII (1963), 440-448.

c. Historical, Regional, Autobiographical

°1. (Argentina) **Enrique Larreta** (1875-1961), minister plenipotentiary to France, 1910-1911, economically independent, lived abroad for long periods of time. He always had a deep love for Spain and Hispanic tradition. He wrote comparatively little. He won immediate and early fame for his *La gloria de don Ramiro* (1908), a masterful reconstruction of Spanish life in the days of Philip II, which is considered to be one of the best historical novels in Spanish of all time. He labored on this novel for five years, and carried out careful research in order to make certain that his facts and descriptions were accurate. The book is a beautifully written example of literary impressionism. *Zogoibi* (1926), his only other important work, represents his attempt to depict life on his native pampas, but the novel does not ring true. Larreta's style is polished and classic.

SUGGESTED READING

La gloria de don Ramiro.

TEXTS

Flores, 269-275.

EDITIONS

La gloria de don Ramiro (1908), 10th ed., Buenos Aires, Espasa-Calpe, 1960 (Col. austral, 74). *Zogoibi* (1926), Buenos Aires, Espasa-Calpe, 1953 (Col. austral, 85). *La calle de la vida y de la muerte,* Buenos Aires, Espasa-Calpe, 1943 (Col. austral, 382). *Tenía que suceder,* Buenos Aires, Espasa-Calpe, 1944 (Col. austral, 411). *La que buscaba don Juan, Artemis, y discursos,* Buenos Aires, Espasa-Calpe, 1945 (Col. austral, 510). *Dramáticas personas,* Buenos Aires, Kraft, 1959. *Obras completas,* 2 vols., Buenos Aires, Zamora, 1959; edited by Arturo Berenguer Carísomo and Enrique de Gandía.

TRANSLATIONS

Jones, 253-257. L. B. Walton (trans.), *The Glory of Don Ramiro,* New York, Dutton, 1924.

CRITICAL REFERENCES

See texts and editions above. Alegría, *Breve hist.,* 129-131. Amado Alonso, *El modernismo en La gloria de don Ramiro,* Buenos Aires, Universidad de Buenos Aires, 1942. Arrieta, IV, 251-260. Arturo

Berenguer Carísimo, *Los valores eternos en la obra de Enrique Larreta,* Buenos Aires, Sopena, 1946. *La gloria de don Ramiro en veinticinco años de crítica, 1908-1933,* Buenos Aires, Rosso, 1934. André Jansen, "El cincuentenario de una gran novela," *Revista hispánica moderna,* XXV (1959), 199-206.

°°2. (Uruguay) **Carlos Reyles** (1868-1938) was born into a wealthy family of Irish ancestry in Uruguay, and inherited a large fortune. After the death of his father in 1886 he went to Europe where he lived for a considerable time in Spain. He married an actress and for a time led a Bohemian café life. One of his first stories, "Doménico," was praised effusively by the great Spanish orator, Emilio Castelar.

Reyles was a man of considerable culture and had read widely in European literatures. He was strongly influenced by naturalism. He was also the first to introduce the psychological novel in Spanish America. His first two novels in the naturalistic vein, *Por la vida* (1888) and *Beba* (1894), caused a riot of protest in Uruguay and Argentina. In works that followed, particularly in *La raza de Caín* (1900) and *El terruño* (1916), he continues to develop his literary techniques and realistic probing. Some of his scenes are pornographic and brutal. His one modernistic novel, *El embrujo de Sevilla* (1922), stands apart from the remainder of his work, and is an impressionistic evocation of the popular song, dance, and bullfight of Andalusia, in which, Reyles affirms, Spain has achieved her essential emotional expression. The city of Seville named him an adopted citizen after the publication of this novel.

After World War I Reyles lost his fortune, and in 1932, already an old man, he produced a work which many call his masterpiece, *El gaucho Florido,* in which he essays to recapture the gaucho past of his region and culture. Aside from his writing, Reyles also served as professor in the fields of philosophy and literature at the University of Montevideo, a position especially created for him by the Chamber of Deputies.

SUGGESTED READING

El embrujo de Sevilla or *El terruño.*

TEXTS

Flores, 467-483. Holmes, *Span. Am.,* 476-478. Torres-Ríoseco, *Ant. lit. hisp.,* 26-30.

EDITIONS

El terruño (1916), Buenos Aires, Losada, 1945 (Bibl. contemporánea, 163). *El embrujo de Sevilla* (1922), Buenos Aires, Espasa-Calpe, 1944 (Col. austral, 208). *El gaucho Florido* (1932), Buenos Aires, Espasa-Calpe, 1940 (Col. austral, 88). *Ego sum, ensayos,* Buenos Aires, Sopena, 1939.

TRANSLATIONS

Jacques LeClerq (trans.), *Castanets (El embrujo de Sevilla),* London and New York, Longmans, 1929.

CRITICAL REFERENCES

See texts and editions above. Alegría, *Breve hist.,* 124-129. Martha Allen, "La personalidad literaria de Carlos Reyles," *Revista iberoamericana,* 23 (1947), 91-117. Barbagelata, 123-132. García Calderón, *Semblanzas,* 163-174. Luis Alberto Menafra, *Carlos Reyles,* Montevideo, Síntesis, 1957. Edwin S. Morby, "Una batalla entre antiguos y modernos: Juan Valera y Carlos Reyles," *Revista iberoamericana,* 7 (1941), 119-143. Torres-Ríoseco, *Grandes novelistas,* I, 175-219. Zum Felde, *Índice crítico,* II, 55-59 *et passim.*

3. (Argentina) **Ricardo Güiraldes (1886-1927) was the greatest stylist among the many gauchesque writers of the River Plate region. He came of a wealthy and cultured Argentine family, and made the first of his many trips to Europe at the age of two. Paris was the axis of his exterior intellectual life, but when he was in his own country he loved to visit the estancia of San Antonio de Areco, in Buenos Aires province, where he knew the prototype of his famous Don Segundo Sombra. From the date of his first short stories, which came out in 1915, to the publication of his last and greatest work, *Don Segundo Sombra* (1926), a year before his death, Güiraldes bent his greatest efforts toward poeticizing and immortalizing the essential and vital aspects of his country's gauchesque past. Utilizing a brilliantly colorful style, replete with striking imagery, and viewing the gaucho nostalgically as from some peak of memory, he recaptures this past of Argentina in unforgettable language. Even his novelette, *Rosaura* (1922), and his novelized travelogue, *Xaimaca* (1923), which are not on gaucho themes, are outstanding for their impressionistic poetic style and imagery. Perhaps better than any other prosist, Güiraldes represents the fusion of a European literary background with vital native themes, and successfully blends the two into an artistic and universal whole.

SUGGESTED READING

Don Segundo Sombra.

TEXTS

Anderson Imbert and Florit, 622-625. Flores, 411-416. Holmes, *Span. Am.*, 75-78. Manzor, 45-50. Noé, 562-564. Onís, 964-967. *Don Segundo Sombra* (ed. Plimpton and Fernández), New York, Holt, 1945. Torres-Ríoseco, *Ant. lit. hisp.,* 73-78.

EDITIONS

Cuentos de muerte y de sangre (1915), Buenos Aires, Losada, 1952 (Bibl. contemporánea, 231). *Raucho* (1917), Buenos Aires, Losada, 1945 (Bibl. contemporánea, 72). *Rosaura y siete cuentos,* Buenos Aires, Losada, 1952 (Bibl. contemporánea, 238). *Xaimaca* (1923), Buenos Aires, Losada, 1950 (Bibl. contemporánea, 129). *Don Segundo Sombra* (1926), vol. 6 of *Obras,* Madrid, Espasa-Calpe, 1931-1933; *ibid.,* Buenos Aires, Losada, 1950 (Bibl. contemporánea, 49). *Pampa (poemas inéditos),* Buenos Aires, Ed. Ollantay, 1954. *Obras completas,* Buenos Aires, Emecé, 1962; prologue by Luis Bernárdez, appendix and bibliography by Horacio Jorge Becco.

TRANSLATIONS

Frank, 181-235. Jones, 242-249. Harriet de Onís (trans.), *Don Segundo Sombra,* New York, Farrar and Rinehart, 1935; *ibid.,* Penguin Books, London, 1948 (paperback); also her *Spanish Stories,* 176-181.

CRITICAL REFERENCES

See texts and editions above. Alegría, *Breve hist.,* 181-190. Guillermo Ara, *Ricardo Güiraldes,* Buenos Aires, La Mandrágora, 1961. Arrieta, IV, 134-143. Horacio Jorge Becco, *Don Segundo Sombra y su vocabulario,* Buenos Aires, Ed. Ollantay, 1952. Ernesto G. Da Cal, "*Don Segundo Sombra,* teoría y simbolismo del gaucho," *Cuadernos americanos,* XLI (1948), 245-259. *Diccionario . . . Argentina,* I, 76-80. Dora Pastoriza de Etchebarne, *Elementos románticos en las novelas de Ricardo Güiraldes,* Buenos Aires, Perrot, 1957. Eunice Joiner Gates, "The Imagery of *Don Segundo Sombra,*" *Hispanic Review,* XVI (1948), 33-49. Michael P. Predmore, "The Function and Symbolism of Water Imagery in *Don Segundo Sombra,*" *Hispania,* XLIV (1961), 428-431. Giovanni Previtali, *Ricardo Güiraldes and Don Segundo Sombra,* New York, Hispanic Institute, 1963. Spell, 191-205. Torres-Ríoseco, *Grandes novelistas,* I, 79-107; also his

"Definición de *Don Segundo Sombra,*" *Memoria del quinto congreso,* 123-133.

°4. (Argentina) **Benito Lynch** (1880-1951) was born in La Plata of mixed Irish, French, and Spanish ancestry. His family belonged to the well-to-do landowning class. At an early age he was taken to live on an estancia in Buenos Aires province called *El Deseado.* Here he learned the gaucho jargon and learned at first hand the psychology of those who live close to the earth. When he was ten the boy was sent back to La Plata to school. His first writing appeared in *El día* of La Plata, and later he became one of the owners of this paper. However, his grand entrance to the literary scene was not made until 1916, when Lynch was 31 years old, with the publication of his novel *Los caranchos de la Florida.* Both Horacio Quiroga and Manuel Gálvez, neither of them professional literary critics, went out of their way to lavish praise on this novel.

Other of Lynch's novels which have attracted wide attention are his masterpiece, *El inglés de los güesos* (1924), which tells of the tragic love of a wild girl of the pampas for an English archaeologist, and *El romance de un gaucho* (1933), which merits a place alongside *Don Segundo Sombra* as a gaucho classic. Many of Lynch's short stories are also extremely effective, and these, too, mainly treat rural themes. Lynch's dialogue is completely spontaneous and natural, without impressionistic or stylized overtones. He is a regional realist in the finest tradition, dedicated heart and soul to his beloved Argentine countryside. He was excessively retiring, and very few details are known about his life or the inner processes of his creative art.

SUGGESTED READING

El inglés de los güesos and "El antojo de la patrona."

TEXTS

Flores, 374-382. Manzor, 63-68. Walsh, *Cuentos,* 67-74. Walsh, *Relatos,* 119-154. G. M. Walsh, 64-72. Torres-Ríoseco, *Ant. lit. hisp.,* 58-66.

EDITIONS

Los caranchos de la Florida (1916), Buenos Aires, Espasa-Calpe, 1945 (Col. austral, 50). *El inglés de los güesos* (1924), México, El Libro Popular, 1955; prologue and bibliography by Xavier Dacal; *ibid.,* Buenos Aires, Ed. Troquel, 1958; *ibid.,* México, La Prensa, 1963. *De los campos porteños,* Buenos Aires, Ed. Anaconda, 1931. *El estanciero,*

Buenos Aires, Rosso, 1933. *El romance de un gaucho* (1933), Buenos Aires, Kraft, 1961. *Palo verde y otras novelas cortas* (1940), Buenos Aires, Espasa-Calpe, 1941 (Col. austral, 127). *Cuentos de nuestra tierra,* Buenos Aires, Raigal, 1952.

CRITICAL REFERENCES

See texts and editions above. Alegría, *Breve hist.,* 190-194. Arrieta, IV, 144-154. Julio Caillet-Bois and Albertina Sonol, *La novela rural de Benito Lynch y bibliografía de Benito Lynch,* La Plata, Univ. Nacional, 1960. Nicolás Cócaro, *Benito Lynch. Algunos aspectos de su obra,* Buenos Aires, Oeste, 1954. *Diccionario . . . Argentina,* I, 124-127. Eunice Joiner Gates, "Charles Darwin and Benito Lynch's *El inglés de los güesos*," *Hispania,* XLIV (1961), 250-254. Marshall R. Nason, "Benito Lynch ¿otro Hudson?," *Revista iberoamericana,* 45 (1958), 65-82. J. Riis Owre, "Los animales en las obras de Benito Lynch," *Revista iberoamericana,* 6 (1941), 357-369. Robert Salama, *Benito Lynch,* Buenos Aires, La Mandrágora, 1959. Torres-Ríoseco, *Grandes novelistas,* I, 111-171.

5. (Chile) **Mariano Latorre** (1886-1955) is the best-known exponent of Chilean regionalism in this century. Born in the south of that country, he completed his education in Valparaíso and Santiago. He studied law but soon gave it up in order to have more time for reading and writing. The French realists and naturalists were his favorites. In Santiago he worked for a time as a librarian but finally became professor of Spanish, and as teacher, writer, and editor, was mentor of a generation of students and leader of the group of Chilean regionalists. From the publication of his first book of short stories, *Cuentos del Maule* (1912), up to his final work, *La Paquera* (1958), which came out posthumously, Latorre stuck to his last and sought variety only in presenting as many types and different regions of his native country as he possibly could: the Chilean South, the mountains, the sea, the desert, the islands. His characters were equally varied: seamen, peasants, *huasos,* rural types of many kinds, Germans of the South. But to Latorre the great character in Chile was the landscape, as he himself stated, and it was to nature that he dedicated his best efforts. Had he belonged to the last century his work would have occupied a high place in Chilean literature, but as a representative of the twentieth century his reputation has diminished somewhat with the passage of the years.

SUGGESTED READING
"El piloto Oyarzo," "La desconocida."
TEXTS
Anthology, 696-707. Anderson Imbert and Florit, 632-637. Flores, 541-557. Leavitt, 53-103. Manzor, 209-220.
EDITIONS
Cuentos del Maule, Santiago, Zig-Zag, 1912. *Cuna de cóndores* (1918), 4th ed., Santiago, Nascimento, 1949; prologue by Emilio Vaïsse, study by Eliodoro Astorquiza. *Sus mejores cuentos* (1925), 3rd ed., Santiago, Nascimento, 1962. *Chilenos del mar,* Santiago, Imp. Universitaria, 1929. *On Panta* (1935) 4th ed., Santiago, Zig-Zag, 1944. *Hombres y zorros* (1937), 2nd ed., Santiago, Nascimento, 1945. *Viento de mallines,* Santiago, Zig-Zag, 1944. *Chile, país de rincones,* Buenos Aires, Espasa-Calpe, 1947 (Col. austral, 680). *Autobiografía de una vocación,* Santiago, Universidad de Chile, 195?.
TRANSLATIONS
Arciniegas, 124-137. Haydn and Cournos, 864-872. H. de Onís, 258-279.
CRITICAL REFERENCES
See texts and editions above. Alegría, *Breve hist.,* 198-199. Magda Arce, "Mariano Latorre," *Revista iberoamericana,* 9 (1942), 121-130; 10 (1942), 359-381; 11 (1943), 303-334; also her "Mariano Latorre, novelista chileno contemporáneo," *Revista hispánica moderna,* IX (1943), 21-58. *Diccionario . . . Chile,* 107-108. Julio Orlandi, *Mariano Latorre,* Santiago, Ed. del Pacífico, 1959. Francisco Santana, *Mariano Latorre,* Santiago, Bello, 1956. Silva Castro, *Panorama nov. chil.,* 141-147.

°6. (Per,) **Ciro Alegría** (1909-1967) was born in northern Peru, and is a descendant of the same Lynch family to which Benito Lynch, famous Argentine novelist, belonged. Alegría's father was named José Alegría Lynch, and was, Ángel Flores tells us, as adept with the plow as he was with the pen. He was the owner of a small estate in northern Peru, and occasionally wrote articles for papers in Trujillo. One of these was a review of his son's first novel, *La serpiente de oro* (1935).

Ciro Alegría was extremely fortunate in having as the teacher of his first grade, César Vallejo, who today is ranked as one of the country's finest poets. After completing his elementary education the boy lived for a time with his grandfather on the edge of the Peruvian jungle. Here he came to know at first hand the lives of the Indians and cholos of that area. Alegría finished his education at the Colegio de San Juan and began to write (mainly for *El norte,* Trujillo) and to participate in politics. He became a member of the APRA party headed by Raúl Haya de la Torre. In 1931 he was imprisoned when that party was persecuted by the national government. Later, when APRA victories at the polls were annulled by a military coup he left Peru permanently, first going to Chile (1934), where he achieved eminence as a writer, and later to the United States, Cuba, and Puerto Rico. Alegría is the author of three good novels about the natives of the Peruvian Andean area, the last of which, *El mundo es ancho y ajeno* (1941), won the international prize offered by the North American publishing house of Farrar and Rinehart for the best Latin American novel. It is a strongly pro-Indian novel of social protest, but contains many passages of very poetic prose and sensitive symbolism. Thomas Mann's *The Magic Mountain* (1924) appears to have influenced the author's presentation of time.

SUGGESTED READING

El mundo es ancho y ajeno.

TEXTS

Flores, 557-561. Jones and Hansen, 187-196. *El mundo es ancho y ajeno* (ed. Wade and Stiefel), New York, Appleton-Century-Crofts, 1945. Walsh, *Relatos,* 88-118.

EDITIONS

La serpiente de oro (1935), Lima, Nuevo Mundo, 1960; *ibid.,* Lima, Populibros, 1963. *Los perros hambrientos* (1939), Santiago, Zig-Zag, 1942; *ibid.,* Lima, Populibros, 1963. *El mundo es ancho y ajeno* (1941), 20th ed., Buenos Aires, Losada, 1961; *ibid.,* 6th ed., México, Ed. Diana, '1963. *Novelas completas,* 2nd ed. Madrid, Aguilar, 1964. *Duelo de caballeros,* Lima, Populibros, 1963.

TRANSLATIONS

Jones, 198-204. Harriet de Onís (trans.), *Broad and Alien Is the World,* New York, Farrar and Rinehart, 1941; *ibid.,* Philadelphia, Dufour Eds., 1962; also *The Golden Serpent,* New York, Farrar and Rinehart, 1943; *ibid.,* New York, Signet Classics, 1963 (paperback); with an afterword by Harriet de Onís. Torres-Ríoseco, *Short Stories,* 111-121.

CRITICAL REFERENCES

See texts and editions above. Ciro Alegría, "Notas sobre el personaje en la novela hispanoamericana," *Memoria del quinto congreso,* 47-59. Alegría, *Breve hist.,* 252-255. Spell, 253-269.

7. (Venezuela) **Teresa de la Parra** (1895-1936), who was born on an hacienda near Caracas received most of her education in Paris, where she spent much of her short life. She is one of the most original and most charming of American women prose writers. In an inimitable personal style, she has penned delightful sketches of Venezuelan rural life. *Las memorias de Mamá Blanca* (1929), a book of childhood reminiscences, ranks high in American autobiographical fiction.

SUGGESTED READING

Las memorias de Mamá Blanca.

TEXTS

Las memorias de Mamá Blanca (ed. García-Prada and Wilson), New York, Macmillan, 1932. Holmes, *Span. Am.,* 537-541. *Blanca Nieves y Compañía* (ed. García-Prada), Boston, Heath, 1946. Latcham, 303-311. Walsh, *Relatos,* 63-87.

EDITIONS

Ifigenia (1924), 3rd ed., Caracas, Las Novedades, 194?; *ibid.,* Lima, Organización Continental de los Festivales del Libro, 1958. *Las memorias de Mamá Blanca,* París, Le Livre Libre, 1929. *Cartas,* Caracas, Cruz del Sur, 1951; prologue by Mariano Picón-Salas. *Tres conferencias inéditas,* Caracas, Garrido, 1961.

TRANSLATIONS

Harriet de Onís (trans.), *Mama Blanca's Souvenirs,* Washington, Pan American Union, 1959.

CRITICAL REFERENCES

See texts and editions above. Alegría, *Breve hist.,* 204-205. Ratcliff, 214-232. Uslar Pietri, *Letras y hombres,* 148-153.

8. (Mexico) **José Rubén Romero** (1890-1952) was born in a village in Michoacán where his father was a merchant and small-town politician. The son was brought up in this lower middle-class atmosphere, and when the Revolution broke out he joined in the Madero revolt and became a part of it. In 1917 Romero himself entered politics and rose rapidly in its hierarchy, serving as ambassador of his country in both Brazil and Cuba for an extended period. His writing reflects

rather faithfully his own racy and colorful life. His masterpieces are *La vida inútil de Pito Pérez* (1938), the life of a Mexican *pícaro* whose search for goodness and beauty in an ugly world is unswerving, and *Rosenda* (1946), the beautiful story of a country girl who gives herself joyfully, without restraint and without question, for love, and thus transcends both faulty knowledge and the false dignity of the man who abandons her. The author's love for his own home region and native town and the kind of simple people who live there is a kind of leitmotif which permeates this tenderly-written novel. In all of Romero's fiction the element of humor, symbolic, ironic, mordant, tender, entertaining, and occasionally downright disgusting, is a distinguishing characteristic, and is perhaps the outstanding trademark of the author.

SUGGESTED READING

La vida inútil de Pito Pérez.

TEXTS

Castro Leal, *Novela,* II, 3-133. *Cuatro siglos lit. mex.,* 790-793, 881-887 (inc. poems).

EDITIONS

Desbandada (1934), 2nd ed., Barcelona, A. Núñez, 1936. *El pueblo inocente* (1934), 3rd ed., Barcelona, A. Núñez, 1936. *La vida inútil de Pito Pérez* (1938), 8th ed., México, Porrúa, 1946. *Breve historia de mis libros,* Habana, La Verónica, 1962. *Rosenda* (1946), 3rd ed., México, Porrúa, 1962. *Obras completas,* México, Eds. Oasis, 1957; prologue by Antonio Castro Leal.

TRANSLATIONS

Flores and Poore, 303-367.

CRITICAL REFERENCES

See texts and editions above. Pedro de Alba, *Rubén Romero y sus novelas populares,* Barcelona, A. Núñez, 1936. Alegría, *Breve hist.,* 156-163. William O. Cord, "José Rubén Romero: the Writer as Seen by Himself," *Hispania,* XLIV (1961), 431-438. González, *Trayectoria,* 223-249. *José Rubén Romero, vida y obra, bibliografía, antología,* New York, Hispanic Institute, 1946; edited by Andrés Iduarte, Juan José Arreola, et al. Gastón La Farga, *La evolución literaria de Rubén Romero,* México, n.p., 1939. Morton, 71-95.

9. (Uruguay) **Enrique Amorim** (1900-1960), born in Salto, was sent to Argentina at the age of seventeen to study. He attended a Colegio

Internacional in Olivos, a small town just outside of Buenos Aires. The Italian humanist and professor Francisco Chelia was the director of this institution, and a group of eager young intellectuals and artists gathered around him. Amorim began to write for a student journal, and eventually became a professor of literature at the college. He also worked as secretary in a tax office in Buenos Aires.

Amorim commenced his literary career writing poetry, but he soon switched to the short story and novel and found in these mediums his principal expression. However, he also wrote plays with a fair amount of success. Amorim is known mainly as a rural or gaucho novelist, but his psychological penetration and stylistic superiority, with many flashy images, have extended his dimension beyond that of mere regionalism or *costumbrismo*. In Amorim's works nature assumes human attributes, and human characters assume the qualities of nature. The gaucho finds his fulfillment in his new role as civilized farmer and tiller of the soil. Amorim's two best-known novels are: *El paisano Aguilar* (1934) and *El caballo y su sombra* (1941); the latter was well received in its English translation. He has also attempted the detective novel, now so popular in the River Plate region.

SUGGESTED READING

El caballo y su sombra.

TEXTS

Anderson Imbert and Florit, 719-722. Flores, 578-583.

EDITIONS

La carreta (1929), Buenos Aires, Rosso, 1937; critical commentary by Martiniano Leguizamón, Daniel Granada, Roberto J. Payró, Fernán Silva Valdés, and others, 235-258; *ibid.*, 6th ed., Buenos Aires, Losada, 1953 (Bibl. contemporánea, 237). *El paisano Aguilar* (1934), Buenos Aires, Losada, 1958 (Bibl. contemporánea, 57). *El caballo y su sombra* (1941), 3rd ed., Buenos Aires, Losada, 1957 (Bibl. contemporánea, 120). *Nueve lunas sobre el Neuquén,* Buenos Aires, Lautaro, 1946. *Corral abierto,* Buenos Aires, Losada, 1956. *La desembocadura,* Buenos Aires, Losada, 1958. *Eva Burgos,* Montevideo, Alfa, 1960. *Mi patria,* Montevideo, Imp. Uruguaya, 1960.

TRANSLATIONS

Richard O'Connell and James Graham Luján (trans.), *The Horse and His Shadow,* New York, Scribner's, 1943.

CRITICAL REFERENCES

See texts and editions above. Alegría, *Breve hist.,* 578-579. Alicia Ortiz, *Las novelas de Enrique Amorim,* Buenos Aires, Imp. Chile, 1949.

10. (Venezuela) **Arturo Uslar Pietri** (1906-   ) received his doctor's degree in political science from the University of Venezuela in 1929, then for the following several years traveled in Europe and North Africa as a diplomatic representative of his country. Later, he taught Spanish American literature for a time at Columbia University. He is well known as a critic, short-story writer, and novelist. In his two best-known works of fiction, *Las lanzas coloradas* (1931) and *El camino de El Dorado* (1947), Uslar Pietri has written impressionistically about two historic epochs of his country. The first deals with the struggle for independence, the second with an episode of the sixteenth century. Landscape, heroic legend, astute psychology, and accurate history are all fused in these two excellent novels which resurrect and recreate the historic reality of Venezuela in a well-ordered literary frame. Uslar Pietri has also distinguished himself as a literary critic, particularly in the field of the Spanish American novel and in the general area of Venezuelan literature.

SUGGESTED READING

Las lanzas coloradas and "La lluvia."

TEXTS

Anderson Imbert and Florit, 726-733. Flores, 635-641. Holmes, *Cont. Span. Amers.,* 184-199. Latcham, 182-186. *Las lanzas coloradas* (ed. D. D. Walsh), New York, Norton, 1944.

EDITIONS

Las lanzas coloradas (1931), Santiago, Zig-Zag, 1940; *ibid.,* 4th ed.; Buenos Aires, Losada, 1962 (Bibl. contemporánea, 64). *Red,* Caracas, Elite, 1936. *El camino de El Dorado* (1947), 3rd ed., Buenos Aires, Losada, 1954. *Letras y hombres de Venezuela,* México, Fondo de Cultura Económica, 1948. *Las nubes* (ensayos), Caracas, Ministerio de Educación, 1951. *Breve historia de la novela hispanoamericana,* Caracas-Madrid, EDIME, 1954. *Un retrato en la geografía,* Buenos Aires, Losada, 1962. *Obras selectas,* Madrid-Caracas, EDIME, 1953.

TRANSLATIONS

Colford, 118-126. Harriet de Onís (trans.), *The Red Lances,* New York, Knopf, 1963.

CRITICAL REFERENCES

See texts and editions above. Alegría, *Breve hist.*, 268-270. Manuel García Hernández, *Literatura venezolana contemporánea*, 1ª serie, Buenos Aires, Eds. Argentinas, 1945, 345-351. González, *Estudios*, 287-296. Emilio González López, "Uslar Pietri y la novela histórica venezolana," *Revista hispánica moderna*, XIII (1947), 44-49. Arturo Uslar Pietri, "The Spanish American Novel Declares its Independence," *Books Abroad*, XI (1938), 150-152; also his "My Debt to Books," *Books Abroad*, XII (1939), 164.

°°11. (Mexico) **Agustín Yáñez** (1904-   ) was born and received his early education in Guadalajara in the state of Jalisco which figures so prominently in his novels. He supported himself as a journalist and teacher until he obtained a law degree there in 1929. Later he attended the National University in Mexico City where he took the degree of doctor in philosophy and then served as a professor of esthetics and literature. His earlier work attracted considerable attention for its impressive poetic style, but it was not until the publication of his magnum opus, *Al filo del agua* (1947), that he achieved national and international renown as a writer.

This unique novel is without question one of the finest to come out of Spanish America. Yáñez's immediate masters were James Joyce, Aldous Huxley and William Faulkner, but there are strong overtones of Freud, and of several writers of the Generation of 1898 in Spain. The polished, poetic, hypnotic language of this novel fits in perfectly with the author's main purpose, which is to present and interpret the strongly repressed inner feelings of the inhabitants of a small town in Jalisco just prior to the outbreak of the Revolution. The hermetic life of this town, with its religious obsessions and sexual inhibitions, reaches several exploding points. In 1953 Yáñez was elected governor of the state of Jalisco, in which position he performed only moderately well. He is still active in both politics and literature, and continues to teach in the latter field. His recent production has been both voluminous and of first-rate quality. *La creación* appeared in 1959, *Ojerosa y pintada* and *La tierra pródiga* came out in 1960, and these were followed by *Las tierras flacas* in 1962. A terse poetic prose, keen psychological insight, and a great talent for establishing emotional moods characterize all of these works.

Al filo del agua.

SUGGESTED READING

TEXTS

Flores, 586-590.

EDITIONS

Archipiélago de mujeres, México, Univ. Nacional, 1943. *Al filo del agua* (1947), 2nd ed., México, Porrúa, 1955; with prologue by Antonio Castro Leal. *La creación* (1959), 2nd ed., México, Fondo de Cultura Económica, 1959. *Ojerosa y pintada,* México, Libro-Mex, 1960. *La tierra pródiga,* México, Fondo de Cultura Económica, 1960. *Las tierras flacas,* México, Joaquín Mortiz, 1962.

TRANSLATIONS

Ethel Brinton (trans.), *The Edge of the Storm,* Austin, Univ. of Texas Press, 1963. Torres-Ríoseco, *Short Stories,* 137-158.

CRITICAL REFERENCES

See texts and editions above. Alegría, *Breve hist.,* 237-242. González, *Trayectoria,* 327-338. Martínez, *Lit. mex. siglo XX,* I, 201-213. Morton, 223-231. George P. Schade, "Augury in *Al filo del agua,*" *Texas Studies in Literature and Language,* Austin, Univ. of Texas Press, 1960, 78-87. José Vázquez Amaral, "Técnica novelística de Agustín Yáñez," *Cuadernos americanos,* XCVIII (1958), 245-251.

III.
Drama

The nativist theater continued to amuse with its superficial depiction of local types and customs. However, Florencio Sánchez had signaled the way to a more serious dramatic effort by probing into the social ills and conflicts of the River Plate scene, and Ibsen's (1829-1906) growing influence bestirred many in the Americas to contribute to the mounting repertoire of somber thesis plays. In Mexico, the Revolution gave birth to an intensely nationalistic theater movement in which the creators of the new order exploited the rich popular heritage, and plastic and lyrical media, to awaken the national pride and purpose. But in spite of such attempts in Mexico, and in other countries, to develop a national dramatic tradition, the theater still lacked perspective and appeal; didactic in tone and shallow in characterization, it failed to produce a dramatist who could interpret the American scene in universal terms.

The change came in the decade following World War I. Earlier efforts on the part of individual groups, variously labeled *Sociedad de Amigos del Teatro,* burgeoned into a rapidly-expanding movement of rededication and revival, as experimental groups, on their own initiative and sometimes with government support, sought to breathe life and art into a theater that had stagnated on the professional stage. Ibsen was no longer alone. In their search for new approaches and techniques, the young Latin American enthusiasts discovered Shaw (1856-1950), Synge (1871-1909), Pirandello (1867-1936), **and** O'Neill (1888–1953); and later, Eliot (1888–1965), Brecht (1898-1956), Sartre (1905-   ), Camus (1913-1960), Tennessee Williams (1914-   ), and Arthur Miller (1915-   ). Translations were performed by university and "little theater" movements everywhere, and national playwrights began to respond by contributing plays that were not long in winning critical and popular acclaim. The better-known and more fruitful of the early experimental theater groups appeared in Mexico in the late twenties: the Teatro de Ulises in 1928, the Teatro de Orientación in 1932. Xavier Villaurrutia (1903–1951) and Celestino Gorostiza (1904–1967) were among the founders and leaders associated with both groups. This experimental theater was largely the creation of poets. Under their guidance Mexican drama took on new poetic and philosophical dimensions; it assumed a life of its own, apart from the immediate environment in which it struggled for survival. The majority of the experimental movements that sprang up in the thirties were short-lived, and largely ineffectual. However, the seed had been planted and a higher sense of professionalism soon made itself felt throughout the theater as a whole. In Argentina, much of the credit for this new focus and emphasis was due to the untiring efforts of the historic Teatro del Pueblo (1930-1943) under the professional guidance of Leónidas Barletta.

The experimental theater continues to be a vital and revitalizing force everywhere in the Americas today. Under the stimulus of such continuing experimentation, writers have begun to portray and to probe more deeply into the national scene, now from the vantage point of broadening universal perspective and sharper psychological perception. Under their guidance the theater is being returned to the professionals and to the people. This revitalized professional stage has become highly receptive to plays of poetic and universal appeal of the quality sustained by Argentina's poet and humorist, Conrado Nalé Roxlo (1898-   ). However, the vast majority of plays of recent years have been written, and often produced and directed, by men born to the theater and no less concerned with the esthetic and technical preoccupations of the poets and the experimentalists. Armando Moock (1894-1942) of Chile, Samuel Eichelbaum (1894-   ) of Argentina, and Rodolfo Usigli (1904-   ) of Mexico have established the theater on a firm and modern professional footing.

REFERENCES

Anderson Imbert, II, *passim*. Jones, *Breve hist.*, *passim*. Magaña Esquivel and Lamb, 99-167. Ordaz, 103-316. Solórzano, *passim*.

1. (Argentina) Samuel Eichelbaum (1894-   ), journalist, short-story writer, and dramatist, was born in Domínguez in the province of

Entre Ríos. He began writing dramatic skits when he was but seven years of age. It was in the provinces, in Rosario, that he was to see the first performance of one of his plays. The play was a *sainete* entitled *El lobo manso*. In 1919, with the presentation of *En la quietud del pueblo,* he was introduced for the first time to the Buenos Aires stage. Since that time he has devoted his life to journalism and to the theater, and he has shared fully in the work of organizations and societies concerned with the welfare and the improvement of all aspects of the theater world. He has written steadily since 1919, and his plays have grown in technique and in substance with the years. Recognition first came in 1930 when his play *Señorita* won him the Premio Municipal. Other awards followed: the Premio Jockey Club in 1933, the Premio Gerchunoff of the Instituto Argentino de Cultura e Información in 1953, and the Premio Nacional, for *Dos brasas,* in 1957. Many consider Eichelbaum fully worthy of the mantle of Florencio Sánchez.

Eichelbaum departed early from the traditional nativist theater of his formative years. Ibsen and others helped him find his way. It is Ibsen who is clearly present in *La mala sed* (1920) and, in general, in his plays of case studies of abnormal types. However, once having freed himself of the techniques and the heavy somber tones inevitably imposed by the thesis drama, he began to write more and more in keeping with his own rapidly-developing concept of dramatic art. Plot, action, external reality, these he accepts as essential, but important above all else is the individual human being in his own peculiar inner world. *El gato y su selva* (1936), *Un guapo del 900* (1940), and *Un tal Servando Gómez* (1942) are among the better plays of his later period. *Pájaro de barro* (1940), generally conceded to be his masterpiece, has been called one of the "best poetic works of the Argentine theater."

SUGGESTED READING

Pájaro de barro and *Un guapo del 900.*

TEXTS

Alpern and Martel, 76-114 (*Divorcio nupcial,* 1941). Jones, *Antología,* 190-238 (*Un guapo del 900*).

EDITIONS

El gato y su selva—Un guapo del 900—Pájaro de barro—Dos brasas, Buenos Aires, Sudamericana, 1952; prologue by Bernardo Canal-Feijóo.

TRANSLATIONS
Jones, 405-411.
CRITICAL REFERENCES
See texts and editions above. Anderson Imbert, II, 137-138. Arrieta, IV, 589-592. Jorge Cruz, *Samuel Eichelbaum,* Buenos Aires, Eds. Culturales Argentinas, 1962. *Diccionario . . . Argentina,* II, 280-284. Jones, *Breve hist.,* 78-81. Ordaz, 160-165.

°2. (Chile) **Armando Moock** (1894-1942) was born in Santiago. However, he spent most of his life in Buenos Aires as a popular and successful dramatist, and it was there that he died at his post as Chile's cultural attaché to Argentina. Having abandoned his studies in architecture at the University of Chile, he turned to writing and to the theater as his life-long career, a career that was interrupted only by his years of service in the consular corps, which he entered in 1926, with appointments to France, Spain, and the Argentine. In 1914 he got off to an indifferent start in the theater with the first public performance of his play *Crisis económica.* A year later he won ready applause for his second play, *Isabel Sandoval, Modas.* For six years he wrote, directed, and acted in plays over much of Chile. By 1919 he realized that his future lay in the theater, and he realized too that he had to seek a wider following elsewhere. Buenos Aires received him and his already popular *Pueblecito* (1918) with warm acclaim. *La serpiente* (1920), *Mocosita o la luna en el pozo* (1929), and *Rigoberto* (1935) were among his most popular prize-winning plays both on the American and the foreign stage. It is said that he wrote some 400 pieces. The majority are one-act plays, most of which are as yet inedited. His success in the theater was probably due in no small measure also to his wide popularity as a short-story writer and novelist.

Moock wrote for an admiring public. He knew that his large middle-class following would respond best to his straight comedy on urban types and scenes. Entertaining and essentially wholesome, his theater affords a faithful mirroring of social customs and problems of his day.

SUGGESTED READING
La serpiente.
TEXTS
Alpern and Martel, 116-167 (*La serpiente*).

EDITIONS

Teatro seleccionado, 2 vols., Santiago, Cultura, 1937; among others, contains *La serpiente, Pueblecito, Cuando venga el amor.*

TRANSLATIONS

Jones, 415-422.

CRITICAL REFERENCES

See texts above. *Diccionario . . . Chile,* 139-142. Willis K. Jones, "Armando Moock, Forgotten Chilean Dramatist," *Hispania,* XXII (1939), 41-50; also his *Breve hist.,* 106-109.

*3. (Mexico) **Xavier Villaurrutia** (1903-1950) dedicated his entire life to poetry and the theater. His first poems appeared in 1923, in the anthology *Ocho poetas,* and his first book of verse, *Reflejos,* in 1927. That same year he joined Salvador Novo in launching *Ulises* (1927-1928), the historical review that nurtured the generation of *Contemporáneos* (1928-1931), the same review that, in 1928, gave its name to Mexico's first experimental theater group, the Teatro de Ulises. Villaurrutia's first play, *Parece mentira,* was performed in 1933 by the Teatro de Orientación, the influential successor to the Ulises group with which Villaurrutia had become identified, in the company of Celestino Gorostiza, but a year before. As the recipient of a Rockefeller Fellowship he left Mexico for a year in 1936 to study drama at Yale University. Multiple activities as literary critic, as professor of literature at the University of Mexico, and as director of the theater program of Bellas Artes, crowded his remaining years. His poetry and his plays alike are, fundamentally, the product of a studied, discreet, and intellectual approach to reality and to art. As a poet he sought dispassionately to plumb the emotional depths of life's passionate embrace of death. As a dramatist he sought to penetrate only that reality that was capable of analysis within the techniques and limitations of the theater itself.

SUGGESTED READING

Poetry: "Ya mi súplica es llanto," "Soledad," "Cuadro," "Calles," "Nocturno miedo," "Nocturno eterno," "Nocturno de estatua," "Estancias nocturnas," "Décima muerte," "Inventar la verdad," "Epitafios." Theater: *Parece mentira* and *Invitación a la muerte.*

TEXTS

Poetry: Anderson Imbert and Florit, 665-666. Caillet-Bois, 1504-1509. Castro Leal, *Poesía,* 317-329. Cuesta, 201-211. Onís, 1171-1174.

Theater: *Teatro mex. cont.* (*¿En qué piensas?, Parece mentira, Sea usted breve*). *Teatro mex. siglo XX*, II (*El yerro candente*).
EDITIONS
Poesía y teatro completos, México, Fondo de Cultura Económica, 1953; prologue by Alí Chumacero.
CRITICAL REFERENCES
See texts and editions above. Vera F. Beck, "Xavier Villaurrutia, dramaturgo moderno," *Revista iberoamericana*, 35 (1952), 27-39. Frank Dauster, "La poesía de Xavier Villaurrutia," *Revista iberoamericana*, 36 (1953), 345-359. Leiva, 151-163. Martínez, *Lit. mex. siglo XX, passim*. Magaña Esquivel and Lamb, 129-131. Ruth S. Lamb, "Xavier Villaurrutia and the Modern Mexican Theater," *Modern Language Forum*, XXXIX (1954), 108-114. Donald L. Shaw, "Pasión y verdad en el teatro de Villaurrutia," *Revista iberoamericana*, 54 (1962), 337-346. Torres-Ríoseco, *Ensayos*, I, 204-207.

⁂4. (Mexico) **Rodolfo Usigli** (1905-   ) was born in Mexico City. His interest in the theater stems from his earliest days when as a child he improvised for puppet performances and as a youth he played on the professional stage. In 1924 he began to write his first impressions of plays and performances, and from that day to the present he has devoted his life to the theater as actor, director, critic, and writer. His talents and ambitions were recognized in 1935 when he was awarded a Rockefeller Fellowship to study dramatic theory and comparative drama at Yale. During 1938-1939 he served as director of the theater division of Bellas Artes. In 1940 he founded and directed the Teatro de Medianoche, for which he translated many of the foreign plays performed by the group. And finally, he has represented his country on numerous occasions at international festivals and congresses on the theater and cinema arts and has served at diplomatic posts in Paris (1944), in Beirut (1957) and, more recently, in Oslo.

Usigli's first attempts at writing for the theater date from 1930, but he was not to see a public performance of his plays until 1936 when *Estado de secreto*, a comedy, was presented in Guadalajara at the Teatro Degollado. He has written more than thirty plays. *El niño y la niebla*, composed in 1936, but not staged until 1951, has been one of the most popular. Obviously influenced by Ibsen, it deals with a case of hereditary insanity. *El gesticulador* (1937), a controversial satire on Mexican life and politics, was favorably received when finally performed for the first time in 1947. His "anti-historical" drama on Maximilian and Carlota, *Corona de sombra* (1943), first performed in 1947, has been more successful abroad than at home. In *Jano es una muchacha* (1952), a box-office triumph, he boldly faces up to the question of sexual license.

Usigli is a dedicated and conscientious dramatist. His serious study of dramatic theory and techniques and his intimate knowledge of the foreign theater—*México en el teatro* (1932) and *Itinerario del autor dramático* (1940)—have served to sharpen his extraordinary powers of observation and analysis. He is a master of dialogue. Thus fortified, he has probed fearlessly beneath the surface of the national scene, not with the thought of contributing to the cure of his country's ills, but solely for the purpose of creating a theater worthy of Mexico's artistic potential.

SUGGESTED READING

El gesticulador and *Corona de sombra*.

TEXTS

Jones, *Antología*, 47-125 (*Corona de sombra*). *Corona de sombra* (ed. Ballinger), New York, Appleton-Century-Crofts, 1961. *Teatro mex. cont.* (*El gesticulador*). *Teatro mex. siglo XX*, II (*El gesticulador*). *El niño y la niebla* (ed. Ballinger), New York, Heath, 1964(paperback).

EDITIONS

Corona de sombra, 3rd ed., México, Cuadernos Americanos, 1959. *El gesticulador*, 3rd ed., México, Ed. Stylo, 1947. *Teatro completo*, 2 vols., México, Fondo de Cultura Económica, (1963-1966).

TRANSLATIONS

Jones, 440-446. William F. Stirling (trans.), *Crown of Shadows*, London, Allan Wingate, 1946. Wayne Wolfe (trans.), *Another Springtime* (*Otra primavera*, 1947), London-New York, S. French, 1961.

CRITICAL REFERENCES

See texts above. Vera F. Beck, "La fuerza motriz en las obras de Usigli," *Revista iberoamericana*, 36 (1953), 369-383. Eunice J. Gates, "Usigli as seen in his prefaces and epilogues," *Hispania*, XXXVII (1954), 432-439. Jones, *Breve hist.*, 170-174. Magaña Esquivel and Lamb, 132-135.

°5. (Argentina) **Conrado Nalé Roxlo** (1898-), poet, humorist, and dramatist, was born in Buenos Aires. Family tradition and early training soon led him into journalism and writing. Recognition first came to him as a poet when in 1923 he received the Babel Prize for his first book of poems, *El grillo*. A year later the same volume was awarded the Premio Municipal for 1924. Other collections of verse, appearing at widely-separated intervals, in 1937 and again in 1952, have established him as one of the best of the deeply sincere and sensitive poets of the postmodernist reaction. His extensive prose writings—articles, sketches, pastiches, short stories—began appearing in book form in 1941 with the publication of his *Cuentos de Chamico*. He ranks high as a "humorist in the Cervantine tradition." His gifts as a short-story writer were recognized in 1956 when he received the Premio Nacional for the collection entitled *Las puertas del purgatorio*.

In 1941 the poet and the humorist joined forces in the production of Nalé's first play, *La cola de la sirena*. Awarded the nation's highest recognition in the theater, it was followed by two other prize-winning plays, *Una viuda difícil*, in 1944, and *El pacto de Cristina*, in 1945. His most recent play, *Judith y las rosas*, appeared in 1956. Poetic and universal in appeal, Nalé's theater takes his audience into a world far removed from that of present-day Argentina. In *La cola de la sirena*, reminiscent of Andersen's "The Little Mermaid," the poet refashions the ancient folkloric theme into a delightful rendition of the age-old and unequal conflict between the hard facts of reality and the illusory dream world of fantasy. Much in the tradition of Spain's classic theater, *Una viuda difícil* gives full play to basic human passions in a complicated and hardly credible plot ostensibly laid in late colonial days. While *El pacto de Cristina*, set in the period of the Crusades, is a variation of the Faust legend, in which it is an innocent maiden who signs the tragic pact. Nalé has given Argentina a theater that transcends traditional themes and techniques to find a permanent place on the international stage.

SUGGESTED READING

Theater: *La cola de la sirena* and *Una viuda difícil*. Poetry: "El grillo," "Los gallos," "Drama nocturno," "Sinceridad," "Se nos ha muerto un sueño," "Lo imprevisto," "Yo quisiera una sombra," "Duo."

IV.
Into the Mainstream

The 1960's and the early 70's witnessed a rich flowering of Spanish American literature. For the first time, wide international attention was drawn to the excellence and versatility of what Spanish American authors were writing, especially in their novels. To the casual reader in New York or Paris this literary "boom" may have seemed a surprising phenomenon, an apparently miraculous birth in virgin lands. Actually, it represented the maturing of literary seeds set out earlier in the century.

In the first place, writers who had shown their mettle in earlier decades forged on to new heights of productivity and fame. Jorge Luis Borges (1899–   ) and Pablo Neruda (1904–1973), especially, continued to develop their genius and to achieve further international recognition. To a lesser degree, this was also true of Eduardo Mallea (1903–   ), Alejo Carpentier (1904–   ), and Augstín Yáñez (1904–   ) in the novel, and Nicolás Guillén (1902–   ) and Jorge Carrera Andrade (1903–   ) in poetry. Among the essayists, Luis Alberto Sánchez (1900–   ) and Germán Arciniegas (1900–   ), have not let age dull their pens.

Furthermore, the imaginative and innovating techniques so much praised in such younger writers such as Carlos Fuentes (1928–   ), Gabriel García Márquez (1928–   ), Guillermo Cabrera Infante (1929–   ) and Mario Vargas Llosa (1936–   ), among others, had years before begun to invigorate the pages of older authors — María Luisa Bombal (1910–   ), Pedro Prado (1886–1952), Horacio Quiroga (1878–1937), and in the early works of Carpentier and Juan Carlos Onetti (1909–   ). In short, the recent upsurge in Spanish American literature has not been a sudden eruption, but the result of an ongoing process of development during the twentieth century.

The rise of a community state in Cuba under Fidel Castro has had, in addition to its political effect in international relations, some palpable influence on the Spanish American literary scene. In Cuba itself, literary activity has been stimulated by the government publishing house,

Casa de las Américas, and, especially in the theatre, several outstanding writers have appeared, e.g., Antón Arrufat (1935-   ) and José Triana (1932-   ). International literary contests sponsored by the Castro regime have encouraged leftist talent in many parts of Spanish America. Some literary production has also burgeoned among Cuban exiles.

Radical socialist ideologies, with the accompanying anti-North American sentiments, have thrived among the younger practitioners of all genres. In the novel and essay, Carlos Fuentes, Mario Vargas Llosa and Mario Benedetti (1920-   ) have professed radical political ideas. In the field of drama, most of the promising writers are in the socialist camp: Jorge Díaz (1930-   ) and Egon Wolff (1926-   ) of Chile, Oswaldo Dragún (1929-   ) of Argentina, and others elsewhere. Among the poets, Ernesto Cardenal (Nicaragua, 1925-   ) has shown his anti-imperialist (United States) attitude in his *Canto nacional* (1973), a long series of poems about his native land, and Enrique Lihn (Chile, 1929-   ) has written verse with leftist sentiments.

It should be emphasized that the radical ideology held by these and other writers has not usually turned their literary production into rank propaganda. Their social criticism is generally an honest and integral part of their view of the human scene.

In fiction, the simple, realistic regionalism of earlier decades, although still practiced by minor authors, especially in Mexico and Colombia, gave away among the major novelists to a more sophisticated type of narrative in which a more sharply-honed style, experimental techniques and more intricate psychological exploration are the dominant characteristics. But under a patina of cosmopolitan universalism, which brought the Spanish American novel into the mainstream of Western literature, there lies in the majority of contemporary novelists a firm substratum of nationalistic concern and even, in some cases, of social protest.

Mario Vargas Llosa, for example, is a master of various literary devices of the novel which are derived in great part from European and North American authors. But at the same time, he is a harsh castigator of those who have been responsible for the social ills of his native Peru. Carlos Fuentes, in his complex *Cambio de piel* (1967), not only is sharply critical of the Mexican "establishment," but also delves into pre-Columbian mythology to give nationalistic substance to his tale. Augusto Roa Bastos (1917   ) skillfully manages surprising structural techniques in his *Hijo de hombre (1960)*, but through them gives us a dreary picture of the social life in his native Paraguay.

The Indian, who claimed the attention of so many regional novelists of earlier days in this century, seldom appears in the pages of contemporary novelists. There have been three signal exceptions: Miguel Angel Asturias (1899-1974), José Maria Arguedas (1911-1969), and Rosario Castellanos (Mexico, 1925-1974). It is significant that all three had training in anthropology; their novels, as a consequence, have an authenticity often lacking in previous *indigenistas*. While they recognize the problems of the Indian, their novels do not usually explode into fiery denunciations.

In the works of some contemporary novelists, the national situation is subordinated to implications of more universal significance. Such is generally the case in the novels of Julio Cortazar (1914-   ), José Donoso (Chile, 1925   ), José Lezama Lima (Cuba, 1912-1976), Manuel Puig (Argentina, 1932-   ), and the short stories of Juan José Arreola (1918-   ) and Mario Benedetti.

A partial explanation of the cosmopolitanism of most recent novelists is the fact that so many of them live or have lived abroad, mostly in Europe, and thus have been in direct contact with avant-garde trends. Miguel Ángel Asturias, Mario Vargas Llosa, Ernesto Sábato and Carlos Fuentes, among others, spent many years in France, and Julio Cortázar is a French citizen. Others, such as Gabriel García Márquez and José Donoso, have lived in Spain. That most of the novelists mentioned dis play a mature attention to craftsmanship is partially due to the fact that they are usually professional writers, not amateurs. In this respect they differ from the majority of their predecessors.

During this period there also continued to flourish a consid erable body of sincere, well-crafted poetry. It is impossible to label it neatly under schools of clearly-defined trends. In form it runs the gamut from bare simplicity to baroque surrealism. Several repeated threads have been woven into a great many contemporary poems—pessimistic existential anguish; philosophical musing; and a desire of the individual to identify with the rest of humanity—sometimes expressed in socialistic terms.

The great poetic voices of the 1960s and early 1970s were those of the older established poets, and above all of Pablo Neruda who continued to write prodigiously until his death in 1973. Others of his generation whose songs were by no means silenced were Carlos Pellicer (1899-1977), José Gorostiza (1901-1973), Nicolás Guillén (1902-   ) and Jorge Carrera Andrade (1903-   ). Octavio Paz (1914-   ), somewhat younger, appears to have lost none of his vigor as a poet and essayist. Nicanor Parra (1914-   ), also younger, has caused spirited controversy with his impish, incongruous poetry.

Among the poets of the newer generation, it is not easy to point to those who will be the master bards in future literary histories. Five names, at least, have impressed critics as poets with outstanding achievement and potentiality: Alberto Girri (Argentina, 1919-   ); Cintio Vitier (Cuba, 1921-   ); Ernesto Cardenal (Nicaragua, 1925 -   ); Jaime Sabines (Mexico, 1925-   ); and Enrique Lihn (Chile, 1929-   ).

Many of the essayists writing during this period who reached a continental public were men past middle age with established reputations: Ezequiel Martínez Estrada (Argentina, 1895-1964); Germán Arciniegas (Colombia, 1900-   ); Luis Alberto Sánchez (Peru, 1900-   ); Mariano Picón Salas (Venezuela, 1901-1965); Arturo Uslar Pietri (Venezuela, 1906-   ); Enrique Anderson Imbert (1910-   ); Ernesto Sábato (1911-   ); Leopoldo Zea (1912-   ); and Octavio Paz (1914   ). Although some of these men (e.g. Martínez Estrada, Sánchez, Paz) have been concerned with political questions, the primary field of interest for most has been literary criticism, and at least three (Sábato, Uslar Pietri, and Paz) have been creative writers themselves.

This central interest in literature has also characterized the younger essayists: Fernando Alegría (1918-   ), Mario Benedetti (1920-   ), Héctor A. Murena (Argentina, 1923-   ), Carlos Fuentes (1928-   ), and Mario Vargas Llosa (1936-   ) are all novelists as well as essayists concerned primarily with literature. The leftists among them still mingle politics with literature (e.g. Benedetti). The theme of national identity, so exercised by the essayists of the 1940s and 1950s, seems to have receded into a limbo of over-worked subjects.

In the realm of drama, the experimental and university theaters so influential in earlier decades, as well as international drama festivals in Spain, France, Cuba, Colombia, Venezuela and elsewhere, continued to infuse vitality and an increasingly professional tone in the more than a dozen important dramatists writing during this period. A few still produced plays portraying and satirizing middle class characters and customs. But the majority followed in the footsteps of European innovators such as Bertolt Brecht (1898-1956), Samuel Beckett (1906-   ) and Eugène Ionesco (1912-   ). Brecht was an especially popular guide because of his Marxist orientation. In its variety and quality, drama during this period almost equalled the status of the novel, although its popularity was more restricted.

Among the younger dramatists, at least four — aside from those treated more fully in the following pages — have received general critical acclaim. Antón Arrufat, influenced by Ionesco, has given Greek myths modern interpretations, underlining man's dignity in the face of an incoherent world. Osvaldo Dragún has presented in a highly theatrical and emotional mood some of the conflicts in modern Argentine life. Luisa Josefina Hernández (Mexico, 1928–   ), after trying her hand at psychological realism and extreme surrealism, has recently written nationalistic plays based on ancient Mexican mythology: *Popol Vuh* (1966) and *Quetzalcoatl* (1968). José Triana has used popular characters and, on occasion, Greek myths to express his pessimistic view of modern bourgeois life. Jorge Díaz of Chile is an angry, satirical, avant-garde dramatist offering sometimes shocking criticism of contemporary mores and shortcomings.

In summary, Spanish American literature today is in a yeasty and healthy state. It offers a great variety of themes and styles which are in step with world literary trends. At the same time, it displays, for the most part, a distinct personality forged in the special experiences which the various republics have undergone. Two somewhat contradictory objectives are evident in a large part of the literary production: on the one hand, some novelists, poets, and dramatists have prided themselves on their virtuosity in creating complex works which are hardly intelligible to the average reader, who is growing in numbers because of increased literacy and greater educational opportunities. Thus the traditional elitism of letters in Spanish America is perpetuated in new forms. On the other hand, some poets and dramatists especially seek to communicate with "the masses," partly for political considerations. This duality of literary aims is a reflection of more general tensions in the social and political life of these Spanish-speaking republics.

REFERENCES

Anderson Imbert, *Spanish American Literature*, 746–756. Baciu, XVII–XLVIII, *passim*. Carrera Andrade, *Reflections*, 39–57. Castagnino, *Experimentos narrativos*, Chaps. 6 and 7. Davis, *Latin American Thought*, Chaps. 8, 9 and 11. Earle and Mead, *passim*. Franco, *Modern Culture*, Chaps. 6–8. Gómez-Gil, Chap. 34. Harss and Dohmann, *Into the Mainstream*, *passim*. Lyday and Woodyard, *Dramatists in Revolt*, XI–XVI. Plaza, Galo, *Latin America: Today and Tomorrow*, Washington, Acropolis Books, 1971, Chaps. 1 and 2. Rodríguez Monegal, *Borzoi Anthology*, II, 799–863. Schwartz, II, 95–112. Whitaker and Jordan, *passim*. *Young Poetry of the Americas*, *passim*. Yurkiévich, *Poesía . . . 1960–1970*, 7–39.

*1. (Argentina) **Enrique Anderson Imbert** (1910–   ) is an essayist in the manner of Alfonso Reyes by the variety of themes treated and by the artistic style employed. First a journalist and then, from 1941–1946, a professor at the National University of Tucumán, he resigned this position in protest against the government of Juan Perón and came to the United States in 1947, where he served successively as a professor of literature at the University of Michigan and at Harvard University. His twenty-seven or more books fall into three categories: (1) fiction, short stories (*Las pruebas del caos*, 1946; *La sandía, y otros cuentos*, 1969) and short novels (*Vigilia*, 1934; *Fuga*, 1951); (2) literary history and criticism (*Historia de la literatura hispanoamericana*, 6th ed., 1974; *El arte de la prosa de Juan Montalvo*, 1948, 1974; *Genio y figura de Sarmiento*, 1967); and (3) essays (*La flecha en el aire*, 1972; *Los domingos del profesor*, 1972). The first category is a collection of journalistic articles written before 1940, the second, first published in Mexico in 1965, revised and enlarged in 1972, is an assembly of wide ranging essays on a cosmopolitan variety of literary personalities, works, and themes. Varying from brief notes to extended essays and written in a conversational and cultivated prose, they reveal the author's broad familiarity with the literature of the western world. "En el fondo," he stated in an interview, "me siento más artista que estudioso." One of his most exciting and challenging adventures in art forms lies in his cultivation of miniature stories—or monads—"psychic atoms," as he describes them, "in which is reflected, from different perspectives, the totality of a view of life."

SUGGESTED READING

Los domingos del profesor.

EDITIONS

El arte de la prosa de Juan Montalvo (1948), 2nd ed., Buenos Aires, Gure, 1974. *La crítica literaria contemporanea*, Buenos Aires, Gure, 1957. *Los domingos del profesor* (1965), 2nd ed., Buenos Aires, Gure, 1972. *Genio y figura de Sarmiento*, Buenos Aires, EUDEBA, 1967. *Análisis de "Fausto,"* Buenos Aires, CEAL, 1968. *La flecha en el aire*, Buenos Aires, Gure, 1972. *Estudios sobre letras hispánicas*, Pittsburg, K & S Enterprises, 1976. *El leve Pedro: antología de cuentos*, Madrid, Alianza, 1976.

TRANSLATIONS

John Falconieri and Elaine Malley (tr.), *Spanish American Literature: A History* (1963), 2nd ed., 2 vols., Detroit, Wayne State Univ. Press, 1969 (paperback). Isabel Reade (tr.), *The Other Side of the Mirror: El grimorio*, Carbondale, Southern Illinois Univ. Press, 1966; also *Cage with Only One Side*, Reno, West Coast Poetry Review, 1974.

CRITICAL REFERENCES

See texts and editions above. Armand J. Baker, "La vision del mundo en los cuentos de Enrique Anderson Imbert," *Revista iberoamericana*, 96-97 (1976), 497-516. Foster, I, 48-53. Helmy Giacoman (ed.), *Homenaje a Enrique Anderson Imbert*, New York, Las Américas, 1973.

*2. (Peru) **José María Arguedas** (1911-1969), one of Peru's great novelists of this century, was born in Andahuaylas, in the Dmpartment of Apurímac, a Quechua-speaking community in the sierra of his country. His father was a lawyer and a judge, and his mother died when the son was only three. His father married again, but the boy's stepmother was cruel to him, and he spent most of his boyhood away from home among the Indians who loved and protected him. He spoke Quechua fluently, and his closest emotional ties were with the Quechua folk with whom he identified completely. In 1920 his father lost his position as judge, and the family suffered financially. A few years later the young Arguedas became a professor of Spanish in a small school where he earned a precarious living. At one time he was jailed for political reasons. After a visit to Mexico with his wife in 1940-1942 he returned to Lima where, in 1948, he received his degree in anthropology from the National University. He worked in the Ministry of Education collecting folklore and folk songs. In 1953 he was named Head of the Institute of Ethnological Studies of the National Museum of History. He committed suicide in 1969.

The great value of Arguedas' fictional world is its compelling authenticity and intense passion. He was able to exteriorize and universalize Quechua Indian life because he had experienced it personally. "I must describe that world exactly as it was," he once commented, "because I have felt joy in it, and I have suffered in it." Arguedas is not identified with any literary school; he is neither Indianist nor Indigenist, neither regionalist nor novelist of the land or of social protest. His internal vision of the Quechua world presents the Indian psychology, culture and manner of speaking and thinking without rhetorical embellishments. He gives the reader the impression that he *is* an Indian writing, thinking, speaking, and there is always a touch of poetry and passion to elevate the reality presented.

Arguedas' most important novels are *Yawar fiesta* (1941), the story of a closed world which emphasizes the Indian's individuality, determination for work and great inner vitality; *Los ríos profundos* (1958), his masterpiece, which begins as a story of individual characters, then moves quickly into the broader arena of collective life where the tragedy of the individual is overpowered by the tragedy of the race; and *Todas las sangres* (1964), a story of violent economic and cultural conflicts which presents a society in crisis, but which underneath is a search for identity, both individual and national. The novel asks and partially answers the questions: "What does it mean to be a Peruvian? Where is Peru headed today?" In the totality of his work Arguedas has presented a better picture of the Indian experience than any other Hispanic writer.

SUGGESTED READING

Los ríos profundos.

TEXTS

Flores, 503-525. Latcham, 269-274. *Los ríos profundos* (ed. Rowe), New York, Pergamon, 1973.

EDITIONS

Agua. Los escoleros. Warma Kuyay (1935), Lima, Universidad Nacional Mayor de San Marcos, 1974; prologue by Antonio Cornejo Polar. *Yawar fiesta* (1941), 2nd ed., Lima, Populibros Peruanos, 1965. *Canciones y cuentos del pueblo quechua*, Lima, Huascarán, 1949. *Los ríos profundos* (1958), Lima, Villanueva, 1972. *Agua y otros cuentos indígenas* (1961), 2nd ed., Lima, Milla Batres, 1974; prologue by Wáshington Delgado. *El sexto* (1961), Lima, Ed. Horizonte, 1973. *Todas las sangres*, Buenos Aires, Losada, 1964; *ibid.*, 2 vols., Lima, Ed. Peisa, 1973. *Amor mundo y todos los cuentos*, Lima, F. Moncloa, 1967. *El zorro de arriba y el zorro de abajo* (1971), 4th ed., Buenos Aires, Losada, 1973. *Páginas escogidas* (1972), 2nd ed., Lima, Ed. Universo, 1974; ed. by Emilio Westphalen, prologue by Abelardo Oquendo. *Temblar-Katatay*, Lima, Instituto Nacional de Cultura, 1972. *La formación de una cultura nacional indoamericana*, México, Siglo Veintiuno, 1975; ed., with prologue, by Ángel Rama. *Relatos completos*, **Buenos** Aires, Losada, ed. by Jorge Lafforgue.

TRANSLATIONS

Howes, 349-357. Ruth Walgreen Stephan (ed. and tr.), *The Singing Mountaineers: Songs and Tales of the Quecha People* (1957), Austin, Univ. of Texas Press, 1971. Ángel and Kate Flores translated the tales. Frances Horning Barraclough (tr.), *Deep Rivers*, Austin, Univ. of Texas Press, 1978.

CRITICAL REFERENCES

See texts and editions above. Alegría, *Historia*, 272-273. Antonio Cornejo Polar, *Los universos narrativos de José María Arguedas*, Buenos Aires, Losada, 1973. Foster, I, 92-98. Helmy F. Giacoman (ed.),

Homenaje a José María Arguedas, New York, Las Américas, 1970. Sara Castro Klarén, *El mundo mágico de José María Arguedas*, Lima, Instituto de Estudios Peruanos, 1973. Juan Larco (ed.), *Recopilación de textos sobre José María Arguedas*, Habana, Casa de las Américas, 1976. César Lévano, *Arguedas: un sentimiento trágico de la vida*, Lima, Labor, 1969. Gladys C. Marín, *La experiencia americana de José María Arguedas*, Buenos Aires, Garcia Cambeiro, 1973. Schwartz, II, 318-328.

3. (Guatemala) **Miguel Ángel Asturias (1899-1974) was awarded the Soviet Union's Peace Prize in 1966, and in this same year was named as the ambassador of his country in Paris. In 1967 he won the Nobel Prize for literature, and quickly became an international celebrity. Asturias is a writer who has always been interested in social problems, especially those concerning the Indian. He graduated from the University of Guatemala in 1923 with a degree in law; his thesis was entitled *The Social Problem of the Indian*. Later that year he departed for France, where he spent the next ten years of his life. In Paris he became acquainted with Professor Georges Raynaud who was giving a course at the Sorbonne in "The Ancient Religions of Central America." Asturias was fascinated by the subject and it changed the course of his life. In 1930 he published in Madrid his *Leyendas dm Guatemala*, in which he recalled stories that he had heard in his youth. The book was translated into French two years later with a prologue by Paul Valéry who warmly praised the tales and characterized them as "historias-sueños-poemas."

During the years 1924-1932 Asturias worked on his masterpiece, *El señor presidente*, which he published at his own expense in a limited edition in Mexico in 1946. The novel was well received, and in 1948 a second edition appeared in Buenos Aires, published by Editorial Losada. Gabriela Mistral called the novel "phenomenal," and further commented: "I do not know where this unique novel came from, written with the very breath and flow of blood of the human body." *El señor presidente* is a dramatic and poetic evocation and condemnation of the dictatorial regime of Manuel Estrada Cabrera, who ruled Guatemala with an iron hand for twenty years early in this century.

From 1947 to 1953 Asturias served as the Ambassador of Guatemala in Buenos Aires. In 1948 appeared his second famous novel, *Hombres de maíz*, based on Maya lore interwoven with comments on the miserable contemporary status of the Indian in Guatemala. This surrealistic novel is so packed with mythology and legendary Mayan beliefs and is so chaotic in structure that it is very disconcerting to the modern reader. Asturias later published a trilogy of anti-imperialistic novels known as the "banana trilogy": *Viento fuerte* (1950), *El Papa verde* (1954) and *Los ojos de los enterrados* (1960), but none of these is on a parity with *El señor presidente* and *Hombres de maíz*.

SUGGESTED READING

El señor presidente.

TEXTS

Flores, 686-694. Gómez-Gil, II, 591-596. Leal and Dauster, 414-417. Sanz y Díaz, 376-379. Stimson and Navas-Ruiz, III, 197-221.

EDITIONS

Leyendas de Guatemala (1930), Buenos Aires, Losada, 1967; also Madrid, Aguilar, 1968. *El señor presidente* (1946), 9th ed., Buenos Aires, Losada, 1974. *Hombres de maíz* (1949), 4th ed., Buenos Aires, Losada, 1971. *Viento fuerte*, Buenos Aires, Losada, 1950. *El Papa verde*, Buenos Aires, Losada, 1954. *Obras escogidas* (1955), 3rd ed., 3 vols., Madrid, Aguilar, 1966; prologue by José María Souviron. *Weekend in Guatemala* (1956), Habana, Imp. Nacional de Cuba, 1960. *Los ojos de los enterrados*, Buenos Aires, Losada, 1960. *El alhajadito*, Buenos Aires, Goyanarte, 1961. *Mulata de tal* (1963), 2nd ed., Buenos Aires, Losada, 1967. Novaro, 1973, *Torotumbo* (1967), Barcelona, Plaza Janes, 1974. *Mi mejor obra; autoantologia, Mexico.*

TRANSLATIONS

Donoso and Henkin, 359-371. Darwin Flakoll and Claribel Alegría (tr.), *The Cyclone*, London, Owen, 1967. Howes, 183-188. Mancini, 70-77. Gerald Martin (tr.), *Men of Maize*, New York, Delacorte, 1975. Frances Partridge (tr.), *The President*, London, Gollancz, 1963; also with the title *El Señor Presidente*, New York, Atheneum, 1964 (paperback 1975). Gregory Rabassa (tr.), *Mulata* (1963), New York, Delacorte, 1967; also *Strong Wind*, New York, Delacorte, 1968; also *The Green Pope*, New York, Delacorte, 1971; also *The Eyes of the Interred*, New York, Delacorte, 1973. Rodríguez Monegal, II, 511-517. Martin Shuttleworth (tr.), *The Bejeweled Boy*, New York, Doubleday, 1971.

CRITICAL REFERENCES

See texts and editions above. Alegría, *Historia*, 215-219. Richard J. Callan, *Miguel Angel Asturias*, New York, Twayne, 1970. Atilio Jorge Castelpoggi, *Miguel Angel Asturias*, Buenos Aires, La Mandrágora, 1961. *Europe* (May-June, 1975, 219 p.) Contains some 30 studies on Asturias. Flores, 684-686. Foster, I, 110-122. Helmy F. Giacoman (ed.), *Homenaje a Miguel Angel Asturias*, New York, Las Américas, 1972.

González del Valle and Cabrera, *passim*. Guibert, 119-179. Harss and Dohmann, 68-101. Eladia León Hill, *Miguel Ángel Asturias, lo ancestral en su obra literaria*, New York, Eliseo Torres, 1972. "Homenaje," *Revista iberoamericana*, 67 (1969). Schwartz, II, 181-191. Aurora Sierra Franco, *Miguel Ángel Asturias en la literatura*, Guatemala, Ed. Istmo, 1969.

*4. (Uruguay) **Mario Benedetti** (1920-   ) is an exceptionally active and versatile writer; he is a poet, dramatist, short-story writer, novelist, essayist and literary historian. In his narrative prose he has concentrated his attention on the urban middle class, which forms a major segment of little Uruguay's population. His people are the office workers, the bureaucrats, the elderly retired, and his themes their boredom, their trivial sexual adventures, and their frustration in seeking some kind of invigorating satisfaction in their dull lives. Although he has four good novels to his credit — *Quien de nosotros* (1953), *La tregua* (1960), *Gracias por el fuego* (1965), and *El cumpleaños de Juan Ángel* (1971), his real forte is the short story. The collection, *Montevideanos* (1959), has been very popular and nicely displays his particular talents. Those talents often include, in contrast to many of his contemporaries, a sense of humor and an ironical lightheartedness, as well as a penchant for surprising, often bizarre endings.

Benedetti's essays are generally serious. As a political leftist, he is unsparingly critical of his society's shortcomings, as in *El país de la cola de paja* (1961), and in his *Cuaderno cubano* (1969) and other essays, he shows his considerable sympathy for the Castro experiment. Many of his essays, and especially his *Literatura uruguaya siglo XX* (1963) and *Letras del continente mestizo* (1967), are outspokenly critical of his country's literature and Spanish American literature in general.

In spite of his critical stance and his existential anguish in the face of an absurd bourgeois environment, Benedetti is frequently compassionate, charitable and even tender toward his fictional characters. In comparison with Vargas Llosa and Fuentes, he has received relatively little international attention and is hardly a major writer in the Alejo Carpentier class. But he is a competent, industrious author who uses his Uruguayan ambience, clever (but not unusual) literary devices, and contemporary social ideologies to produce a solid and interesting literature.

SUGGESTED READING

Short stories: *Montevideanos*. Novel: *La tregua*. Essays: *El país de la cola de paja.*

TEXTS

Alegría, *Novelistas,* 184-198. Brotherston and Vargas Llosa, 42-65. Castro Arenas, 291-296. Englekirk, *Anthology,* 761-765. Latcham, 440-446. Lewald and Smith, 38-50. Rodríguez Alcalá, 145-163. Solórzano, I, 64-123.

EDITIONS

Novels: *Quien de nosotros* (1953), 4th ed., Montevideo, Alfa, 1969; *ibid.,* Buenos Aires, Alfa Argentina, 1974. *La tregua* (1960), 6th ed., Montevideo, Alfa, 1970; *ibid.,* 10th ed., Buenos Aires, Alfa Argentina, 1974; *ibid.,* Barcelona, Planeta, 1973. *Gracias por el fuego* (1965), 5th ed., Montevideo, Alfa, 1969; *ibid.,* Habana, Casa de las Américas, 1969; *ibid.,* Barcelona, Laia, 1974. *El cumpleaños de Juan Ángel,* México, Siglo XXI, 1971.

Short Stories: *Esta mañana* (1949), Montevideo, Arca, 1968; *ibid.,* Montevideo, Arca-Calicanto, 1975. *Montevideanos: Cuentos* (1959), 5th ed., Montevideo, Alfa, 1972; prologue by Emir Rodríguex Monegal; *ibid.,* Habana, Casa de las Américas, 1968. *La muerte y otras sorpresas* (1968), 4th ed., Mexico, Siglo XXI, 1972; *ibid.,* Montevideo, Alfa, 1969. *Cuentos completos,* Santiago, Ed. Universitaria, 1970.

Essays: *El país de la cola de paja* (1961), 8th ed., Montevideo, Arca, 1970. *Literatura uruguaya siglo XX* (1963), 2nd ed., Montevideo, Alfa, 1969. *Genio y figura de José Enrique Rodó,* Buenos Aires, EUDEBA, 1966. *Letras del continente mestizo* (1967), 2nd ed., Montevideo, Arca, 1969. *Sobre artes y oficios: Ensayo,* Montevideo, Alfa, 1968. *Cuaderno cubano* (1969), 2nd ed., Montevideo, Arca, 1969. *Crítica cómplice,* Habana, Instituto Cubano del Libro, 1971. *El escritor latinoamericano y la revolución posible,* Buenos Aires, Alfa Argentina, 1974. *Antología natural,* Montevideo, Alfa, 1967.

TRANSLATIONS

Cohen, *Latin American Writing Today,* 143-149. Flakoll and Alegría, 121-127. Benjamin Graham (tr.), *The Truce,* New York, Harper and Row, 1969. Mancini, 366-376.

CRITICAL REFERENCES

See texts and editions above. Alegría, *Historia,* 286-287. Englekirk and Ramos, 121-123. Foster, I, 148-153. Ricardo Latcham, *Carnet crítico,* Montevideo, Alfa, 1962, 141-153. Rodríguez Monegal, *Narradores,* II, 209-225. Schwartz, II, 176-178.

5. (Mexico) **Emilio Carballido** (1925-   ) was born in Córdoba. He

studied at the National University, where he later taught drama and playwriting. He has also taught at the Universidad Veracruzana and at a number of universities in the United States. He has been the recipient of national and international drama awards.

Carballido is not only the best known of the large group of contemporary Mexican dramatists, but also exemplifies in his many plays the evolution experienced by the Spanish American drama in the last quarter of a century. His first full-length play, *Rosalba y los Llaveros* (1950), is a more or less realistic drama of provincial manners, not far removed, in spite of its Freudian ingredient, from the earlier *costumbrista* plays so beloved by the public. There are several other plays that followed in the same tradition.

La hebra de oro (1956) marked a definite change in theme, viewpoint, and technique. Beginning with a realistic enough situation, the play soon transports the spectator into a supernatural dream world of the subconscious in which time turns back, space is capricious, and various symbolic elements are introduced. Most of Carballido's later works, especially *El día que se soltaron los leones* (1963) and *Yo también hablo de la rosa* (1966) continue this pattern of melding the realistic, the fantastic and the symbolic to present what the playwright considers a truer vision of our life and its relation to cosmic forces. Frequently, there is a sharp note of social criticism in these plays, as in *Medusa* (1958), a modern interpretation of the Greek myth, that is also laden with symbolism. And all the later plays are studded with a number of novel theatrical devices that clearly relate them to the experimental drama of Ionesco, Beckett, Brecht, et al. Carballido has also written stories and novels and has collaborated in film and operatic productions.

SUGGESTED READING

Yo también hablo de la rosa and *Rosalba y los Llaveros*.

TEXTS

Castillo and Castillo, 131-183 *(El relojero de Córdoba)*. Dauster, *Teatro . . . tres piezas*, 13-108 *(Rosalba y los Llaveros)*. Dauster and Lyday, 5-19 *(El censo)*. Lamb, 135-184 *(Yo también hablo de la rosa)*. *Teatro mex. siglo XX*, 133-206 *(La danza que sueña la tortuga)*; also V, 231-276 *(Yo también hablo de la rosa)*. *Teatro mexicano* (1963), 99-168 *(¡Silencio, pollos, pelones, ya les van a echar su maíz!)*; also (1968), 31-104 *(Medusa)*.

EDITIONS

D. F. (1957), 2nd ed., Xalapa, Universidad Veracruzana, 1962. Fourteen one-act plays. *La hebra de oro: auto sacramental en tres jornadas*, México, UNAM, 1957. *Teatro* (1960), México, FCE, 1976.

TRANSLATIONS

Oliver, *Voices of Change*, 3–46 *(The Day They Let the Lions Loose)*. Margaret Sayers Peden (tr.), *The Norther* (novel, *El norte*, 1958), Austin, Univ. of Texas Press, 1968; also *The Golden Thread and Other Plays*, Austin, Univ. of Texas Press, 1970. Woodyard, 289–331 *(I Too Speak of the Rose)*.

CRITICAL REFERENCES

Dauster, *Hist. teatro*, 101–102. *Diccionario . . . mexicanos*, 59–61. Jones, *Behind . . . Footlights*, 508–509. Lyday and Woodyard, 21–36. Magaña Esquivel, *Medio siglo*, ·134–135. Solórzano, *Teatro . . . siglo XX*, 75–77.

*.*6. (Argentina) **Julio Cortázar** (1914–   ) was born in Brussels of Argentine parents, but was reared and educated mainly in Buenos Aires. When he was 35 he left his country as a self-willed exile from the dictatorship of Perón and established himself in Paris, where he has lived ever since. Cortázar is a translator for UNESCO, and he has become a French citizen. He is a dedicated Marxist, and when queried about politics is verbosely dogmatic in his Marxist convictions.

Cortázar is the author of several books of excellent short stories, set in a frame of magical realism, which frequently shifts to and fro in time and place while maintaining the unity of human experience. Imagination and reality are intermingled so deftly that the line between them is blurred and often indistinguishable. Among his best collections of short stories are: *Final del juego* (1956), *Las armas secretas* (1959), and *Relatos* (1970).

In his novelistic world Cortázar represents a reality that is deeply subjective, and it is not easy for the reader to discern the author's meaning. *Los premios* (1960) is the story of a group of people who win tickets for a cruise, and their ship (somewhat like Katherine Anne Porter's *Ship of Fools*) becomes their temporary universe. *Rayuela* (1963) is a novel like the ocean, replete with universal symbols and cryptic, often abstruse, parallels and allusions. It begins in Paris and then moves to Buenos Aires, the two worlds that Cortázar knows best, and the characters from Paris merge completely with those of Buenos Aires as the same alienation continues. It is a novel of acute existential anguish in which children's games become the symbols of life's most critical rituals. The absurd and the grotesquely tragi-comic scenes of the novel slough off the veneer imposed on man by civilization and reveal the gut feelings of the characters who are always seeking, but never find, the forgotten kingdom. They are invariably "on the brink" of some experience which might enable them to capture the perishable dream, only to realize that life's perishable quality is its primary essence and meaning. Cortázar believes that human beings follow not only their individual patterns and destinies, but that they are also participants in a larger constellation or collectivity, the understanding of which continuously escapes them.

Cortazar's style and approach to the novel is encyclopedic, and he literally overwhelms his reader with a plethora of neurotic emotions, an imposing vocabulary, an amazing range of knowledge, and a recondite portrait of the human condition. His work suggests a twentieth-century Plato's cave. He presents the most serious problems of life in a grotesque and comic manner, thinking thus to give them a vitality and validity that would be denied by a more solemn approach. The evanescent quality of life is apparent on every page, and agony is a constant.

SUGGESTED READING

Final del juego.

TEXTS

Brotherston and Vargas Llosa, 10–19. Coleman, 57–113. Gómez-Gil, II, 681–686. Leal and Dauster, 438–442. Lewald and Smith, 52–65. Hugo and Sally Rodríguez Alcalá, 7–31. Stimson and Navas-Ruiz, III, 360–372. Vázquez, 316–332.

EDITIONS

Final del juego (1956), 11th ed., Buenos Aires, Sudamericana, 1970. *Las armas secretas,* Buenos Aires, Sudamericana, 1959. *Los premios* (1960), 14th ed., Buenos Aires, Sudamericana, 1975. *Rayuela* (1963), 12th ed., Buenos Aires, Sudamericana, 1975. *Cuentos,* Habana, Casa de las Américas, 1964; ed., with prologue, by Antoń Arrufat. *Todos los fuegos el fuego* (1966), 11th ed., Buenos Aires, Sudamericana, 1970. *62. Modelo para armar,* Buenos Aires, Sudamericana, 1968. *Libro de Manuel* (1973), 5th ed., Buenos Aires, Sudamericana, 1975. *Los relatos,* 3 vols., Madrid, Alianza, 1976.

TRANSLATIONS

Paul Blackburn (tr.), *End of the Game and Other Stories,* New York, Pantheon, 1967; also by Harper and Row, 1978 (paperback); also *Blow-up and Other Stories,* New York, Collier, 1968; also *Cronopios and Famas,* New York, Pantheon, 1969. Cohen, *Latin American Writing Today,* 72–86. Donoso and Henkin, 375–390. Howes, 369–382. Elaine Kerrigan (tr.), *The Winners,* New York, Pantheon, 1965. Suzanne Jill Levine (tr.), *All Fires the Fire and Other Stories,* New York, Pantheon, 1973. Mancini, 176–187. Gregory Rabassa (tr.), *Hopscotch,* New York, Ran-

dom House, 1966; and New American Library, 1967 (paperback); also *62: A Model Kit*, New York, Pantheon, 1972. Rodríguez Monegal, II, 717-732.
CRITICAL REFERENCES
See texts and editions above. Alegría, *Historia*, 297-299. Manuel Durán, (ed.), *La vuelta a Cortázar en nueve ensayos*, Buenos Aires, Carlos Pérez, 1968. Roberto Escamilla Molina, *Julio Cortázar. Visión de conjunto*, México, Novaro, 1970. Malva E. Filer, *Los mundos de Julio Cortázar*, New York, Las Américas, 1970. Foster, I, 257-274. Fuentes, 67-78. Evelyn Picón Garfield, *Julio Cortázar*, New York, Frederick Ungar, 1975. Kathleen Genover, *Claves de una novelística existencial: Rayuela de Cortázar*, Madrid, Playor, 1973. Helmy F. Giacoman (ed.), *Homenaje a Julio Cortázar*, New York, Las Americas, 1972. Guibert, 277-302. Harss and Dohmann, 206-245. "Homenaje," *Revista iberoamericana*, 84-85 (1973). David Sagmanovich (ed.), *Estudios Sobre los cuentos de Julio Cortázar*, Barcelona, Sololibros, 1975. Leal, *Historia*, 115-117. Antonio Planells, *Cortázar: metafísica y erotismo*, Madrid, Porrua, 1977. Pupo-Walker, 165-179. Joaquín Roy, *Julio Cortázar ante su sociedad*, Barcelona, Ed. Península, 1974. Schwartz, II, 261-270. Ana María Simo (ed.) *Cinco miradas sobre Cortázar*, Buenos Aires, Ed. Tiempo Contemporáneo, 1968. Graciela de Sola, *Julio Cortázar y el hombre nuevo*, Buenos Aires, Sudamericana, 1968. Saúl Sosnowski, *Julio Cortázar: una búsqueda mítica*, Buenos Aires, Ed. Noe, 1973.
7. (Mexico) **Carlos Fuentes (1928-   ) was born in Mexico City but has lived for extensive periods of time in the United States, Europe and South America. He speaks and writes perfect English. Fuentes is a graduate of the National University of Mexico, from which he holds a degree in law. During the presidency of Echeverría Álvarez he became Mexican Ambassador in Paris, subordinating his strong Marxist leanings in the hope of improving Mexico's image abroad. Earlier in his life, with Emmanuel Carballo as co-founder, Fuentes helped to launch the literary review, *Revista mexicana de literatura* (1955-1958). His first fictional work was a collection of short stories in a surrealistic vein, *Los días enmascarados* (1954). Four years later, in 1958, he attracted wide attention with his novel, *La región más transparente*, a scathing, kaleidoscopic, chaotic examination of post-revolutionary society in Mexico. This work was followed by a short, conventional novel, *Las buenas conciencias* (1959), an incisive psychological study of a provincial Mexican family.

In 1962 appeared two works: *Aura*, a novella of fantasy in which an old lady wills herself temporarily young and beautiful again, and *La muerte de Artemio Cruz*, perhaps Fuentes' masterpiece, which gives a panoramic view of Mexico from the early 1900's to the 1960's. The story of the dying Cruz is told in flashbacks showing his change from a revolutionary idealist to a post-revolutionary opportunist and man of property. The twelve crucial decisions in the life of Cruz are told with considerable dramatic impact. Fuentes concludes that Mexico is not prosperous enough to support a revolutionary rhetoric of the kind that keeps the present politicians and economic bosses in power.

In 1967 Fuentes published *Cambio de piel,* which is a return to his early highly convoluted style, but with a changed perspective. Mexico is the locale, but not the primary concern of this novel, in which Fuentes attempts, not entirely successfully, to universalize his characters and concepts in examining man's condition. *Zona sagrada,* which also appeared in 1967, is a psychological novel, with almost clinical overtones, showing the relationship between a Mexican motion picture actress and her neurotic son. In 1975 appeared a tremendously long novel, *Terra nostra,* a veritable potpourri into which Fuentes poured, like a torrent, every thought, feeling and anecdote that he could muster about the symbolic history of Hispanic culture. The novel loses its focus as a work of fiction, and becomes mainly an essay propounding many of the author's ideas.

SUGGESTED READING

La muerte de Artemio Cruz or *Las buenas conciencias.*

TEXTS

Alegría, *Novelistas,* 116-131. Castillo and Castillo, 51-75. Gómez-Gil, II, 714-725. Kadir, 71-113. Leal and Dauster, 449-454. Stimson and Navas Ruiz, III, 344-360.

EDITIONS

Los días enmascarados (1954), 2nd ed., México, Novaro, 1966. *La región más transparente* (1958), 5th ed., México, FCE, 1966. *Las buenas conciencias* (1959), 5th ed., México, FCE, 1969. *Aura* (1962), México, Alacena, 1968. *La muerte de Artemio Cruz* (1962). 6th ed., México, FCE, 1970. *Cantar de ciegos* (1964), México, Joaquín Mortiz, 1976. *Zona sagrada* (1967), México, Siglo XXI, 1969. *Cambio de piel* (1967), México, Joaquin Mortiz, 1968. *Obras completas,* Mexico, Aguilar, 1974; biography and prologue by Fernando Bénitez. *Terra nostra,* (1975), Barcelona, Seix Barral, 1977. *Cumpleaños,* México, Joaquín Mortiz, 1976.

TRANSLATIONS

Cohen, *Latin American Writing Today,* 107-137. Sam Hileman (tr.), *Where the Air is Clear,* New York, Ivan Obolensky, 1960; also *The Good Conscience,* New York, Ivan Obolensky, 1961; also *The Death of Artemio Cruz,* New York, Farrar, Straus, Giroux, 1964; also *A Change of Skin,*

New York, Farrar, Straus, Giroux, 1968. Howes, 505-519. Lysander Kemp (tr.), *Aura*, New York, Farrar, Straus, Giroux, 1965. Mancini, 258-280. Margaret Sayers Peden (tr.), *Terra Nostra*, New York, Farrar, Straus, Giroux, 1976. Rodríguez Monegal, II, 853-876.

CRITICAL REFERENCES

See texts and editions above. Alegría, *Historia*, 304-306. Carballo, 425-448. Durán, 51-134. Gloria Durán, *La magia y las brujas en la obra de Carlos Fuentes*, México, UNAM, 1976. Foster, I, 331-346. Helmy F. Giacoman (ed.), *Homenaje a Carlos Fuentes*, New York, Las Américas, 1971. Daniel de Guzmán, *Carlos Fuentes*, New York, Twayne, 1972. *Diccionario . . . mexicanos*, 120-123. Harss and Dohmann, 276-310. Pupo-Walker, 249-264. Richard M. Reeve, "An Annotated Bibliography on Carlos Fuentes: 1949-69." *Hispania*, 53 (1970), 597-652. Schwartz, II, 303-311. Sommers, 97-164 and 178-181.

8. (Colombia) **Gabriel García Márquez (1928-   ) spent his childhood in the small town of Aracataca, near the northern coast of Colombia. He attended the universities of Bogotá and Cartagena without obtaining a degree. He was a voluminous reader and was especially fond of James Joyce, Virginia Woolf and William Faulkner. Faulkner's decaying Southern world seems to him to bear a remarkable resemblance to his own familiar tropical universe.

The literary career of García Márquez began with the publication of *La hojarasca* in 1955, which had previously been rejected by an Argentine publishing house with the suggestion that he follow some other profession. His next work was the short novel, *El coronel no tiene quien le escriba* (1958), the character sketch of a seedy retired army officer who anxiously awaits the arrival of his non-existent pension. A whole world of emotions and experiences is created by the pension that never comes, but the colonel is able to maintain a deep core of dignity despite the vicissitudes of fate. In 1962 appeared two works, *La mala hora* and *Los funerales de la Mamá Grande*, and in 1967 his masterpiece, *Cien años de soledad*. In 1975 *El otoño del patriarca*, the tale of a mythic Latin American dictator who lived for almost two centuries, marked the continuance of García Márquez's strange fantastic world.

Cien años de soledad is one of the great works of Hispanic literature. It is a vast canvas of mythic proportions in which is depicted the 100-year life of the author's imaginary Macondo, a microcosm of Latin American towns, which in a larger frame of reference recapitulates the symbolic history of Spanish America from its earliest beginnings. As the novel opens, Macondo is on the brink of its own creation. We see it progress from Genesis to Armageddon, when the town is destroyed by a tremendous wind. *Cien años de soledad* is a fantasy whose realism is absolutely convincing. People die to reappear, generations repeat themselves, there is a four-year flood, a rain of birds, another of yellow flowers, a young woman rises to heaven along with the sheets she is hanging out, an old gypsy lives for four hundred years, the entire population of Macondo is overcome with amnesia.

The novel has the mixed flavor of the Bible, the Arabian Nights, and the mythic unconscious, and it presents life in a subjective cyclical manner which is outside the flow of time. Indeed, in this novel "time moves in circles," and there are moments of eternal return. We repeatedly feel the nostalgia of *ubi sunt* (Where are they now? Where are the snows of yesteryear?) as the luminous wheel time and again repeats its infinite round. *Cien años de soledad* catches the eternal pulse of Latin American life in a way that no realistic work possibly could, and in this lies its quality of uniqueness. By almost universal critical consensus this strangely compelling novel stands alone in world fiction; there can never be another like it.

SUGGESTED READING

Cien anos de soledad.

TEXTS

Brotherston and Vargas Llosa, 1–10. Coleman, 221–272. Gómez-Gil, II, 707–713. Kadir, 1–69. Latcham, 241–246. Stimson and Navas Ruiz, III, 388–409.

EDITIONS

Ojos d perro azul (1950), Rosario, Equiseditorial, 1972. *La hojarasca* (1955), 3rd ed., Barcelona, Plaza & Janés, 1976. *Relato de un náufrago* (1955), Barcelona, Tusquets, 1970. *El coronel no tiene quien le escriba* (1958), 4th ed., Barcelona, Plaza & Janés, 1976. *Los funerales de la Mamá Grande* (1962), 3rd ed., Barcelona, Plaza & Janés, 1976. *La mala hora* (1962), 3rd ed., Barcelona, Plaza & Janés, 1976. *Cien años de soledad* (1967), 10th ed., Buenos Aires, Sudamericana, 1973. *Isabel viendo llover en Macondo*, Buenos Aires, Estuario, 1967. *La increíble y triste historia de la cándida Erendira y de su abuela desalmada*, Buenos Aires, Sudamericana, 1972. *Cuando era feliz e indocumentado* (1973), 3rd ed., Barcelona, Plaza & Janés, 1975. *El otoño del patriarca*, Barcelona, Plaza & Janés, 1975. *Todos los cuentos de Gabriel García Márquez*, 3rd ed., Barcelona, Plaza & Janés, 1976.

INTO THE MAINSTREAM

TRANSLATIONS

J. S. Bernstein (tr.), *No One Writes to the Colonel and Other Stories*, New York, Harper and Row, 1968 (paperback, Avon, 1973). Cohen, *Latin American Writing Today*, 182-202. Donoso and Henkin, 179-186. Howes, 489-497. Mancini, 280-292. Gregory Rabassa (tr.), *One Hundred Years of Solitude*, New York, Harper and Row, 1970 (paperback, Avon, 1973); also *Leaf Storm and Other Stories*, New York, Harper and Row, 1972 (paperback, Avon, 1973); also *The Autumn of the Patriarch*, New York, Harper and Row, 1975. Rodriguez Monegal, II, 886-901.

CRITICAL REFERENCES

See texts and editions above. Alegría, *Historia*, 299-304. Germán Darío Carrillo, *La narrativa de Gabriel García Márquez*, Madrid, Castalia, 1975. Miguel Fernández-Braso, *La soledad de Gabriel García Márquez (Una conversación infinita)*, Barcelona, Planeta, 1972. Foster, I, 374-391. Fuentes, 58-67. Gallagher, 144-163. García Márquez and Vargas Llosa, *passim*. Helmy F. Giacoman (ed.), *Homenaje a Gabriel García Marquez*, New York, Las Américas, 1972. González del Valle and Cabrera, *passim*. Guibert, 303-307. Ricardo Gullón, *García Márquez o el olvidado arte de contar*, Madrid, Taurus, 1970. Harss and Dohmann, 310-342. Leal, *Historia*, 137-139. Josefina Ludmer, *Cien años de soledad: una interpretación crítica*, Buenos Aires, Ed. Tiempo Contemporáneo, 1972. Pedro Simón Martínez (ed.), *Sobre García Márquez*, Montevideo, Marcha, 1971. Graciela Maturo, *Claves simbólicas de García Marquez*, Buenos Aires, García Cambeiro, 1972. George R. McMurray, *Gabriel García Márquez*, New York, Frederick Ungar, 1977. Roseanne B. de Mendoza, "Bibliografía de y sobre Gabriel García Márquez," *Revista iberoamericana*, 90 (1975), 107-143. *9 asedios a García Márquez*, Santiago, Ed. Universitaria, 1969. Francisco E. Porrata and Fausto Avendaño (ed.), *Explicación de Cien años de soledad*, Sacramento, SCUC Foundation, 1976. Pupo-Walker, 235-249. *Recopilación de textos sobre Gabriel García Márquez*, Habana, Casa de las Américas, 1969. Schwartz, II, 140-145. Mario Vargas Llosa, *García Márquez: historia de un deicidio*, Barcelona, Barral, 1971; also Caracas, Monte Ávila, 1971.

*9. (Mexico) **José Gorostiza** (1901-1973) was born in Villahermosa. He was educated in Mexico where he completed his studies in letters in 1920. He taught literature for a time during the years that followed. In 1929 he was named to an honorary professorship at the University of Mexico. The rest of his life was to be dedicated almost exclusively to government service: at home, in public health, education, and foreign affairs; abroad, at diplomatic posts and on missions to many countries in Europe and America. He represented Mexico at the United Nations and at other political and cultural gatherings around the world. He was a member of the Academia Mexicana de la Lengua (1955).

Gorostiza was one of the most promising poets of the generation of *Contemporaneos* (1928–1931). The deceptive simplicity and popular tone of his first brief collection of lyrics, *Canciones para cantar en las barcas,* that appeared in 1925, won him instant recognition as a disciple of the Gongora renaissance: the "canciones," though few in number, have appeared and reappeared in anthologies of international scope that were quick to follow the lead taken by Onís in 1934. But Gorostiza did not rush into a facile and faulty expression of the profound metaphysical themes already present in the subtle undercurrents of "las barcas," themes that were to crystallize in his masterpiece, *Muerte sin fin,* of 1939. This "indispensable" poem of lucid meditation is, essentially, an "epic" on the eternal verities of humankind: love, solitude, anguish, "god," death — a "morir a gotas" — in which the only certainty is the futile conflict between form and matter, logic and passion, hope and silence ... a striving that can only end, inescapably, in the final disappearance of man himself. Although constantly immersed in the political turmoil of the day, Gorostiza steadfastly continued to reserve a spot wherein to forge a language that would flower into what critics unanimously acclaim as "la pureza más acendrada de la poesía lírica."

Except for some of the earlier lyrics, Gorostiza's poetry does not lend itself readily to the anthologist's game: clearly, *Muerte sin fin* must be read in its entirety.

SUGGESTED READING

Selections from *Canciones para cantar en las barcas* and *Muerte sin fin.*

TEXTS

Anderson Imbert and Florit, 663–664. Flores, III (2), 433–446. Florit and Jiménez, 353–360. Gómez-Gil, II, 388–392. Onís, 1145–1149.

EDITIONS

Canciones para cantar en las barcas, México, Cultura, 1925. Muerte sin fin (1939), 2nd ed., México, Imp. Universitaria, 1952; commentary by Octavio Paz. *Poesía* (1964), México, FCE, 1971; includes poet's "Notas sobre poesía."

TRANSLATIONS

Benson, 10–47. Hays, 170–191. Rodríguez Monegal, II, 600–603. Laura Villaseñor (tr.), *Death Without End,* Austin, Univ. of Texas Press, 1969; bilingual edition.

CRITICAL REFERENCES

See texts and editions above. Anderson Imbert, II, 159-160. Andrew P. Debicki, *La poesía de José Gorostiza*, México, Studium, 1962. *Diccionario . . . mexicanos*, 156-158. Foster, I, 412-415. Leiva, 109-122. Paz, *Las peras*, 105-114. Mordecai S. Rubin, *Una poética moderna. Muerte sin fin de José Gorostiza*, México, Imp. Universitaria, 1966; prologue by Eugenio Florit. Xirau, 13-20.

*10. (Uruguay) **Juan Carlos Onetti** (1909-   ) was born in Montevideo, but lived in Argentina for two extensive periods of time totalling seventeen years. During the 1940s and 1950s he served as editor or coeditor of several magazines: *Vea y lea, Marcha, Ímpetu* and *Acción*. In 1957 he became the director of the municipal libraries of Montevideo. He has always been a withdrawn and solitary man, and this lifetime of emotional isolation turned him into an agonizing existential writer. In Onetti's complex fictional world, life is seen as decay and doom "only partly mitigated by the transcending possibilities of love and art." He writes with biting irony, but also with compassion, in a convoluted Faulknerian style, and with a touch of paranoia which strongly suggests a Hispanic Walter Mitty. In his novels and short stories all action is simultaneous, imagination becomes reality, and the patchwork plots emphasize the fragmentation of man in a hostile universe. The only salvation is "to keep the consciousness of death alive in every cell of our bones." Within this frame, his protagonists (really anti-heroes) struggle courageously to escape their doomed condition. Like Sisyphus they find it necessary to say "yes" to a life of effort which is beyond all hope. Only the struggle itself has the power to redeem man's heart.

The novella, *El pozo* (1939), whose protagonist appears to be a thinly veiled counterpart of the author, is a tense, almost psychiatric confessional in which Onetti probes the alienated life of an egocentric writer. In *La vida breve* (1950) the protagonist replaces his own degraded identity with a series of shorter-lived but more palatable fictional selves. Onetti's fictional universe centers mainly around his imaginary Santa María, which takes its place along with the Macondo of García Márquez, the Jefferson of Faulkner, and the Comala of Rulfo as a symbolic microcosm. The novel *El astillero* (1961) further delineates the absurd reality of contemporary life, and at times brings to mind the grotesque logic of Kafka. The fiction of this strange Uruguayan writer is strongly influenced by Joyce, Faulkner and Roberto Arlt, but Onetti is always able to maintain his own identity and style. His intensely subjective, introverted presentation of human character is one of the strongest elements in the "new novel" of Latin America today.

SUGGESTED READING

"Jacob y el otro" and *La vida breve*.

TEXTS

"Jacob y el otro," in *Ceremonia secreta y otros cuentos de América Latina* (*Life en español*), Garden City, New York, Doubleday, 1961, 349-389. Kadir, 115-184. Latcham, 428-434.

EDITIONS

El pozo (1939), Montevideo, Arca, 1965; with "Origen de un novelista y de una generación" by Ángel Rama. *Tierra de nadie* (1941), Montevideo, Ed. Banda Oriental, 1965. *Para esta noche* (1943), Montevideo, Arca, 1967. *La vida breve* (1950), Buenos Aires, Sudamericana, 1970. *Un sueño realizado y otros cuentos,* Montevideo, Numero, 1951; prologue by Mario Benedetti. *Los adioses* (1954), Montevideo, Arca, 1967. *Una tumba sin nombre* (1959), Montevideo, Alfa, 1968. *El astillero* (1961), 2nd ed., Buenos Aires, Fabril, 1969. *Tan triste como ella y otros cuentos* (1963), Montevideo, Ed. Lumen, 1976; prologue by Joaquín Marco. *Juntacadávares* (1964), Madrid, Revista de Occidente, 1969. *La novia robada* (1967), Buenos Aires, Siglo XXI, 1973. *Novelas cortas completas,* Caracas, Monte Ávila, 1968. *Cuentos completos,* Buenos Aires, Corregidor, 1974. *Requiem por Faulkner y otros escritos,* Buenos Aires, Calicanto, 1976.

TRANSLATIONS

Rachel Caffyn (tr.), *The Shipyard,* New York, Scribner's, 1968. Hortense Carpentier (tr.), *A Brief Life,* New York, Grossman, 1976. Cohen, *Latin American Writing Today,* 34-48. Howes, 267-313. Mancini, 354-366. *Prize Stories,* 319-360. Rodríguez Monegal, II, 536-576.

CRITICAL REFERENCES

See texts and editions above. Adams, 37-80. Fernando Áinsa, *Las trampas de Onetti,* Montevideo, Alfa, 1970. Alegría, *Historia,* 226-227. Benedetti, 76-95. Englekirk and Ramos, 225-226. Foster, II, 134-142. Reinaldo García Ramos (ed.), *Recopilación de textos sobre Juan Carlos Onetti,* Habana, Casa de las Américas, 1969. Helmy F. Giacoman (ed.), *Homenaje a Juan Carlos Onetti,* New York, Las Américas, 1974. Harss and Dohmann, 173-205. Pupo-Walker, 150-165. Jorge Ruffinelli (ed.), *Onetti,* Montevideo, Marcha, 1973. Schwartz, II, 168-173. Hugo J. Verani, "Contribución a la bibliografía de Juan Carlos Onetti," *Cuadernos hispanoamericanos,* 292-294 (1974), 731-750.

11. (Mexico) **Juan Rulfo (1918-   ) was born in the village of Sayula in the state of Jalisco. This once green and thriving village, like many others in the area, was abandoned during the Revolution, and in

Rulfo's mind became a symbolic lost Eden. Many such Mexican villages have never since been repopulated and restored to their former state; the process of sterility begun by the Revolution was irreversible. Apparently, Rulfo's parents also abandoned him at birth, and he was turned over to his maternal grandparents who shortly thereafter placed him in a religious orphanage. His father was killed by an irate peon, and his mother died two years later, when Rulfo was only nine. He never knew either parent well. All of his literary work reflects the tragic trauma of these formative years of his life.

In 1933 Rulfo went to Mexico City where for ten years he worked in the Immigration Department, and then for another seven years for the Goodrich Rubber Company. In 1953 he received a Rockefeller grant as a promising writer, which permitted him to complete his masterpiece, *Pedro Paramo*, a short novel published in 1955. Rulfo's only other published work is a brief collection of fifteen short stories written over a period of several years and later published in a volume entitled *El llano en llamas* (1953). At a recent literary gathering in Mexico City Rulfo was asked why he has not published anything since 1955, and the writer rose to his feet to give this impassioned reply: "Because I do not want to keep on bloodying up Mexican literature!"

Rulfo's literary world is one of fantasy and reality so intertwined that the line of demarcation between them is indefinable. In *Pedro Páramo* he creates a timeless, frozen zone in which the dead and the living co-exist and co-suffer. The son, Juan Preciado, is searching for his father, Pedro Páramo, who years previously had abandoned him and his mother; but his father is already dead. Most of the novel is composed of a surrealistic converation between two animated corpses (Juan Preciado and Dorotea) in the village graveyard. The story takes place in a sterile land and revolves around the polarities of the search for beauty and the eruption into violence when beauty is lost. The locus of this search, the village Comala, is a symbolic and mythic microcosm of all rural Mexican towns. Because of its lack of a time frame, many flashbacks and interpolated memories, *Pedro Páramo* is not an easy novel to read, but it is undoubtedly one of the great novels to come out of Latin America in this century, and merits a most careful reading and rereading. The mythic psyche of Mexico itself is implicit in this book, whose style is as stark, laconic, and cutting as the grim story it tells.

SUGGESTED READING

Pedro Páramo.

TEXTS

Alegría, Novelistas, 95–116. Brotherston and Vargas Llosa, 33–41. Coleman, 115-163. Englekirk, *Anthology*, 758-760. Flores, 658-664. Gómez-Gil, II, 693-700. Leal, *Antología*, 155-162. Leal and Dauster, 443-448. *El llano en llamas* (ed. Rodríguez Alcalá and Raya Verzaconi), Englewood Cliffs, Prentice-Hall, 1973. Menton, *El cuento*, 191-199. *Pedro Páramo* (ed. Leal), New York, Appleton-Century-Crofts, 1970. Vázquez, 340-348.

EDITIONS

El llano en llamas (1953), 8th ed., México, FCE, 1970. *Pedro Páramo* (1955), 12th ed., México, FCE, 1971. *Pedro Páramo y El llano en llamas*, Barcelona, Planeta, 1975.

TRANSLATIONS

Cohen, *Latin American Writing Today*, 174-178. Howes, 413-419. Lysander Kemp (tr.), *Pedro Páramo*, New York, Grove, 1959. Mancini, 246-258. Rodríguez Monegal, II, 752-759. George D. Schade (tr.), *The Burning Plain and Other Stories*, Austin, Univ. of Texas Press, 1967.

CRITICAL REFERENCES

See texts and editions above. Alegría, *Historia*, 287-288. Carlos Blanco Aguinaga, "Realidad y estilo de Juan Rulfo," in Lafforgue, I, 85-113. *Diccionario . . . mexicanos*, 346-347. Durán, 9-51. Flores, 657-658. Foster, II, 295-304. Fuentes, 15-18. Helmy F. Giacoman (ed.), *Homenaje a Juan Rulfo*, New York, Las Américas, 1974. Donald K. Gordon, *Los cuentos de Juan Rulfo*, Madrid, Playor, 1976. Harss and Dohmann, 246-275. Leal, *Historia*, 134-137. Pupo-Walker, 195-215. Arthur Ramírez, "Hacia una bibliografía de y sobre Juan Rulfo," *Revista iberoamericana* 86 (1974), 135-171. *Recopilación de textos sobre Juan Rulfo*, Habana, Casa de las Américas, 1969. Hugo Rodríguez Alcalá, *El arte de Juan Rulfo*, México, INBA, 1965. Schwartz, II, 289-292. Sommers, 69-96; also (ed.), *La narrativa de Juan Rulfo, Interpretaciones críticas*, México, Secretaría de Educación Pública, 1975.

*12. (Argentina) **Ernesto Sábato** (1911-   ) was born in the town of Rojas in Buenos Aires province. In 1937 he received his doctorate in physics from La Plata University. A fellowship took him to the Curie Laboratory in Paris and to the Massachusetts Institute of Technology to further pursue his scientific studies.

Early in his career, the scientific conception of the world in which he was trained began to seem insufficient as an explanation of the enigma of human relations with the universe. Consequently, when he was still a university student, he was attracted to literature, and in 1945 he definitely forsook science in favor of the literary experience; since then he has lived as a journalist, essayist and novelist.

Sábato has used both the essay and the novel to elucidate his quest for an understanding of man's true nature. Perhaps his most significant volumes of essays are *Uno y el universo* (1945), *Hombres y engranajes* (1951), *El escritor y sus fantasmas* (1963), and *La cultura en la encrucijada nacional* (1973). They cover a wide range of philosophical and speculative themes, as well as penetrating meditations on modern literature.

Although he has only produced three novels to date, they place him in the first rank of contemporary novelists. *El túnel* (1948), a novelette, is the confession of a painter-murderer, a lonely and tormented soul. Partly because of its element of suspense, it has achieved great popular appeal. The usual critical view is that the painter in his alienation is symbolic of contemporary man.

Sobre héroes y tumbas (1961) is a complex novel with several interesting plots. The most discernible one concerns an odd love affair between Martín, a naive adolescent, and Alejandra, an anguished, neurotic woman. It is not a happy affair and ends with the suicide of Alejandra when she burns her ancestral home along with her paranoid father, Fernando Vidal. Another seemingly autonomous plot is the "Informe sobre ciegos," a document left by Vidal detailing his delusion that the world is ruled by the Sect of the Blind and his hallucinatory experiences with their vengeance on him. Two other subsidiary plots are woven into this lengthy, symbolic and overpowering novel.

Sábato's third novel, *Abaddón, el exterminador* (1974), is a long and, in the conventional sense, formless work. It has little plot and consists of a meandering series of episodes in which characters from the previous novels appear. Sábato himself turns up occasionally to be ridiculed by his own creations. The novel reflects the author's desperation and anxiety as he seeks meaning in an incoherent world.

SUGGESTED READING

El tunel and "Informe sobre ciegos" which appears in *Sobre héroes y tumbas*.

TEXTS

Alegría, *Novelistas*, 27–62. *Cuentos de la metrópoli* (ed. Yates), Englewood Cliffs, Prentice-Hall, 1975; chapters XII and XIII of *El túnel*. Lewald and Smith, 192–212. *El túnel* (ed. Pérez), New York, Macmillan, 1965.

EDITIONS

Novels: *El túnel* (1948), 10th ed., Buenos Aires, Sudamericana, 1972; ibid., Buenos Aires, EUDEBA, 1966. *Sobre héroes y tumbas* (1961), 14th ed., Buenos Aires, Sudamericana, 1973. *Abaddón, el exterminador,* Buenos Aires, Sudamericana, 1974. *Obras de ficción,* Buenos Aires,

Losada, 1966; introduction by Harley D. Oberhelman.
Essays: *Uno y el universo* (1945), 3rd ed., Buenos Aires, Sudamericana, 1970. *Hombres y engranajes* (1951), 3rd ed., Buenos Aires, Emecé, 1970. *Heterodoxia* (1953), Buenos Aires, Emecé, 1972. *El escritor y sus fantasmas* (1963), 4th ed., Madrid, Aguilar, 1971. *La cultura en la encrucijada nacional*, Buenos Aires, Crisis, 1973. *Obras: ensayos*, Buenos Aires, Losada, 1970.

TRANSLATIONS

Stuart M. Gross (tr.), "Report on the Blind," *TriQuarterly*, 13-14 (1968-69), 95-105. Harriet de Onís (tr.), *The Outsider (El túnel)*, New York, Knopf, 1950. Rodríguez Monegal, II, 733-741.

CRITICAL REFERENCES

Alegría, *Historia*, 276-279. Arrieta, IV, 202-204. Mariá Angélica Correa, *Genio y figura de Ernesto Sábato*, Buenos Aires, EUDEBA, 1971. Angela B. Dellepiane, *Ernesto Sábato, el hombre y su obra*, New York, Las Américas, 1968. *Diccionario . . . Argentina*, II, 368-371. Foster, *Currents*, chap. IV; also Foster, II, 305-314. Helmy F. Giacoman, *Los personajes de Sábato*, Buenos Aires, Emecé, 1972; also Giacoman (ed.), *Homenaje a Ernesto Sábato*, New York, Las Américas, 1973. Harley D. Oberhelman, *Ernesto Sábato*, New York, Twayne, 1970. Rodríguez Monegal, *El arte de narrar*, 219-248. Schwartz, II, 241-246. Zum Felde, *Índice crítico: La narrativa*, 328-332.

13. (Guatemala) **Carlos Solórzano** (1922-   ) is known, not only as an outstanding playwright, but also as a prolific publicist for the contemporary Spanish American theatre. He was born in the small Guatemalan town of San Marcos, but as a young man of seventeen he went to Mexico and has worked there ever since. After acquiring a diploma in architecture, he earned a doctor's degree in literature from the National University. Thereafter he spent three years in France with a Rockefeller grant studying drama. He has been Professor of Dramatic Art in the National University and has lectured in American universities and in the Soviet Union. For ten years (1952-1962) he was Director of the Teatro Universitario in Mexico City, a strictly professional group.

Solórzano's first play, *Doña Beatriz* (1952), is a historical, nationalistic drama. Beatriz was the wife of Pedro de Alvarado, the conqueror of Guatemala in the sixteenth century. The plot deals with her tragic life and the love affairs of Alvarado's children. The characters have a symbolic significance: Alvarado's natural mestiza daughter represents the dynamic, life-giving spirit of the New World, while Beatriz embodies the tradition-bound, decadent outlook of the Old World.

Another notable play by Solórzano is *Las manos de Dios*

(1956), a sort of modern *auto sacramental* in which another Beatriz's brother occupies farm land he believes to be his. For this he is imprisoned. The Stranger (the Devil) advises Beatriz to steal jewels from the church to buy her brother's freedom. She does so and is condemned to death by a furious mob. The Stranger swears to her that he will continue the battle for justice.

Solórzano has also written a number of one-act plays, the most interesting of which are perhaps *Tres actos* (1959). These short pieces deal with rural religious customs in a symbolic fashion. Besides his plays, he has edited four anthologies of Spanish American dramas and has written a useful study of the contemporary theatre.

SUGGESTED READING

Las manos de Dios.

TEXTS

Dauster and Lyday, 21-40 (*Los fantoches*). Earle, 91-142 (*Las manos de Dios*). Gaucher-Shultz and Morales, 3-24 (*Los fantoches*). Gómez-Gil, II, 655-681 (*Las manos de Dios*). Rodríguez-Sardiñas and Suárez Radillo, 293-364 (*El hechicero*). Solórzano, *Teatro hispanoam. contemp.*, II, 303-358 (*Las manos de Dios*); also *Teatro breve*, 323-342 (*Los fantoches*); also *Teatro contemporáneo guatemalteco*, 263-327 (*Doña Beatriz*).

EDITIONS

Doña Beatriz, México, Helios, 1954 (Col. "Teatro mexicano"). *El hechicero*, México, Cuadernos americanos, 1955. *Tres actos*, México, El Unicornio, 1959; the three are: *Los fantoches, Cruce de vías, El crucificado*. *Testimonios teatrales de México*, México, UNAM, 1973. *Los falsos demonios*, México, Joaquín Mortiz, 1966; a novel.

TRANSLATIONS

Colecchia and Matas, 53-68 (*Crossroads*). Luzuriaga and Rudder, 137-153 (*The Crucifixion*).

CRITICAL REFERENCES

See texts and editions above. *Diccionario . . . mexicanos*, 369-370. Foster, II, 347-352. Jones, *Behind . . . Footlights*, 456-457. Esteban Rivas, *Carlos Solórzano y el teatro hispanoamericano*, México, Anáhuac, 1970.

14. (Peru) **Mario Vargas Llosa (1936-   ) is, along with Carlos Fuentes and Gabriel García Márquez, a leading figure in the campaign to trumpet the maturity of the contemporary Spanish American novel. Like the other two, he has been an active publicist for the so-called "boom."

He was born in Arequipa and initiated his peripatetic life early by moving to Bolivia. Back in Peru, he attended a military school in the capital, and eventually graduated from San Marcos University. Subsequently, he lived in Spain (a doctorate in 1958) and Paris (1959–1966). Later he taught in several United States universities. In spite of his international connections, his fiction all concerns his homeland and its ills.

To date, Vargas Llosa has published four major novels: *La inciudad y los perros* (1962); *La casa verde* (1966); *Conversación en la Catedral* (1969); and *Pantaleón y las visitadoras* (1973). The first records the evils that take place among the freshmen (*los perros*) of the Leoncio Prado military academy in Lima, where the author had been a student. Because of its devastating criticism of the military mind and of the system, some copies were officially burned. In this novel, as in later works, he displays a whole show window of stylistic innovations, among which the capricious alteration of normal time and space relations is perhaps the most confusing.

La casa verde is hardly less brutal than *La ciudad*, but it is considerably more complicated. There are five intertwined plots, many characters, and a variety of novelistic techniques, including dream states, stream-of-consciousness, chronological shifts, and varying views of the same incident. The action takes place over a forty-year period in Piura, a semi-desert town, and a jungle post on the Marañón river. There are two "green houses," both of prostitution.

While the condemnation of the Peruvian social and political system is implicit in *La casa verde,* it is painfully explicit in *Conversación en la Catedral.* The awful sins and corruption of Peruvian politics are set forth in a series of conversations in a Lima bar called "La Catedral."

Although his latest novel, *Pantaleón y las visitadoras,* is an unsavory tale of prostitution organized by the army, it does have some flashes of humor, an element notably lacking in previous works.

The author's first fictional publication was a collection of six short stories, *Los jefes* (1959), that concern violence among adolescents in a provincial town. The novelette, *Los cachorros* (1967), also concerns an adolescent, a pitiful, castrated lad, and his frustrations.

Both Vargas Llosa's novels and his shorter works are a strange blend of revolutionary criticism of social conditions, repugnant naturalism, and unusual stylistic devices. They are not pleasant reading for a gentle and sensitive person: prostitution, bestiality, homosexuality, sadism, violence and poverty—physical and spiritual—are the themes with which this leftist author illustrates the decadence of the "upper" and lower Peruvian classes in his novels and stories. In addition to his fiction,

Vargas Llosa has also produced many journalistic articles and pieces of literary criticism.

SUGGESTED READING

La ciudad y los perros or *Los cachorros*.

TEXTS

Castro Arenas, 279-289. Gomez-Gil, II, 725-734.

EDITIONS

Los jefes (1959), Barcelona, Barral, 1972; prologue by José María Castellet; *ibid.*, Madrid, Aguilar, 1974; bibliography by José Miguel Oviedo. *La ciudad y los perros* (1962), Barcelona, Seix Barral, 1971. *La casa verde* (1966), 13th ed., Barcelona, Seix Barral, 1974. *Los cachorros* (1967), 6th ed. Barcelona, Lumen, 1976. *Conversación en la Catedral* (1969), 2 vols., Barcelona, Seix Barral, 1972. *La historia secreta de una novela*, Madrid, Tusquets, 1971 (the genesis of *La casa verde*.) *García Márquez: historia de un deicidio*, Barcelona, Barral, 1971. *Novelas y cuentos*, Madrid, Aguilar, 1973. *Pantaleón y las visitadoras*, Barcelona, Seix Barral, 1973. *La orgía perpetua: Flaubert y Madame Bovary*, Madrid, Taurus, 1975.

TRANSLATIONS

Howes, 535-556. Lysander Kemp (tr.), *The Time of the Hero* (*La ciudad y los perros*), New York, Grove, 1966; also Harper and Row, 1979 (paperback). Gregory Kolovakos and Ronald Christ (tr.), *Captain Pantoja and the Special Service*, New York, Harper and Row, 1978. Mancini, 410-434. Gregory Rabassa (tr.), *The Green House*, New York, Harper and Row, 1968; also *Conversation in the Cathedral*, New York, Harper and Row, 1975. Rodríguez Monegal, II, 941-950.

CRITICAL REFERENCES

Alegría, *Historia*, 306-309. Rosa Boldori, de Baldussi, *Vargas Llosa: un escritor y sus demonios*, Buenos Aires, Garcia Cambeiro, 1974. Brushwood, *Spanish American Novel*, 212-213, *passim*. Flores and Silva Castro, 221-286. Foster, II, 402-412. Franco, *Introduction*, 337-341. Fuentes, 35-48. Gallagher, 122-143. García Márquez and Vargas Llosa, *passim*. Helmy F. Giacoman (ed.), *Homenaje a Mario Vargas Llosa*, New York, Las Américas, 1972. Harss and Dohmann, *Into the Mainstream*, 342-376. Lafforgue, I, 209-240. José Luis Martín, *La narrativa de Vargas Llosa*, Madrid, Gredos, 1974. José Miguel Oviedo, *Mario Vargas Llosa: la invención de una realidad*, Barcelona, Barral, 1970. Rodríguez Monegal, *Narradores*, II, 394-420; also Rodríguez Monegal (ed.), *Asedios a Mario Vargas Llosa*, Santiago, Ed. Universitaria, 1972. Charles Rossman and Alan Warren Friedman (ed.), *Mario Vargas Llosa. A Collection of Critical Essays*, Austin, Univ. of Texas Press, 1978. Schulman,

15. (Chile) **Egon Wolff** (1926–   ) was born of German middle-class parents. He began his career as a chemical engineer after studies at the Catholic University of Santiago and in England. But even as a young student he showed literary inclinations, and finally, when he was thirty years old, he devoted his talents primarily to the theatre. Incidentally, it is said that he plans his plays in English before writing them in Spanish—doubtless as a result of his training in Great Britain.

He has been successful in his second career and is generally recognized as a serious, competent playwright. In his first plays, *Mansión de lechuzas* (1957), *Discípulos de miedo* (1958), and *Niñamadre* (1960) he displays excellent ability in the psychological theatre. His first play skillfully shows the conflict between a worried mother, clinging to old fashioned customs and values, and her two sons, who want to make their way in a changed world. *Niñamadre,* which had its premiere at the Yale Drama School while the author was on a fellowship in the United States, tells of the struggle of a prostitute to win the lasting love of the man who fathered her child.

While the plays mentioned incorporate a certain amount of social criticism, their emphasis is on the subtle development of character. But, beginning with *Los invasores* (1963), perhaps his best-known work, the themes become more directly polemical. In this play a wealthy industrialist dreams that people of the poor and oppressed class invade his palatial home, smash it up, threaten his family, and establish a kind of socialist rule. The rest of the drama shows with surprising techniques how the dream is essentially reenacted as reality. There is some of the usual leftist criticism of North American imperialism.

A more recent play, *Flores de papel* (1971), which has won considerable praise, is basically another version of *Los invasores*. Eva, a middle-class widow, lives in a snug, cute apartment. It is invaded by Merluza, a tramp, who moves in. Gradually he tears apart the bourgeois trappings of the place and substitutes his own tattered decor, especially bunches of paper flowers. Eva is beaten down and finally goes to live with Merluza in his own disorderly milieu. This play links Wolff quite clearly with the theater of the absurd, but it also underlines his social concern, which seems to encompass the destruction or revision of bourgeois values.

In spite of his leftist ideology, Wolff is in no way a blatant propagandist, and his control of the dramatic craft is firm and highly skilled.

SUGGESTED READING

Los invasores.

TEXTS

Coloquio, 100-106. Schwartz, II, 325-332.
Durán Cerda, 131-209 (*Los invasores*). Lamb, 73-134 (*Los invasores*).
Rodríguez-Sardiñas and Suárez Radillo, 106-196 (*Flores de papel*).
Solórzano, *Teatro hispano. contemp.,* I, 126-190 (*Los invasores*). *Tres obras de teatro,* Habana, Casa de las Américas, 1970, 125-245 (*Flores de papel*).

EDITIONS

Niñamadre, Santiago, Instituto Chileno-Norteamericano de Cultura, 1961. *Mansión de lechuzas,* Santiago, Zig-Zag, 1966. *El signo de Caín. Discípulos del miedo,* Santiago, Ed. Valores Literarios, 1971.

TRANSLATIONS

Margaret Sayers Peden (tr.), *Paper Flowers: A Play in Six Scenes,* Columbia, Univ. of Missouri Press, 1974.

CRITICAL REFERENCES

See texts and editions above. Gómez-Gil, 732-733. Lyday and Woodyard, 190-200.

16. (Mexico) **Leopoldo Zea (1912-   ), the leading thinker and philosopher of a brilliant group of Mexican scholars who emerged from El Colegio de Mexico and the Universidad Nacional around 1945. Specializing in philosophy as an undergraduate at the National University, Zea began teaching this subject in the National Preparatory School and El Colegio de México. In 1944 he became a professor of history at the National University, and the philosophy of the history of America was soon his primary interest. Strongly influenced by the Spanish philosopher, José Ortega y Gasset (1883-1955), and the latter's well known dictum *Yo soy yo y mi circunstancia,* Zea's main thesis, developed in a series of books, asserts that the basic problem of Mexico and, by extension, all Hispanic America, is to achieve cultural independence. Both must completely cast off the psychological heritage of a colonial paternalism and, especially Mexico owing to its proximity to the United States, the "Colossus of the North," they must reject a fatalistic inferiority complex, both with respect to this northern neighbor and to their European origins. "Our coming of age depends on honest recognition of our American circumstance" is largely the theme of Zea's *Apogeo y decadencia del positivismo en Mexico* (1944); *Dos etapas del pensamiento en Hispanoamerica: del romanticismo al positivismo* (1949); *America en la historia* (1957); and *Conciencia y posibilidad del mexicano: el occidente y la conciencia de Mexico* (1974).

SUGGESTED READING

America en la historia.

TEXTS

Martinez, II, 280-296.

EDITIONS

El positivismo en Mexico (1943), 2nd ed., Mexico, El Colegio de Mexico, 1953 . *Apogeo y decadenci del positivismo en Mexico,* Mexico, El Colegio de Mexico, 1944. *En torno a una filosofia americana,* Mexico, El Colegio de Mexico, 1945. *Dos etapas del pensamiento en Hispanoamerica: del romanticismo al positivismo,* Mexico, El Colegio de Mexico, 1949. *America como conciencia,* Mexico, Cuadernos americanos, 1953. *America en la historia* (1957), Madrid, Revista de Occidente, 1970. *Conciencia y posibilidad del mexicano: el occidente y la conciencia de Mexico,* Mexico, Porrua, 1974.

TRANSLATIONS

James H. Abbott and Lowell Dunham (tr.), *The Latin American Mind* (1963), 3rd ed., Norman, Univ. of Oklahoma Press, 1970. Frances K. Hendricks and Beatrice Berler (tr.), *Latin America and the World,* Norman, Univ. of Oklahoma Press, 1969. Martinez, 423-436. Josephine H. Schulte (tr.), *Positivism in Mexico,* Austin, Univ. of Texas Press, 1977.

CRITICAL REFERENCES

See texts and editions above. Earle and Mead, 143-145. Patrick Romanell, *Making of the Mexican Mind,* Lincoln, Univ. of Nebraska Press, 1952, 166-176.

Bibliography

For the sake of brevity, only the name of the author (or editor or translator) of the following works is cited in the text unless two or more works of the same author have been used. In that case an abbreviated title is also quoted.

Works not listed below to which reference is made only once are cited in full immediately after the topic which they treat.

HISTORICAL BACKGROUND

BAILEY, Helen Miller and NASATIR, Abraham P., *Latin America: The Development of Its Civilization,* Englewood Cliffs, N.J., Prentice-Hall, 1960.
BERNSTEIN, Harry, *Modern and Contemporary Latin America,* Philadelphia, Lippincott, 1952.
CASTRO, Américo, *Iberoamérica,* rev. ed., New York, Dryden, 1946.
CHANG-RODRÍGUEZ, Eugenio, *La América Latina de hoy,* New York, Ronald, 1961.
CHAPMAN, Charles E., *Colonial Hispanic America: A History,* New York, Macmillan, 1933.
———, *Republican Hispanic America,* New York, Macmillan, 1937.
Crow, John A., *The Epic of Latin America,* Garden City, N.Y., Doubleday, 1952.
DAVIS, HAROLD E., *Latin American Leaders,* New York, Wilson, 1949.
———, *Makers of Democracy in Latin America,* New York, Wilson, 1945.
DIFFIE, Bailey W., *Latin American Civilization: Colonial Period,* Harrisburg, Pa., Stackpole, 1945.
FAGG, John Edwin, *Latin America: A General History,* New York, Macmillan, 1963.
HANKE, Lewis, *Modern Latin America: Continent in Ferment,* 2 vols., Princeton, Van Nostrand, 1959 (paperback).
HARING, Clarence H., *The Spanish Empire in America,* New York, Oxford, 1952; *ibid.,* New York, Harbinger Books, 1963 (paperback).

HARRIS, Marvin, *Race, Tradition and Culture in Latin America*, New York, Walker, 1963.
HERRING, Hubert C., *A History of Latin America*, 2nd ed., New York, Knopf, 1961.
JAMES, Preston E., *Latin America*, rev. ed., New York, Odyssey, 1950.
MADARIAGA, Salvador de, *The Rise of the Spanish American Empire*, New York, Macmillan, 1947.
PATTEE, Richard, *Introducción a la civilización hispanoamericana*, rev. ed., New York, Heath, 1948.
PICÓN-SALAS, Mariano, *A Cultural History of Spanish America, from the Conquest to Independence* (trans. by Irving A. Leonard), Berkeley and Los Angeles, Univ. of California, 1962 (paperback, 1963).
———, *De la conquista a la independencia: tres siglos de historia cultural hispanoamericana*, 3rd ed., México, Fondo de Cultura Económica, 1958.
RIPPY, James Fred, *Latin America: A Modern History*, Ann Arbor, Univ. of Michigan, 1958.
ROBERTSON, William S., *History of Latin American Nations*, New York, Appleton-Century, 1943.
SCHURZ, William L., *This New World: The Civilization of Latin America*, 2nd ed., New York, Dutton, 1963.
TANNENBAUM, Frank, *Ten Keys to Latin America*, New York, Knopf, 1962.
THOMAS, Alfred B., *Latin America, A History*, New York, Macmillan, 1956.
WILGUS, A. Curtis, *The Development of Hispanic America*, New York, Farrar and Rinehart, 1941.
———, (ed.), *Colonial Hispanic America*, Washington, D.C., The George Washington Univ., 1936.
———, (ed.), *Modern Hispanic America*, Washington, D.C., The George Washington Univ., 1933.
WORCESTER, Donald E. and SCHAEFFER, Wendell G., *The Growth and Culture of Latin America*, New York, Oxford, 1956.

LITERARY HISTORY AND CRITICISM

ALEGRÍA, Fernando, *Breve historia de la novela hispanoamericana*, México, Studium, 1959.
———, *La poesía chilena*, Berkeley and Los Angeles, Univ. of California, 1954.
———, *Walt Whitman en Hispanoamérica*, México, Studium, 1954.
"Alone": see DÍAZ ARRIETA, Hernán.
AMUNÁTEGUI SOLAR, Domingo, *Las letras chilenas*, Santiago, Nascimento, 1934.
ANDERSON IMBERT, Enrique, *Historia de la literatura hispanoamericana*, 3rd ed., 2 vols., México, Fondo de Cultura Económica, 1961.

———, *Spanish American Literature: A History* (trans. by John V. Falconieri), Detroit, Wayne State Univ., 1963.
ARANGO FERRER, Javier, *La literatura de Colombia*, Buenos Aires, Coni, 1940.
ARGÜELLO, Santiago, *Modernismo y modernistas*, 2 vols., Guatemala, Tipografía Nacional, 1935.
ARIAS, Augusto, *Panorama de la literatura ecuatoriana*, 2nd ed., Quito, Imp. de la Universidad, 1948.
ARRIETA, Rafael Alberto, and others, *Historia de la literatura argentina*, 6 vols., Buenos Aires, Peuser, 1958.
ARROM, José Juan, *Historia de la literatura dramática cubana*, New Haven, Yale Univ., 1944.
———, *El teatro de Hispanoamérica en la época colonial*, Habana, Anuario Bibliográfico Cubano, 1956.
AUBRUN, Charles Vincent, *Histoire des lettres hispanoaméricaines*, Paris, Armand Colin, 1954.
AZUELA, Mariano, *Cien años de novela mexicana*, México, Botas, 1947.
BALAGUER, Joaquín, *Literatura dominicana*, Buenos Aires, Américalee, 1950.
BALSEIRO, José A., *Expresión de Hispanoamérica*, 2 vols., San Juan, Instituto de Cultura Puertorriqueña, 1960-63.
BARBAGELATA, Hugo D., *La novela y el cuento en Hispanoamérica*, Montevideo, Enrique Miguez, 1947.
BARRERA, Isaac J., *Historia de la literatura ecuatoriana*, 4 vols., Quito, Ed. Ecuatoriana, 1953-55.
———, *Literatura hispanoamericana*, Quito, Univ. Central, 1934.
BAZIN, Robert, *Histoire de la littérature américaine de langue espagnole*, Paris, Hachette, 1953.
Bibliographies of Spanish American Literature prepared by the Harvard Council on Hispano-American Studies, 3 vols., Cambridge, Harvard Univ., 1931-35.
BLANCO-FOMBONA, Rufino, *Grandes escritores de América*, Madrid, Renacimiento, 1917.
———, *El modernismo y los poetas modernistas*, Madrid, Mundo Latino, [1929].
BRUSHWOOD, John S., *The Romantic Novel in Mexico*, Columbia, Univ. of Missouri, 1954.
——— and ROJAS GARCIDUEÑAS, José, *Breve historia de la novela mexicana*, México, Studium, 1959.
CARILLA, Emilio, *El gongorismo en América*, Buenos Aires, Univ. de Buenos Aires, 1946.
———, *El romanticismo en la América hispánica*, Madrid, Gredos, 1958.
CARRIÓN, Benjamín, *Los creadores de la nueva América*, Madrid, Soc. Gen. Esp. de Lib., 1928.
CARTER, Boyd G., *Las revistas literarias de Hispanoamérica*, México, Studium, 1959.
CASTILLO, Homero and SILVA CASTRO, Raúl, *Historia bibliográfica de la novela chilena*, Charlottesville, Univ. of Virginia, 1961.

Centurión, Carlos R., *Historia de las letras paraguayas,* 3 vols., Buenos Aires and Asunción, Ayacucho, 1947-51.
Coester, Alfred, *The Literary History of Spanish America,* 2nd ed., New York, Macmillan, 1928.
Cometta Manzoni, Aida, *El indio en la poesía de América española,* Buenos Aires, Joaquín Torres, 1939.
Corvalán, Octavio, *El postmodernismo,* New York, Las Américas, 1961.
Crawford, William Rex, *A Century of Latin American Thought,* rev. ed., Cambridge, Harvard Univ., 1961.
[Crispo Acosta, Osvaldo] "Lauxar", *Motivos de crítica hispanoamericanos,* Montevideo, Mercurio, 1914.
Cruz, Salvador de la, *La novela iberoamericana actual,* México, Secretaría de Educación Pública, 1956.
Curcio Altamar, Antonio, *Evolución de la novela en Colombia,* Bogotá, Instituto Caro y Cuervo, 1957.
Dauster, Frank, *Breve historia de la poesía mexicana,* México, Studium, 1956.
Del Greco, Arnold A., *Leopardi in Hispanic Literature,* New York, Vanni, 1952.
Del Río, Ángel, *Historia de la literatura española,* 2 vols., New York, Dryden, 1948.
[Díaz Arrieta, Hernán] "Alone," *Historia personal de la literatura chilena,* 2nd ed., Santiago, Zig-Zag, 1962.
Diccionario de la literatura latinoamericana: Argentina, 2 vols., Washington, D.C., Unión Panamericana, 1960-61.
Diccionario de la literatura latinoamericana: Bolivia, Washington, D.C., Unión Panamericana, [1957].
Diccionario de la literatura latinoamericana: Chile, Washington, D.C., Unión Panamericana, 1958.
Diccionario de la literatura latinoamericana: Colombia, Washington, D.C., Unión Panamericana, 1959.
Diccionario de la literatura latinoamericana: Ecuador, Washington, D.C., Unión Panamericana, 1962.
Díez-Canedo, Enrique, *Letras de América,* México, Fondo de Cultura Económica, 1944.
Díez de Medina, Fernando, *Literatura boliviana,* 2nd ed., Madrid, Aguilar, 1954.
Englekirk, John E., *La literatura y la revista literaria en Hispanoamérica,* México, Revista Iberoamericana, 1961-63.
―――, *Poe in Hispanic Literature,* New York, Instituto de las Españas, 1934.
――― and Wade, Gerald E., *Bibliografía de la novela colombiana,* México, Imp. Universitaria, 1950.
Finot, Enrique, *Historia de la literatura boliviana,* 2nd ed., La Paz, Gisbert, 1955.
Gallo, Ugo, *Storia della letteratura ispano-americana,* Milano, Nuova Accademia Editrice, 1954.

GARCÍA CALDERÓN, Ventura, *Del romanticismo al modernismo,* Paris, Ollendorff, 1910.
———, *Semblanzas de América,* [Madrid], Cervantes, [1920?].
GARCÍA GODOY, Federico, *Americanismo literario,* Madrid, América, [1917].
GARCÍA-PRADA, Carlos, *Estudios hispanoamericanos,* México, Fondo de Cultura Económica, 1945.
GOLDBERG, Isaac, *Studies in Spanish American Literature,* New York, Brentano's, 1920.
GÓMEZ RESTREPO, Antonio, *Historia de la literatura colombiana,* 4 vols., Bogotá, Imp. Nacional, 1945-47.
GÓMEZ TEJERA, Carmen, *La novela en Puerto Rico,* San Juan, Univ. de Puerto Rico, 1947.
GONZÁLEZ, Manuel Pedro, *Estudios sobre literaturas hispanoamericanas,* México, Cuadernos Americanos, 1951.
———, *Notas en torno al modernismo,* México, Imp. Universitaria, 1958.
———, *Trayectoria de la novela en México,* México, Botas, 1951.
GONZÁLEZ, PEÑA, Carlos, *Historia de la literatura mexicana,* 7th ed., México, Porrúa, 1960.
———, *History of Mexican Literature,* rev. ed. (trans. by Gusta Barfield Nance and Florence Johnson Dunstan),* Dallas, Southern Methodist Univ., 1943.
GUTIÉRREZ, Juan María, *Escritores coloniales americanos,* Buenos Aires, Raigal, 1957.
GUZMÁN, Augusto, *La novela en Bolivia,* La Paz, Juventud, 1955.
HAMILTON, Carlos, *Historia de la literatura hispanoamericana,* 2 vols., New York, Las Américas, 1960.
HENRÍQUEZ UREÑA, Max, *Breve historia del modernismo,* 2nd ed., México, Fondo de Cultura Económica, 1962.
———, *Panorama histórico de la literatura cubana,* New York, Las Américas, 1963.
———, *Panorama histórico de la literatura dominicana,* Rio de Janeiro, [Companhia Brasileira de Artes Gráficas], 1945.
HENRÍQUEZ UREÑA, Pedro, *Las corrientes literarias en la América hispánica,* 2nd ed., México, Fondo de Cultura Económica, 1954.
———, *Historia de la cultura en la América hispánica,* 3rd ed., México, Fondo de Cultura Económica, 1955.
———, *A Brief History of Hispanic American Culture* (trans., with supplementary chap. to 1962, by Gilbert Chase), Baton Rouge, Louisiana State Univ., 1964.
———, *Literary Currents in Hispanic America,* Cambridge, Harvard Univ., 1945.
IGUÍNIZ, Juan B., *Bibliografía de novelistas mexicanos,* México, Monografías Bibliográficas Mexicanas, 1926.
JIMÉNEZ RUEDA, Julio, *Historia de la literatura mexicana,* 4th ed., México, Botas, 1946.
———, *Letras mexicanas en el siglo XIX,* México, Fondo de Cultura Económica, 1944.

JONES, Willis Knapp, *Breve historia del teatro latinoamericano*, México, Studium, 1956.
LAMB, Ruth S., *Bibliografía del teatro mexicano del siglo XX*, México, Studium, 1962.
LATORRE, Mariano, *La literatura de Chile*, Buenos Aires, Coni, 1941.
"Lauxar": see CRISPO ACOSTA, Osvaldo.
LEAL, Luis, *Breve historia del cuento mexicano*, México, Studium, 1956.
LEAVITT, Sturgis E., NICHOLS, Madaline W. and SPELL, Jefferson Rea, *Revistas hispanoamericanas: Índice bibliográfico 1843-1935*, Santiago, Fondo Histórico y Bibliográfico, José Toribio Medina, 1960.
LEGUIZAMÓN, Julio A., *Historia de la literatura hispanoamericana*, 2 vols., Buenos Aires, Editoriales Reunidas, 1945.
LEIVA, Raúl, *Imagen de la poesía mexicana contemporánea*, México, Imp. Universitaria, 1959.
LEONARD, Irving A., *Baroque Times in Old Mexico*, Ann Arbor, Univ. of Michigan, 1959.
———, *Books of the Brave*, Cambridge, Harvard Univ., 1949.
———, *Los libros del conquistador*, México, Fondo de Cultura Económica, 1953.
LICHTBLAU, Myron I., *The Argentine Novel in the Nineteenth Century*, New York, Hispanic Institute, 1959.
LOPRETE, Carlos Alberto, *La literatura modernista en la Argentina*, Buenos Aires, Poseidón, 1955.
MCGRADY, Donald, *La novela histórica en Colombia, 1844-1959*, Bogotá, Kelly, 1962.
MAGAÑA ESQUIVEL, Antonio and LAMB, Ruth S., *Breve historia del teatro mexicano*, México, Studium, 1958.
MARINELLO, Juan, *Literatura hispanoamericana*, México, Univ. Nacional, 1937.
MARTÍNEZ, José Luis, *La expresión nacional. Letras mexicanas del siglo XIX*, México, Imp. Universitaria, 1955.
———, *Literatura mexicana. Siglo XX*, 2 vols., México, Robredo, 1949-50.
MATLOWSKY, Bernice D., *Antologías del cuento hispanoamericano: guía bibliográfica*, Washington, D.C., Unión Panamericana, 1950.
———, *Bibliografía del modernismo*, Washington, D.C., Unión Panamericana, 1952.
MAYA, Rafael, *Los orígenes del modernismo en Colombia*, Bogotá, Imp. Nacional, 1961.
MEAD, Robert G., *Breve historia del ensayo hispanoamericano*, México, Studium, 1956.
———, *Temas hispanomericanos*, México, Studium, 1959.
——— (ed.), *Iberoamérica: Sus lenguas y literaturas vistas desde los Estados Unidos*, México, Studium, 1962.
MELÉNDEZ, Concha, *La novela indianista en Hispanoamérica*, 2nd ed., San Juan, Univ. de Puerto Rico, 1961.
Memoria del primer congreso internacional de catedráticos de literatura iberoamericana, México, Univ. Nacional, 1939.

Memoria del segundo congreso internacional de catedráticos de literatura iberoamericana, Berkeley and Los Angeles, Univ. of California, 1941.

Memoria del tercer congreso internacional de catedráticos de literatura iberoamericana, New Orleans, Tulane Univ., 1944.

Memoria del cuarto congreso del Instituto Internacional de Literatura Iberoamericana, Habana, Ministerio de Educación, 1949.

Memoria del quinto congreso internacional de literatura iberoamericana: La novela iberoamericana, Albuquerque, Univ. of New Mexico, 1952.

Memoria del sexto congreso del Instituto Internacional de Literatura Iberoamericana, México, Imp. Universitaria, 1954.

Memoria del séptimo congreso del Instituto Internacional de Literatura Iberoamericana: La cultura y la literatura iberoamericanas, Berkeley and Los Angeles, Univ. of California, 1957.

Memoria del octavo congreso del Instituto Internacional de Literatura Iberoamericana: La literatura del Caribe y otros temas, México, Cultura, 1961.

MENÉNDEZ Y PELAYO, Marcelino, *Historia de la poesía hispanoamericana*, 2 vols., Santander, 1948 (Ed. Nacional de las Obras Completas, 27-28).

MENTON, Seymour, *Historia crítica de la novela guatemalteca*, Guatemala, Ed. Universitaria, 1960.

MEZA FUENTES, Roberto, *De Díaz Mirón a Rubén Darío*, Santiago, Nascimento, 1940.

MILLÁN, María del Carmen, *Literatura mexicana*, México, Esfinge, 1962.

MIRANDA, Estela, *Poetisas de Chile y Uruguay*, Santiago, Nascimento, 1937.

MONGUIÓ, Luis, *Estudios sobre literatura hispanoamericana y española*, México, Studium, 1958.

———, *La poesía postmodernista peruana*, Berkeley and Los Angeles, Univ. of California, 1954.

MONTERDE, Francisco, *Bibliografía del teatro en México*, México, Monografías Bibliográficas Mexicanas, 1934.

MORALES, Ernesto, *Historia del teatro argentino*, Buenos Aires, Lautaro, 1944.

MORTON, F. Rand, *Los novelistas de la Revolución Mexicana*, México, Cultura, 1949.

MOSES, Bernard, *The Intellectual Background of the Revolution in South America, 1810-1824*, New York, Hispanic Society, 1926.

———, *Spanish Colonial Literature in South America*, New York, Hispanic Society, 1922; ibid., 2nd ed., New York, Kraus Reprint, 1961.

NAVARRO, Joaquina, *La novela realista mexicana*, México, La Carpeta, 1955.

OLAVARRÍA Y FERRARI, Enrique, *Reseña histórica del teatro en México*, 3rd ed., 5 vols., prologue by Salvador Novo, México, Porrúa, 1961.

OLIVERA, Otto, *Breve historia de la literatura antillana*, México, Studium, 1957.

ORDAZ, Luis, *El teatro en el Río de la Plata*, 2nd ed., Buenos Aires, Leviatán, 1957.

ORTEGA, José J., *Historia de la literatura colombiana*, Bogotá, Cromos, 1935.

PAYRÓ, Roberto P., *Historias de la literatura americana: guía bibliográfica*, Washington, D.C., Unión Panamericana, 1950.

PICÓN-SALAS, Mariano, *Literatura venezolana*, 3rd ed., Caracas, Las Novedades, 1948.

RATCLIFF, D. F., *Venezuelan Prose Fiction*, New York, Instituto de las Españas, 1933.

READ, J. Lloyd, *The Mexican Historical Novel, 1826-1910*, New York, Instituto de las Españas, 1939.

REMOS, Y RUBIO, Juan J., *Historia de la literatura cubana*, 3 vols., Habana, Lectura, 1944.

REYES, Alfonso, *Letras de la Nueva España*, México, Fondo de Cultura Económica, 1948.

ROJAS, Ángel F., *La novela ecuatoriana*, México, Fondo de Cultura Económica, 1948.

ROJAS, Ricardo, *Historia de la literatura argentina*, 4th ed., 9 vols., Buenos Aires, Kraft, [1957].

ROJAS GARCIDUEÑAS, José, *El teatro de Nueva España en el siglo XVI*, México, Luis Álvarez, 1935.

ROSENBAUM, Sidonia Carmen, *Modern Women Poets of Spanish America*, New York, Hispanic Institute, 1945.

ROXLO, Carlos, *Historia crítica de la literatura uruguaya*, 6 vols., Montevideo, Barreiro y Ramos, 1912-15.

SÁNCHEZ, Luis Alberto, *Escritores representativos de América*, 2 vols., Madrid, Gredos, 1957.

———, *La literatura del Perú*, 2nd ed., *Buenos Aires*, Imp. de la Univ., 1943.

———, *La literatura peruana: Derrotero para una historia espiritual del Perú*, 6 vols., Lima, Ed. P.T.C.M., Buenos Aires, Guaranía, 1950-51.

———, *Nueva historia · de la literatura americana*, 5th ed., Buenos Aires, Guaranía, 1950.

———, *Proceso y contenido de la novela hispanoamericana*, Madrid, Gredos, [1953].

SANÍN CANO, Baldomero, *Letras · colombianas*, México, Fondo de Cultura Económica, 1944.

SANTOS GONZÁLEZ, C., *Poetas y críticos de América*, Paris, Garnier, [1913].

SILVA CASTRO, Raúl, *Historia crítica de la novela chilena (1843-1956)*, Madrid, Cultura Hispánica, 1960.

———, *Panorama de la novela chilena*, México, Fondo de Cultura Económica, 1955.

———, *Panorama literario de Chile*, Santiago, Ed. Universitaria, 1961.

———, *Retratos literarios*, Santiago, Ercilla, 1932.

SOLAR CORREA, Eduardo, *Semblanzas literarias de la colonia*, 2nd ed., Santiago, Difusión Chile, 1945.

SOLÓRZANO, Carlos, *Teatro latinoamericano del siglo XX*, Buenos Aires, Eds. Nueva Visión, 1961.

SPELL, Jefferson Rea, *Contemporary Spanish American Fiction*, Chapel Hill, Univ. of North Carolina, 1944.

———, *Rousseau in the Spanish World before 1833*, Austin, Univ. of Texas, 1938.
TORRE, Guillermo de, *Literaturas europeas de vanguardia*, Madrid, Caro Raggio, 1925.
TORRES-RÍOSECO, Arturo, *Aspects of Spanish American Literature*, Seattle, Univ. of Washington, 1964.
———, *Breve historia de la literatura chilena*, México, Studium, 1956.
———, *Ensayos sobre literatura latinoamericana*, 2 vols., Berkeley and Los Angeles, Univ. of California, 1953-58.
———, *The Epic of Latin American Literature*, Berkeley and Los Angeles, Univ. of California, 1959 (paperback).
———, *Grandes novelistas de la América hispana*, 2nd ed., 2 vols., Berkeley and Los Angeles, Univ. of California, 1949.
———, *New World Literature*, Berkeley and Los Angeles, Univ. of California, 1949.
———, *La novela en la América hispana*, Berkeley and Los Angeles, Univ. of California, 1939.
———, *Nueva historia de la gran literatura iberoamericana*, Buenos Aires, Emecé, 1960.
———, *Precursores del modernismo* (1925), 2nd ed.,· New York, Las Américas, 1963.
TRENTI ROCAMORA, José Luis, *El teatro en la América colonial*, Buenos Aires, Huarpes, 1947.
UGARTE, Manuel, *Escritores iberoamericanos de 1900*, Santiago, Orbe, 1943.
USLAR PIETRI, Arturo, *Breve historia de la novela hispanoamericana*, Caracas-Madrid, Edime, 1954.
———, *Letras y hombres de Venezuela*, México, Fondo de Cultura Económica, 1948.
VALBUENA BRIONES, Ángel, *Literatura hispanoamericana*, Barcelona, Gustavo Gili, 1963.
VALERA, Juan, *Cartas americanas*, 4 vols., Madrid, Imp. Alemana, 1915-16 (Obras Completas, vols. 41-44).
VEGA, Miguel Ángel, *Literatura chilena de la conquista y de la colonia*, Santiago, Nascimento, 1954.
VELA, David, *Literatura guatemalteca*, 2 vols., Guatemala, Tipografía Nacional, 1943.
VITIER, Medardo, *Del ensayo americano*, México, Fondo de Cultura Económica, 1945.
WARNER, Ralph E., *Historia de la novela mexicana en el siglo XIX*, México, Robredo, 1953.
ZEA, Leopoldo, *Dos etapas del pensamiento en Hispanoamérica. Del romanticismo al positivismo*, México, El Colegio de México, 1949.
———, *The Latin American Mind* (trans. by James Abbot and Lowell Dunham), Norman, Univ. of Oklahoma, 1963.
ZUM FELDE, Alberto, *Índice crítico de la literatura hispanoamericana*, 2 vols., México, Guaranía, 1954-59.

———, *La literatura del Uruguay*, Buenos Aires, Imp. de la Universidad, 1940.
———, *Proceso intelectual del Uruguay*, rev. ed., 2 vols., Montevideo, Claridad, 1944.

ANTHOLOGIES IN SPANISH

ALBAREDA, Ginés de and GARFIAS, Francisco, *Antología de la poesía hispanoamericana*, 9 vols., Madrid, Bibl. Nueva, 1957-61.
ALPERN, Hymen and MARTEL, José, *Teatro hispanoamericano*, New York, Odyssey, 1956.
ALTOLAGUIRRE, Manuel, *Presente de la lírica mexicana*, México, El Ciervo Herido, [1946].
ANDERSON IMBERT, Enrique and FLORIT, Eugenio, *Literatura hispanoamericana*, New York, Holt, Rinehart and Winston, 1960.
ANDERSON IMBERT, Enrique and KIDDLE, Lawrence B., *Veinte cuentos hispanoamericanos del siglo XX*, New York, Appleton-Century-Crofts, 1956.
Antología boliviana, Cochabamba, Atlantic, 1948.
ARELLANO, Jesús, *Antología de los 50 poetas contemporáneos de México*, México, Eds. Alatorre, 1952.
ARJONA, Doris King and VÁZQUEZ ARJONA, Carlos, *Siglo de aventuras*, New York, Macmillan, 1943.
ARRATIA, Alejandro and HAMILTON, Carlos D., *Diez cuentos hispanoamericanos*, New York, Oxford Univ., 1958.
BALLAGAS, Emilio, *Antología de la poesía negra hispanoamericana*, Madrid, Aguilar, 1944.
———, *Mapa de la poesía negra americana*, Buenos Aires, Pleamar, 1946.
BELTRÁN, Oscar R., *Antología de poetas y prosistas americanos*, 4 vols., Buenos Aires, Anaconda, 1937.
BELTROY, Manuel, *Las cien mejores poesías (líricas) peruanas*, Lima, Euforión, 1921.
BUZO GOMES, Sinforiano, *Índice de la poesía paraguaya*, Asunción and Buenos Aires, Tupâ, 1943.
CAILLET-BOIS, Julio, *Antología de la poesía hispanoamericana*, Madrid, Aguilar, 1958.
CASAL, Julio J., *Exposición de la poesía uruguaya*, Montevideo, Claridad, 1940.
CASTILLO, Carlos, *Antología de la literatura mexicana*, Chicago, Univ. of Chicago, 1944.
CASTRO LEAL, Antonio, *La novela de la Revolución Mexicana*, 2 vols., México, Aguilar, 1958-60.
———, *La poesía mexicana moderna*, México, Fondo de Cultura Económica, 1953.

BIBLIOGRAPHY

COESTER, Alfred, *An Anthology of the Modernista Movement in Spanish America*, Boston, Ginn, 1924.
———, *Cuentos de la América española*, 2nd ed., Boston, Ginn, 1941.
CROW, John A., *Cuentos hispánicos*, New York, Holt, 1939.
CUADRA DOWLING, Orlando, *Nueva poesía nicaragüense*, Madrid, Cultura Hispánica, 1949.
Cuatro siglos de literatura mexicana (ed. by Abreu Gómez, Zavala, López Trujillo and Henestrosa), México, Leyenda, 1946.
CUESTA, Jorge, *Antología de la poesía mexicana moderna*, México, Contemporáneos, 1928.
D'SOLA, Otto, *Antología de la moderna poesía venezolana*, 2 vols., Caracas, Ministerio de Educación Nacional, 1940.
DE VITIS, Michael A., *Florilegio del parnaso americano*, Barcelona, Maucci, n.d. (1927).
——— and TORREYSON, Dorothy, *Tales of Spanish America*, New York, Macmillan, 1933.
ELLIOT, Jorge, *Antología crítica de la nueva poesía chilena*, Santiago, Nascimento, 1957.
FERNÁNDEZ SPENCER, Antonio, *Nueva poesía dominicana*, Madrid, Cultura Hispánica, 1953.
FLORES, Ángel, *Historia y antología del cuento y la novela en Hispanoamérica*, New York, Las Américas, 1959.
GARCÍA CALDERÓN, Ventura, *Los mejores cuentos americanos*, Barcelona, Maucci, n.d.
——— (ed.), *Biblioteca de cultura peruana*, 13 vols., Paris, Desclée, De Bruuwer, 1938.
GARCÍA-PRADA, Carlos, *Antología de líricos colombianos*, 2 vols., Bogotá, Imp. Nacional, 1936.
———, *Poetas modernistas hispanoamericanos*, Madrid, Cultura Hispánica, 1956.
GÜIRAO, Ramón, *Órbita de la poesía afrocubana—1928-37*, Habana, Úcar, García, 1938.
HENRÍQUEZ UREÑA, Pedro and BORGES, Jorge Luis, *Antología clásica de la literatura argentina*, 2nd ed., Buenos Aires, Kapelusz, [1937].
HESPELT, E. Herman, LEONARD, Irving A., REID, John T., CROW, John A. and ENGLEKIRK, John E., *An Anthology of Spanish American Literature*, New York, Appleton-Century-Crofts, 1946.
HILLS, E. C., *Bardos cubanos*, Boston, Heath, 1901.
———, *The Odes of Bello, Olmedo and Heredia*, New York and London, Putnam, 1920.
——— and MORLEY, S. G., *Modern Spanish Lyrics*, New York, Holt, 1913.
HOLMES, Henry Alfred, *Contemporary Spanish Americans*, New York, Crofts, 1942.
———, *Spanish America in Song and Story*, New York, Holt, 1932.
JIMÉNEZ RUEDA, Julio, *Antología de la prosa en México*, 2nd ed., México, Botas, 1938.

JONES, Willis Knapp, *Antología del teatro hispanoamericano*, México, Studium, 1958.

────── and HANSEN, Miriam M., *Hispanoamericanos: Stories about Typical Latin Americans*, New York, Holt, [1941].

LABARTHE, Pedro Juan, *Antología de poetas contemporáneos de Puerto Rico*, México, Ed. Clásica, 1946.

LAGUARDIA, C. G. B., *Cuentos hispanoamericanos*, New York, Scribner's, 1920.

LATCHAM, Ricardo A., *Antología del cuento hispanoamericano contemporáneo, 1910-1956*, 2nd ed., Santiago, Zig-Zag, 1962.

LEAL, Luis, *Antología del cuento mexicano*, México, Studium, 1957.

LEAVITT, Sturgis E., *Tres cuentos sudamericanos*, New York, Crofts, 1935.

LILLO, Samuel A., *Literatura chilena con una antología contemporánea*, 5th ed., Santiago, Nascimento, 1930.

MANZOR, Antonio R., *Antología del cuento hispanoamericano*, Santiago, Zig-Zag, 1939.

MAPLES ARCE, Manuel, *Antología de la poesía mexicana moderna*, Roma, Poligráfica Tiberina, 1940.

MARTÍNEZ, José Luis, *El ensayo mexicano moderno*, 2 vols., México, Fondo de Cultura Económica, 1958.

MAURINO, Ferdinando D. and FUCILLA, Joseph G., *Cuentos hispanoamericanos de ayer y hoy*, New York, Scribner's, 1956.

MÉNDEZ PLANCARTE, Alfonso, *Poetas novohispanos: (1521-1721)*, 3 vols., México, Imp. Universitaria, 1942-45.

MÉNDEZ PLANCARTE, Gabriel, *Humanismo mexicano del siglo XVI*, México, Imp. Universitaria, 1946.

──────, *Humanistas del siglo XVIII*, 2nd ed., México, Imp. Universitaria, 1962.

MENÉNDEZ Y PELAYO, Marcelino, *Antología de poetas hispanoamericanos*, 4 vols., Madrid, Tip. de la Rev. de Archivos, 1893-95, reprinted 1927-28.

MERINO, Félix, *Poesía épica de la edad de oro: Ercilla, Balbuena, Hojeda*, Zaragoza, Ebro, 1955.

MONTERDE, Francisco, *Antología de poetas y prosistas hispanoamericanos modernos*, México, Univ. Nacional, 1931.

NOÉ, Julio, *Antología de la poesía argentina moderna (1896-1930)*, 2nd ed., Buenos Aires, El Ateneo, 1932.

ONÍS, Federico de, *Antología de la poesía española e hispanoamericana (1882-1932)*, 2nd ed., New York, Las Américas, 1961.

OYUELA, Calixto, *Antología poética hispanoamericana*, 5 vols., Buenos Aires, Estrada, 1919-20.

PAGANO, José León, *El parnaso argentino*, 9th ed., Barcelona, Maucci, n.d.

PALCOS, Alberto, *Grandes escritores argentinos*, 100 vols., Buenos Aires, Jackson, 193?-44.

PANERO, Leopoldo, *Poesía hispanoamericana*, 2 vols., Madrid, Ed. Nacional, 1944.

PEREDA VALDÉS, Ildefonso, *Antología de la moderna poesía uruguaya*, Buenos Aires, El Ateneo, 1927.

PIERCE, Frank, *The Heroic Poem of the Spanish Golden Age: Selections*, New York, Oxford Univ., 1947.

―――, *La poesía épica del Siglo de Oro*, Madrid, Gredos, 1961.

Poemas clásicos: La cautiva, El Fausto, Santos Vega, Buenos Aires, Claridad, n.d.

Prize Stories from Latin America (winners of *Life en español* literary contest), New York, Doubleday, 1963.

PUIG, Juan de la C., *Antología de poetas argentinos*, 10 vols., Buenos Aires, Biedma, 1910.

ROJAS GARCIDUEÑAS, José, *Autos y coloquios del siglo XVI*, México, Imp. Universitaria, 1939.

ROSENBERG, S. L. Millard and TEMPLIN, Ernest H., *A Brief Anthology of Mexican Prose*, Stanford, Calif., Stanford Univ., 1928.

―――, *A Brief Anthology of Mexican Verse*, Stanford, Calif., Stanford Univ., 1928.

SANTOS GÒNZÁLEZ, C., *Antología de poetas modernistas americanos con un ensayo acerca del modernismo en América por R. Blanco-Fombona*, Paris, Garnier, [1913].

SAZ, Agustín del, *Nueva· poesía panameña*, Madrid, Cultura Hispánica, 1953.

SCARPA, Roque Esteban, *Lecturas americanas*, 2nd ed., Santiago, Zig-Zag, 1948.

SILVA CASTRO, Raúl, *Antología crítica del modernismo hispanoamericano*, New York, Las Américas, 1963.

―――, *Antología de cuentistas chilenos*, 2nd ed., Santiago, Zig-Zag, [1957].

―――, *Antología general de la poesía chilena*, Santiago, Zig-Zag, [1959].

SOLAR CORREA, Eduardo, *Poetas de hispanoamérica*, Santiago, Cervantes, 1926.

STARR, Frederick, *Central America, Readings in Prose and Poetry from Central American Writers*, New York, Sanborn, 1930.

―――, *Readings from Modern Mexican Authors*, Chicago, Open Court, 1904.

Teatro mexicano contemporáneo, prologue by Antonio Espina, Madrid, Aguilar, 1959.

Teatro mexicano del siglo XX, 3 vols. (ed. by Francisco Monterde, Antonio Magaña Esquivel and Celestino Gorostiza), México, Fondo de Cultura Económica, 1956.

TENTORI, Francesco, *Poesia ispano-americana del 900*, Bologna, Guanda, 1927.

TISCORNIA, Eleuterio F., *Poetas gauchescos: Hidalgo, Ascasubi, Del Campo*, Buenos Aires, Losada, 1940.

TORRES-RÍOSECO, Arturo, *Antología de la literatura hispanoamericana*, 2nd ed., New York, Appleton-Century-Crofts, 1941 (paperback).

―――, *Antología' de poetas precursores del modernismo*, Washington, D.C., Unión Panamericana, [1954].

――― and KRESS, Margaret K., *Chilean Short Stories*, New York, Prentice-Hall, 1929.

TORRES-RÍOSECO, Arturo and SIMS, E. R., *Mexican Short Stories,* New York, Prentice-Hall, 1932.
TURRELL, Charles Alfred, *Cuentos hispanoamericanos,* Boston, Allyn and Bacon, 1921.
VALBUENA BRIONES, Ángel and HERNÁNDEZ AQUINO, L., *Nueva poesía de Puerto Rico,* Madrid, Cultura Hispánica, 1952.
VALLE, Rafael Heliodoro, *Índice de la poesía centroamericana,* Santiago Ercilla, 1941.
VARGAS UGARTE, Rubén, *De nuestro antiguo teatro: Colección de piezas dramáticas de los siglos XVI, XVII, y XVIII,* Lima, Univ. Católica del Perú, 1943.
———, *Nuestro romancero,* 2 vols., Lima, 1951-58 (Clásicos peruanos: 4, 6).
VÁZQUEZ, Alberto, *Cuentos de la América española,* New York, Longmans, Green, 1952.
VITIER, Cintio, *Cincuenta años de poesía cubana (1902-1952),* Habana, Ministerio de Educación, 1952.
WALSH, Donald Devenish, *Cuentos americanos y algunos versos,* New York, Norton, 1949.
———, *Seis relatos americanos,* New York, Norton, 1943.
WALSH, Gertrude M., *Cuentos criollos,* Boston, Heath, [1941].
WEISINGER, Nina Lee, *Readings from Spanish American Authors,* Boston, Heath, 1929.
WEYLAND, W. G. (ed.), *Poetas coloniales de la Argentina,* Buenos Aires, Estrada, 1949.
WILKINS, Lawrence A., *Antología de cuentos americanos,* Boston, Heath, 1924.
ZUM FELDE, Alberto, *Índice de la poesía uruguaya contemporánea,* Santiago, Ercilla, 1935.

ANTHOLOGIES IN ENGLISH TRANSLATION

Anthology of Mexican Poetry (comp. by Octavio Paz; pref. by C. M. Bowra; trans. by Samuel Beckett), Bloomington, Indiana Univ., 1958.
ARCINIEGAS, Germán, *The Green Continent,* New York, Knopf, 1944.
BLACKWELL, Alice Stone, *Some Spanish American Poets,* 2nd ed., Philadelphia, Univ. of Pennsylvania, 1937.
COLFORD, William E., *Classic Tales from Spanish America,* Great Neck, New York, Barron's Educational Series, 1962.
CRAIG, G. Dundas, *The Modernist Trend in Spanish American Poetry,* Berkeley, Univ. of California, 1934.
CRANFILL, Thomas Mabry, *The Muse in Mexico,* Austin, Univ. of Texas, 1959.
FITTS, Dudley, *Anthology of Contemporary Latin American Poetry,* rev. ed., New York, New Directions, 1947.

FLAKOLL, Darwin J. and ALEGRÍA, Claribel, *New Voices of Hispanic America*, Boston, Beacon, 1962.
FLORES, Ángel, *An Anthology of Spanish Poetry*, New York, Doubleday, 1961 (paperback).
——— and POORE, Dudley, *Fiesta in November: Stories from Latin America*, Boston, Houghton Mifflin, 1942.
FRANK, Waldo (ed.), *Tales from the Argentine*, New York, Farrar and Rinehart, 1930.
GREEN, Ernest S. and VON LOWENFELS, H., *Mexican and South American Poems*, San Diego, Calif., Dodge and Burbeck, 1892.
HAYDN, Hiram and COURNOS, John, *A World of Great Stories*, New York, Crown, 1947.
HAYS, H. R., *12 Spanish American Poets*, New Haven, Yale Univ., 1943.
JOHNSON, Mildred E., *Swan, Cygnets, and Owl: An Anthology of Modernist Poetry in Spanish America: Translations*, Columbia, Univ. of Missouri, 1956.
JONES, Willis Knapp (ed.), *Spanish American Literature in Translation: A Selection of Poetry, Fiction and Drama Since 1888*, New York, Frederick Ungar, 1963.
ONÍS, Harriet de, *The Golden Land: An Anthology of Latin American Folklore in Literature*, 2nd ed., New York, Knopf, 1961.
———, *Spanish Stories and Tales*, New York, Pocket Books, 1956 (paperback).
PATTERSON, Helen Wohl (ed. and trans.), *Poetisas de América*, Washington, Mitchell, 1960.
POOR, Agnes Blake, *Pan-American Poems*, Boston, Gorham, 1918.
Three Spanish American Poets: Pellicer, Neruda, Andrade (trans. by Lloyd Mallan, Mary and C. V. Wicker and Joseph L. Grucci), Albuquerque, Swallow and Critchlow, 1942.
TORRES-RÍOSECO, Arturo (ed.), *Short Stories of Latin America* (trans. by Zoila Nelken and Rosalie Torres-Ríoseco), New York, Las Américas, 1963.
Translations from Hispanic Poets, New York, Hispanic Society, 1938.
UNDERWOOD, Edna Worthley, *Anthology of Mexican Poets*, Portland, Me., Mosher, 1932.
WALSH, Thomas, *The Catholic Anthology*, rev. ed., New York, Macmillan, 1942.
———, *Hispanic Anthology*, New York and London, Putnam, 1920.

OTHER WORKS OF GENERAL REFERENCE

ARJONA, Doris King and ARJONA, Jaime Homero, *A Bibliography of Textbooks of Spanish Published in the United States (1795-1939)*, Ann Arbor, Michigan, Edwards Brothers, 1939.
Diccionario enciclopédico de las Américas: Geografía, historia, economía,

política, literatura, arte, música, deporte, cine, teatro, etnografía, fauna, flora, ciencias generales, Buenos Aires, Ed. Futuro S.R.L., 1947.

ENGLEKIRK, John E., *Obras norteamericanas en traducción española,* México, Instituto Internacional de Literatura Iberoamericana, 1944.

GRISMER, Raymond L., *A Reference Index to Twelve Thousand Spanish American Authors,* New York, Wilson, 1939.

HANKE, Lewis, BURGIN, Miron, AGUILERA, Francisco, HAVERSTACK, Nathan A. and PARISEAU, Earl J. (eds.), *Handbook of Latin American Studies,* 25 vols., Cambridge, Harvard Univ., 1935-51; Gainesville, Univ. of Florida, 1951-

HILTON, Ronald (ed.), *Who's Who in Latin America,* 3rd ed., Stanford, Calif., Stanford Univ., 1945.

JONES, Willis Knapp, *Latin American Writers in English Translation,* Washington, Pan American Union, 1944.

KEEN, Benjamin, *Readings in Latin American Civilization,* Boston, Houghton Mifflin, 1955 (paperback).

LEAVITT, Sturgis E., BARRETT, Linton Lomas, and SMITHER, William J., "A Bibliography of Theses dealing with Hispano-American Literature," *Hispania,* XVIII (1935), 169-182, and subsequent years.

PANE, Remigio U., "Two Hundred Latin American Books in English Translation: A Bibliography," *Modern Language Journal,* XXVII (1943), 593-604.

WILGUS, A. Curtis, *Latin America in Maps,* New York, Barnes and Noble, 1943.

———, *Readings in Latin American Civilization,* New York, Barnes and Noble, 1946.

Addenda to Bibliography

Historical Background

Burns, E. Bradford, *Latin America: A Concise Interpretive History* (1972), 2nd ed., Englewood Cliffs, Prentice-Hall, 1977.
Davis, Harold E., *Latin American Thought; A Historical Introduction*, Baton Rouge, Louisiana State Univ. Press, 1972.
Griffin, Charles C. (ed.), *Latin America: A Guide to the Historical Literature*, Austin, Univ. of Texas Press, 1971.
Harris, Louis K. and Alba, Victor, *The Political Culture and Behavior of Latin America*, Kent, Kent State Univ. Press, 1974.
Herring, Hubert C., *A History of Latin America*, 3rd ed., New York, Knopf, 1968.
Reid, John T., *Spanish American Images of the United States: 1790–1960*, Gainesville, Univ. Presses of Florida, 1977.
Rivera, Julius, *Latin America: A Socio-Cultural Interpretation*, New York, Irvington, 1971.
Whitaker, Arthur Preston and Jordan, David C., *Nationalism in Contemporary Latin America*, New York, Free Press, 1966.

Literary History and Criticism

Adams, M. Ian, *Three Authors of Alienation: Bombal, Onetti, Carpentier*, Austin, Univ. of Texas Press, 1975.
Aldrich, Earl M., *The Modern Short Story in Peru*, Madison, Univ. of Wisconsin Press, 1966.
Aldridge, A. Owen (ed.), *The Ibero-American Enlightenment*, Urbana, Univ. of Illinois Press, 1971.
Alegria, Fernando, *Historia de la novela hispanoamericana* (1959), 4th ed., Mexico, Andrea, 1974.
——, *La novela hispanoamericana del siglo XX*, Buenos Aires, CEAL, 1967.
——, *Literatura y praxis en America Latina*, Caracas, Monte Avila, 1975.
Amoros, Andres, *Introduccion a la novela hispanoamericana actual* (1969), Salamanca, Anaya, 1976.
Anderson, Robert Roland, *Spanish American Modernism: A Selected Bibliography*, Tucson, Univ. of Arizona Press, 1970.
Ara, Guillermo, *La novela naturalista hispanoamericana*, Buenos Aires, EUDEBA, 1965.

ARROM, Jose Juan, *Certidumbre de America* (1959), 2nd ed., Madrid, Gredos, 1971.

——, *Esquema generacional de las letras hispanoamericanas*, Bogota, Instituto Caro y Cuervo, 1963.

——, *El teatro de Hispanoamerica*, 2 vols., Mexico, Andrea, 1967.

——, *Hispanoamerica: Panorama contemporanea de su cultura*, New York, Harper and Row, 1969.

AVALLE-ARCE, Juan Bautista (ed.), *Narradores hispanoamericanos de hoy*, Chapel Hill, Univ. of North Carolina Press, 1973.

BALSEIRO, Jose A., *Expresion de Hispanoamerica* (1960–1963), 2nd ed., 2 vols., Madrid, Gredos, 1970.

BAQUERO, Gaston, *Escritores hispanoamericanos de hoy*, Madrid, Cultura Hispanica, 1961.

BECCO, Horacio Jorge, *Fuentes para el estudio de la literatura hispanoamericana*, Buenos Aires, CEAL, 1968.

BEDREGAL DE CONITZER, Yolanda, *Poesia de Bolivia*, Buenos Aires, EUDEBE, 1964.

BENEDETTI, Mario, *Literatura uruguaya siglo XX*, Montevideo, Alfa, 1963.

BLEZNICK, Donald W. (ed.), *Variaciones interpretativas en torno a la nueva narrativa hispanoamericana*, Santiago, Ed. Universitaria, 1972.

——, *A Sourcebook for Hispanic Literature and Language*, Philadelphia, Temple Univ. Press, 1974.

BOLLO, Sarah, *Literatura uruguaya, 1807–1965.* 2 vols., Montevideo, Orfeo, 1965.

BONILLA, Abelardo, *Historia de la literatura costarricense*, San Jose, Ed. Costa Rica, 1967.

BRAVO-ELIZONDO, Pedro, *Teatro hispanoamericano de critica social*, Madrid, Playor, 1975. Comments on plays by Carballido, Solorzano, Wolff, and five others.

BROTHERSTON, Gordon, *Latin American Poetry: Origins and Presence*, New York, Cambridge Univ. Press, 1975.

——, *The Emergence of the Latin American Novel*, New York, Cambridge Univ. Press, 1977. Essays on J. J. Arguedas, Asturias, Carpentier, Cortazar, Garcia Marquez, Onetti, Rulfo, Vargas Llosa.

BRUSHWOOD, John S., *Mexico in its Novel: A Nation's Search for Identity*, Austin, Univ. of Texas Press, 1966.

——, *The Spanish American Novel: A Twentieth-Century Survey*, Austin, Univ. of Texas Press, 1975.

BRYANT, Shasta M., *A Selective Bibliography of Bibliographies of Hispanic American Literature* (1966), 2nd ed., Austin, Univ. of Texas Press, 1976.

BUENO, Salvador, *Historia de la literatura cubana* (1954), Habana, Minerva, 1963.

CAMBOURS OCAMPO, Arturo, *El problema de las generaciones literarias*, Buenos Aires, Pena Lillo, 1963.

CAPARROSO, Carlos Arturo, *Dos ciclos de lirismo colombiano*, Bogota, Instituto Caro y Cuervo, 1961.
CARBALLO, Emmanuel, *Diecinueve protagonistas de la literatura mexicana del siglo XX*, Mexico, Empresas Editoriales, 1965.
CARILLA, Emilio, *El romanticismo en la America hispanica* (1958), 3rd ed., 2 vols., Madrid, Gredos, 1975.
——, *Estudios de literatura argentina*, 4 vols., Tucuman, Universidad Nacional de Tucuman, 1961-!1968.
——, *La literatura de la independencia hispanoamericana*, Buenos Aires, EUDEBA, 1964.
——, *Hispanoamerica y su expresion literaria: caminos del americanismo*, Buenos Aires, EUDEBA, 1969.
——, *La literatura barroca en Hispanoamerica*, New York, Anaya, 1972.
CARTER, Boyd G., *Historia de la literatura hispanoamericana a traves de sus revistas*, Mexico, Andrea, 1968.
CASTAGNARO, R. Anthony, *The Early Spanish American Novel*, New York, Las Americas, 1971.
CASTAGNINO, Raul H., *Escritores hispanoamericanos, desde otros angulos de simpatia*, Buenos Aires, Ed. Nova, 1971.
——, *Experimentos narrativos*, Buenos Aires, Goyanarte, 1971.
——, *Semiotica, ideologia y teatro hispanoamericano contemporaneo*, Buenos Aires, Ed. Nova, 1974.
CASTILLO, Homero (ed.), *Estudios criticos sobre el modernismo*, Madrid, Gredos, 1968.
CHADWICK, John R., *Main Currents in the Venezuelan Novel from Romero Garcia to Gallegos*, Berkeley, Univ. of California Press, 1956.
CHANG-RODRIGUEZ, Raquel and YATES, Donald A. (ed.), *Homage to Irving A. Leonard*, East Lansing, Michigan State University, 1977. Essays on Hispanic art, history and literature.
CHRISTENSEN, George K., "A Bibliography of Latin American Plays in English Translation," *Latin American Theater Review* 6 (1973), 29-39.
COMETTA MANZONI, Aida, *El indio en la novela de America*, Buenos Aires, Ed. Futuro, 1960.
CONDE, Carmen, *Once grandes poetisas americo-hispanas*, Madrid, Cultura Hispanica, 1967.
COULTHARD, George Robert, *Race and Colour in Caribbean Literature* (Spanish, 1958), London, Oxford Univ. Press, 1962.
CRAWFORD, William Rex, *A Century of Latin American Thought* (1961), New York, Praeger, 1966 (paperback).
CUEVA, Agustin, *La literatura ecuatoriana*, Buenos Aires, CEAL, 1968.
CUNEO, Dardo, *Aventura y letra de America Latina* (1964), Caracas, Monte Avila, 1975.
DAUSTER, Frank, *Ensayos sobre poesia mexicana: asedio a los "Contemporaneos,"* Mexico, Andrea, 1963.
——; *Historia del teatro hispanoamericano: siglos XIX y XX* (1966),

2nd ed., Mexico, Andrea, 1973.
———, *Ensayos sobre teatro hispanoamericano*, Mexico, SEP Setentas, 1975.
DAVISON, Ned J., *The Concept of Modernism in Hispanic Criticism*, Boulder, Pruett Press, 1966.
———, *El concepto del modernismo en la critica hispanica*, Buenos Aires, Ed. Nova, 1971.
DEBICKI, Andrew P. (ed.), *Poetas hispanoamericanos contemporaneos*, Madrid, Gredos, 1976. Includes studies on Borges, Marti, Neruda, Pacheco, Parra, Paz, Pellicer, Sabines, Vallejo, Villaurrutia.
——— and PUPO-WALKER, Enrique (ed.), *Estudios de literatura hispanoamericana en honor a Jose J. Arrom*, Chapel Hill, Univ. of North Carolina Press, 1974.
DESCALZI, Ricardo, *Historia critica del teatro ecuatoriano*, 6 vols., Quito, CCE, 1968.
DESSAU, Adalbert, *La novela de la Revolucion mexicana*, Mexico, FCE, 1972.
Diccionario de escritores mexicanos, Mexico, UNAM, 1967; ed. by Aurora Maura Ocampo de Gomez and Prado Velazquez, Ernesto.
Diccionario de la literatura latinoamericana: America Central, Washington, Union Panamericana, 1963.
DONOSO, Jose, *The Boom in Spanish American Literature* (1972, Spanish), New York, Columbia Univ. Press, 1977; tr. by Gregory Kolovakos.
DORFMAN, Ariel, *Imaginacion y violencia en America* (1970), Barcelona, Anagrama, 1972. On Arguedas, Asturias, Borges, Carpentier, Garcia Marquez, Rulfo, Vargas Llosa.
DURAN, Manuel, *Triptico mexicano: Juan Rulfo, Carlos Fuentes, Salvador Elizondo*, Mexico, Secretaria de Educacion Publica, 1973.
DURAN CERDA, Julio, *Repertorio del teatro chileno*, Santiago, Instituto de Literatura Chilena, 1962.
EARLE, Peter G. and MEAD, Robert G., *Historia del ensayo hispanoamericano*, Mexico, Andrea, 1973.
ENGLEKIRK, John E., *De lo nuestro y lo ajeno*, Mexico, Cultura, 1966.
——— and RAMOS, Margaret M., *La narrativa uruguaya*, Berkeley, Univ. of California Press, 1967.
EYZAGUIRRE, Luis B., *El heroe en la novela hispanoamericana del siglo XX*, Santiago, Ed. Universitaria, 1973.
FELL, C., *Estudios de literatura hispanoamericana contemporanea*, Mexico, SepSetentas, 1976.
FERNANDEZ DE LA VEGA, Oscar and PAMIES, Albert N., *Iniciacion a la poesia afroamericana*, Miami, Eds. Universal, 1973.
FERRO, Hellen, *Historia de la poesia hispanoamericana*, New York, Las Americas, 1964.
FLORES, Angel, *Bibliografia de escritores hispanoamericanos, 1609-1974*, New York, Gordian Press, 1975.
——— and SILVA CACERES, Raul (ed.), *La novela hispanoamericana actual*, New York, Las Americas, 1971.

ADDENDA TO BIBLIOGRAPHY

FOGELQUIST, Donald F., *Espanoles de America y americanos de Espana*, Madrid, Gredos, 1967.
FORSTER, Merlin H. (ed.), *Tradition and Renewal: Essays on Twentieth Century Latin American Literature and Culture*, Urbana, Univ. of Illinois Press, 1975.
FOSTER, David William, *Currents in the Contemporary Argentine Novel*, Columbia, Univ. of Missouri Press, 1975. On Arlt, Cortazar, Mallea, Sabato.
——, *A Dictionary of Contemporary Latin American Authors*, Tempe, Arizona State University, 1975.
——, *The 20th Century Spanish American Novel: A Bibliographic Guide*, Metuchen, Scarecrow Press, 1975.
——, and FOSTER, Virginia Ramos, *Manual of Hispanic Bibliography*, Seattle, Univ. of Washington Press, 1970.
——, *Research Guide to Argentine Literature*, Metuchen, Scarecrow Press, 1970.
—— (ed.), *Modern Latin American Literature*, 2 vols., New York, Frederick Ungar, 1975.
FRANCO, Jean, *The Modern Culture of Latin America: Society and the Artist* (1967), Baltimore, Penguin, 1970.
——, *An Introduction to Spanish American Literature* (1969), London, Univ. of Cambridge Press, 1975 (paperback).
——, *Introduccion a la literatura hispanoamericana*, Caracas, Monte Avila, 1971; tr. by Francisco Rivera.
——, *Spanish American Literature Since Independence*, New York, Barnes and Noble, 1973.
——, *Historia de la literatura hispanoamericana a partir de la independencia*, Barcelona, Ariel, 1975.
FUENTES, Carlos, *La nueva novela hispanoamericana (1969)*, Mexico, Joaquin Mortiz, 1974.
GALLAGHER, David P., *Modern Latin American Literature*, New York, Oxford Univ. Press, 1973. On Borges, Cabrera Infante, Garcia Marquez, Neruda, Paz, Vallejo, Vargas Llosa.
GARCIA MARQUEZ, Gabriel and VARGAS LLOSA, Mario, *La novela en America Latina: dialogo* (1968), Barcelona, Peninsula, 1971.
GERTEL, Zunilda, *La novela hispanoamericana contemporanea*, Buenos Aires, Columba, 1970.
GHIANO, Juan Carlos, *Fuentes para el estudio de la literatura hispanoamericana*, Buenos Aires, CEAL, 1968.
GICOVATE, Bernardo, *Conceptos fundamentales de literatura comparada; iniciacion de la poesia modernista*, San Juan, Asomante, 1962.
——, *Ensayos sobre poesia hispanica: del modernismo a la vanguardia*, Mexico, Andrea, 1967.
GOIC, Cedomil, *La novela chilena*, Santiago, Ed. Universitaria, 1968.
——, *Historia de la novela hispanoamericana*, Valparaiso, Ed. Universitaria, 1972.
GOMEZ-GIL, Orlando, *Historia critica de la literatura hispanoamericana*, New York, Holt, Rinehart, Winston, 1968.
GONZALEZ DEL VALLE, Luis and CABRERA, Vicente, *La nueva ficcion*

hispanoamericana a traves de Miguel Angel Asturias y Gabriel Garcia Marquez, New York, Eliseo Torres, 1972.

GONZALEZ PENA, Carlos, *History of Mexican Literature* (Porrua, 10 ed.), 3rd ed., Dallas, Southern Methodist University, 1968; tr. by Nance and Dunstan.

GROSSMANN, Rudolf, *Historia y problemas de la literatura latinoamericana,* Madrid, Revista de Occidente, 1972.

GUIBERT, Rita (ed.), *Seven Voices,* New York, Knopf, 1973; tr. by Frances Partridge, with introduction by Emir Rodriguez Monegal. The seven voices are Asturias, Borges, Cabrera Infante, Cortazar, Garcia Marquez, Neruda, Paz.

GULLON, Ricardo, *Direcciones del modernismo* (1964), 2nd ed., Madrid, Gredos, 1971.

HAMILTON, Carlos, *El ensayo hispanoamericano,* Madrid, EISA, 1972.

HARSS, Luis and DOHMANN, Barbara, *Los nuestros* (1966), 6th ed., Buenos Aires, Sudamericana, 1975.

——, *Into the Mainstream,* New York, Harper and Row, 1967. On Asturias, Borges, Carpentier, Cortazar, Fuentes, Garcia Marquez, Guimaraes Rosa, Onetti, Rulfo, Vargas Llosa.

HEBBLETHWAITE, Frank P., *A Bibliographical Guide to the Spanish American Theatre,* Washington, Pan American Union, 1969.

HENRIQUEZ URENA, Pedro, *A Concise History of Latin American Culture* (tr. from Spanish edition of 1955 by Gilbert Chase), New York, Praeger, 1966.

IRBY, James East, *La influencia de William Faulkner en cuatro narradores hispanoamericanos,* Mexico, UNAM, 1956. The four are Novas Calvo, Onetti, Revueltas, Rulfo.

JACKSON, Richard L., *The Black Image in Latin American Literature,* Albuquerque, Univ. of New Mexico Press, 1976.

JANSEN, Andre, *La novela hispanoamericana actual y sus antecedentes,* Barcelona, Labor, 1973. On Asturias, Carpentier, Cortazar, Fuentes, Gallegos, Garcia Marquez, Vargas Llosa.

JIMENEZ, Jose Olivio, *Estudios criticos sobre la prosa modernista hispanoamericana,* New York, Eliseo Torres, 1975.

JITRIK, Noe, *Produccion literaria y produccion social,* Buenos Aires, Sudamericana, 1975.

JOHNSON, Harvey L. and TAYLOR, Philip B. (ed.), *Contemporary Latin American Literature,* Houston, Univ. of Houston, 1973.

JONES, Willis Knapp, *Behind Spanish American Footlights,* Austin, Univ. of Texas Press, 1966.

JOZEF, Bela, *O espaco reconquistado: linguagem e criacao no romance hispanoamericano contemporaneo,* Petropolis, Editora Vozes, 1974.

LAFFORGUE, Jorge (ed.), *Nueva novela latinoamericana,* 2 vols., Buenos Aires, Paidos, 1969-1972.

LAFLEUR, Hector Rene, PROVENZANO, Sergio D. and ALONSO, Fernando P., *Las revistas literarias argentinas 1893-1967* (1962), 2nd ed., Buenos Aires, CEAL, 1968.

LANGFORD, Walter M., *The Mexican Novel Comes of Age,* Notre Dame,

Univ. of Notre Dame Press, 1972.
LAZO, Raimundo, *Historia de la literatura hispanoamericana*, 2 vols., Mexico, Porrua, 1965-1967.
——, *La novela andina*, Mexico, Porrua, 1973. On C. Alegria, A. Arguedas, J. M. Arguedas, Icaza, Vallejo, Vargas Llosa.
——, *Historia de la literatura cubana*, Mexico, UNAM, 1974.
LEAL, Luis, *Panorama de la literatura mexicana actual*, Washington, Union Panamericana, 1968.
——, *Breve historia de la literatura hispanoamericana*, New York, Knopf, 1971.
——, *Historia del cuento hispanoamericano* (1966), 2nd ed., Mexico, Andrea, 1971.
LEON HAZERA, Lydia de, *La novela de la selva hispanoamericana*, Bogota, Instituto Caro y Cuervo, 1971; prologue by James Willis Robb.
LEONARD, Irving A., *Books of the Brave* (1949), 2nd ed., New York, Gordian Press, 1964.
LITVAK, Lily (ed.), *El modernismo*, Madrid, Taurus, 1975. Essays by **Fogelquist**, J. R. Jimenez, M. Machado, Mejia Sanchez, Monguio, **Paz, Schulman**, Valle-Inclan and others.
LOVELUCK, Juan (ed.), *La novela hispanoamericana* (1963), 4th ed., Santiago, Ed. Universitaria, 1972.
——, (ed.), *Descolonizacion, mitoespacio: la novela hispanoamericana actual*, Madrid, Taurus, 1975.
LYDAY, Leon F. and WOODYARD, George W., *A Bibliography of Latin American Theater Criticism 1940-1974*, Austin, Univ. of Texas Press, 1977.
——, *Dramatists in Revolt: The New Latin American Theater*, Austin, Univ. of Texas Press, 1975.
MACADAM, Alfred J., *Modern Latin American Narratives: The Dreams of Reason*, Chicago, Univ. of Chicago Press, 1977.
MAGANA ESQUIVEL, Antonio, *Medio siglo de teatro mexicano*, Mexico, INBA, 1966.
——, *Teatro mexicano del siglo XIX*, Mexico, FCE, 1972.
MARTIN, Jose Luis, *Literatura hispanoamericana contemporanea*, San Juan, EDIL, 1973.
Memoria del IX congreso del Instituto Internacional de Literatura Iberoamericana (IILI): Influencias extranjeras en la literatura iberoamericana y otros temas, Mexico, Cultura, 1963.
Memoria del X congreso del IILI: Influjos locales, Mexico, UNAM, 1965.
Memoria del XI congreso del IILI: Movimientos literarios de vanguardia en Iberoamerica, Austin, Univ. of Texas, 1965.
Memoria del XII congreso del IILI: El teatro en Iberoamerica, Mexico, Cultura, 1966.
Memoria del XIII Congreso del IILI: Homenaje a Ruben Dario (1867-1967), Primera Sesion, Los Angeles, Univ. of California Press, 1970.

Memoria del XIII Congreso del IILI: La novela iberoamericana contemporanea, Segunda Sesion, Caracas, Universidad Central de Caracas, 1968.

Memoria del XIV Congreso del IILI: El ensayo y la critica literaria en Iberoamerica, Toronto, Univ. of Toronto, 1970.

Memoria del XV Congreso del IILI: La literatura iberoamericana del siglo XIX, Primera Sesion, Tucson, Univ. of Arizona, 1974.

Memoria del XV Congreso del IILI: Literatura de la emancipacion hispanoamericana y otros ensayos, Segunda Sesion, Lima, Universidad Nacional Mayor de San Marcos, 1972.

Memoria del XVI Congreso del IILI: Otros mundos, otros fuegos, Fantasia y realismo magico en Iberoamerica, East Lansing, Michigan State University, 1975.

Memoria del XVII Congreso del IILI: Surrealismo/Surrealisimos-Latinoamerica y Espana, Sequnda Sesion, Philadelphia, Univ. of Pennsylvania Press, n.d. (1977).

MENTON. Seymour, *Prose Fiction of the Cuban Revolution,* Austin, Univ. of Texas Press, 1975.

MONTES HUIDOBRO, Matias and GONZALEZ, Yara, *Bibliografia critica de la poesia cubana (exilio: 1959-1971),* Madrid, Playor, 1972.

MORENO-DURAN. Rafael Humberto, *De la barbarie, a la imaginacion,* Barcelona, Tusqueto, 1976.

NOMLAND, John B., *Teatro mexicano contemporaneo (1900-1950),* Mexico, INBA, 1967; tr. by Paloma Gorostiza de Zozaya and Luis Reyes de la Maza.

OCAMPO DE GOMEZ, Aurora Maura, *Literatura mexicana contemporanea. Biobibliografia critica,* Mexico, UNAM, 1965.

———— (ed.), *Critica de la novela iberoamericana contemporanea,* Mexico, UNAM, 1973.

ORGAMBIDE, Pedro G. and YAHNI, Roberto, *Enciclopedia de la literatura argentina,* Buenos Aires, Sudamericana, 1970.

ORJUELA, Hector H., *Las antologias poeticas de Colombia: Estudio y bibliografia,* Bogota, Instituto Caro y Cuervo, 1966.

————, *Bibliografia del teatro colombiano,* Bogota, Instituto Caro y Cuervo, 1974.

ORTEGA, Julio, *Relato de la utopia: notas sobre narrativa cubana de la Revolucion,* Barcelona, La Gaya Ciencia, 1973.

———— (ed.), *La contemplacion y la fiesta* (1968), Caracas, Monte Avila, 1969. don Cabrera Infante, Cortazar, Fuentes, Garera Marquez, Rulfo, Nestor Sanchez, Vargas Llosa.

PEREZ, Galo Rene, *Pensamiento y literatura del Ecuadoar,* Quito, CCE, 1972. History and anthology.

PHILLIPS, Allen W., *Estudios y notas sobre literatura hispanoamericana,* Mexico, Cultura, 1965.

————, *Cinco estudios sobre la literatura mexicana moderna,* Mexico, SEPSetentas, 1974.

————, *Temas del modernismo hispanico y otros estudios,* Madrid, Gredos, 1974.

PUPO-WALKER, Enrique (ed.), *El cuento hispanoamericano ante la cri-*

tica, Madrid, Castalia, 1973.
RELA, Walter, *Guia bibliografica de la literatura hispanoamericana desde el siglo XIX hasta 1970,* Buenos Aires, Pardo, 1971.
RODMAN, Selden, *South America of the Poets,* New York, Hawthorn, 1970. On Asturias, Borges, Cortazar, Fuentes, Garcia Marquez, Neruda, Parra.
RODRIGUEZ ALCALA, Hugo, *Historia de la literatura paraguaya,* Mexico, Andrea, 1970.
———, *Narrativa hispanoamericana,* Madrid, Gredos, 1973. On Carpentier, Guiraldes, Roa Bastos, Rulfo.
RODRIGUEZ FERNANDEZ, Mario, *El modernismo en Chile y en Hispanoamerica,* Santiago, Instituto de Literatura Chilena, 1967.
RODRIGUEZ MONEGAL, Emir, *El juicio de los parricidas: la nueva generacion argentina y sus maestros,* Buenos Aires, Deucalion, 1956. On Borges, Mallea, Martinez Estrada.
———, *Narradores de esta America* (1962), 2nd ed., 2 vols., Montevideo, Alfa, 1969–1974.
———, *Literatura uruguaya del medio siglo,* Montevideo, Alfa, 1966.
———, *El arte de narrar,* Caracas, Monte Avila, 1968.
———, *El "boom" de la novela latinoamericana,* Caracas, Tiempo Nuevo, 1972.
——— (ed.), "Literatura y revolucion en las letras cubanas," *Revista iberoamericana,* 92–93 (1975). On Carpentier, Lezama Lima, et al.
ROGGIANO, Alfredo A., *En este aire de America,* Mexico, Cultura, 1966.
ROSA-NIEVES, Cesareo, *Historia panoramica de la literatura puertorriquena,* 2 vols., San Juan, Campos, 1963.
ROY Joaquin (ed.), *Narrativa y critica de nuestra America,* Madrid, Castalia, 1978. On Asturias, Borges, Carpentier, Cortazar, Fuentes, Garcia Marquez, Onetti, Rulfo, Sabato, Sarduy, Vargas Llosa.
RUTHERFORD, John, *An Annotated Bibliography of the Novels of the Mexican Revolution of 1910-1917 in English and Spanish,* Troy, Whitston, 1972.
SACOTO, Antonio, *El indio en el ensayo do la America espanola,* New York, Las Americas, 1973.
SALVADOR, Nelida, *La nueva poesia argentina,* Buenos Aires, Columba, 1969.
SANCHEZ, Luis Alberto, *Escritores representativos de America* (1957) 3rd ed., 3 vols., Madrid, Gredos, 1976.
SANCHEZ TRINCADO Jose, *Literatura hispanoamericana, siglo XX,* Buenos Aires, Pena Lillo, 1964.
SCHULMAN, Ivan A., *Genesis del modernismo: Marti, Najera, Silva, Casal* (1966), 2nd ed., Mexico, El Colegio de Mexico, 1968.
——— (ed.), *Coloquio sobre la novela hispanoamericana,* Mexico, Tezontle, 1967.
———, *El modernismo hispanomericano,* Buenos Aires, CEAL, 1969.
——— and GONZALEZ, MANUEL PEDRO, *Marti, Dario y el modernismo* (1969), Madrid, Gredos, 1974.
SCHWARTZ, KESSEL, *A New History of Spanish American Fiction,* 2 vols.,

Coral Gables, Univ. of Miami Press, 1972.
SOLORZANO, CARLOS. *El teatro latinoamericano en el siglo XX* (1961), 2nd ed., Mexico, Pormaca, 1964.
SOMMERS, Joseph, *After the Storm*, Albuquerque, Univ. of New Mexico Press, 1966; also published, under title, *Yanez, Rulfo, Fuentes*, Caracas, Monte Avila, 1970.
SOUZA, Raymond D., *Major Cuban Novelists: Innovation and Tradition*, Columbia, Univ. of Missouri Press, 1976.
STABB Martin S., *In Quest of Identity: Patterns in the Spanish American Essay of Ideas, 1890-1960*, Chapel Hill, Univ. of North Carolina Press, 1967.
STIMSON Frederick S., *The New Schools of Spanish American Poetry*, Madrid, Castalia, 1970.
TAMAYO VARGAS, Augusto, *Literatura peruana*, Lima, Universidad Nacional Mayor de San Marcos, 1967.
VALDIVIESO, Jaime, *Realidad y ficcion en Latinoamerica*, Mexico, Joaquin Mortiz, 1975.
VAZQUEZ AMARAL, Jose, *The Contemporary Latin American Narrative*, New York, Las Americas, 1970.
WOODYARD, George W. and LYDAY, Leon F., "Studies on the Latin American Theatre, 1960-69," *Theatre Documentation*, 2(1969-70), 49-84.
XIRAU, Ramon, *Tres poetas de la soledad*, Mexico, Robredo, 1955. The poets are Jose Gorostiza, Paz, Villaurrutia.
YURKIEVICH, Saul, *Fundadores de la nueva poesia latinoamericana* (1971), 2nd ed., Barcelona, Barral, 1973. The "fundadores" are Borges, Girondo, Huidobro, Neruda, Paz, Vallejo..
———, *Celebracion del modernismo*, Barcelona, Tusquets, 1976.
ZUM FELDE, Alberto, *La narrativa hispanoamericana* (1959), 2nd ed., Madrid, Aguilar, 1964.

Anthologies in English Translation

Beckett, Samuel (tr.), *An Anthology of Mexican Poetry* (1958), 2nd ed., Bloomington, Indiana Univ. Press, 1965 (paperback); ed. by Octavio Paz, with preface by C. M. Bowra.

Benson, Rachel (tr.), *Nine Latin American Poets*, New York, Las Américas, 1968. A bilingual edition. The poets are Gorostiza, Huidobro, Neruda, Palés Matos, Paz, Pellics, Storni, Vallejo, Villaurrutia.

Bly, Robert (ed. and tr.), *Neruda and Vallejo: Selected Poems*, Boston, Beacon, 1971. A bilingual edition, with translations by Robert Bly, John Knoepfle, James Wright.

Caracciolo-Trejo, Enrique, *The Penguin Book of Latin American Verse*, Baltimore, Penguin, 1971. A bilingual edition, with translations in prose and an introduction by Henry Gifford.

Carpentier, Hortense and Brof, Janet, *Doors and Mirrors: Fiction and Poetry from Spanish America (1920-1970)*, New York, Grossman, 1972.

Cohen, John Michael (ed.), *Latin American Writing Today*, Baltimore, Penguin, 1967. Translations from works of 32 writers.

—— (ed. and tr.), *Writers in the New Cuba: An Anthology*, Baltimore, Penguin, 1967.

—— (ed.), *En tiempos difíciles. La poesía cubana de la Revolución*, Barcelona, Tusquets, 1970; tr. by Isabel Vericat.

Colecchia, Francesca and Matas, Julio, *Selected Latin American One-Act Plays*, Pittsburgh, Univ. of Pittsburgh Press, 1973.

Crow, John A. (ed. and tr.), *An Anthology of Spanish Poetry* (Spain and Spanish America), Baton Rouge, Louisiana State Univ. Press, 1979.

Franco, Jean (ed.), *Short Stories in Spanish. Cuentos hispánicos*, Baltimore, Penguin, 1966. A bilingual edition of eight stories by Benedetti, Borges, Cela, García Márquez, Martínez Moreno, Murena, Onetti, Rulfo.

Fremantle, Anne (ed. and tr.), *Latin-American Literature Today*, New York, New American Library, 1977 (Mentor). Translations, with preface, by editor and others (Christofer Fremantle, James E. Irby, Susan Kaufman, Margaret S. Peden, Gregory Rabassa, et al) from works of 38 writers (several are in their twenties). A good number of the translations are here published for the first time; many of the remainder have already been listed in this *Outline History*.

Howes, Barbara (ed.), *The Eye of the Heart*, New York, Bobbs-Merrill, 1973; also Avon, 1974 (paperback). Forty-two short stories from Latin America, rendered by various translators.

Jones, Willis Knapp, *Men and Angels. Three South American Comedies*, Carbondale, Southern Illinois Univ. Press, 1970.

Luzuriaga, Gerardo and Rudder, Robert S. (tr.), *The Orgy. Modern One-Act Plays from Latin America*, Los Angeles, Univ. of California Press, 1974. Plays by Adellach, Buenaventura, Denevi, Díaz,

Dragún, Martinel, Queirolo, Menén Desleal, Solorzano.
MANCINI, Pat McNees (ed.), *Contemporary Latin American Short Stories,* Greenwich, Fawcett, 1974.
——, *A Treasury of Latin American Literature;* Greenwich, Fawcett, 1974.
MÁRQUEZ, Robert, *Latin American Revolutionary Poetry,* New York, Monthly Review Press, 1974.
MARTÍNEZ, José Luis, *The Modern Mexican Essay* (Spanish, 1958), Toronto, Univ. of Toronto Press, 1965; tr. by Harry Warren Hilborn.
OLIVER, William I., *Voices of Change in the Spanish American Theatre,* Austin, Univ. of Texas Press, 1971. Plays by Buenaventura, Carballido, Gámbaro, Hernández, Maggi, Vodanović.
Poesía cubana, Habana, Casa de las Américas, 1968. A bilingual edition.
Prize Stories from Latin America, New York, Doubleday, 1963; prologue by Arturo Uslar Pietri.
RESNICK, Seymour, *Spanish American Poetry: A Bilingual Selection,* New York, Harvey House, 1964.
RODRIGUEZ MONEGAL, Emir (ed., "with the assistance of Thomas Colchie"), *The Borzoi Anthology of Latin American Literature,* 2 vols., New York, Knopf, 1977. Historical, critical and biographical commentary on each author's work and on each major period in the literature as a whole. Most of the translations gathered herein have already been cited in the third edition of this *Outline History.* References to the *Anthology* are made only when applicable to the new authors presented in this fourth edition.
STRAND, Mark (ed. and tr.), *New Poetry of Mexico, 1915-1966,* New York, Dutton, 1970; also London, Secker & Warburg, 1972. A bilingual edition, with selections from twenty-four contemporary poets taken from *Poesía en movimiento, México, 1915-1966* (see Anthologies in Spanish).
Three Spanish American Poets: Pellicer, Neruda, Andrade (1942), New York, Gordon Press, 1977.
WOODYARD, George, *The Modern Stage in Latin America: Six Plays,* New York, Dutton, 1971 (paperback). Plays by Carballido, Díaz, Dragún, Gomes, Marqués, Triana.
Young Poetry of the Americas, Washington, Pan American Union, 1967. A bilingual edition.

OTHER WORKS OF GENERAL REFERENCE

BRYANT, Shasta M., *A Selective Bibliography of Bibliographies of Hispanic American Literature* (1966), 2nd ed., Austin, Univ. of Texas Press, 1976.
DELPAR, Helen (ed.), *Encyclopedia of Latin America,* New York, McGraw-Hill, 1974.
DORN, Georgette M., *Latin America, Spain and Portugal: An*

Annotated Bibliography of Paperback Books (1971), 2nd ed., Washington, Library of Congress, 1976.

GROPP, Arthur E., *A Bibliography of Latin American Bibliographies*, Metuchen, Scarecrow Press, 1968; with Supplement, 1971.

——, *A Bibliography of Latin American Bibliographies Published in Periodicals*, 2 vols., Metchuen, Scarecrow Press, 1976. Companion work to his *Bibliography of Latin American Bibliographies*.

HULET, Claude Lyle, *Latin American Prose in English Translation: A Bibliography*, Washington, Pan American Union, 1964.

——, *Latin American Poetry in English Translation: A Bibliography*, Washington, Pan American Union, 1965.

LEAVITT, Sturgis E., Barrett, Linton Lomas, Smither William J., and Hulet, Claude L., "A Bibliography of Theses dealing with Hispano-American Literature," *Hispania*, *XVIII* (1935), 169-182, and subsequent years.

SHAW, Bradley A., *Latin American Literature in English Translation: An Annotated Bibliography*, New York, New York Univ. Press, 1976.

WILGUS, Karna S., *Latin American Books: An Annotated Bibliography*, New York, Center for Inter-American Relations, 1974.

FLORIT, Eugenio and JIMENEZ, Jose Olivio, *La poesia hispanoamericana desde el modernismo*, New York, Appleton-Century-Crofts, 1968.

FRANCO, Jean, *Cuentos americanos de nuestros dias*, London, Harrap, 1965.

GALLY C., Hector, *Treinta cuentos de autores mexicanos jovenes*, Mexico, Ed. Pax-Mexico, 1967.

GARGANIGO, John and RELA, Walter, *Antologia de la literatura gauchesca y criolla*, Montevideo, Ed. Delta, 1967.

GAUCHER-SHULTZ, Jeanine and MORALES, Alfredo O., *Tres dramas mexicanos en un acto*, New York, Bobbs-Merrill, 1971. Plays by Garro, Magana, Solorzano.

GHIANO, Juan Carlos, *Poesia argentina del siglo XX*, Mexico, FCE, 1957.

GLEAVES, Robert M. and VANCE, Charles M., *Hispanoamerica magica y misteriosa: once relatos*, New York, Holt, Rinehart, Winston, 1973.

GOMEZ GIL, Orlando, *Literatura hispanoamericana: antologia critica*, 2 vols., New York, Holt, Rinehart, Winston, 1971.

ISAACSON, Jose and URQUIA, Carlos Enrique, *40 anos de poesia argentina*, 3 vols., Buenos Aires, Americalee, 1964.

JIMENEZ, Jose Olivio, *Cien de las mejores poesias hispanoamericanas*, New York, Las Americas, 1965.

——, *Antologia de la poesia hispanoamericana contemporanea, 1914-1970*, Madrid, Alianza, 1971.

——, *Grandes poetas de Hispanoamerica del siglo XV al XX*, Barcelona, Salvat, 1972.

—— and CAMPA, Antonio R. de la, *Antologia critica de la prosa modernista hispanoamericana*, New York, Eliseo Torres, 1976.

KADIR, Djelal, *Triple espera: novelas cortas de Hispanoamerica*, New York Harcourt, Brace, Jovanovich, 1976. The novels are by Fuentes

(*Aura*), Garcia Marquez (*El coronel no tiene quien le escriba*), Onetti (*Los adioses*).
LAMB, Ruth S., *Three Contemporary Latin American Plays*, Waltham, Ginn, 1971. The plays are by Carballido, Marques, Wolff.
LEAL, Luis, *Cuentistas hispanoamericanos del siglo veinte*, New York, Random, 1972.
—— and DAUSTER, Frank, *Literatura de Hispanoamerica*, New York, Harcourt, Brace, World, 1970.
LEVINE, Suzanne Jill and TAYLOR, Hollie D., *Triple Cross*, New York, Dutton, 1972. Translations from J. Donoso, Fuentes, Sarduy.
LEWALD, H. Ernest, *Antologia de veinte poetas post-modernistas latinoamericanos*, Buenos Aires, Instituto de Amigos del Libro Argentino, 1967.
——, *Latino-America: sus culturas y sociedades*, New York, McGraw-Hill, 1973.
——, and SMITH, George E., *Escritores platenses, ficciones del siglo XX*, Boston, Houghton Mifflin, 1971.
LEZAMA LIMA, Jose, *Antologia de la poesia cubana*, Habana, Consejo Nacional de Cultura, 1965.
LIPP, Solomon and LIPP, S. E., *Hispanoamerica vista por sus ensayistas*, New York, Scribner's, 1969.
LOPEZ, MORALES, Humberto, *Poesia cubana contemporanea*, New York, Las Americas, 1967.
LUZURIAGA, Gerardo and REEVE, Richard, *Los clasicos del teatro hispanoamericano*, Mexico, FCE, 1975.
MARCELESE, Mario, *Antologia poetica hispanoamericana actual*, 2 vols., La Plata, Ed. Platense, 1969.
MATUS, Eugenio, *Literatura hispanoamericana de la conquista y de la colonia: antologia*, Habana, Ed. Nacional de Cuba, 1963.
MENESES, Guillermo, *El cuento venezolano, 1900-1940*, Buenos Aires, EUDEBA, 1966.
MENTON, Seymour, *El cuento hispanoamericano: antologia criticohistorica*, 2 vols., Mexico, FCE, 1964.
MILLAN, Maria del Carmen, *Antologia de cuentos mexicanos, 3 vols.*,
MENTON, Seymour, *El cuento hispanoamericano: antologia criticohistorica*, 2 vols., Mexico, FCE, 1964.
MILLAN, Maria del Carmen, *Antologia de cuentos mexicanos, 3 vols.*, Mexico, SEPSetentas, 1976.
MIRO, Rodrigo, *Cien anos de poesia en Panama, 1852-1952*, Panama, Imp. Nacional, 1953.
MONTES DE OCA, Francisco, *Poesia mexicana*, Mexico, Porrua, 1968.
PACHECO, Jose Emilio, *Antologia del modernismo, 1884-1921*, 2 vols., Mexico, UNAM, 1970.
PELLEGRINI, Aldo, *Antologia de la poesia viva latinoamericana*, Barcelona, Seix Barral, 1966.
PERCAS, Helena, *La poesia femenina argentina, 1810-1950*, Madrid, Cultura Hispanica, 1958.
PICON SALAS, Mariano, *Dos siglos de prosa venezolana*, Madrid, Edime,

1965.
Poesia en movimiento, Mexico, 1915-1966 (1966), 9th ed., Mexico, Siglo XXI, 1976; ed. by Octavio Paz ("Prologo"), Ali Chumacero, Jose Emilio Pacheco, Homero Aridjis.

PORRATA, Francisco E. and SANTANA, Jorge A., *Antologia comentada del modernismo*, Sacramento, CSUC Foundation, 1974. Texts of 14 poets analyzed by 75 scholars.

RAMIREZ, Sergio, *Antologia del cuento centroamericano*, 2 vols., San Jose, Ed. Universitaria Centroamericana, 1973.

REEDY, Daniel and JONES, Joseph R., *Narraciones ejemplares de Hispanoamerica (1836-1959)*, New York, Las Americas, 1966.

——— and VALDESPINO, Andres, *Teatro hispanoamericano: antologia critica*, 2 vols., New York, Anaya, 1972-1973.

RODRIGUEZ ALCALA, Hugo and Sally, *Cuentos nuevos del sur*, Englewood Cliffs, Prentice-Hall, 1967.

RODRIGUEZ SARDINAS, Orlando, *La ultima poesia cubana: antologia reunida (1959-1973)*, Madrid, Hispanova, 1973.

——— and SUAREZ RADILLO, Carlos Miguel, *Teatro contemporaneo hispanoamericano*, 3 vols., Madrid, Escelicer, 1971.

ROGERS, Paul, *Florilegio de cuentos hispanoamericanos*, New York, Macmillan, 1968.

SANZ Y DIAZ, Jose, *Antologia de cuentistas hispanoamericanos* (1946), 2nd ed., Madrid, Aguilar, 1956.

SAZ, Agustin del, *Teatro hispanoamericano*, 2 vols., Barcelona, Vergara, 1964.

SCARPA, Roque Esteban and MONTES, Hugo, *Antologia de la poesia chilena contemporanea*, Madrid, Gredos, 1968.

SOLORZANO, Carlos, *Teatro guatemalteco contemporaneo*, Madrid, Aguilar, 1964.

———, *El teatro hispanoamericano contemporaneo. Antologia*, 2 vols., Mexico, FCE, 1964.

———, *Teatro breve hispanoamericano contemporaneo*, Madrid, Aguilar, 1969.

———, *El teatro actual latinoamericano*, Mexico, Andrea, 1972.

STIMSON, Frederick S. and NAVAS-RUIZ, Ricardo, *Literatura de la America Hispanica*, 3 vols., New York, Dodd, Mead, 1971-1975.

Teatro latinoamericano de agitacion, Habana, Casa de las Americas, 1972.

Teatro mexicano, Mexico, Aguilar, 1958-1972; ed. by Antonio Magana Esquivel.

Teatro mexicano del siglo XX, 5 vols., Mexico, FCE, 1956-1970.

Works and Studies

ACEVEDO DÍAZ, Eduardo
WORKS
El combate de la tapera y otros cuentos, Montevideo, Arca, 1965; ed. by Angel Rama.
STUDIES
Englekirk and Ramos, 45–48, 98–103. Emir Rodriguez Monegal, *Vinculo de sangre: Eduardo Acevedo Diaz, novelista,* Montevideo, Alfa, 1968.

ACUÑA, Manuel
WORKS
Manuel Acuna: biografia, obras completas, epistolario y juicios, Mexico, Ed. "Mexico," 1971; ed. by Jose Farias Galindo.

AGUSTINI, Delmira
WORKS
Poesias completas, Barcelona, Labor, 1971; ed. by Manuel Alvar.
STUDIES
Foster, I, 16–20. Clara Silva, *Pasion y gloria de Delmira Agustini; su vida y su obra,* Buenos Aires, Losada, 1972.

ALEGRÍA, Ciro
STUDIES
Foster, I, 20–30.

ALTAMIRANO, Ignacio Manuel
WORKS
La navidad en las montanas, Mexico, Porrua, 1972; ed. by Marta R. Gomez and Harvey L. Johnson.
STUDIES
Chris N. Nacci, *Ignacio Manuel Altamirano,* New York, Twayne, 1970.

AMORIM, Enrique
>
> WORKS

El asesino desvelado del "Septimo Circulo," (ed. Herman and Brady), Boston, Houghton Mifflin, 1952. Crow and Dudley, 138–149. Latcham, 414–424.

> STUDIES

Englekirk and Ramos, 85–88, 107–112. Foster, I, 42–48. K. E. A. Mose, *Enrique Amorim: The Passion of a Uruguayan*, Madrid, Playor, 1972. Hugo Rodriguez Urruty, *Para la bibliografia de Amorim*, Montevideo, Agon, 1958. Schwartz, II, 162–166.

ANDRADE, Olegario Victor

> WORKS

Poesia de Olegario V. Andrade, Buenos Aires, EUDEBA, 1966; ed. by Teresita Frugoni de Fritsche.

ARCINIEGAS, Germán

> WORKS

El continente de siete colores, Buenos Aires, Sudamericana, 1965; tr. by Joan MacLean, *Latin America. A Cultural History*, New York, Knopf, 1967. *El continente de siete colores* (ed. McVickers and Soto), New York, Harcourt, Brace, World, 1968. *Paginas escogidas (1932–1973)*, Madrid, Gredos, 1974.

> STUDIES

Foster, I, 78–84.

ARÉVALO MARTINEZ, Rafael

> WORKS

Crow and Dudley, 301–375. *El hombre que parecia un caballo y otros cuentos*, 9th ed., Guatemala, Ministerio de Educacion Publica, 1963.

> STUDIES

Alegria, *Historia*, 125–127. Teresa Arevalo, *Rafael Arevalo Martinez, de 1884 hasta 1926*, Guatemala, Tipografia Nacional, 1971. Hugo Estrada, *La poesia de Rafael Arevalo Martinez*, Guatemala, Universidad de San Carlos, 1971. Foster, I, 84–89. Joseph Anthony Lonteen, *Interpretacion de una amistad intelectual y su producto literario El hombre que parecia un caballo*, Guatemala, Ed. Landivar, 1969. Schwartz, II, 112–116.

AZUELA, Mariano
> WORKS

Epistolario y archivo, Mexico, UNAM, 1969; ed. by Beatrice Berler. *Los de abajo* (ed. Englekirk and Kiddle, 1939), New York, Appleton-Century-Crofts, 1971; complete edition.

> STUDIES

Foster, I, 122-133. Luis Leal, *Mariano Azuela,* New York, Twayne, 1971. Stanley L. Robe, *Azuela and the Mexican Underdogs,* Los Angeles, Univ. of California Press, 1979; contains text, together with background data and English translation, of the original late — 1915 *folletin* edition of *Los de abajo.*

BARRIOS, Eduardo
> WORKS

Castillo and Castillo, 5-26. Edmundo Garcia Giron (tr.), *Brother Ass,* New York, Las Americas, 1969

> STUDIES

Ned Davison, *Eduardo Barrios,* New York, Twayne, 1970. Foster, I, 143-148. Mariano Morinigo, *Eduardo Barrios, novelista,* Tucuman, Universidad Nacional, 1971. Schwartz, I, 225-231.

BELLO, Andrés
> WORKS

Antologia, Caracas, Kapelusz, 1970; ed. by Pedro Grases.

> STUDIES

Emir Rodriguez Monegal, *El otro Andres Bello,* Caracas, Monte Avila, 1969. Angel Rosenblat, *Andres Bello,* Caracas, Universidad Central de Venezuela, 1967. Raul Silva Castro, *Don Andres Bello, 1781-1865,* Santiago, Ed. Andres Bello, 1965.

BLANCO- FOMBONA, Rufino
> WORKS

Obras selectas, Madrid, Edime, 1958; ed. by Edgar Gabaldon Marquez.

> STUDIES

Fogelquist, 319-326. Angel Rama, *Rufino Blanco-Fombona intimo,* Caraeas, Monte Avila, 1976.

BOLÍVAR, Simón
> WORKS

The Political Thought of Bolivar: Selected Writings, The Hague, Martinus Nijnoff, 1971; ed. by Gerald E. Fitzgerald.

> STUDIES

The Liberator, Simon Bolivar: Man and Image, New York, Knopf, 1970;

BOMBAL, María Luisa
>WORKS
>Crow and Dudley, 207-218. Howes, 323-335. Mancini, 232-246.
>STUDIES
>Adams, 15-35. *Diccionario . . . Chile*, 34-35.

BORGES, Jorge Luis
>WORKS
>*Borges, sus mejores paginas* (ed. Enguidanos), Englewood Cliffs, Prentice-Hall, 1970. Coleman, 1-55. Crow and Dudley, 222-227; 242-248. Leal and Dauster, 407-414. *Nueva antologia personal*, Buenos Aires, Emece, 1968. *Obra poetica, 1923-1967* (1964), 8th ed., Buenos Aires, Emece, 1969. *Obras completas*, 9 vols., Emece, 1953-1960. The separate volumes are reprints of part of the author's total production. Norman Thomas di Giovanni (tr.), *The Book of Imaginary Beings*, New York, Dutton, 1969; also (ed. and tr.) *The Aleph and Other Stories, 1933-1969*, New York, Dutton, 1970; also *Doctor Brodie's Report*, New York, Dutton, 1972; also (ed. and tr.) *Selected Poems, 1923-1967*, New York, Delacorte, 1972; also *A Universal History of Infamy*, New York, Dutton, 1972; also *In Praise of Darkness*, New York, Dutton, 1974. Howes, 173-183. Anthony Kerrigan (tr.), *A Personal Anthology*, New York, Grove, 1967. Mancini, 134-150. Ruth L.C. Simms (tr.), *Other Inquisitions, 1937-1952* (1964), New York, Simon and Schuster, 1968.
>STUDIES
>Jaime Alazraki, *La prosa narrativa de Jorge Luis Borges* (1968), 2nd ed., Madrid, Gredos, 1975; also (ed.), *Jorge Luis Borges*, Madrid, Taurus, 1976. Anna Maria Barrenechea, *La expresion de la irrealidad en la obra de Jorge Luis Borges* (1957); tr. by Robert Lima, *Borges, the Labyrinth Maker*, New York, New York Univ. Press, 1965. Maria Luisa Bastos, *Borges ante la critica argentina: 1923-1960*, Buenos Aires, Eds. Hispamerica, 1974. Horacio Jorge Becco, *Jorge Luis Borges, bibliografia total, 1923-1973*, Buenos Aires, Pardo, 1973. Richard Burgin, *Conversations with Jorge Luis Borges*, New York, Holt, Rinehart, Winston, 1969. *The Cardinal Points of Borges*, Norman, Univ. of Oklahoma Press, 1971; ed. by Lowell Dunham and Ivar Ivask. Ronald J. Christ, *The Narrow Act; Borges' Art of Allusion*, New York, New York Univ. Press, 1969. John Michael Cohen, *Jorge Luis Borges*, New York, Barnes and Noble, 1974. David W. Foster, *A Bibliography of the Works of Jorge Luis Borges*, Tempe, Arizona State Univ., 1971; also Foster, I, 167-194. Zunilda Gertel, *Jorge Luis Borges y su retorno*

CABEZA DE VACA, Álvar Núñez

Fanny Bandelier (tr.), *The Narrative of Alvar Nunez Cabeza de Vaca*, Barre, Mass., The Imprint Society, 1972.

STUDIES

Cleve Hallenback, *Alvar Nunez Cabeza de Vaca: Journey and Route* (1940), Port Washington, Kennikat Press, 1971.

CAMPO, Estanislao del

STUDIES

Enrique Anderson Imbert, *Analisis del Fausto*, Buenos Aires, CEAL, 1968.

CARO, José Eusebio

WORKS

A la sombra del alero, Bogota, Instituto Caro y Cuervo, 1964; ed. by Eduardo Esponda.

STUDIES

Jose Luis Martin, *La poesia de Jose Eusebio Caro*, Bogota, Instituto Caro y Cuervo, 1966.

CARPENTIER, Alejo

WORKS

Brotherston and Vargas Llosa, 68-87. *!Ecue Yamba-O!* (1933), Mexico, Ed. Diez, 1976. Leal and Dauster, 430-438. *Los pasos perdidos* (1953), Buenos Aires, Ed. Andina, 1969. *El reino de este mundo* (1949), Barcelona, Seix Barral, 1969. *Tientos y diferencias* (1964), Montevideo, Arca, 1967. Cohen, *Latin American Writing Today*, 53-66. Howes, 205-221. Mancini, 150-170. Frances Partridge (tr.), *War of Time* (Spanish, 1958), New York, Knopf, 1970.

STUDIES

Adams, 81-105. Foster, I, 212-226. Helmy F. Giacoman (ed.), *Homenaje a Alejo Carpentier*, New York, Las Americas, 1970. Roberto Gonzalez Echevarria, *Alejo Carpentier. The Pilgrim at Home*, Ithaca, Cornell Univ. Press, 1977. Alexis Marquez Rodriguez, *La obra narrativa de Alejo Carpentier*, Caracas, Universidad Central de Venezuela, 1970. Nora Mazziotti (ed.), *Historia y mito en la obra de Alejo Carpentier*, Buenos Aires, Garcia Cambeiro, 1972. Klaus Muller-Bergh, *Alejo Carpentier: estudio biografico-critico*, New York, Las Americas, 1972; also (ed.), *Asedios a Carpentier. Once ensayos criticos sobre el novelista cubano*, Santiago, Ed. Universitaria, 1972. Pupo-Walker, 126-150. Jose Sanchez-Boudy, *La tematica novelistica de Alejo Carpentier*, Miami,

Eds. Universal, 1969. Schwartz, II, 194–204. Esther P. Morega-Gonzalez, *La narrativa de Alejo Carpentier: el concepto del tiempo como tema fundamental*, New York, Eliseo Torres, 1975.

CARRASQUILLA, Tomás

WORKS

Frutos de mi tierra, Bogota, Instituto Caro y Cuervo, 1972; ed. by Seymour Menton. *La marquesa de Yolombo*, Bogota, Instituto Caro y Cuervo, 1974; ed. by Kurt L. Levy.

CARRERA ANDRADE, Jorge

WORKS

Obra poetica completa, Quito, CCE, 1976. *Poesia ultima*, New York, Las Americas, 1968; ed. by Enrique Ojeda. Don C. and Gabriela de C. Bliss (tr.), *Reflections on Spanish American Poetry*, Albany, SUNY Press, 1973. H. R. Hays (ed. and tr.), *Selected Poems of Jorge Carrera Andrade*, Albany, SUNY Press, 1972.

STUDIES

Diccionario... Ecuador, 94–99. Foster, I, 226–232. Enrique Ojeda, *Jorge Carrera Andrade: introduccion al estudio de su vida y de su obra*, New York, Eliseo Torres, 1972.

CASAL, Julián del

WORKS

Julian del Casal, vida y obra poetica, New York, Las Americas, 1970; ed. by Rosa M. Cabrera. *The Poetry of Julian del Casal: A Critical Edition*, 3 vols., Gainesville, Univ. Presses of Florida, 1976–1977; ed. by Robert Jay Glickman. *Prosas*, 3 vols., Habana, Consejo Nacional de Cultura, 1963–1964.

STUDIES

Esperanza Figueroa (ed.), *Julian del Casal: estudios criticos sobre su obra*, Miami, Eds. Universal, 1974. Fogelquist, 268–279. Jose Antonio Portuondo, *Angustia y evasion de Julian del Casal*, Habana, Cultural, 1940.

CHOCANO, José Santos

STUDIES

Fogelquist, 167-204. Foster, I, 246-250. Phyllis W. Rodriguez-Peralta, *Jose Santos Chocano*, New York, Twayne, 1971.

CORTÉS, Hernón

WORKS

Cartas y documentos de Hernan Cortes, Mexico, Porrua, 1963.

STUDIES

J. Bayard Morris (ed. and tr.), *Five Letters*, New York, Norton, 1962 (paperback). Leslie Byrd Simpson (ed. and tr.), *Cortes: The Life of the Conqueror by his Secretary Francisco Lopez de Gomara*, Berkeley, Univ. of California Press, 1964.

CRUZ, Sor Juana Inés

WORKS

Poesia, teatro y prosa, Mexico, Porrua, 1965; ed. by Antonio Castro Leal.

STUDIES

Gerard C. Flynn, *Sor Juana Ines de la Cruz*, New York, Twayne, 1971. Raul Leiva, *Introduccion a Sor Juana*, Mexico, UNAM, 1975. Maria Esther Perez, *Lo americano en el teatro de Sor Juana Ines de la Cruz*, New York, Eliseo Torres, 1975.

DARÍO, Rubén

WORKS

Antologia, Mexico, FCE, 1967; ed. by Jaime Torres Bodet. *Antologia poetica*, Buenos Aires, Losada, 1966; ed. by Guillermo de Torre. Howes, 85–91. Lysander Kemp (tr.), *Selected Poems*, Austin, Univ. of Texas Press, 1965: prologue by Octavio Paz. Mancini, 32–40. *Poesias completas*, Buenos Aires, Eds. Zamora, 1967; ed. by Luis Alberto Ruiz.

STUDIES

Enrique Anderson Imbert, *La originalidad de Ruben Dario*, Buenos Aires, CEAL, 1967. Jose A. Balseiro, *Seis estudios sobre Ruben Dario*, Madrid, Gredos, 1967. *Ruben Dario*, La Plata, Universidad Nacional, 1968; estudios reunidos en conmemoracion del centenario, 1867–1967. Arnold Armand Del Greco, *Repertorio bibliografico del mundo de Ruben Dario*, New York, Las Americas, 1969. Keith Ellis, *Critical Approaches to Ruben Dario*, Toronto, Univ. of Toronto Press, 1974. Fogelquist, 89–112, *passim*. Foster, I, 280–296. "Homenaje," *Revista iberoamericana*, 64 (1967). *Homenaje a Ruben Dario (1867–1967)*. See *Memoria del XIII Congreso del IILI* (Los Angeles, 1967). Carlos Lozano, *Ruben Dario y el modernismo en Espana, 1888–1920; ensayo de bibliografia comentada*, New York, Las Americas, 1968. Ernesto Mejia Sanchez (ed.), *Estudios sobre Ruben Dario*, Mexico, FCE, 1968. Andres R. Quintian, *Cultura y literatura espanolas en Ruben Dario*, Madrid, Gredos, 1974. Pedro Salinas, *La poesia de Ruben Dario* (1948), Barcelona, Seix Barral, 1975. Charles D. Watland, *Poet-errant: A Biography of Ruben Dario*, New York, Philosophical Society, 1965.

Hensley C. Woodbridge, *Ruben Dario. A Selective, Classified, and Annotated Bibliography*, Metuchen, Scarecrow Press, 1975.

DÍAZ DEL CASTILLO. Bernal

WORKS

John Michael Cohen (ed. and tr.), *Conquest of New Spain*, Baltimore, Penguin, 1963.

STUDIES

Herbert Cerwin, *Bernal Diaz: Historian of the Conquest*, Norman, Univ. of Oklahoma Press, 1963.

DIAZ RODRIGUEZ, Manuel

WORKS

Manuel Diaz Rodriguez, 2 vols., Carácas, Clasicos Venezolanos de la Lengua: 10-11, 1964; prologue by Rafael Angarita Arvelo, study by Lowell Dunham. *Obras selectas*, Caracas, Edime, 1968.

STUDIES

Fogelquist, 319-330, *passim*. Foster, I, 300-305.

ECHEVERRÍA, Esteban

STUDIES

Noe Jitrik, *Esteban Echeverria*, Buenos Aires, CEAL, 1967.

ERCILLA Y ZUÑIGA. Alonso de

STUDIES

August J. Aquila, *Alonso de Ercilla y Zuniga: A Basic Bibliography*, London, Grant and Cutler, 1975. Julio Caillet-Bois, *Analisis de La araucana*, Buenos Aires, CEAL, 1967.

FERNÁNDEZ DE LIZARDI, José Joaquín

WORKS

Don Catrin de la Fachenda y Noches tristes y un dia alegre (1959), 2nd ed., Mexico, Porrua, 1970.

STUDIES

Schwartz, I, 18-22.

GALLEGOS, Rómolo

Antologia, Mexico, Costa-Amic, 1966; ed. by Pedro Diaz Seijas. *Dona Barbara*, Caracas, Monte Avila, 1970. Howes, 115-123. Mancini, 60-70.

STUDIES

Foster, I, 347-362. Andres Iduarte, *Con Romulo Gallegos*, Caracas, Monte Avila, 1969. Ulrich Leo, *Romulo Gallegos. El arte de novelar*, Caracas, INCIBA, 1968. Juan Liscano, *Romulo Gallegos y su tiempo*,

Caracas, Monte Avila, 1969. Hilda Marban, *Romulo Gallegos: El hombre y su obra,* Madrid, Playor, 1973. Schwartz, I, 168–184.

GÁLVEZ, Manuel

WORKS

La maestra normal, Buenos Aires, Losada, 1964.

STUDIES

Foster, I, 362–371. Natilio Kisnerman, *Bibliografia de Manuel Galvez,* Buenos Aires, Fondo Nacional de las Artes, 1964. Myron I. Lichtblau, *Manuel Galvez,* New York, Twayne, 1972. Schwartz, I, 217–225.

GOMEZ DE AVELLANEDA, Gertrudís

WORKS

Obras de dona Gertrudis de Avellaneda, Madrid, BAE: 272, 1974; ed. by Jose Maria Castro y Calvo. *Poesias selectas,* Barcelona, Bruguera, 1968; ed. by Benito Varela Jacome.

STUDIES

Carmen Bravo-Villasante, Gaston Baquero and Jose Escarpanter, *Gertrudis Gomez de Avellaneda,* Madrid, FUE, 1974.

GONZÁLEZ MARTÍNEZ, Enrique

WORKS

Antologia de su obra poetica, Mexico, FCE, 1971; ed. by Jaime Torres Bodet. *Obras completas,* Mexico, El Colegio Nacional, 1971; ed. by Antonio Castro Leal.

STUDIES

John S. Brushwood, *Enrique Gonzalez Martinez,* New York, Twayne, 1969. *Diccionario . . . mexicanos,* 148–151. Foster, I, 399–405. Jose Manuel Topete, *El mundo poetico de Enrique Gonzalez Martinez,* Guadalajara, "Fenix," 1967.

GONZÁLEZ-PRADA, Manuel

WORKS

Ensayos escogidos (2nd ed., 1958), 3rd ed., Lima, Ed. Universo, 1970.

STUDIES

Foster, I, 405–412. Hugo Garcia Salvatecci, *El pensamiento de Gonzalez Prada,* Lima, Ed. Arica, 1972; prologue by Jose Miguel Oviedo.

GUILLÉN, Nicolás

WORKS

Antologia mayor: El son entero y otros poemas, Habana, Eds. Union, 1964; prologue by Angel Augier. *Summa poetica,* Madrid, Catedra, 1976; ed. by Luis Inigo Madrigal. Richard J. Carr (tr.), *Tengo,* Detroit, Broadside Press, 1974; prologue by Jose Antonio Portuondo. Robert Marquez (tr.), *!Patria o Muerte! The Great Zoo and Other Poems by Nicolas Guillen,* New York, Monthly Review Press, 1972. Robert Marquez and David Arthur McMurray (ed. and tr.), *Man-Making Words: Selected Poems,* Amherst, Univ. of Massachusetts Press, 1972.

STUDIES

Angel Augier, *Nicolas Guillen; notas para un estudio biografico-critico,* 2 vols., Santa Clara, Universidad Central de las Villas, 1962-1964. Foster, I, 415-421. Ezequiel Martinez Estrada, *La poesia afrocubana de Nicolas Guillen,* Montevideo, Arca, 1966. Nancy Morejon (ed.), *Recopilacion de textos sobre Nicolas Guillen,* Habana, Casa de las Americas, 1974.

GUIRALDES, Ricardo

WORKS

Crow and Dudley, 278-296. *Don Segundo Sombra,* Mexico, Porrua, 1971. *Don Segundo Sombra* (ed. Dellepiane), Englewood Cliffs, Prentice-Hall, 1971. *Don Segundo Sombra* (ed. Beardsell), New York, Pergamon, 1973. Howes, 123-131.

STUDIES

Ivonne Bordelois, *Genio y figura de Ricardo Guiraldes,* Buenos Aires, EUDEBA, 1967. Foster, I, 421-436. Juan Carlos Ghiano, *Ricardo Guiraldes,* Buenos Aires, Pleamar, 1966. Schwartz, I, 202-211.

GUTIÉRREZ NÁJERA, Manuel

WORKS

Crow and Dudley, 195-200; 249-255. Martinez, 60-64.

STUDIES

Diccionario . . . mexicanos, 163-166. Fogelquist, 244-252. *passim,*

GUZMÁN, Martín Luis

WORKS

Antologia de Martin Luis Guzman, Mexico, Eds. Oasis, 1970; ed. by Ermilo Abreu Gomez. *Obras completas,* 2 vols., Mexico, Cia. General de Ediciones, 1961-1963; prologue by Andres Iduarte. Martinez, 115-119. Harriet de Onis (tr. 1930), *The Eagle and the Serpent,* New York, Doubleday, 1965. Virginia H. Taylor (tr.), *Memoirs of Pancho Villa,* Austin, Univ. of Texas Press, 1965.

STUDIES

Ermilo Abreu Gomez, *La expresion literaria de Martin Luis Guzman,* Mexico, Secretaria de Education Publica, 1968. *Diccionario...mexicanos,* 66-168. Larry M. Grimes, *The Revolutionary Cycle in the Literary Production of Martin Luis Guzman,* Cuernavaca, CIDOC, 1969.

HENRÍQUEZ UREÑA, Pedro
WORKS
Ensayos (1965), Habana, Casa de las Americas, 1973; ed. by Jose Rodriguez Feo. *Pedro Henriquez Urena*, Buenos Aires, Eds. Culturales Argentinas, 1966; ed. by Carmelina de Castellanos and Luis Alberto Castellanos; prologue by Ernesto Sabato.
STUDIES
Diccionario . . . mexicanos, 170 171. Foster, I, 436–439.

HEREDIA Jose María
WORKS
Poesias completas, Miami, Eds. Universal, 1970; ed. by Angel Aparicio Laurencio.
STUDIES
Tomas F. Robaina, *Bibliografia sobre Jose Maria Heredia*, Habana, Biblioteca Nacional, 1970.

HERNÁNDEZ-CATÁ, Alfonso
WORKS
Crow and Dudley, 69–78; 200–207; 228–237
STUDIES
Gaston Fernandez de la Torriente, *La novela dè Hernandez-Cata*, Madrid, Playor, 1976.

HERNÁNDEZ, José
WORKS
Martin Fierro, Madrid, Aguilar, 1971; ed. by E. F. Tiscornia. *Martin Fierro,* Barcelona, Labor, 1972; ed. by Emilio Carilla. C. E. Ward (tr.), *The Gaucho Martin Fierro,* Albany, SUNY Press, 1967 (paperback); bilingual edition.
STUDIES
Emilio Carilla, *La creacion del Martin Fierro,* Madrid, Gredos, 1973. John B. Hughes, *Arte y sentido de Martin Fierro,* Madrid, Castalia, 1970. Noe Jitrik, *Jose Hernandez,* Buenos Aires, CEAL, 1971. *Martin Fierro en su centenario,* Washington, Embajada de la Republica Argentina, 1973. Walter Sava, "Jose Hernandez: cien anos de bibliografia, aporte parcialmente anotado," *Revista iberoamericana,* 81 (1972), 681 774. Daniel C. Scroggins, *A Concordance of Jose Hernandez' Martin Fierro,* Columbia, Univ. of Missouri Press, 1971.

HERRERA Y REISSIG, Julio
STUDIES
Foster, I, 440-445.

HIDALGO, Bartolomé
WORKS
Cielitos y dialogos patrioticos, Buenos Aires, CEAL, 1967; ed. by Horacio J. Becco.

HOSTOS, Eugenio María
WORKS
Antologia, Madrid, Juan Bravo, 1952; ed. by Eugenio Carlos de Hostos, with prologue by Pedro Henriquez Urena. *Moral social* (1888), 9th ed., New York, Las Americas, 1964; prologue by Rufino Blanco-Fombona. Ripoll, 150-179.
STUDIES
Antonio S. Pereira, *Hostos, ciudadano de America,* San Juan, Instituto de Cultura Puertorriquena, 1964.

HUIDOBRO, Vincente
WORKS
Obras completas, 2 vols., Santiago, Zig-Zag, 1964; prologue by Braulio Arenas.
STUDIES
David Bary, *Huidobro o la vocacion poetica,* Granada, CSIC, 1963. Enrique Caracciolo Trejo, *La poesia de Vicente Huidobro y la vanguardia,* Madrid, Gredos, 1974. Rene De Costa (ed.), *Vicente Huidobro y el creacionismo,* Madrid, Taurus, 1975. Foster, I, 445-452. Cedomil Goic, *La poesia de Vicente Huidobro,* Santiago, Universidad de Chile, 1956. Nicholas Hey, "Bibliografia de y sobre Vicente Huidobro," *Revista iberoamericana,* 91 (1975), 293-353.

IBARBOUROU, Juana de
WORKS
Antologia poetica, Madrid, Cultura Hispanica, 1970; ed. by Dora Isella Russell.
STUDIES
Foster, I, 453-457.

ISAACS, Jorge
WORKS
Maria, Barcelona, Labor, 1970; ed. by Donald McGrady. *Maria,* 5th ed., Mexico, Porrua, 1972; ed. by Daniel Moreno.
STUDIES

German Arciniegas, *Genio y figura de Jorge Isaacs*, Buenos Aires, EUDEBA, 1967. Donald McGrady, *Bibliografia sobre Jorge Isaacs*, Bogota, Instituto Caro y Cuervo, 1971; also *Jorge Isaacs*, New York, Twayne, 1972.

JAIMES FREYRE, Ricardo

STUDIES

Foster, I, 467-470. Mireya Jaimes Freyre, *Modernismo y 98 a traves de Ricardo Jaimes Freyre*, Madrid, Gredos, 1969.

LARRETA, Enrique

WORKS

La gloria de don Ramiro (ed. Sedgwick and Hatton), Boston, Heath, 1966.

STUDIES

Fogelquist, 330-334. Andre Jansen, *Enrique Larreta, novelista hispano-argentino (1875-1961)*, Madrid, Cultura Hispanica, 1967. Maria Luisa Montero and Angelica L. Tortola, *Contribucion a la bibliografia de Enrique Larreta*, Buenos Aires, Fondo Nacional de las Artes, 1964.

LATORRE, Mariano

STUDIES

Mariano Latorre: vida y obra, bibliografia, antologia, New York, Hispanic Institute, 1944.

LILLO, Baldomero

WORKS

Crow and Dudley, 112-121. *Obras completas*, Santiago, Nascimento, 1968; ed. by Raul Silva Castro.

STUDIES

Alegria, *Historia*, 127-129.

LÓPEZ ALBÚJAR, Enrique

WORKS

La mujer Diogenes. Cuentos de arena y sol. Palos al viento, Lima, Consejo Nacional de la Universidad Peruana, 1972; ed. by Raul Estuardo Cornejo.

STUDIES

Raul Estuardo Cornejo, *Lopez Albujar, narrador de America*, Madrid, Anaya, 1961. Tomas Gustavo Escajadillo, *La narrativa de Lopez Albujar*, Lima, CONUP, 1972.

LÓPEZ, Luis Carlos

WORKS

Sus versos, Medellin, Bedout, 1973.

STUDIES

Martha S. Bazik, *The Life and Works of Luis Carlos Lopez,* Chapel Hill Univ. of North Carolina Press, 1977.

LÓPEZ-PORTILLO Y ROJAS, José

WORKS

Novelas de Federico Gamboa, Mexico, FCE, 1965; prologue by Francisco Monterde.

STUDIES

Alexander C. Hooker, *La novela de Federico Gamboa,* Madrid, Plaza Mayor, 1971.

LÓPEZ VELARDE, Ramón

WORKS

Obras, Mexico, FCE, 1972. *Poesias, cartas, documentos e iconografia,* Mexico, Imp. Universitaria, 1952; ed. by Elena Molina Ortega. Martinez, 120-137.

STUDIES

Calendario de Ramon Lopez Velarde, Mexico, Eds. Olimpia, 1971. *Diccionario . . . mexicanos,* 200-203. Foster, I, 496-501. Concepcion Galvez de Tovar, *Ramon Lopez Velarde en tres tiempos,* Mexico, Porrua, 1971. Guillermo Lopez de Lara, *Hablando de Lopez Velarde,* Mexico, Eds. Ateneo, 1973. Frederic W. Murray, *La imagen arquetipica en la poesia de Ramon Lopez Velarde,* Chapel Hill, Univ. of North Carolina Press, 1972. Schwartz, I, 298-302.

LUGONES, Leopoldo

WORKS

Las fuerzas extrañas (1906), Buenos Aires, Centurion, 1948. *Lunario sentimental* (1909), Buenos Aires, Centurion, 1971. *Obras en prosa,* Madrid, Aguilar, 1962; ed. by Leopoldo Lugones (h). Howes, 91-101. Mancini, 40-52.

STUDIES

Fogelquist, 306-310, *passim.* Foster, I, 501-510. "Homenaje," *Revista iberoamericana,* 57 (1964). Noe Jitrik, *Leopoldo Lugones, mito nacional,* Buenos Aires, Eds. Palestra, 1960. Alfredo A. Roggiano, "Bibliografia de y sobre Leopoldo Lugones," *Revista iberoamericana,* 53 (1962), 155-213.

LYNCH, Benito

STUDIES
Foster, I, 510-513. Ulises Petit de Murat, *Genio y figura de Benito Lynch*, Buenos Aires, EUDEBA, 1968.

MALLEA, Eduardo

WORKS
Lewald and Smith, 170-189. *Todo verdor perecera* (ed. Shaw), New York, Pergamon, 1968. Maria Mercedes Aspiazu (ed. and tr.), *Chaves and Other Stories*, London, Calder and Boyars, 1970. John B. Hughes (ed. and tr.), *All Green Shall Perish and Other Novellas and Stories*, New York, Knopf, 1966.

STUDIES
Foster, II, 18-33. H. Ernest Lewald, *Eduardo Mallea*, Boston, Twayne, 1977. Myron I. Lichtblau, *El arte estilistico de Eduardo Mallea*, Buenos Aires, Goyanarte, 1967. Mercedes Pintar Genaro, *Eduardo Malles, novelista*, Rio Piedras, Ed. Universitaria, 1976. Carmen Rivelli, *Eduardo Mallea: La continuidad tematica de su obra*, New York, Las Americas, 1969. Schwartz, II, 226-236. Oscar Hermes Villardo, *Genio y figura de Eduardo Mallea*, Buenos Aires, EUDEBA, 1973.

MÁRMOL, José

WORKS
Cantos del peregrino; seleccion, Buenos Aires, EUDEBA, 1966; ed. by Elvira Burlando de Meyer.

MARTÍ, José

WORKS
Antologia critica, New York, Las Americas, 1968; ed. by Susana Redondo de Feldman and Anthony Tudisco. *Ensayos sobre arte y literatura*, Habana, Instituto Cubano del Libro, 1972; ed. by Roberto Fernandez Retamar. *Jose Marti: poesia mayor* (1972), Habana, Instituto Cubano del Libro, 1973; ed. by Juan Marinello. *Obras completas*, 28 vols., Habana, Ed. Nacional de Cuba, 1963-1973. Luis A. Baralt (ed. and tr.), *Marti on the U.S.A.*, Carbondale, Southern Illinois Univ. Press, 1966; foreword by J. Cary Davis. Philip S. Foner (ed.), *Inside the Monster by Jose Marti*, New York, Monthly Review Press, 1975; tr. by Elinor Randall et al. "Writings on the United States and American Imperialism." Esther Elise Schuler (tr.), *Marti, Martyr of Cuban Independence* (Lizaso, 1940), Albuquerque, Univ. of New Mexico Press, 1953.

STUDIES

Roberto D. Agramonte, *Marti y su concepcion del mundo*, Rio Piedras, Ed. Universitaria, 1971. Fogelquist, 253–268. Richard Butler Gray, *Jose Marti, Cuban Patriot*, Gainesville, Univ. of Florida Press, 1962. Andres Iduarte, *Marti, escritor* (1945), 2nd ed. Habana, Ministerio de Educacion, 1951. Carlos Ripoll, *Archivo Jose Marti: repertorio critico; medio siglo de estudios martianos*, New York, Eliseo Torres, 1971; also *Indice universal de la obra de Jose Marti*, New York, Eliseo Torres, 1971. Fryda Schultz de Mantovani, *Genio y figura de Jose Marti*, Buenos Aires, EUDEBA, 1968.

MARTÍNEZ ESTRADA, Ezequiel

WORKS

Antologia, Mexico, FCE, 1964. *Cuentos completos*, Madrid, Alianza, 1975; ed. by Roberto Yakni. *Poesia*, Buenos Aires, Argos, 1947. Alain Swietlicki (tr.), *X-Ray of the Pampa*, Austin, Univ. of Texas Press, 1971; introduction by Thomas F. McGann.

STUDIES

Carlos Adam, *Bibliografia y documentos de Ezequiel Martinez Estrada*, La Plata, Universidad Nacional, 1968. Peter G. Earle, *Prophet in the Wilderness; The Works of Ezequiel Martinez Estrada*, Austin, Univ. of Texas Press, 1971. Foster, II, 44–52. Astur Morsella, *Martinez Estrada*, Buenos Aires, Plus Ultra, 1973.

MATO DE TURNER, Clorinda

WORKS

Indole (1891), Lima, Instituto Nacional de Cultura, 1974.

MENA, Juan León

WORKS

Cumanda, Quito, Ed. Universitaria, 1969; ed. by Miguel Sanchez Astudillo.

STUDIES

Dario C. Guevara, *Juan Leon Mera: El hombre de cimas* (1944), Quito, Ministerio de Educacion Publica, 1965.

MISTRAL, Gabriela

WORKS

Poesias, Habana, Casa de las Americas, 1967; ed. by Eliseo Torres. *Poesias completas* (1958), 2nd ed., Madrid, Aguilar, 1962; introductory study by Julio Saavedra Molina. Doris Dana (tr.), *Selected Poems of Gabriela Mistral*, Baltimore, The Johns Hopkins Press, 1971; bilingual edition.

STUDIES

Fernando Alegria, *Genio y figura de Gabriela Mistral*, Buenos Aires, EUDEBA, 1966. Margot Arce de Vazquez, *Gabriela Mistral, persona y poesia* (1958); tr. by Helene Masslo Anderson, *Gabriela Mistral, the Poet and her Work*, New York, New York Univ. Press, 1964. Carmen Conde, *Gabriela Mistral*, Madrid, EPESA, 1970. Foster, II, 64–74. Mary C.A. Preston, *A Study of Significant Variants in the Poetry of Gabriela Mistral*, Washington, Catholic Univ. of America Press, 1964. Margaret T. Rudd, *Gabriela: The Chilean Years*, University, Univ. of Alabama Press, 1968. Martin C. Taylor, *Gabriela Mistral's Religious Sensibility*, Berkeley, Univ. of California Press, 1968; also *Sensibilidad religiosa de Gabriela Mistral*, Madrid, Gredos, 1975.

MONTALVO, Juan

WORKS

El pensamiento vivo de Montalvo, Buenos Aires, Losada, 1961; ed. by Benjamin Carrion. Ripoll, 107–142.

STUDIES

Plutarco Naranjo and Carlos A. Rolando, *Juan Montalvo; estudio bibliografico*, 2 vols., Quito, Casa de la Cultura Ecuatoriana, 1966. Antonio Sacoto Salamea, *Juan Montalvo: El escritor y el estilista*, Quito, Casa de la Cultura Ecuatoriana, 1973.

MOOCK, Armando

STUDIES

Raul Silva Castro, *La dramaturgia de Armando Moock*, Santiago, SECH, 1964.

NERVDA, Pablo

WORKS

Canto general, Barcelona, Lumen El Bardo, 1976. *Confieso que he vivido: memorias*, Buenos Aires, Losada, 1974. *Fulgor y muerte de Joaquin Murieta*, Santiago, Zig-Zag, 1966; tr. by Ben Belitt, *Splendor and Death of Joaquin Murieta*, New York, Farrar, Straus, Giroux, 1972; bilingual edition. *Memorial de Isla Negra*, 5 vols., Buenos Aires, Losada, 1964. *Obra poetica*, 10 vols., Santiago, Cruz del Sur, 1947–1948; ed. by Juvencio Valle. *Obras completas* (1957), 4th ed., 3 vols., Buenos Aires, Losada, 1973; "Cronologia de Pablo Neruda" by Margarita Aguirre, "Guias bibliograficas" by Alfonso M. Escudero and Hernan Loyola. *Pablo Neruda: A Basic Anthology*, Oxford, Dolphin, 1975; ed. by Robert Pring-Mill. *Plenos poderes*, Buenos Aires, Losada, 1962; tr. by Alistair Reid, *Fully Empowered*, New York, Farrar, Straus,

Giroux, 1974; bilingual edition. *Poesías*, 2 vols., Madrid, Noguer y Gredos, 1976; prologue by Luis Rosales. Ben Belitt (tr.), *New Poems (1968-1970)*, New York, Grove, 1972; bilingual edition. Ben Belitt (ed. and tr.), *Pablo Neruda. Five Decades (1925-1970)*, New York, Grove, 1974; bilingual edition. Ben Belitt and Alistair Reid (tr.), *A New Decade; Poems: 1958-1967*, New York, Grove, 1969; bilingual edition. Bly (see Anthologies in English Translation). W. S. Merwin (tr.) *Twenty Love Songs and a Song of Despair*, New York, Grossman, 1971. Elsa Newberger (tr.), *Bestiary*, (1965), New York, Harcourt, Brace, Jovanovich, 1974, bilingual edition. David Ossman and Carlos B. Hagen (tr.), *The Early Poems*, New York, New Rivers Press, 1969. Alastair Reid (tr.), *We Are Many* (1967), New York, Grossman, 1972; bilingual edition; also *Extravagaria*, New York, Farrar, Straus, Giroux, 1974; bilingual edition. Hardie St. Martin (tr.), *Memoirs*, New York, Farrar, Straus, Giroux, 1977. Nathaniel Tarn (ed.), *Selected Poems* (1970), New York, Delacorte, 1972; bilingual edition; tr. by Anthony Kerrigan, et al. Nathaniel Tarn (tr.), *The Heights of Macchu Picchu*, New York, Farrar, Straus, Giroux, 1967; bilingual edition. *Three Spanish American Poets* (see Anthologies in English Translation). Donald D. Walsh (tr.), *The Captain's Versos*, New York, New Directions, 1972 (paperback); bilingual edition; also *Residence on Earth*, New York, New Directions, 1973; bilingual edition. James Wright and Robert Bly (tr.), *Twenty Poems*, Madison, Sixties Press, 1967; bilingual edition.

STUDIES

Margarita Aguirre, *Genio y figura de Pablo Neruda*, Buenos Aires, EUDEBA, 1964; later published as *Las vidas de Pablo Neruda*, Mexico, Grijalbo, 1973. Jaime Alazraki, *Poetica y poesia de Pablo Neruda*, New York, Las Americas, 1965. Amado Alonso, *Poesia y estilo de Pablo Neruda* (1940), 4th ed., Buenos Aires, Sudamericana, 1968. Angel Flores (ed.), *Aproximaciones a Pablo Neruda*, Barcelona, Ocnos, 1974. Foster, II, 98-122. Guibert, 1-74. "Homenaje," *Revista iberoamericana*, 82-83 (1973). Juan Larrea, *Del surrealismo a Machupicchu*, Mexico, Joaquin Mortiz, 1967. Frank Riess, *The Word and the Stone: Language and Imagery in Neruda's Canto general*, London, Oxford Univ. Press, 1972. Eliana S. Rivero, *El gran amor de Pablo Neruda: Estudio critico de su poesia*, Madrid, Plaza Mayor, 1971. Emir Rodriguez Monegal, *Neruda, el viajero inmovil* (1966), Caracas, Monte Avila, 1976. Raul Silva Castro, *Pablo Neruda*, Santiago, Ed. Universitaria, 1964. Juan Villegas, *Estructuras miticas y arquetipos en el Canto general de Neruda*, Barcelona, Planeta, 1976.

NERVO, Amado
WORKS
Martinez, 182-190
STUDIES
Diccionario . . . mexicanos, 250-252. Manuel Duran, *Genio y figura de Amado Nervo,* Buenos Aires, EUDEBA, 1968. Fogelquist, 113-140. Foster, II, 122-127.

PALMA, Ricardo
WORKS
Tradiciones peruanas, Lima, Universidad Nacional Mayor de San Marcos, 1969; ed. by Alberto Tauro. *Tradiciones peruanas,* Oxford, Pergamon, 1969; ed. by Pamela Francis.
STUDIES
Shirley L. Arora, *Proverbial Comparisons in Ricardo Palma's Tradiciones peruanas,* Berkeley, Univ. of California Press, 1966. Jose Miguel Oviedo, *Genio y figura de Ricardo Palma,* Buenos Aires, EUDEBA, 1965.

PARRA, Teresa de la
WORKS
Obras completas, Caracas, Ed. Arte, 1965.

PAYRÓ, Roberto J.
WORKS
Roberto J. Payro, Buenos Aires, Ministerio de Educacion, 1962; ed. by Walter G. Weyland.
STUDIES
Stella Maris Fernandez de Vidal, *Bibliografia de Roberto J. Payro, 1867–1928,* Buenos Aires, Fondo Nacional de las Artes, 1962. Foster, II, 161-167. Eduardo Gonzalez Lanuza, *Genio y figura de Roberto J. Payro,* Buenos Aires, EUDEBA, 1965. Schwartz, I, 155-159.

PAZ, Octavio
WORKS
El arco y la lira, Mexico, FCE, 1956; tr. by Ruth L. C. Simms, *The Bow and the Lyre,* Austin, Univ. of Texas Press, 1973. *Conjunciones y disyuntivas* (ensayos), Mexico, Joaquin Mortiz, 1969; tr. by Helen R. Lane, *Conjunctions and Disjunctions,* New York, Viking, 1974. *Corriente alterna,* Mexico, Eds. Siglo XXI, 1967; tr. by Helen R. Lane, *Alternating Current,* New York, Viking, 1973. *El laberinto de la soledad* (1950), Mexico, FCE, 1972. *Posdata,* Mexico, Siglo XXI, 1970; tr. by Lysander Kemp, *The Other Mexico; Critique of the Pyramid,* New York, Grove,

1972. G. Aroul (ed. and tr.), *Configurations,* New York, New Directions, 1971; selected poems, bilingual edition. Cohen, *Latin American Writing Today,* 87-96. Lysander Kemp and Margaret Sayers Peden (tr.), *The Siren and the Seashell and Other Essays on Poets and Poetry,* Austin, Univ. of Texas Press, 1976. Mancini, 170-174. Martinez, 437-471. Rachel Phillips (tr.), *Children of the Mire,* Cambridge, Harvard Univ. Press, 1974. Muriel Rukeyser (ed. and tr.), *Early Poems (1935-1955),* New York, New Directions, 1973. Eliot Weinberger (tr.), *?Aguila o sol? Eagle or Sun?,* New York, October House, 1970.

STUDIES

Diccionario . . . mexicanos, 278-280. Angel Flores (ed.), *Aproximaciones a Octavio Paz,* Mexico, Joaquin Mortiz, 1974. Foster, II, 168-182. Guibert, 183-275. "Homenaje," *Revista iberoamericana,* 74 (1971); see especially Alfredo A. Roggiano, "Bibliografia de y sobre Octavio Paz," 269-297. Ivar Ivask (ed.), *The Perpetual Present: The Poetry and Prose of Octavio Paz,* Norman, Univ. of Oklahoma Press, 1973. Luisa M. Perdigo, *La estetica de Octavio Paz,* Madrid, Playor, 1975. Rachel Phillips, *The Poetic Modes of Octavio Paz,* New York, Oxford, 1972; tr. as *Las estaciones poeticas de Octavio Paz,* Mexico, FCE, 1976. Ramon Xirau, *Octavio Paz: el sentido de la palabra,* Mexico, Joaquin Mortiz, 1970.

PELLICER, Carlos

WORKS

Primera antologia poetica, Mexico, FCE, 1969; ed. by Guillermo Fernandez, with prologue by Jose Alvarado, Gabriel Zaid, Guillermo Fernandez. Cohen, *Lat. Am. Writing Today,* 49-52. *Three Spanish American Poets* (see Anthologies in English Translation).

STUDIES

Diccionario . . . mexicanos, 281-283. Foster, II, 182-186. Edward J. Mullen, *Carlos Pellicer,* Boston, Twayne, 1977. Maria Teresa Ponce de Hurtado, *El ruisenor lleno de muerte; aproximacion a Carlos Pellicer,* Mexico, Ed. Meridiano, 1970.

PERALTA BARNUEVO, Pedro de

STUDIES

Luis Alberto Sanchez, *El doctor Oceano: estudios sobre don Pedro de Peralta Barnuevo,* Lima, Universidad Nacional Mayor de San Marcos, 1967.

PÉREZ BONALDO, Juan Antonio

WORKS

J. A. Perez Bonalde, 2 vols., Caracas, Academia Venezolana de la

Lengua, 1964; ed. by Pedro Pablo Paredes.
STUDIES
Ernest A. Johnson, *Juan A. Perez Bonalde: Los anos de formacion; documentos, 1846-1870,* Merida, Universidad de los Andes, 1971.

PICÓN-SALAS, Mariano
WORKS
Los malos salvajes, Buenos Aires, Sudamericana, 1962; tr. by Herbert Weinstock, *The Ignoble Savages,* New York, Knopf, 1965.
STUDIES
Foster, II, 187-190. Pedro Grases, *Mariano Picon Salas, o la inquietud hispanoamericana,* Caracas, Ed. Arte, 1966.

POMBO, Rafael
WORKS
Hector H. Orjuela (ed.), *Poesia inedita y olvidada,* 2 vols., Bogota, Instituto Caro y Cuervo, 1970; also *Antologia poetica,* Bogota, Eds. La Candelaria, 1975; also *La obra poetica de Rafael Pombo,* Bogota, Instituto Caro y Cuervo, 1975.
STUDIES
Hector H. Orjuela and Ruben Perez Ortiz, *Biografia y bibliografia de Rafael Pombo,* Bogota, Instituto Caro y Cuervo, 1965.

PRADO, Pedro
WORKS
Alsino (1920), 9th ed., Santiago, Nascimento, 1968. *Antologia,* Santiago, Ed. Gabriela Mistral, 1975; ed. by Enrique Pascal, G. H. *Un juez rural* (1924), 3rd. ed., Santiago, Nascimento, 1957; tr. by Lesley Byrd Simpson, *Country Judge,* Berkeley, Univ. of California Press, 1968; introduction by Arturo Torres-Rioseco.
STUDIES
John R. Kelly, *Pedro Prado,* New York, Twayne, 1973.

QUIROGA, Horacio
WORKS
Castillo and Castillo, 27-50. Crow and Dudley, 1-10, 15-20, 101-111, 121-127. *Cuentos,* Mexico, Porrua, 1970; ed. by Raimundo Lazo. *Cuentos escogidos* (ed. Franco), Oxford, Pergamon, 1968. *Seleccion de cuentos,* 2 vols., Montevideo, Bibl. Artigas, 1966; ed. by Emir Rodriguez Monegal. Yates, Sommers, Palley, 9-59. Howes, 110-115. Mancini, 52-60. Margaret Sayers Peden (tr.), *The Decapitated Chicken and Other Stories,* Austin, Univ. of Texas Press, 1976.

STUDIES

Angel Flores (ed.), *Aproximaciones a Horacio Quiroga*, Caracas, Monte Avila, 1976. Englekirk and Ramos, 74-76, 241-257. Foster, II, 202-212. Noe Jitrik, *Horacio Quiroga*, Buenos Aires, CEAL, 1967. Ezequiel Martinez Estrada, *El hermano Quiroga*, Montevideo, Arca, 1967. Pupo-Walker, 64-81. Walter Rela, *Horacio Quiroga; repertorio bibliografico anotado, 1897-1971*, Buenos Aires, Pardo, 1973. Emir Rodriguez Monegal, *Genio y figura de Horacio Quiroga*, Buenos Aires, EUDEBA, 1967; also *El desterrado. Vida y obra de Horacio Quiroga*, Buenos Aires, Losada, 1968.

REYES, Alfonso

WORKS

Poesia y prosa (ed. Robb), Madrid, Catedra, 1975. Martinez, 138-176.

STUDIES

Barbara Bockus Aponte, *Alfonso Reyes and Spain*, Austin, Univ. of Texas Press, 1972. *Diccionario... mexicanos*, 318-322. Foster, II, 237-245. "Homenaje," *Revista iberoamericana*, 59 (1965). James Willis Robb, *El estilo de Alfonso Reyes*, Mexico, FCE, 1965; also *Repertorio bibliografico de Alfonso Reyes*, Mexico, UNAM, 1974; also *Estudios sobre Alfonso Reyes*, Bogota, Eds. El Dorado, 1976.

REYLES, Carlos

WORKS

Ensayos, 3 vols., Montevideo, Bibl. Artigas (84-86), 1965; prologue by Arturo Sergio Visca.

STUDIES

Englekirk and Ramos, 261-266. Foster, II, 245-248. Gervasio Guillot Munoz, *La conversacion de Carlos Reyles*, Montevideo, Arca, 1966. Schwartz, I, 183-188.

RIVERA, José

WORKS

Obras completas, Medellin, Montoya, 1963. *La voragine*, Santiago, Zig-Zag, 1959; ed. by Juan Loveluck. *La voragine*, Bogota, Caja de Credito Agrario, 1974; ed. by Luis C. Herrera.

STUDIES

Alegria, *Historia*, 165-168. Foster, II, 253-259. Luis Carlos Herrera Molina, *Jose Eustasio Rivera*, Bogota, Instituto Caro y Cuervo, 1968. Schwartz, I, 253-260.

RODÓ, José Enrique

WORKS

Ariel (ed. Brotherston), Cambridge, Univ. of Cambridge Press, 1967. *Paginas de Jose Enrique Rodo,* Buenos Aires, EUDEBA, 1963; ed. by Emir Rodriguez Monegal.

STUDIES

Mario Benedetti, *Genio y figura de Jose Enrique Rodo,* Buenos Aires, EUDEBA, 1966. Fogelquist, 306-310, *passim.* Foster, II, 264-272. Emir Rodriguez Monegal, *Jose Enrique Rodo en el novecientos,* Montevideo, Numero, 1950. Hugo Torrano, *Rodo: accion y libertad; restauracion de su imagen,* Montevideo, Barreiro y Ramos, 1973.

ROMERO, José Rubén

WORKS

Cuentos y poesias ineditos, Mexico, Andrea, 1964; ed. by William D. Cord. *La vida inutil de Pito Perez* (ed. Cord), Englewood Cliffs, Prentice-Hall, 1972. William O. Cord (tr.), *The Futile Life of Pito Perez,* New York, Prentice-Hall, 1967.

STUDIES

Diccionario . . . mexicanos, 336-338. Foster, II, 277-283. Jose J. Larraz, *Idealismo y realidad. Analisis critico de las novelas de Jose Ruben Romero,* Madrid, Oscar, 1971. Schwartz, I, 291-296.

ROJAS, Manuel

WORKS

La ciudad de los Cesares, (ed. Sangiorgi and Knopp), New York, Appleton-Century-Crofts, 1951. Crow and Dudley, 161-175; 187-195. Yates, Sommers, Palley, 126-178.

STUDIES

Foster, II, 273-277. Rosa Rodriquez de Reeves, "Bibliografia de y sobre Manuel Rojas," *Revista iberoamericana,* 95 (1976), 285-313. Schwartz, I, 245-248.

SANCHEZ, Florencio

WORKS

Castillo and Castillo, 78-129.

STUDIES

Jorge Cruz, *Genio y figura de Florencio Sanchez,* Buenos Aires, EUDEBA, 1966. Foster, II, 327-338. Luis Ordaz, *Florencio Sanchez,* Buenos Aires, CEAL, 1971. Walter Rela, *Florencio Sanchez: guia bibliografica,* Montevideo, Ed. Delta, 1967.

SARMIENTO, Domingo Faustino

WORKS

Facundo, 2nd ed., Mexico, Porrua, 1969, ed. by Raimundo Lazo. *Facundo*, Buenos Aires, El Ateneo Editorial, 1974; ed. by Jorge Luis Borges. *Recuerdos de provincia*, 4th ed., Buenos Aires, EUDEBA, 1970. Michael A. Rockland (tr.), *Travels in the United States in 1847*, Princeton, Princeton Univ. Press, 1970.

STUDIES

Enrique Anderson Imbert, *Genio y figura de Sarmiento*, EUDEBA, 1967. Ana Maria Barrenechea and Beatriz R. Lavandera, *Domingo Faustino Sarmiento*, Buenos Aires, CEAL, 1967. Frances G. Crawley, *Domingo Faustino Sarmiento*, New York, Twayne, 1972. Noe Jitrik, *Muerte y resurreccion de Facundo*, Buenos Aires, CEAL, 1968.

SIGÜENZA Y GÓNGORA, Carlos de

WORKS

Infortunios de Alonso Ramirez, San Juan, Ed. Cordillera, 1967; ed. by Alba Valles Formosa.

SILVA, José Asunción

WORKS

Obras completas, 2 vols., Buenos Aires, Plus Ultra, 1968; ed. by Hector H. Orjuela.

STUDIES

Diccionario . . . Colombia, 113–115. Fogelquist, 279–289, *passim*. Juan Loveluck, "De sobremesa, novela desconocida del modernismo," *Revista iberoamericana*, 59 (1965), 17–32. Betty T. Osiek, *Jose Asuncion Silva; estudio estilistico de su poesia*, Mexico, Andrea, 1968.

STORNI, Alfonsina

WORKS

Obra poetica completa, Buenos Aires, Eds. Meridion, 1961

STUDIES

Marta Baralis, *Contribucion a la bibliografia de Alfonsina Storni*, Buenos Aires, Fondo Nacional de las Artes, 1964. Foster, II, 363–366. Conrado Nale Roxlo and Mabel Marmol, *Genio y figura de Alfonsina Storni*, Buenos Aires, EUDEBA, 1964. Rachel Phillips, *Alfonsina Storni; From Poetess to Poet*, London, Tamesis, 1975.

TORRES BODET, Jaime

WORKS

Memorias, 5 vols., Mexico, Porrua, 1969-1974. *Tiempo de arena*, Mexico, FCE. 1955. *Versos y prosas,* Madrid, EISA, 1966; ed. by Sonja Karsen. Martinez, 280-299.

STUDIES

Emmanuel R. Carballo, *Jaime Torres Bodet,* Mexico, Empresas Editoriales, 1968. *Diccionario... mexicanos,* 379-382. Foster, II, 370-376. Sonja P. Karsen, *Jaime Torres Bodet,* New York, Twayne, 1971. Beth Curti Miller, *La poesia constructiva de Jaime Torres Bodet; un estudio de Cripta y de sus conceptos,* Mexico, Porrua, 1974.

USIGLI, Rodolfo

WORKS

Corona de luz (ed. Ballinger), New York, Appleton-Century-Crofts, 1967. Martinez, I, 169-178. Thomas Bledsoe (tr.), *Two Plays: Crown of Light, One of These Days,* Carbondale, Southern Illinois Univ. Press, 1971; introduction by Willis Knapp Jones, foreword by J. Cary Davis. Wilder P. Scott (tr.), *Mexico in the Theatre* (Spanish, 1932), University, Univ. of Mississippi, 1976.

STUDIES

Diccionario... mexicanos, 393-395. Foster, II, 377-385.

USLAR PIETRÍ, Arturo

WORKS

El globo de colores, Caracas, Monte Avila, 1976. *La otra America,* Madrid, Alianza, 1975.

STUDIES

Foster, II, 385-391. Domingo Miliani, *Uslar Pietri, renovador del cuento venezolano,* Caracas, Monte Avila, 1969.

VALENCIA, Guillermo

STUDIES

Diccionario... Colombia, 123-126. Alberto Duarte French, *Guillermo Valencia,* Bogota, Ed. Jotade, 1941. Oscar Echeverri Mejia, *Guillermo Valencia, estudio y antologia,* Madrid, Cia. Bibliografia Espanola, 1965.

VALDÉS, Gabriel de la Concepción ("Placido")

WORKS

Los poemas mas representativos de Placido, Madrid, Castalia, 1976 (Estudios de *Hispanofila:* 40); ed. by Frederick S. Stimson and Humberto E. Robles.

VALLEJO, César

WORKS

Cesar Vallejo: An Anthology of His Poetry, New York, Pergamon, 1970;

ed. by James Higgins. *Novelas y cuentos completos,* Lima, F. Moncloa, 1967. *Obra poetica completa,* Lima, F. Moncloa, 1968; ed. by Georgette de Vallejo, with prologue by Americo Ferrari. Bly (see Anthologies in English Translation). Clayton Eshleman, (tr.), *Poemas humanos. Human Poems,* New York, Grove, 1968. Clayton Eshleman and Jose Rubia Barcia (tr.), *Spain, Take This Cup From Me,* New York, Grove, 1974; bilingual edition. Clayton Eshleman and Jose Rubia Barcia (tr.), *Cesar Vallejo. The Complete Posthumous Poetry,* Berkeley, Univ. of California Press, 1979; critical, bilingual edition.

STUDIES

Xavier Abril, *Cesar Vallejo y la teoria poetica,* Madrid, Taurus, 1962. Cesar A. Angeles Caballero, *Cesar Vallejo, su obra,* Lima, Minerva, 1964. Andre Coyne, *Cesar Vallejo,* Buenos Aires, Nueva Vision, 1968. Juan Espejo Asturrizaga, *Cesar Vallejo. Itinerario del hombre, 1892 1923,* Lima, Juan Mejia Baca, 1965. Americo Ferrari, *El universo poetico de Cesar Vallejo,* Caracas, Monte Avila, 1972. Angel Flores (ed.), *Aproximaciones a Cesar Vallejo,* 2 vols., New York, Las Americas, 1971. Foster, II, 392-402. Jean Franco, *Cesar Vallejo: The Dialectics of Poetry and Silence,* New York, Cambridge Univ. Press, 1976. James Higgins, *Vision del hombre y de la vida en las ultimas obras poeticas de Cesar Vallejo,* Mexico, Siglo XXI, 1970. "Homenaje", *Revista iberoamericana,* 71 (1970); see Alfredo A. Roggiano, "Minima guia bibliografies;" 353-358. Juan Larrea, *Cesar Vallejo y el surrealismo,* Madrid, A. Corazon, 1976. Eduardo Neale-Silva, *Cesar Vallejo en su fase trilcica,* Madison, Univ. of Wisconsin Press, 1975. Julio Ortega (ed.), *Cesar Vallejo,* Madrid, Taurus, 1975.

VASCONCELOS, José

WORKS

Ulises criollo (ed. Hilton), Boston, Heath, 1960. *Vasconcelos,* Mexico, Secretaria de Educacion Publica, 1942; ed., with prologue, by Genaro Fernandez MacGregor. Martinez, 95-109.

STUDIES

Itzhak Bar-Lewaw, M., *Jose Vasconcelos, vida y obra,* Mexico, Ed. Librera Intercontinental, 1965. *Diccionario . . . mexicanos,* 403-404. John H. Haddox, *Vasconcelos of Mexico: Philosopher and Prophet,* Austin, Univ. of Texas Press, 1967.

VIANA, Javier de

WORKS

Guri, y otras novelas (1901), Montevideo, C. Garcia, 1946. *Seleccion de cuentos*, 2 vols., Montevideo, Bibl. Artigas, 1965; ed. by Arturo Sergio Visca.

STUDIES

Englekirk and Ramos, 299-308. John F. Garganigo, *Javier de Viana*, New York, Twayne, 1972.

VILLAURRUTIA, Xavier

WORKS

Obras (1953), Mexico, FCE, 1966; ed. by Miguel Capistran, Ali Chumacero, Luis Mario Schneider. Martinez, 300-325.

STUDIES

Frank N. Dauster, *Xavier Villaurrutia*, New York, Twayne, 1971. *Diccionario... mexicanos*, 410-412. Merlin H. Forster, *Fire and Ice: The Poetry of Xavier Villaurrutia*, Chapel Hill, Univ. of North Carolina Press, 1976. Foster, II, 422-429. Adolfo Snaidas, *El teatro de Xavier Villaurrutia*, Mexico, SepSetentas, 1973.

YÁÑEZ, Agustín

WORKS

Al filo del agua (1947), 10th ed., Mexico, Porrua, 1969. *Obras escogidas*, Mexico, Aguilar, 1968; prologue by Jose Luis Martinez. Ethel Brinton (tr.), *The Lean Lands*, Austin, Univ. of Texas Press, 1968. Martinez, 355-367.

STUDIES

Diccionario... mexicanos, 413-417. John J. Flasher, *Mexico contemporaneo en las novelas de Agustin Yanez*, Mexico, Porrua, 1969. Foster, II, 433-442. Helmy F. Giacoman (ed.), *Homenaje a Agustin Yanez*, New York, Las Americas, 1973. Alfonso Rangel Guerra, *Agustin Yanez*, Mexico, Empresas Editoriales, 1969; "Vida y obra," "Antologia," "Critica y juicios," Bibliografia." Schwartz, II, 280-285. Linda M. Van Conant, *Agustin Yanez, interprete de la novela mexicana moderna*, Mexico, Porrua, 1969.

ZORRILLA DE SANMARTIN, Juan

WORKS

Conferencias y discursos (1905), 3 vols., Montevideo, Bibl. Artigas, 1965; prologue by Jose Q. Antuna. *Obras escogidas*, Madrid, Aguilar, 1967.

STUDIES

Enrique Anderson Imbert, *Analisis de Tabare*, Buenos Aires, CEAL, 1968. Domingo Luis Bordoli, *Vida de Juan Zorrilla de San Martin*, Montevideo, Concejo Departamental de Montevideo, 1961. Norma Suiffet, *Analisis estilistico de Tabare*, Montevideo, s. e., 1960.

Index of Authors

Acevedo Díaz, Eduardo, 55, *93-94*
Acosta, José de, 11
Acuña, Manuel, 60, 63, *71-72*
Agustini, Delmira, 137, 142, *147-148*
Alatorre, Antonio, 174
Alberdi, Juan Bautista, 78
Alegría, Ciro, 137, 170, 190, 192, 193, *214-216*
Alegría, Fernando, 174
Altamirano, Ignacio Manuel, 55, 56, 78, *82-83*
Álvarez de Toledo, Hernando, 19
Amorim, Enrique, 170, *217-219*
"Anastasio el Pollo," 76
Andersen, Hans Christian, 113, 229
Anderson Imbert, Enrique, 174
Andrade, Olegario Víctor, *69-70,* 72
"Aniceto el Gallo," 75, 76
Apollinaire, Guillaume, 138, 156
"Apostle of the Indians," 16
Araya, Enrique, 172
Arciniegas, Germán, 174, *183-184*
Arévalo Martínez, Rafael, 142, *153-154,* 172, 203
Arguedas, Alcides, 170, *189-190*
Arguedas, José María, 170, 190
Ariosto, Ludovico, 4, 19, 26
Arreola, Juan José, 173
Arrieta, Rafael Alberto, 142, *146*
Asbaje y Ramírez de Santillana, Juana Inés (Sor Juana Inés de la Cruz),. 6, 25, *27-28,* 31, 33, 34, 121

Ascasubi, Hilario ("Aniceto el Gallo"), 54, *74-75*, 76, 243
Ascencio Segura, Manuel, 88
Asturias, Miguel Ángel, 170
Azuela, Mariano, 169, *194-195*

Balbuena, Bernardo de, 24, *25-26,* 30
Balzac, Honoré de, 91, 96
Banchs, Enrique, 142, *145*
Barco Centenera, Martín del, 19
Barletta, Leónidas, 223
Barrios, Eduardo, 171, *199-200,* 203
Baudelaire, Charles, 112, 114
Beckett, Samuel, 159
Bécquer, Gustavo Adolfo, 63, 114, 115
Bello, Andrés, 8, 38, *41-43,* 83, 175, 184, 241
Benavente, Toribio de (Motolinía), 4, 11
Benedetti, Mario, 173
Blanco-Fombona, Rufino, *175-176,* 243
Blest Gana, Alberto, *91-92,* 101
Boiardo, Matteo Maria, 26
Bolívar, Simón, 7, 9, 39, 45, 46, *48-49,* 85
Bombal, María Luisa, 172, *202-203*
Borges, Jorge Luis, 138, 143, *158-160,* 172, 204
Boursault, Edmé, 6
Bramón, Francisco, 30
Brecht, Bertolt, 222
Breton, André, 142
Bretón de los Herreros, Manuel, 88

INDEX OF AUTHORS

Brunet, Marta, 202
Bryant, William Cullen, 69
Bustamante Carlos Inga, Calixto, 45
Byron, 63, 64, 69, 79, 109

Cabeza de Vaca, Álvar Núñez, 11, *14-15*
Caesar, Julius, 13
Calderón, Fernando, 88
Calderón de la Barca, Pedro, 34
Cambaceres, Eugenio, 90, 101
Campo, Estanislao del ("Anastasio el Pollo"), *75-76*, 243
Campoamor, Ramón de, 114, 115
Camus, Albert, 172, 222
Caro, José Eusebio, 63, *67-68*
Carpentier, Alejo, 172, *206-208*
Carrasquilla, Tomás, *98-99*
Carrera Andrade, Jorge, 143, *161-162*, 245
Carrió de la Vandera, Alonso ("Concolorcorvo"), 44, *45-46*
Casal, Julián del, 104, *112-113*
Casas, Bartolomé de las ("Apostle of the Indians"), 4, 11, *16-17*
Castelar, Emilio, 209
Castellanos, Juan de, 19
Castillo Andraca y Tamayo, Francisco del ("The Blind Mercedarian"), 25, 29, 34, *35-36*
Castillo y Guevara, Sor Francisca Josefa del (Madre Castillo), 25
Cernuda, Luis, 166
Cervantes, 85, 229
Cetina, Gutierre de, 19
Chateaubriand, François René, 9, 49, 63, 80
Chesterton, Gilbert Keith, 159
Chocano, José Santos, 55, 60, 109, 116, *127-128*
Cieza de León, Pedro, 4, 11
Cocteau, Jean, 171
Coloane, Francisco, 173
Colón, Cristóbal, 11, *12-13*
Columbus, Christopher, *12-13*
"Concolorcorvo," 44, *45-46*

Corneille, Pierre, 6, 34
Coronado, Martín, 102
Cortazar, Julio, 173
Cortés, Hernán, 4, 11, *13-14*, 15, 19, 89
Cruz, Sor Juana Inés de la Cruz, 6, 25, *27-28*, 31, 33, 34, 121
Cuervo, Rufino José, 42
Cueva, Juan de la, 19

D'Annunzio, Gabriele, 119
Darío, Rubén, 55, 60, 104, 108, 109, *115-118*, 119, 121, 123, 124, 153, 201, 237
Delgado, Rafael, 91
Denevi, Marco, 173
D'Halmar, Augusto, 201
Díaz del Castillo, Bernal, 4, 11, *15-16*
Díaz Dufóo, Carlos, 110
Díaz Mirón, Salvador, 104, *109-110*, 237
Díaz Rodríguez, Manuel; *118-119*, 168
Diderot, Denis, 6
Domínguez Camargo, Hernando, 25
Donoso, José, 173
Dos Passos, John, 171
Dostoievsky, 171

Echeverría, Esteban, 54, 56, 63, *64-65*, 72, 73, 77, 90
Eichelbaum, Samuel, 137, *223-225*·
"El cholo Vallejo," 160
"El Duque Job," 110-111
"El Pensador Mexicano," 7, *47-48*
"El tuerto López," 151
Eliot, Thomas Stearns, 142, 222
Éluard, Paul, 142
Ercilla y Zúñiga, Alonso de, 4, 19, *20*, 21
Espinosa Medrano, Juan de, 30
Espronceda, José de, 63
Evia, Jacinto de, 25

Faulkner, William, 171, 220
Feijóo, Benito, 47
Fernández, Juanita, 148
Fernández de Lizardi, José Joaquín ("El Pensador Mexicano"), 7, 44, 45, *47-48*

INDEX OF AUTHORS

Fernández de Oviedo, Gonzalo, 11
Fernández Madrid, José, 49
Fernández Moreno, Baldomero, 142, *143-145*
Flaubert, Gustave, 115, 169
Flores, Manuel, 63
Fuentes, Carlos, 172

Gallego, Juan Nicasio, 8, 37
Gallegos, Rómulo, 137, 168, 170, *192-194*
Gálvez, Manuel, 169, *186-187*, 212
Gamboa, Federico, 57, 90, *100*
García Calderón, Francisco, 48, *177-178*
García Calderón, Ventura, 177
García Gutiérrez, Antonio, 88
García Lorca, Federico, 138, 157, 205
García Velloso, Enrique, 102
Garcilaso de la Vega, El Inca, 11, *17-18*
Gautier, Théophile, 110
Gide, André, 165, 171
Giraudoux, Jean, 165
Giusti, Roberto, 174
Godoy Alcayaga, Lucila (Gabriela Mistral), 149
Goethe, 69, 181
Gómez de Avellaneda, Gertrudis (La Avellaneda), 60, 63, *66-67*, 88
Goncourt, Edmond and Jules, 90, 91, 100
Góngora y Argote, Luis de, 6, 30, 31, 109
González de Eslava, Fernán, *22-23*
González Martínez, Enrique, *129-131*, 135
González-Prada, Manuel, 58, 101, *105-107*, 119
Gorostiza, Celestino, 223, 226
Gorostiza, José, 143
Grimm, J. L. K. and W. K., 113
Guillén, Nicolás, 143, *162-163*
Güiraldes, Ricardo, 137, 170, *210-212*
Gutiérrez, Juan María, 55, 78
Gutiérrez González, Gregorio, 63

Gutiérrez Nájera, Manuel ("El Duque Job"), 104, *110-112*
Guzmán, Martín Luis, *195-196*

Haya de la Torre, Raúl, 105, 106, 174, 215
Hebreo, León, 17, 18
Heine, Heinrich, 63, 71, 114
Hemingway, Ernest, 171
Henríquez Ureña, Max, 174, 179
Henríquez Ureña, Pedro, 174, 178, *179-181*
Heredia, José María, 8, 38, *43-44*, 49, 62, 67, 241
Heredia, José María de (French), 69
Hernández, José, 72, *76-77*
Hernández, Pero, 14
Hernández-Catá, Alfonso, 172, *203-204*
Herrera y Reissig, Julio, *128-129*
Hidalgo, Bartolomé, 40, 243
Hojeda, Diego de, 24, *26-27*
Homer, 69
Horace, 39, 40, 69
Hostos, Eugenio María, 55, 78, *86*
Hudson, Guillermo Enrique, 183, 213
Hugo, Victor, 42, 64, 70, 71, 109
Huidobro, Vicente, 138, 143, *155-157*
Huxley, Aldous, 171, 220

Ibarbourou, Juana de ("Juana de América"), 137, 142, *148-149*
Ibsen, Hendrik, 102, 222, 224, 227
Icaza, Jorge, 170, *191-192*
Ingenieros, José, 96
Isaacs, Jorge, 57, 78, *81-82*

Jaimes Freyre, Ricardo, *123-124*
Jiménez, Juan Ramón, 118, 138
Joyce, James, 139, 171, 220
"Juana de América," 148

Kafka, Franz, 159, 171, 172
Kierkegaard, Sören, 205
Kipling, Rudyard, 198

La Avellaneda, 63, 88

INDEX OF AUTHORS

Laforgue, Jules, 125
Lamartine, Alphonse de, 69
Larra, Mariano José de, 105
Larreta, Enrique, 168, *208-209*
Latorre, Mariano, *213-214*
Lavardén, Manuel José de, 37, 50
Lawrence, D. H., 171
Leguizamón, Martiniano P., 59, *95*, 102
Leopardi, Giacomo, 69, 234
Lillo, Baldomero, 57, *92-93*
Lobo Lasso de la Vega, Gabriel, 19
Longfellow, Henry Wadsworth, 69
López, Luis Carlos ("El tuerto López"), 142, *150-151*
López Albújar, Enrique, *190-191*
López de Gómara, Francisco, 15
López de Jerez, Francisco, 11
López-Portillo y Rojas, José, *99-100*
López Velarde, Ramón, 142, *154-155*
López y Fuentes, Gregorio, 170, *196-197*
López y Planes, Vicente, 38
Luca, Esteban de, 38
Lugones, Leopoldo, 96, *124-125*, 145
Lynch, Benito, 137, 168, 170, *212-213*, 214

Madre Castillo, 25
Mallea, Eduardo, 139, 171, 174, 183, *204-206*
Mann, Thomas, 215
Mariátegui, José Carlos, 105, 106, 174
Mármol, José, 54, 63, 68, 78, *79-80*, 88
Martí, José, 104, *107-109*, 116, 118, 120, 204
Martínez de la Rosa, Francisco, 65
Martínez Estrada, Ezequiel, 140, 174, *182-183*
Matto de Turner, Clorinda, 58, *97-98*, 101, 190
Maupassant, Guy de, 198, 203
Mendès, Catulle, 115
Menéndez Pidal, Ramón, 181
Mera, Juan León, 57, 78, *80*, 85
Milanés, José Jacinto, 88
Miller, Arthur, 222

Milton, John, 26
Mistral, Gabriela, 137, 142, *149-150*, 178
Mitre, Bartolomé, 78
Molière, 6
Molinari, Ricardo, 143
Montalvo, Juan, 55, 78, *85*, 105
Monteagudo, Bernardo de, 7, 45, *46-47*
Monteforte Toledo, Mario, 170
Monterroso, Augusto, 173
Moock, Armando, 223 *225-226*
Moreno, Mariano, 7
Motolinía, 11
Musset, Alfred de, 64, 110

Nalé Roxlo, Conrado, 142, 223, *228-230*
Nariño, Antonio, 7
Navarrete, Manuel de, 37
Neruda, Pablo, 137, 143, *157-158*, 245
Nervo, Amado, *121-123*
Novo, Salvador, 226
Núñez, Rafael, 115
Núñez Cabeza de Vaca, Álvar, 11, *14-15*
Núñez de Pineda y Bascuñán, Francisco, 30, *32-33*

Obligado, Rafael, *72-73*
Ocampo, Victoria, 174
Ocantos, Carlos María, 57, *95-96*
Olmedo, José Joaquín, 8, 9, 37, *38-40*, 42, 241
Oña, Pedro de, 19, *20-21*
O'Neill, Eugene, 222
Onetti, Juan Carlos, 172, 173
Ortiz, José Joaquín, 67
Ovalle, Alonso de, 30, 31
Oyuela, Calixto, 72

Palafox y Mendoza, Juan de, 30
Palés Matos, Luis, 143
Palma, Ricardo, 36, 78, *86-88*, 97, 190
Pardo, Felipe, 50
Parra, Teresa de la, 170, *216*
Payró, Roberto J., 59, *96-97*, 102

INDEX OF AUTHORS

Paz, Octavio, 140, 143, *166-167*, 174, 186
Pellicer, Carlos, 143, *163-164*, 245
Perálta Barnuevo, Pedro de, 6, 33, *34-35*
Pereda, José María, 91, 98
Pérez Bonalde, Juan Antonio, *70-71*
Pérez Galdós, Benito, 86, 91, 96, 98, 203
Peza, Juan de Dios, 63, 64
Picón-Salas, Mariano, 139, 174, *184-186*
Pirandello, Luigi, 222
"Plácido," 55, 56, 63, *65-66*, 72
Poe, Edgar Allan, 71, 114, 115, 159, 198, 234
Pombo, Rafael, *68-69*
Pope, Alexander, 39
Prado, Pedro, 168, *200-201*
Prieto, Jenaro, 172
Proust, Marcel, 139, 165, 171

Quintana, Manuel José, 8, 37
Quintana Roo, Andrés, 38
Quiroga, Horacio, 128, 172, *197-199*, 212

Reverdy, Pierre, 142
Revueltas, José, 172
Reyes, Alfonso, 140, 148, 174, 178, 180, *181-182*
Reyes, Neftalí Ricardo (Pablo Neruda), 157
Reyles, Carlos, 119, 169, 170, *209-210*
Rilke, Rainer Maria, 142
Rivera, José Eustasio, 142, *151-153*, 168, 170, 192
Rodó, José Enrique, 60, *119-121*, 177
Rodríguez Freile, Juan, 30
Rodríguez Galván, Ignacio, 88
Rojas, Manuel, 172, *188-189*
Rojas, Ricardo, 50
Romains, Jules, 139, 171
Romero, Francisco, 174
Romero, José Rubén, 137, 170, *216-217*
Rosales, Diego de, 31

Rousseau, Jean Jacques, 6
Rulfo, Juan, 172, 173

Sábato, Ernesto, 171, 172
Sahagún, Bernardino de, 11
Saint Phalle, Fal de, 202
Salazar Bondy, Sebastián, 173
Sánchez, Florencio, 59, *102-103*, 222, 224
Sánchez, Luis Alberto, 90, 105
Sanín Cano, Baldomero, 140, 174, 184
Sarmiento, Domingo Faustino, 42, 55, 78, *83-84*, 183, 186
Sartre, Jean-Paul, 172, 222
Scarron, Paul, 6
Schiller, Friedrich, 64
Scott, Walter, 64
Scribe, Augustin Eugène, 88
Shaw, George Bernard, 222
Sigüenza y Góngora, Carlos de, 6, 30, *31-32*
Silva, José Asunción, 104, *113-115*, 126
Spota, Luis, 171
Storni, Alfonsina, 137, 142, *146-147*
Subercaseaux, Benjamín, 174
Synge, John Millington, 222

Tasso, Torquato, 4, 19
Tennyson, Alfred, 69
Terralla y Landa, Esteban de, 37
Terrazas, Francisco de, 19
"The Blind Mercedarian," 25, 34
Tolstoi, 201
Torres Bodet, Jaime, 143, *164-166*
Torres-Ríoseco, Arturo, 174
Trejo, Pedro de, 19
Tzara, Tristan, 142

Ugarte, Manuel, 60, 174, *176-177*
Unamuno, Miguel de, 183
Usigli, Rodolfo, 137, *227-228*
Uslar Pietri, Arturo, 170, 173, *219-220*

Valdelomar, Abraham, 190
Valdés, Antonio, 50

INDEX OF AUTHORS

Valdés, Gabriel de la Concepción ("Plácido"), 55, *65-66*
Valencia, Guillermo, 55, *126-127*
Valenzuela, Jesús E., 121
Valera, Juan, 91, 104, 115, 210
Valéry, Paul, 138, 142
Valle y Caviedes, Juan del, 25, *29*, 35
Vallejo, César ("El cholo Vallejo"), 143, *160-161*, 214
Varela, Juan Cruz, 38, *40-41*, 49
Vasconcelos, José, 174, *178-179*
Vela, Eusebio, 33
Velarde, Hector, 173
Vergil, 19, 39, 40, 69
Verlaine, Paul, 110, 112, 116
Viana, Javier de, *94-95*
Villarroel, Gaspar de, 30
Villaurrutia, Xavier, 143, 166, 223, *226-227*
Voltaire, 6

Werfel, Franz, 171
Whitman, Walt, 70, 107, 138, 232
Williams, Tennessee, 222
Woolf, Virginia, 171

Xenophon, 13

Yáñez, Agustín, 171, *220-221*

Zea, Leopoldo, 139, 174
Zola, Émile, 90, 92, 94, 96, 100
Zorrilla de San Martín, Juan, 57, *73-74*
Zum Felde, Alfredo, 174
Zweig, Arnold, 171